D1085280

Designing for Cisco Internetwork Solutions (DESGN) Foundation Learning Guide
Third Edition

Sean R. Wilkins

Cisco Press

800 East 96th Street

Indianapolis, IN 46240

Designing for Cisco Internetwork Solutions (DESGN) Foundation Learning Guide, Third Edition

Sean R. Wilkins

Copyright© 2012 Cisco Systems, Inc.

Published by:
Cisco Press
800 East 96th Street
Indianapolis, IN 46240 USA

All rights reserved. No part of this book may be reproduced or transmitted in any form or by any means, electronic or mechanical, including photocopying, recording, or by any information storage and retrieval system, without written permission from the publisher, except for the inclusion of brief quotations in a review.

First Printing August 2011

Library of Congress Cataloging-in-Publication Number:

Wilkins, Sean, 1975–
    Designing for CISCO internetwork solutions (desgn) foundation
learning guide / Sean R Wilkins. — 3rd ed.
        p. cm.
    Rev. ed. of: Designing for Cisco internetwork solutions (DESGN) /
Diane Teare. c2008.
    ISBN 978-1-58720-424-1 (hardcover)
  1. Computer networks—Examinations—Study guides.
  2. Telecommunications engineers—Certification.   3. Internetworking
(Telecommunication)—Examinations—Study guides.   I. Teare, Diane.
Designing for Cisco internetwork solutions (DESGN)   II. Title.
    TK5105.5.T418 2012
    004.6—dc23
                                                    2011022265

ISBN-13: 978-1-58720-424-1

ISBN-10: 1-58720-424-x

Warning and Disclaimer

This book is designed to provide information about designing Cisco networks. Every effort has been made to make this book as complete and as accurate as possible, but no warranty or fitness is implied.

The information is provided on an "as is" basis. The author, Cisco Press, and Cisco Systems, Inc., shall have neither liability nor responsibility to any person or entity with respect to any loss or damages arising from the information contained in this book or from the use of the discs or programs that may accompany it.

The opinions expressed in this book belong to the author and are not necessarily those of Cisco Systems, Inc.

Trademark Acknowledgments

All terms mentioned in this book that are known to be trademarks or service marks have been appropriately capitalized. Cisco Press or Cisco Systems, Inc. cannot attest to the accuracy of this information. Use of a term in this book should not be regarded as affecting the validity of any trademark or service mark.

Corporate and Government Sales

The publisher offers excellent discounts on this book when ordered in quantity for bulk purchases or special sales, which may include electronic versions and/or custom covers and content particular to your business, training goals, marketing focus, and branding interests . For more information, please contact: U.S. Corporate and Government Sales 1-800-382-3419 corpsales@pearsontechgroup.com

For sales outside the U.S., please contact: International Sales international@pearsoned.com

Feedback Information

At Cisco Press, our goal is to create in-depth technical books of the highest quality and value. Each book is crafted with care and precision, undergoing rigorous development that involves the unique expertise of members from the professional technical community.

Readers' feedback is a natural continuation of this process. If you have any comments regarding how we could improve the quality of this book, or otherwise alter it to better suit your needs, you can contact us through email at feedback@ciscopress.com. Please make sure to include the book title and ISBN in your message.

We greatly appreciate your assistance.

Publisher: Paul Boger

Associate Publisher: Dave Dusthimer

Executive Editor: Brett Bartow

Managing Editor: Sandra Schroeder

Senior Project Editor: Tonya Simpson

Editorial Assistant: Vanessa Evans

Book Designer: Sandra Schroeder

Composition: Mark Shirar

Business Operation Manager, Cisco Press: Anand Sundaram

Manager, Global Certification: Erik Ullanderson

Development Editor: Marianne Bartow

Copy Editor: John Edwards

Technical Editors: Diane Teare and Richard Piquard

Proofreader: Sheri Cain

Indexer: Larry Sweazy

CISCO.

Americas Headquarters
Cisco Systems, Inc.
San Jose, CA

Asia Pacific Headquarters
Cisco Systems (USA) Pte. Ltd.
Singapore

Europe Headquarters
Cisco Systems International BV
Amsterdam, The Netherlands

Cisco has more than 200 offices worldwide. Addresses, phone numbers, and fax numbers are listed on the Cisco Website at **www.cisco.com/go/offices.**

CCDE, CCENT, Cisco Eos, Cisco HealthPresence, the Cisco logo, Cisco Lumin, Cisco Nexus, Cisco StadiumVision, Cisco TelePresence, Cisco WebEx, DCE, and Welcome to the Human Network are trademarks; Changing the Way We Work, Live, Play, and Learn and Cisco Store are service marks; and Access Registrar, Aironet, AsyncOS, Bringing the Meeting To You, Catalyst, CCDA, CCDP, CCIE, CCIP, CCNA, CCNP, CCSP, CCVP, Cisco, the Cisco Certified Internetwork Expert logo, Cisco IOS, Cisco Press, Cisco Systems, Cisco Systems Capital, the Cisco Systems logo, Cisco Unity, Collaboration Without Limitation, EtherFast, EtherSwitch, Event Center, Fast Step, Follow Me Browsing, FormShare, GigaDrive, HomeLink, Internet Quotient, IOS, iPhone, iQuick Study, IronPort, the IronPort logo, LightStream, Linksys, MediaTone, MeetingPlace, MeetingPlace Chime Sound, MGX, Networkers, Networking Academy, Network Registrar, PCNow, PIX, PowerPanels, ProConnect, ScriptShare, SenderBase, SMARTnet, Spectrum Expert, StackWise, The Fastest Way to Increase Your Internet Quotient, TransPath, WebEx, and the WebEx logo are registered trademarks of Cisco Systems, Inc. and/or its affiliates in the United States and certain other countries.

All other trademarks mentioned in this document or website are the property of their respective owners. The use of the word partner does not imply a partnership relationship between Cisco and any other company. (0812R)

About the Author

Sean Wilkins is an accomplished networking consultant for SR-W Consulting (www.sr-wconsulting.com) and has been in the field of IT since the mid-1990s working with companies such as Cisco, Lucent, Verizon, and AT&T, as well as several other private companies. Sean currently holds certifications with Cisco (CCNP/CCDP), Microsoft (MCSE), and CompTIA (A+ and Network+). He also retains a Master of Science degree in information technology with a focus in network architecture and design, a Master of Science in organizational management, a Master's Certificate in network security, a Bachelor of Science degree in computer networking, and an Associate of Applied Science degree in computer information systems. In addition to working as a consultant, Sean is a technical writer and editor for various companies.

About the Technical Reviewers

Diane Teare, P. Eng., CCNP, CCDP, PMP, is a professional in the networking, training, project management, and e-learning fields. She has more than 25 years of experience in designing, implementing, and troubleshooting network hardware and software and has been involved in teaching, course design, and project management. She has extensive knowledge of network design and routing technologies and is an instructor with one of the largest authorized Cisco Learning Partners. She was the director of e-learning for the same company, where she was responsible for planning and supporting all the company's e-learning offerings in Canada, including Cisco courses. Diane has a bachelor degree in applied science in electrical engineering and a master's degree in applied science in management science. She authored or coauthored the Cisco Press titles *Implementing Cisco IP Routing (ROUTE) Foundation Learning Guide*; *Designing Cisco Network Service Architectures (ARCH)*, Second Edition; *Campus Network Design Fundamentals*; the three editions of *Authorized Self-Study Guide Building Scalable Cisco Internetworks (BSCI)*; and *Building Scalable Cisco Networks*. Diane edited the two previous editions of the *Authorized Self-Study Guide Designing for Cisco Internetwork Solutions (DESGN) and Designing Cisco Networks*.

Richard Piquard is a senior network consultant for NovaNet Technologies, LLC, a Washington, D.C., area IT consulting firm. Richard has more than 16 years of industry experience in design and implementation of both Cisco and multivendor environments. His experience in the industry ranges from his military background as the network chief of the Marine Corps Systems Command, Quantico, Virginia, to a field engineer for the Xylan Corporation (Alcatel), Calabasas, California, to a member of a four-person, worldwide network planning and implementation team for the Household Finance Corporation, Chicago, Illinois. He is a certified Cisco instructor and has more than 11 years of experience teaching introductory and advanced routing, switching, design, voice, and data center courses throughout North America and Europe for one of the largest authorized Cisco Learning Partners. In addition, he has served as a technical reviewer for the Cisco Press titles *Authorized Self Study-Guide Designing for Cisco Internetwork Solutions (DESGN)*, Second Edition and *Authorized Self-Study Guide Designing Cisco Network Service Architectures (ARCH)*, Second Edition.

Dedication

I dedicate this book to my girls (Stacy, Anij, and Saliah), one of whom was born during the development of this book. Without all of you, none of this would be possible.

—Sean Wilkins

Acknowledgments

I want to take this opportunity to thank all the people who have helped take the words in this text and transform them into a readable, organized, and formatted text for all of you to read and learn from. Without their efforts, this book would not have been possible. Because I only work directly with a few of these people, there are many people I will be unable to directly thank. For these people, I take this opportunity to thank you for your work in developing this project and look forward to working with you in the future.

Contents at a Glance

Contents

Icons Used in This Book

Access Point

Cisco Unified
Communications
Manager

Router

Bridge

Hub

DSU/CSU

Cisco IP Phone

H.323
Device

PBX

Catalyst
Switch

Multilayer
Switch

ATM
Switch

ISDN/Frame
Relay
Switch

Content Switch

Voice-Enabled
Router

Router with
Firewall

Communication
Server

Gateway

Access
Server

Phone

Netflow
Router

VPN
Concentrator

Network
Management
Appliance

DSLAM

Wide Area
Application
Engine

WiSM

Optical
Services Router

Lightweight
Double Radio
Access Point

WLAN
Controller

PC with
Software

Terminal

File
Server

Web
Server

Cisco Works
Workstation

Modem

PC

Printer

Laptop

Cisco Security
MARS

NAC
Appliance

PIX Security
Appliance

Network Cloud

Cisco MDS
9000 SSM

Optical
Transport

NAS

InfiniBand

WAFS

IDS

Token Ring

FDDI

Line: Ethernet

Line: Serial

Line: Switched Serial

Wireless Connection

Command Syntax Conventions

The conventions used to present command syntax in this book are the same conventions used in the IOS Command Reference. The Command Reference describes these conventions as follows:

- **Boldface** indicates commands and keywords that are entered literally as shown. In actual configuration examples and output (not general command syntax), boldface indicates commands that are manually input by the user (such as a **show** command).

- *Italic* indicates arguments for which you supply actual values.

- Vertical bars (|) separate alternative, mutually exclusive elements.

- Square brackets ([ ]) indicate an optional element.

- Braces ({ }) indicate a required choice.

- Braces within brackets ([{ }]) indicate a required choice within an optional element.

Introduction

Modern networks are both extremely complex and critical to business success. As organizational processes continue to increase the requirements for bandwidth, reliability, and functionality from their networks, network designers are challenged to rapidly develop and evolve networks that use new protocols and technologies. Network designers are also challenged to stay current with the internetworking industry's constant and rapid changes. Designing robust, reliable, scalable networks is a necessary skill for network operators and designers in the modern organizational environment.

This book teaches the concepts required to design enterprise networks. Specific topics include campus and data center infrastructure, remote connectivity, IP addressing (IPv4 and IPv6) design, routing protocol selection, voice network design, wireless network design, and including security in these designs.

Chapter-ending review questions illustrate and help solidify the concepts presented in this book.

This book provides you with the knowledge and skills that are needed to achieve associate-level competency in network design. It starts the reader down the path to attaining the CCDA certification, because it provides in-depth information to help you prepare for the DESGN exam.

DESGN is the first step in the design curriculum that supports the Cisco network design certification track. This book focuses on the technology and methods currently available.

Objectives of This Book

The goal of this book is to provide the knowledge needed to gather internetworking requirements, identify solutions, and design the network infrastructure and services to ensure basic functionality, using the principles of hierarchical network design to structure and modularize a converged enterprise network design. Design tasks might include understanding the design methodology; structuring and modularizing the network design; designing the Enterprise Campus, Enterprise Data Center, Enterprise Edge, and remote modules as needed; designing an addressing plan and selecting suitable routing protocols; designing basic voice transport across the network; designing a basic wireless solution; and evaluating security solutions.

Who Should Read This Book

This book is intended for network and sales engineers who are involved in network design, planning, and implementation, and for those who plan to take the 640-864 DESGN exam toward the CCDA certification. This book provides in-depth study material for that exam. To fully benefit from this book, the reader should have the following prerequisite skills:

- CCNA-level knowledge (or CCNA certification), which can best be achieved by completing the related CCNA courses and using CCNA books from Cisco Press. You can find more information on the CCNA certification at www.cisco.com/go/ccna.

- Knowledge of wired and wireless networking, quality of service (QoS), network security, and multilayer switching is highly recommended. This is the level equivalent to that covered in the professional-level Cisco networking certification track (ROUTE, SWITCH, and TSHOOT).

- Practical experience deploying and operating networks based on Cisco network devices and the Cisco IOS.

Summary of the Contents

The chapters and appendixes of this book are as follows:

- Chapter 1, "Network Fundamentals Review," introduces some fundamental concepts and terminology that are the foundation for the material in the rest of this book.

- Chapter 2, "Network Design Methodology," introduces the Cisco vision of intelligent networks and the Cisco Network Architectures for the Enterprise framework. The lifecycle of a network and a network design methodology based on the lifecycle are presented, and each phase of the network design process is explored in detail.

- Chapter 3, "Structuring and Modularizing the Network," introduces a modular hierarchical approach to network design: the Cisco Network Architectures for the Enterprise. The chapter includes a detailed description of hierarchical model layers and of the different modules inside the Cisco Network Architectures for the Enterprise.

- Chapter 4, "Designing Basic Campus and Data Center Networks," examines the design of the enterprise campus and enterprise data center network infrastructure.

- Chapter 5, "Designing Remote Connectivity," discusses WAN technologies and design considerations. This chapter describes the enterprise WAN architectures and enterprise branch and teleworker architectures, and discusses the selection of the best technologies to use in each potential situation.

- Chapter 6, "Designing IP Addressing," discusses the design of IP version 4 (IPv4) and version 6 (IPv6) addressing schemes. The chapter also discusses IPv4-to-IPv6 migration strategies.

- Chapter 7, "Designing and Selecting Routing Protocols," describes considerations for selecting the most appropriate network routing protocol depending on the specific network characteristics and customer requirements. The chapter discusses why certain protocols are suitable for specific modules in the enterprise architecture.

- Chapter 8, "Evaluating Security Solutions for the Network," describes the different security concepts that are required for an organized and secure network design. It introduces the Cisco SAFE architecture strategy and reviews how a modular network design can be used to isolate potential security threats.

- Chapter 9, "Identifying Voice and Video Networking Considerations," describes the wireless design principles that must be understood for integrating voice and data networks. The chapter introduces wireless technologies and explores considerations when designing a unified communications network in enterprise environments.

- Chapter 10, "Identifying Design Considerations for Basic Wireless Networking," introduces the Cisco Unified Wireless Network and discusses the design technologies and considerations when implementing a controller-based wireless network.

- Appendix A, "Answers to Review Questions," contains answers to the review questions that appear at the end of the chapters.

- Appendix B, "Acronyms and Abbreviations," spells out the abbreviations, acronyms, and initialisms used in this book.

Review Questions

Starting in Chapter 2, each chapter includes review questions on the subjects covered in that chapter so that the reader can test his or her knowledge. To find the correct answers to these review questions, compare your answers to those provided in Appendix A.

What's New in This Edition

This book is an update to *Authorized Self-Study Guide Designing for Cisco Internetwork Solutions (DESGN)*, Second Edition (ISBN 1-58705-272-5). This third edition reflects changes to the DESGN course. The following are the major changes in this edition:

- Every chapter has been rewritten. Some material was removed from the main portion of the previous edition due to course changes. The appendixes have been updated to reflect the book's content.

- An effort was made to condense the material and focus on the concepts that are directly covered on the associated exam. Much of the detailed explanations of certain concepts have been removed.

Author's Notes, Key Topics, Sidebars, and Cautions

The notes, Key Topics, sidebars, and cautions found in this book provide extra information on a subject. The Key Topics highlight information that is important for understanding the topic at hand and specific points of interest.

Resources for Further Study

Within each chapter are references to other resources that provide you with further information on specific topics. For more information about Cisco exams, training, and certifications, refer to the Training and Events area on the Cisco website, at www.cisco.com/web/learning/index.html.

> **Note**   The website references in this book were accurate at the time of writing; however, they might have since changed. If a URL is unavailable, try conducting a search using the title as keywords in your favorite search engine.

Chapter 1

Network Fundamentals Review

This chapter describes the fundamental concepts that relate to networks and includes the following sections:

- Introduction to Networks

- Protocols and the OSI Model

- LANs and WANs

- Network Devices

- Introduction to the TCP/IP Suite

- Routing

- Addressing

- Switching Types

- Spanning Tree Protocol

- Virtual LANs

This chapter introduces some fundamental concepts and terminology that act as the foundation for additional material in the book. After a brief introduction to networks, the communication protocols that are used by the devices on the network will be reviewed. LANs and WANs are described, as are the various devices found in a network. This chapter also includes an introduction to TCP/IP, which is used extensively in the Internet. Routing and addressing, including IP addresses, are explored. Layer 2 and Layer 3 switching are described. The Spanning Tree Protocol (STP) and its operation are introduced, followed by a discussion of VLANs.

Introduction to Networks

In the 1960s and 1970s, prior to the invention of the PC, a company would typically have one central computer: a mainframe. Users connected to the mainframe through terminals on their desks. These terminals lacked intelligence; their only function was to display a text-based user interface provided by the mainframe. For this reason, they were usually called dumb terminals. The only network was the connection between the terminals and the mainframe.

In 1981, the IBM PC was released, an event that significantly changed the industry. The PC had intelligence of its own, allowing users to perform tasks on their desktops that previously required a mainframe. Networks were introduced to interconnect these distributed PCs.

The term *network* is used frequently. For example, people network with one another, telephones are networked in the public telephone system, and data networks connect different computers. Definitions of the term have a common thread: communication. Networks make it possible for people or devices to communicate with each other.

A data network is a network that allows computers to exchange data. The simplest data network is two PCs connected through a cable. However, most data networks connect various devices.

An internetwork is a collection of individual networks connected by networking devices and functions as a single large network. The public Internet is the most common example. It is a single network that connects millions of computers. *Internetworking* refers to the industry and products that are involved in the design, implementation, and administration of internetworks.

The first networks were LANs; they enabled multiple users in a relatively small geographic area to exchange files and messages and to access shared resources such as printers and disk storage. WANs were introduced to interconnect these LANs so that geographically dispersed users could also share information. These two types of networks are described in more detail later in this chapter in the section "LANs and WANs."

Note   Appendix B, "Acronyms and Abbreviations," lists many of the acronyms that appear in this book.

Protocols and the OSI Model

The following sections describe the Open Systems Interconnection (OSI) model and protocols used in internetworking. They introduce the OSI model, which outlines the communication functions and their relationships with each other.

OSI Model

The ISO standards committee created a list of all the network functions required for sending data (such as an email) and divided them into seven categories. This model is known as the OSI seven-layer model. The OSI seven-layer model was released in 1984. It is illustrated in Figure 1-1.

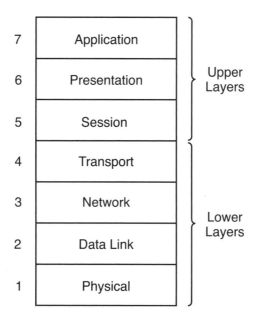

Figure 1-1   *Seven Layers of the OSI Model*

Also shown in Figure 1-1, the seven layers can be thought of in two groups: the upper layers and the lower layers. *Upper layers* often refer to Layers 5 through 7, and the *lower layers* pertain to Layers 1 through 4, although this terminology is relative. The term *upper layer* also refers to any layer above another layer.

The upper layers are concerned with application issues; for example, the interface to the user and the format of the data. The lower layers relate to transport issues, for example, travel of data to the network and the physical characteristics of that network.

Protocols

A protocol is a set of rules. The OSI model provides a framework for the communication protocols used between computers. Computers require a unified set of rules to success- fully communicate. Two computers must use the same protocol to communicate. Computers that attempt to employ different protocols would be analogous to speaking Italian to someone who understands only English.

Many different networking protocols are employed in a variety of categories. For example, LAN and WAN protocols (found at the lower two OSI layers) specify how communication is accomplished across various media types. Routed protocols (associated with Layer 3) specify the data's format and process of transport throughout a network. Routing protocols (some of which also operate at Layer 3) specify how routers communicate with one another to indicate the best paths through the network.

Today, the most widely used network protocol suite is the TCP/IP suite. It is named after two protocols within the suite. This network protocol suite is utilized for many purposes. Organizations use it to facilitate their networks. It is also the backbone of the Internet. Apple Corporation's AppleTalk and IBM's System Network Architecture (SNA) are two other examples of network protocol suites, although both are rarely used on modern networks.

OSI Layers

The following sections briefly describe each of the seven layers of the OSI model, starting at the lowest layer.

Physical Layer: Layer 1

The OSI physical layer defines specifications such as the electrical and mechanical conditions necessary for activating, maintaining, and deactivating the physical link between devices. Specifications include voltage levels, maximum cable lengths, connector types, and maximum data rates. The physical layer is concerned with the binary transmission of data. This binary data is represented as bits (binary digits) A bit has a single binary value, either 0 or 1.

Data Link Layer: Layer 2

Layer 2, the data link layer, defines the format of data to be transmitted across the physical network. It indicates how the physical medium is accessed, including physical addressing, error handling, and flow control. The data link layer sends frames of data. Different media have distinct types of frames.

A *frame* is a defined set of data that includes addressing and control information and is transmitted between network devices. A frame can contain a header field (in front of the data) and a trailer field (after the data). These two fields are said to "frame" the data.

For LANs, the Institute of Electrical and Electronics Engineers (IEEE) split Layer 2 into two sublayers: Logical Link Control (LLC) and Media Access Control (MAC). The LLC sublayer (defined by the IEEE 802.2 specification) allows multiple network layer (Layer 3) protocols to communicate over the same physical data link by allowing the Layer 3 protocol to be specified in the LLC portion of the frame.

Some examples of MAC sublayer protocols are IEEE 802.3 Ethernet and IEEE 802.5 Token Ring. The MAC sublayer specifies the physical MAC address that uniquely identifies a device on a network. Each frame that is sent specifies a destination MAC address;

only the device with that MAC address should receive and process the frame. Each frame also includes the MAC address of the frame's source.

Network Layer: Layer 3

Logical network addresses (as opposed to physical MAC addresses) are specified at Layer 3. Layer 3 protocols include routed and routing protocols. Routing protocols determine the best path that should be used to forward the routed data through the internetwork to its destination, while routed protocols are contained within this routed data.

Note   A datagram is a defined set of data that includes addressing and control information and is routed between the data's source and destination.

If a datagram needs to be sent across a network that can only handle a certain amount of data at one time, the datagram can be fragmented into multiple packets and then reassembled at the destination. Therefore, a *datagram* is a unit of data, whereas a *packet* is what physically goes on the network. If fragmentation is not required, a packet is a datagram; the two terms are often used interchangeably.

Transport Layer: Layer 4

Layer 4, the transport layer, is concerned with end-to-end connections between the source and the destination. The transport layer provides network services to the upper layers.

Connection-oriented reliable transport establishes a logical connection and uses sequence numbers to ensure that all data is received at the destination. Connectionless best-effort transport only sends the data and relies on upper-layer error-detection mechanisms to report and correct problems. Reliable transport has more overhead than best-effort transport.

Note   Best-effort delivery means that the protocol will not check to see whether the data was delivered intact; a higher-level protocol, or the end user, must confirm that the data was delivered correctly.

Multiplexing allows many applications to use the same physical connection. For example, data is tagged with a number that identifies the application from which it came. Both sides of the connection can interpret the data in the same way.

The transport layer sends segments. A segment is a defined set of data that includes control information and is sent between the transport layers of the sender and receiver.

Upper Layers: Layers 5 Through 7

From the lower layers' perspective, the three upper layers represent the data that must be transmitted from the source to the destination. The network does not comprehend the contents of these layers. The following points briefly describe the functions of these layers:

- **Session layer:** Layer 5 is responsible for establishing, maintaining, and terminating communication sessions between applications running on different hosts.

- **Presentation layer:** Layer 6 represents the data in various ways. It specifies format, data structure, coding, and compression, just to name a few. It ensures that information sent from one host's application layer can be read by the destination host.

- **Application layer:** Layer 7 is the closest to the end user. It interacts directly with software applications necessary to communicate over the network.

Communication Among OSI Layers

This section describes how communication among the seven OSI layers is accomplished. When an email is sent from Toronto to a recipient in San Francisco, think of the email application in Toronto as sending a message to the email application on the recipient's computer in San Francisco. In OSI model terms, information is exchanged between peer OSI layers. The application layer on the transmitting computer is communicating with the application layer on the recipient's computer. However, to accomplish this, the email must go through all the other layers on the computer. For example, it must have the correct network layer address, be put in the correct frame type, and so on. The email must then go over the network, and then back through all the layers on the recipient's computer, until it finally arrives at the recipient's email application.

Control information from each layer is added to the email data before it passes to lower layers. This control information is necessary to allow the data to go through the network properly. Thus, the data at each layer is encapsulated or wrapped in the information appropriate for that layer. This process includes addressing and error checking. The right side of Figure 1-2 illustrates the following encapsulation process:

- At Layer 4, the email is encapsulated in a segment.

- At Layer 3, this segment is encapsulated in a packet.

- At Layer 2, this packet is encapsulated in a frame.

- At Layer 1, the frame is sent out on the wire (or air, if wireless is used) in bits.

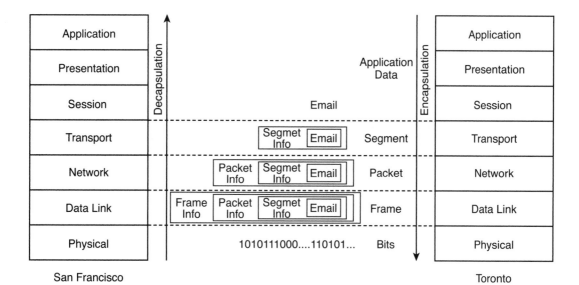

Figure 1-2   *Data Encapsulation and Decapsulation*

The grouping of data used to exchange information at a particular OSI layer is known as a protocol data unit (PDU). Thus, the PDU at Layer 4 is a segment. At Layer 3, it is a packet, and at Layer 2, it is a frame.

Notice how the overall size of the information increases as the data goes down through the lower layers. When data is received at the other end of the network, this additional information is analyzed and then removed as the data is passed to the higher layers toward the application layer. In other words, the data is *decapsulated*, or unwrapped. This process is shown on the left side of Figure 1-2.

Note   For simplicity, Figure 1-2 shows only two systems, one in San Francisco and one in Toronto, and does not show the details of email protocols or email servers. Later sections in this chapter describe what occurs when intermediate devices, such as routers, are encountered between the two systems.

At each layer, different protocols are available. For example, the packets sent by IP are different from those sent by Internetwork Packet Exchange (IPX) because different protocols (rules) must be followed. Both sides of peer layers that are communicating must support the same protocol.

LANs and WANs

LANs were first employed for PCs when users needed to integrate with other PCs in the same location to share resources. A LAN is a high-speed, yet relatively inexpensive, network that allows connected computers to communicate. LANs have limited reach (hence the term *local-area network*), typically less than a few hundred meters, so they can merge only devices in the same room or building, or possibly within the same campus.

A LAN is an always-on connection. In other words, the connection does not require a dialup or other connection step to send data. LANs usually belong to the organization in which they are deployed, so there is not an incremental cost associated with sending data. A variety of LAN technologies are available, some of which are shown in the center of Figure 1-3 and briefly described here:

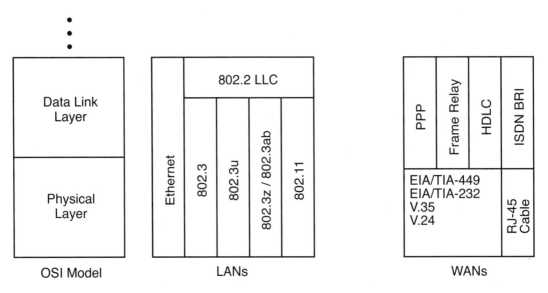

Figure 1-3   *Several LAN and WAN Standards*

- **Ethernet and IEEE 802.3:** It runs at 10 megabits per second (Mbps) and uses a carrier sense multiple access collision detection (CSMA/CD) technology. When a CSMA/CD device has to send data, it verifies that it is the only device in use on the wire (multiple access) and allows it to transmit data (carrier sense). The detection process is continuous to avoid a situation where another device might erroneously attempt to transmit data at the same time (collision detect).

■ **Fast Ethernet (at 100 Mbps):** It is covered by the IEEE 802.3u specification and also uses the CSMA/CD technology.

■ **Gigabit Ethernet (running at 1 and 10 gigabits per second [Gbps]):** It is covered by the IEEE 802.3z, 802.3ab, and 802.3ae specifications and uses the CSMA/CD technology.

■ **Wireless LAN (WLAN) standards:** They are defined by the IEEE 802.11 specifications and are capable of speeds up to 600 Mbps under the 802.11n specification. WLANs use a carrier sense multiple access collision avoidance (CSMA/CA) mechanism (versus the CSMA/CD mechanism used by the wired Ethernet standards).

WANs interconnect devices, are usually connected to LANs, and are located over a relatively broad geographic area (hence the term *wide-area network*). Compared to a LAN, a typical WAN is slower and requires a connection request when data is to be sent. A WAN usually belongs to another organization (called a service provider). A fee might be charged by the service provider (known as a tariff) for the use of the WAN. The rate is either a fixed monthly amount or a variable based on usage and distance.

Many types of WANs are available, some of which are illustrated on the right side of Figure 1-3. Similar to LANs, WANs function at the lower two layers of the OSI model. A few, such as ISDN, also function at Layer 3. The service that is implemented depends on many factors, including location availability and cost of service. Some of the common WAN technologies include the following:

■ **Packet-switched network:** This network shares the service provider's facilities. The service provider creates permanent virtual circuits and switched virtual circuits that deliver data between subscribers' sites. Frame Relay is an example of a packet-switched network.

■ **Leased line:** This is a point-to-point connection reserved for transmission. Common data link layer protocols used in this case are Point-to-Point Protocol (PPP) and High-Level Data Link Control (HDLC).

■ **Circuit-switched network:** This is a physical path reserved for the duration of the connection between two points. ISDN Basic Rate Interface (BRI) is an example of this type of network.

Two other technologies, digital subscriber line (DSL) and cable, connect residential and business premises to service providers' premises and are described here:

■ **DSL:** It utilizes unused bandwidth on traditional copper telephone lines to deliver traffic at higher speeds than allowed by traditional modems. The most common DSL implementation is asymmetric DSL (ADSL). It is called asymmetric because the download speed is faster than the upload speed. It reflects the needs of most users and more efficiently uses the available bandwidth on standard two-wire telephone lines. ADSL allows regular telephone traffic to simultaneously share the line with high-speed data traffic. Only one telephone line is required to support both high-speed Internet access and normal telephone services.

■   **Cable:** It utilizes vacant bandwidth on cable television networks to deliver data at higher speeds than traditional modems allow.

Note   These and other WAN technologies are discussed in Chapter 5, "Designing Remote Connectivity."

Network Devices

The main devices that interconnect networks are hubs, switches, and routers. They are described in the following sections.

Note   Many other devices can be used in networks to provide specific functionality. These devices are introduced in the appropriate chapters in this book.

Terminology: Domains, Bandwidth, Unicast, Broadcast, and Multicast

Table 1-1 lists the most common terminology associated with the operation of network devices.

Devices in the same bandwidth domain are also in the same broadcast domain. However, devices in the same broadcast domain can be in different bandwidth domains.

Table 1-1   *Network Terminology*

Term	Description
Domain	Specific part of a network.
Bandwidth	The amount of data that can be carried across a network in a given time period.
Unicast data	Data meant for a specific device.
Broadcast data	Data meant for all devices. A special broadcast address indicates this.
Multicast data	Data destined for a specific group of devices. A special address indicates this.
Collision domain (or *bandwidth domain)* for Ethernet LANs	Includes all devices that share the same bandwidth.
Broadcast domain	Includes all devices that receive each other's broadcasts (and multicasts).

Hubs

A hub works at Layer 1 and connects multiple devices so that they are strategically placed on a single LAN.

Physical Interfaces and Ports

Note   The physical connection point on a network device, hub, switch, or router is called an *interface* or a *port*.

Do not confuse this definition of *port* with the application layer port numbers discussed later in this chapter in the section, "TCP/IP Transport Layer Protocols."

A hub lacks intelligence. It sends all data received on any port to all the other ports. Consequently, devices connected through a hub receive everything that the other devices transport, regardless of the intended recipient. This is analogous to being in a room with many people, and if one person speaks, everyone can hear that person. If more than one person speaks at the same time, everyone hears nothing but noise.

All devices connected to a hub are in one collision domain and one broadcast domain.

Note   A hub just repeats all the data received on any port to all the other ports. Thus, hubs are also known as repeaters.

Switches

Using hubs in anything but a small network is not efficient. To improve performance, LANs are usually divided into smaller and numerous LANs interconnected by a Layer 2 LAN switch. The devices connected to a switch now appear as if they are unified on one LAN. This process allows multiple conversations between devices connected through the switch to occur simultaneously.

Note   This section discusses Layer 2 LAN switches. Layer 3 switching is discussed in the section, "Switching Types," later in this chapter.

LAN switches are typically Layer 2 devices and have some intelligence. They send data to a port only if it is required. A device connected to a switch port does not receive any of the information addressed to devices on other ports. Therefore, the main advantage of using a switch instead of a hub is a reduction of traffic received by a device. Only frames that are addressed to a specific device are forwarded to the port on which the device is connected.

Switches read the source and destination MAC addresses in the frames. They keep track of who is where and who is talking to whom, and they have the ability to send data to the appropriate locations. However, if the switch receives a frame whose destination address indicates that it is a broadcast (information meant for everyone) or multicast (information meant for a group), by default, it sends the frame out to all ports (except for the one on which it was received).

All devices connected to one switch port are located in the same collision domain, but devices connected to different ports are in different collision domains. By default, all devices connected to a switch are in the same broadcast domain.

Switches do not allow devices on different logical LANs to communicate with each other. This requires a router, as described in the next section.

Switches Versus Bridges

Note Both *bridges* (an older method) and *switches* describe connection devices that are similar in nature. Switches and bridges are logically equivalent. The main differences are as follows:

■ Switches are significantly faster because they switch in hardware, whereas bridges switch in software.

■ Switches typically have more ports than bridges.

■ Modern switches have additional features not found on bridges; these features are described in later chapters.

Routers

A router extends the reach of a switch. It is a Layer 3 device that possesses more intelligence than a hub or switch. By using logical Layer 3 addresses, routers allow devices on different LANs to communicate with each other and with distant devices such as connections through the Internet or through a WAN. Examples of logical Layer 3 addresses include TCP/IP's IP addresses.

A device connected to a router does not receive any of the information allocated for devices on other ports, or broadcasts (destined for all networks) from devices on other ports.

The router reads the source and destination logical addresses in the packets and keeps track of who is where and who is talking to whom, and then sends data to the appropriate locations. It supports communication between LANs but blocks broadcasts (destined for all networks).

All devices connected to one router port are in the same collision domain, but devices connected to different ports are in different collision domains.

All the devices connected to one router interface are in the same broadcast domain, but devices connected to different interfaces are in different broadcast domains. Routers block broadcasts (destined for all networks) and multicasts by default. Routers forward only unicast packets (destined for a specific device) and packets of a special type called *directed broadcasts*.

Note   An IP-directed broadcast is an IP packet that is destined for all devices on an IP subnet. IP subnets are described in the "Addressing" section, later in this chapter.

The significant difference between a router and a switch is that a router does not forward broadcasts (destined for all networks). A router also helps control the amount of traffic on the network. For example, many protocols, such as IP, might use broadcasts for routing protocol advertisements, discovering servers, and so on. These broadcasts are a necessary part of local LAN traffic, but they are not required on other LANs and can even overwhelm slower WANs. Routers can generate broadcasts themselves if necessary (for example, to send a routing protocol advertisement), but they do not pass on a received broadcast.

Routing operation is discussed in further detail in the "Routing" section, later in this chapter.

Note   The concepts of unicast, multicast, and broadcast apply to Layer 2 and Layer 3 individually. Although a router does not forward any type of frame, it can forward a unicast, multicast, or directed broadcast packet that it receives in a frame. A switch, however, can forward a unicast, multicast, or broadcast frame.

Introduction to the TCP/IP Suite

As mentioned earlier, TCP/IP is the most widely used protocol suite. The relationship among the five layers of the TCP/IP protocol suite and the seven layers of the OSI model is illustrated in Figure 1-4.

The five layers of the TCP/IP suite are

- Application layer
- Transport layer
- Internet layer
- Data link layer
- Physical layer

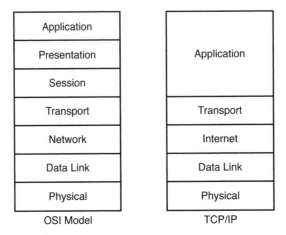

Figure 1-4   *TCP/IP Protocol Suite*

Note   The data link and physical layers are sometimes grouped as one layer, called the *network interface layer*.

The TCP/IP application layer includes the functionality of the OSI application, presentation, and session layers. Applications defined in the TCP/IP suite are shown in Table 1-2.

Table 1-2   *TCP/IP Suite Applications*

Application	Function
FTP	Transfers files between devices
Trivial File Transfer Protocol (TFTP)	Transfers files between devices
SMTP	Provides email services
POP3	Provides email services
HTTP	Transfers information to and from a World Wide Web server through web-browser software
Telnet	Emulates a terminal to connect to devices
Domain Name System (DNS)	Translates network device names into network addresses and vice versa
Simple Network Management Protocol (SNMP)	Used for network management, including setting threshold values and reporting network errors
Dynamic Host Configuration Protocol (DHCP)	Assigns dynamic IP addressing information to devices as they require it

The transport layer and Internet layer protocols are detailed the sections that follow.

The data link and physical layers can support a wide variety of LANs and WANs (including those discussed in the "LANs and WANs" section, earlier in this chapter).

TCP/IP Transport Layer Protocols

The TCP/IP transport layer includes the following two protocols:

- **Transmission Control Protocol (TCP):** Provides connection-oriented, end-to-end reliable transmission. Before sending any data, TCP on the source device establishes a connection with TCP on the destination device, ensuring that both sides are synchronized. Data is acknowledged. Any data not received properly is retransmitted. FTP is an example of an application that uses TCP to guarantee that the data sent from one device to another is received successfully.

- **User Datagram Protocol (UDP):** Provides connectionless, best-effort unacknowledged data transmission. In other words, UDP does not ensure that all the segments arrive at the destination undamaged. UDP does not have the capabilities of TCP, such as establishing the connection and acknowledging the data. However, this means that upper-layer protocols or the user must determine whether all the data arrives successfully. The user must retransmit if necessary. TFTP is an example of an application that uses UDP. When all the segments have arrived at the destination, TFTP computes the file check sequence and reports the results to the user. If an error occurs, the user must resend the entire file.

Note DNS is an example of an application layer protocol that may use either TCP or UDP, depending on the function it is performing.

TCP and UDP, being at the transport layer, send segments. Figure 1-5 illustrates the fields in a UDP segment and in a TCP segment. Notice that the UDP segment headers contain at least 8 bytes, whereas TCP segment headers contain at least 20 bytes.

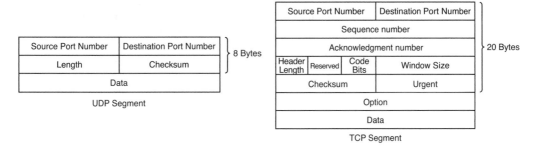

Figure 1-5 *UDP Segment Headers and TCP Segment Headers*

The UDP segment fields are listed in Table 1-3.

Table 1-3   *UDP Segment Fields*

Field	Length	Description
Source and destination port numbers	16 bits each	Identifies the upper-layer protocol (the application) in the sending and receiving devices
Length	16 bits	The total number of 32-bit words in the header and the data
Checksum	16 bits	The checksum of the header and data fields, used to ensure that the segment is received correctly
Data	Variable length	The upper-layer data (the application data)

The TCP segment fields are listed in Table 1-4.

Table 1-4   *TCP Segment Fields*

Field	Length	Description
Source and destination port numbers	16 bits each	Identifies the upper-layer protocol (the application) in the sending and receiving hosts
Sequence and acknowledgment numbers	32 bits each	Ensures the correct order of the received data and that the data reached the destination
Header length	4 bits	The number of 32-bit words in the header
Reserved	6 bits	For future use, set to 0
Code bits	6 bits	Indicates different types of segments. For example, the SYN (synchronize) bit is used for setting up a session, the ACK (acknowledge) bit is used for acknowledging a segment, and the FIN (finish) bit is used for closing a session.
Window size	16 bits	The number of octets that the receiving device is willing to accept before it must send an acknowledgment
Checksum	16 bits	The checksum of the header and data fields, used to ensure that the segment is received correctly
Urgent	16 bits	Indicates the end of urgent data
Option	0 or 32 bits	The options available for the packet
Data	Variable	The upper-layer data (the application data)

Note   An octet is 8 bits of data.

Notice that the UDP header is much smaller than the TCP header. UDP does not need the sequencing, acknowledgment, or windowing fields, because it does not establish and maintain connections.

Port number operation, which is the same for both TCP and UDP, is described in the next section. Following that section, the operation of sequence and acknowledgment numbers and windowing are described; these are crucial to understanding TCP operation.

Port Numbers

Well-known, or standardized, port numbers are assigned to applications so that different implementations of the TCP/IP protocol suite can interoperate. Well-known port numbers are numbers up to 1023. Some examples are listed in Table 1-5.

Table 1-5   *Standardized Port Numbers*

Applications	Port Numbers
FTP	TCP port 20 (data) and port 21 (control)
TFTP	UDP port 69
SMTP	TCP port 25
POP3	TCP port 110
HTTP	TCP port 80
Telnet	TCP port 23
DNS	TCP and UDP port 53
SNMP	UDP port 161

Note   TCP and UDP use protocol port numbers to distinguish among multiple applications that are running on a single device.

Port numbers from 1024 through 49151 are called registered port numbers; these are registered for use by other applications. The dynamic ports numbers are those from 49152 through 65535; these can be dynamically assigned by hosts as source port numbers when they create and end sessions.

For example, Figure 1-6 illustrates a device in Toronto that is opening a Telnet session (TCP port 23) with a device in London. Note that the source port from Toronto is 50051. Toronto records this Telnet session with London as port 50051 to distinguish it from any other Telnet sessions it might have running (because simultaneous multiple Telnet sessions can be running on a device). The London device receives port number 23 and therefore knows that this is a Telnet session. In its reply, it uses a destination port of 50051, which Toronto recognizes as the Telnet session it opened with London.

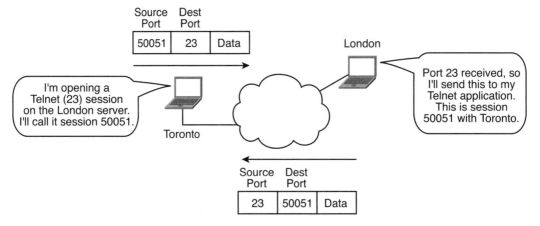

Figure 1-6   *Port Numbers Example*

TCP Sequencing, Acknowledgment, and Windowing

To illustrate TCP operation, this section follows a TCP session as it is established, acknowledges that data is sent, and the session is closed.

Note   A TCP connection is established by a process called a *three-way handshake*. This process uses the SYN and ACK bits (in the code bits field in the TCP segment) as well as the sequence and acknowledgment number fields.

The TCP three-way handshake is shown in Figure 1-7.

In this example, a user in Toronto wants to establish a TCP session with a device in London to start a Telnet session. The first step in the handshake involves the initiator, Toronto. Toronto sends a segment with the SYN bit set to indicate that it wants to begin a session and synchronize with London. This segment also includes the initial sequence number (21) that Toronto is using.

Assuming that the device in London is willing to establish the session, it returns a segment that also has the SYN bit set. This segment also includes the ACK bit set because

London is acknowledging that it successfully received a segment from Toronto. The acknowledgment number is set to 22, indicating that London is now expecting to receive segment 22 and successfully received number 21. This is known as an *expectational acknowledgment*. The new segment includes the initial sequence number (75) that London is using.

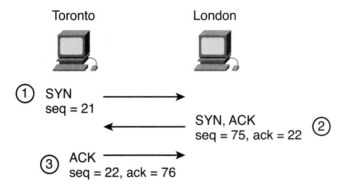

Figure 1-7   *TCP Three-Way Handshake*

Finally, Toronto replies with an acknowledgment segment, sequence number 22 (as London is expecting), and acknowledgment number 76. The reply indicates that it is now expecting number 76 and has successfully received number 75. The session is now established, and data can be exchanged between Toronto and London.

Note   The sequence and acknowledgment numbers specify octet numbers, not segment numbers. For ease of illustration, this example assumes that a segment is 1 octet of data. This is not the case in real life, but it simplifies the example so that the concepts are easier to understand.

The window size field in the segment controls the flow of the session. It indicates the number of octets a device is willing to accept before it must send an acknowledgment. Because each host can have different flow restrictions, each side of the session can have different window sizes. For example, one host might be busy and therefore require that a smaller amount of data be sent at one time, as illustrated in Figure 1-8.

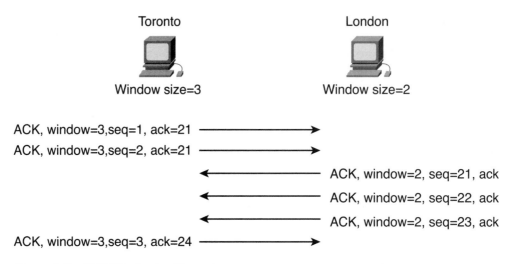

Figure 1-8   *TCP Windowing Example*

In this example, the window size on Toronto is set to 3, and on London it is set to 2. When Toronto transmits data to London, it can send 2 octets prior to waiting for an acknowledgment. When London relays data to Toronto, it can send 3 octets prior to an acknowledgment.

Note   The window size specifies the number of octets that can be sent, not the number of segments. For ease of illustration, this example assumes that a segment is 1 octet of data. This is not the case in real life, but it simplifies the example so that the concepts are easier to understand. The window sizes shown in the example are also small for ease of explanation. In reality, the window size would be much larger, allowing a lot of data to be sent between acknowledgments.

After all the data for the session is transmitted, the session can be closed. The process is similar to how it was established: using a handshake. In this case, four steps are used, hence the four-way handshake illustrated in Figure 1-9.

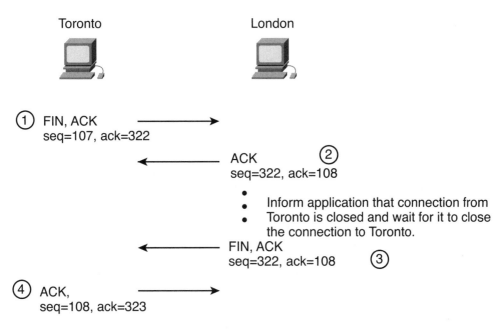

Figure 1-9   *TCP Session Closure Example*

For a more detailed explanation of the four stages that occur, see the following steps:

Step 1.   In this example, Toronto wants to close its Telnet session with London. The first step in the handshake involves Toronto transmitting a segment with the FIN bit set, indicating that it wants to complete the session. This segment also includes the sequence number (107) that Toronto is currently using.

Step 2.   London immediately acknowledges the request. This segment has the ACK bit set with the acknowledgment number set to 108, indicating that London successfully received number 107. The segment includes the sequence number (322) that London is currently using. London then informs its Telnet application that half of the session, the connection from Toronto, is now closed.

Step 3.   When the application on the London device requests that the other half of the connection (to Toronto) be closed, London transmits a new segment with the FIN bit set, indicating that it wants to close the session.

Step 4.   Finally, Toronto replies with a confirmation segment including acknowledgment number 323. This indicates that Toronto has successfully received number 322. The session is now closed in both directions.

Note   In many common TCP/IP implementations, this four-way handshake can be reduced to a three-way handshake by combining a FIN and ACK into a single segment.

TCP/IP Internet Layer Protocols

The TCP/IP Internet layer corresponds to the OSI network layer and includes the IP-routed protocol as well as a protocol for message and error reporting.

Protocols

The protocols at this layer include the following:

- **IP:** Provides connectionless, best-effort delivery of datagrams through the network. A unique IP address is assigned to each interface of every device in the network.

- **Internet Control Message Protocol (ICMP):** Sends messages and error reports through the network. For example, the ping application included in most TCP/IP protocol suites sends an ICMP echo message to a destination. It replies with an ICMP echo reply message. Ping confirms that the destination can be reached and measures the length of time for the long packets to travel between the source and destination.

Note   These protocols are all at the TCP/IP Internet layer, corresponding to the OSI model network layer, Layer 3. They run on top of the TCP/IP physical and data link layers, Layers 1 and 2.

IPv4 Datagrams

Figure 1-10 illustrates the fields of an IPv4 datagram.

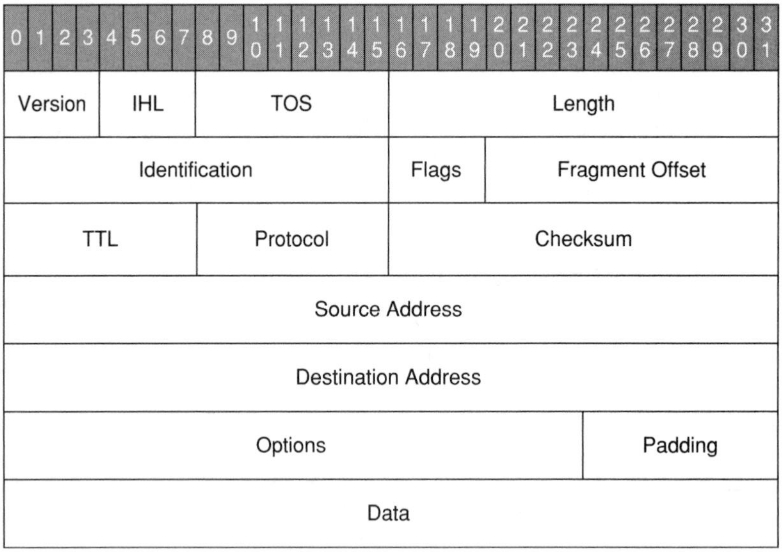

Figure 1-10   *IPv4 Datagram*

The IPv4 datagram fields are listed in Table 1-6.

Table 1-6   *IPv4 Datagram Fields*

Field	Length	Description
Version	4 bits	Identifies the IP version, version 4.
Internet Header Length (IHL)	4 bits	The number of 32-bit words in the header (including the options).
Type of service (ToS)	8 bits	Specifies how the datagram should be handled within the network. These bits mark traffic for a specific quality of service (QoS).
Length	16 bits	The total number of octets in the header and data fields.
Identification Flags Fragment offset	16 bits 3 bits 13 bits	Handles cases where a large datagram must be fragmented—split into multiple packets—to go through a network that cannot handle datagrams of that size.
Time to Live (TTL)	8 bits	Ensures that datagrams do not loop endlessly in the network. This field must be decremented by 1 by each router that the datagram is forwarded through.
Protocol	8 bits	Indicates the upper or transport layer (Layer 4) protocol that is specific to the data. This field might indicate the type of segment that the datagram is carrying. It is similar to how the port number field in the UDP and TCP segments indicates the type of application that the segment is carrying. A protocol number of 6 means that the datagram is carrying a TCP segment, whereas a protocol number of 17 means that the datagram is carrying a UDP segment. The protocol can have other values, including a value that indicates that traffic from a specific routing protocol is being carried inside the datagram.
Checksum	16 bits	Ensures that the header is received correctly.
Source and destination IP addresses	32 bits each	Ensures that logical IP addresses are assigned to the source and destination of the datagram, respectively.
Options and padding	Variable length; 0 or a multiple of 32 bits	Used for network testing and debugging.
Data	Variable	The upper-layer (transport layer) data.

IPv6 Datagrams

Figure 1-11 illustrates the fields of an IPv6 datagram.

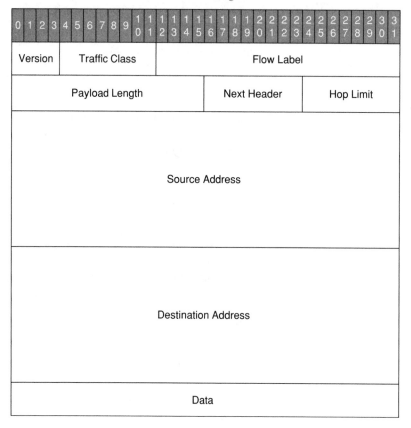

Figure 1-11   *IPv6 Datagram*

The IPv6 datagram fields are listed in Table 1-7.

Table 1-7   *IPv6 Datagram Fields*

Field	Length	Description
Version	4 bits	Identifies the IP version, in this case, version 6.
Traffic Class	8 bits	Works similarly to the IPv4 ToS field. Provides the ability to place traffic into different classes.
Flow Label	20 bits	Can be used to assist in the identification of traffic flows and relate traffic in different classes.
Payload Length	16 bits	Contains the overall length of the packet payload.

Table 1-7 *IPv6 Datagram Fields*

Field	Length	Description
Next Header	8 bits	Works similarly to the IPv4 Protocol field by defining the type of traffic that is contained within the payload (which header to expect, for example, tcp).
Hop Limit	8 bits	Works similarly to the IPv4 TTL field to ensure that datagrams do not loop endlessly in the network. This field must be decremented by 1 by each router that the datagram is forwarded through.
Source and Destination IP addresses	128 bits each	Ensures that logical IP addresses are assigned to the source and destination of the datagram, respectively.
Data	Variable	The upper-layer (transport layer) data.

Routing

The following sections examine how routers work and introduce routing tables and routing protocols. Routers perform at the OSI model network layer. The main functions of a router are to determine the best path that each packet should take to get to its destination and to send the packet on its way. This process is called *switching the packet* because the packet is encapsulated in a new frame with the appropriate framing information.

Therefore, a router's job is much like that of a worker at a post office. The postal worker looks at the address label on the letter (the network layer address on the packet), determines which way the letter (the packet) should be sent, and then sends it. The comparison between the post office and a router is illustrated in Figure 1-12.

Note   This explanation of routers is focused on the traditional role of routers in a network: at the OSI model network layer. Routers are now taking on more functions, particularly in QoS and security areas. These and other tasks are described in the relevant chapters throughout this book.

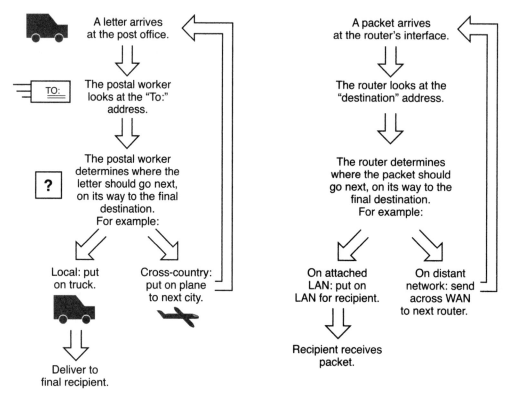

Figure 1-12 *Routing Behavior Example*

Routers Work at the Lower Three OSI Layers

Traditionally, routers are not responsible for activity at the higher layers. Their main objective is to send the packet the correct way. The router does have to be concerned with the data link and physical layers because it might have to receive and send data on different media. For example, a packet received on an Ethernet LAN might have to be sent out on a Frame Relay WAN circuit. This would require the router to know how to communicate on both these types of media. In terms of layers, a router decapsulates received data up to the network layer and then encapsulates the data again into the appropriate frame and bit types. This process is illustrated in Figure 1-13, where the PC on the left is transmitting data to the PC on the right. The routers have determined that the path marked with the arrows is the best path between the PCs.

In this figure, notice that only the two PCs are engaged with the upper layers, whereas all the routers in the path concern themselves with only the lower three layers.

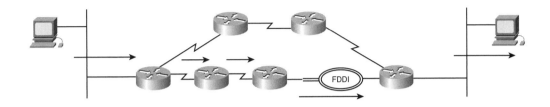

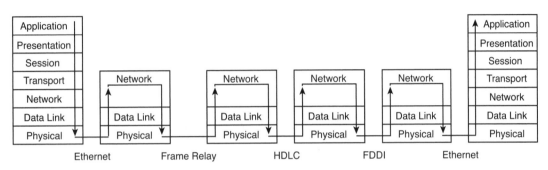

Figure 1-13 *Network Layer Router Example*

Routing Tables

To determine the best path on which to send a packet, a router must know how to reach the destination network. When the router obtains destination network information, it keeps the best path (or multiple best paths) to each destination in a routing table. A routing table contains a list of all the networks that are attainable by the router. For each network, the routing table typically contains the following items:

■ How the route to the network was learned (for example, statically or by using a routing protocol).

■ The network address of the router from which the route to the network was learned (if applicable).

■ The interface (port) on the router through which the network can be reached.

■ The metric of the route. The metric is a measurement, such as the number of other routers that the path goes through. This is used by the routing protocols when determining the best path.

Note   The best path that is determined by the router depends on the protocol in use. For example, some routing protocols define *best* as the path that goes through the fewest additional routers (the fewest hops). Others define the best path with a metric calculated from the path's bandwidth and delay (and possibly other) information.

For example, in the network shown in Figure 1-14, the metric used is hop count. This is the number of other routers between this router and the destination network. Both routers are aware of all three networks. Router X, on the left, acknowledges networks A and B because it is connected to them (hence the metric of 0) and also knows about network C from Router Y (hence the metric of 1). Router Y, on the right, acknowledges networks B and C because it is connected to them (hence the metric of 0) and knows about network A from Router X (hence the metric of 1).

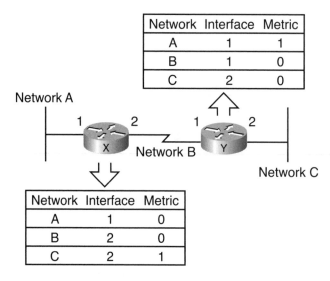

Figure 1-14   *Routing Table Example*

Routing Protocols

Routers employ routing protocols to exchange routing information. Routing protocols allow routers to acquire the necessary data from other routers to determine the availability of networks so that data can be sent in the correct direction. Remember that two routers communicating with each other must use the same routing protocol or they cannot understand each other.

The TCP/IP protocol suite includes the following routing protocols:

- Routing Information Protocol (RIP), versions 1 and 2 (RIPv1 and RIPv2)

- Enhanced Interior Gateway Routing Protocol (EIGRP)

- Open Shortest Path First (OSPF)

- Integrated Intermediate System–to–Intermediate System (IS-IS)

- Border Gateway Protocol (BGP) version 4 (BGP-4)

Note   These routing protocols are discussed further in Chapter 7, "Designing and Selecting Routing Protocols."

The previous sections introduced the basics of routing and described how routers identify the available networks so that data can be sent along the correct path. Routers analyze the packet's destination address to determine the final location so that they can then select the best route to transmit the packet. The following sections discuss these addresses.

Addressing

The following sections describe physical and network layer addressing and discuss how routers use them. The sections conclude with a brief introduction to IP addressing.

Physical Addresses

As discussed earlier, MAC addresses reside at the data link layer and are considered physical addresses. When a network interface card is manufactured, it is assigned an address called a burned-in address (BIA). This does not change when the network card is installed in a device and moved from one network to another. Typically, the BIA is copied to interface memory and used as the interface's MAC address. MAC addresses are analogous to United States Social Security numbers: One is assigned to each person, and the numbers do not change when that person changes his or her address. These numbers are associated with the physical person, not the person's location.

Note   Some organizations set the MAC addresses of their devices to something other than the BIA. For example, sometimes it is based on the location of the device in the network for management purposes.

Knowing the MAC address assigned to a PC or to a router's interface does not reflect its location or to what network it is attached. It also cannot assist a router to determine the best route to transport the data. Logical network layer addresses are needed to accomplish the task. Logical network layers are assigned when a device is installed on a network and should be changed when the device is moved.

Logical Addresses

When sending a letter to someone, a postal address is required. Every postal address in the world is unique, so a letter can potentially be sent to anyone in the world. The addresses are logical and hierarchical. For example, they include the country, province/state, street, and building/house number. The top portion of Figure 1-15 illustrates Main Street with various houses. All these houses have one portion of their address in common: Main Street. They also have one portion that is unique: the house number.

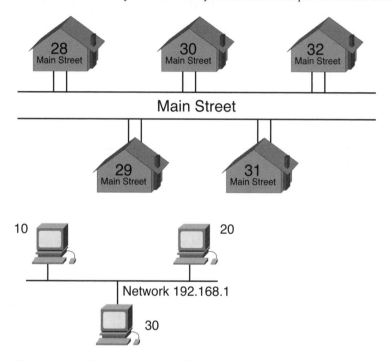

Figure 1-15 *Network Layer Address Example*

> **Note** Network layer addresses are also logical and hierarchical, and they are either defined statically by an administrator or obtained automatically from a server. They have two main parts: the network that the device is on (similar to the street, city, province, and so on) and the device number on that network (similar to the building number).

> **Note** The terms *device*, *host*, and *node* are used interchangeably to represent the entity that is communicating.

The lower portion of Figure 1-15 illustrates a network (17) with various PCs on it. All of these PCs have one portion of their address in common (17) and one part that is unique: their device number. Devices on the same logical network must share the same network portion of their address and have different device portions.

Routing and Network Layer Addresses

A router's primary interest is the network portion of a destination address. It compares the network portion to its routing table, and if it finds a match, it sends the packet out the appropriate interface and toward its destination.

A router's main concern is the device portion of a destination address. It must confirm that it is directly connected to the same network as the destination. In this case, the router must send the packet directly to the appropriate device. The entire destination address is required for this process. A router on a LAN uses the Address Resolution Protocol (ARP) to determine the MAC address of the device with that IP address and then creates an appropriate frame with that MAC address as the destination MAC address.

IPv4 Addresses

IP addresses are network layer addresses. As mentioned earlier, IPv4 addresses are 32-bit numbers. As shown in Figure 1-16, the 32 bits are usually written in dotted-decimal notation. They are grouped into 4 octets (8 bits each), separated by dots, and each octet is represented in decimal format. Each bit in the octet has a binary weight (the highest is 128 and the next is 64, followed by 32, 16, 8, 4, 2, and 1). Thus, the minimum value for an octet is 0, and the maximum decimal value for an octet is 255.

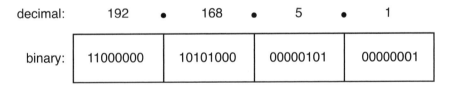

Figure 1-16 *IPv4 Dotted-Decimal Notation*

Note The maximum value of an octet is when all 8 bits are binary 1. The decimal value of an octet is calculated by adding all the weighted bits, in this case, 128 + 64 + 32 + 16 + 8 + 4 + 2 + 1 = 255.

IPv4 Address Classes

IPv4 addresses are categorized into five classes: A, B, C, D, and E. Only Class A, B, and C addresses are utilized for addressing devices. Class D is used for multicast groups, and Class E is reserved for experimental use.

The first octet of an IPv4 address defines which class it resides in, as illustrated in Table 1-8 for Class A, B, and C addresses. The address class determines which part of the address represents the network bits (N) and which part represents the host bits (H), as shown in this table. The number of networks available in each class and the number of hosts per network are also shown.

Table 1-8 *IP Address Classes*

Class	Format	Higher-Order Bits	Address Range	Number of Networks	Number of Hosts per Network
A	N.H.H.H	0	1.0.0.0 to 126.0.0.0	126	16,777,214
B	N.N.H.H	10	128.0.0.0 to 191.255.0.0	16,386	65,534
C	N.N.N.H	110	192.0.0.0 to 223.255.255.0	2,097,152	254

*N=network number bits; H=host number bits

Note Class A addresses are any addresses that have the higher-order bit set to 0, which would include 0 through 127 in the first octet. However, network 0.0.0.0 is reserved, and network 127.0.0.0 (any address starting with decimal 127) is reserved for loopback functionality. Therefore, the first octet of Class A addresses ranges from 1 to 126.

Note Class D addresses have higher-order bits 1110 and are in the range of 224.0.0.0 to 239.255.255.255. Class E addresses have higher-order bits 1111 and are in the range of 240.0.0.0 to 255.255.255.255.

For example, 192.168.5.1 is a Class C address. Therefore, it is in the format N.N.N.H; the network part is 192.168.5 and the host part is 1.

Private and Public IPv4 Addresses

The IPv4 address space is divided into public and private sections. Private addresses are reserved for internal purposes within a company's network. The addresses are not to be routed on the Internet. Only public IPv4 address ranges are used for Internet communication.

If using private addresses internally, they must be mapped to a public IPv4 address before being routed to the Internet.

Note RFC 1918, "Address Allocation for Private Internets," defines the private IPv4 addresses as follows:

10.0.0.0 to 10.255.255.255

172.16.0.0 to 172.31.255.255

192.168.0.0 to 192.168.255.255

The remaining addresses are public addresses.

Note Internet RFC documents are written definitions of the Internet's protocols and policies. A complete list and the documents can be found at www.rfc-editor.org/rfc.html.

Note All the IP addresses used in this book are private addresses to avoid publishing anyone's registered address.

IPv4 Subnets

As illustrated in Table 1-9, Class A addresses have little use in a normal organization.
Most companies would not want a single network with more than 16 million PCs on it!
This would not be physically possible or desirable. Because of this limitation on address-
es when only their class is considered (called classful addressing) and the finite number of
such addresses, subnets were introduced by RFC 950, "Internet Standard Subnetting
Procedure."

Table 1-9 *IPV4 Address Default Subnet Masks*

Class	Default Mask in Binary Format	Default Mask in Decimal Format
A	11111111.00000000.00000000.00000000	255.0.0.0
B	11111111.11111111.00000000.00000000	255.255.0.0
C	11111111.11111111.11111111.00000000	255.255.255.0

Class A, B, and C addresses can be divided into smaller networks, called *subnetworks* or
subnets. This results in a larger number of possible networks, each with fewer host
addresses available than the original network.

The addresses used for the subnets are created by borrowing bits from the host field and
using them as subnet bits. A subnet mask indicates which bits have been borrowed. A
subnet mask is a 32-bit value associated with an IPV4 address. It specifies which bits in
the address represent network and subnet bits and which represent host bits. Using subnet masks creates a three-level hierarchy: network, subnet, and host.

In binary format, a subnet mask bit of 1 indicates that the corresponding bit in the IPV4
address is a network or subnet bit. A subnet mask bit of 0 indicates that the corresponding bit in the IPV4 address is a host bit. Subnet bits come from the higher-order (left-
most) bits of the host field; therefore, the 1s in the subnet mask are contiguous.

The default subnet masks for Class A, B, and C addresses are shown Table 1-9.

When all of an address's host bits are 0, that is the address for the subnet itself (sometimes called the wire). When all of an address's host bits are 1, the address is the directed
broadcast address for that subnet (in other words, for all the devices on that subnet).

Note   An IP-directed broadcast is an IP packet destined for all devices on an IP subnet. When the directed broadcast originates from a device on another subnet, routers that are not directly connected to the destination subnet forward the IP-directed broadcast. The same process is used to forward unicast IP packets destined for a host on that subnet.

On Cisco routers, the **ip directed-broadcast** interface command determines the operation of the last router in the path, the one connected to the destination subnet. It accomplishes this by using a directed broadcast packet. If **ip directed-broadcast** is enabled on the interface, the router changes the directed broadcast to a broadcast. It sends the packet, encapsulated in a Layer 2 broadcast frame, onto the subnet. However, if the **no ip directed-broadcast** command is configured on the interface, directed broadcasts destined for the subnet to which that interface is attached are dropped. In Cisco IOS Release 12.0, the default for this command was changed to **no ip directed-broadcast.**

Note   The formula 2^s calculates the number of subnets created, where s is the number of subnet bits (the number of bits borrowed from the host field).

The formula $2^h - 2$ calculates the number of host addresses available on each subnet, where h is the number of host bits.

For example, 10.0.0.0 is a Class A address. It has a default subnet mask of 255.0.0.0, indicating 8 network bits and 24 host bits. To use 8 of the host bits as subnet bits, a subnet mask of 11111111.11111111.00000000.00000000 is required, which is 255.255.0.0 in decimal format. The 8 subnet bits can be used to address 256 subnets. Each of these subnets could support up to 65,534 hosts. The address of one of the subnets is 10.1.0.0. The broadcast address on this subnet is 10.1.255.255.

Another way of indicating the subnet mask is to use a prefix. A prefix is a slash (/) followed by a numeral that is the number of bits in the network and subnet portion of the address—in other words, the number of contiguous 1s that would be in the subnet mask. For example, the subnet mask of 255.255.240.0 is 11111111.11111111.11110000.00000000 in binary format, which is 20 1s followed by 12 0s. Therefore, the prefix would be /20 for the 20 bits of network and subnet information, the number of 1s in the mask.

IP address planning is discussed in Chapter 6, "Designing IP Addressing."

IPv6 Addresses

The decline of free IPv4 addresses will accelerate the implementation of IPv6 to become the global standard for device addressing. The IPv6 address and packet structure is a bit different, as shown in previous sections. The IPv6 address is 128 bits long, as opposed to 32 bits. This difference in address size gives a significantly larger pool of addresses for allocation purposes. The notation of an IPv6 address is also different from its IPv4 counterpart. Typically, IPv4 addresses are written in decimal form and are easier to remember and work with. IPv6 addresses are typically notated in hexadecimal form and look quite foreign to many people. Figure 1-17 shows an example of an IPv6 address notated as hexadecimal and binary.

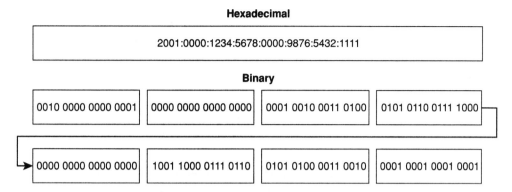

Hexadecimal

2001:0000:1234:5678:0000:9876:5432:1111

Binary

| 0010 0000 0000 0001 | 0000 0000 0000 0000 | 0001 0010 0011 0100 | 0101 0110 0111 1000 |

| 0000 0000 0000 0000 | 1001 1000 0111 0110 | 0101 0100 0011 0010 | 0001 0001 0001 0001 |

Figure 1-17 *IPv6 Address Notation*

This address notation can be further confusing. A number of rules enable the address to be shortened:

■ Leading 0s in each grouping can be omitted. However, at least one hex digit is required per grouping.

■ Consecutive groups of 0s across groupings can be replaced by a double colon (::). This can only be done once per address.

Using these rules, the address shown in Figure 1-17 can be displayed in a number of ways; some of these are shown in Figure 1-18.

Hexadecimal

2001:0000:0034:5600:0000:9876:5432:1111
2001:0:0034:5600:0000:9876:5432:1111
2001:0000:34:5600:0000:9876:5432:1111
2001::34:5600:0000:9876:5432:1111
2001::34:5600:0:9876:5432:1111
2001:0000:0034:5600:0:9876:5432:1111

Figure 1-18 *IPv6 Shortened Address Notation*

IPv6 Address Types

As with IPv4, there are a number of different types that are used to segment the IPv6 address space. With IPv6, these include

- Aggregatable Global Unicast

- Link-Local Unicast

- Unique Local Unicast

- Multicast

- Anycast

The Aggregatable Global Unicast address type is equivalent to what most people refer to as public addresses. These addresses are given out to individual devices on the public Internet and will be able to be publicly routed. Addresses in the Aggregatable Global Unicast range always start with a binary 001. This works out to all addresses starting from hexadecimal 2000 through 3FFF. This is also notated as 2000::/3.

The Link-Local Unicast address type is assigned to all IPv6 device interfaces and is used specifically for local link traffic. Addresses in the Link-Local Unicast range always start with a binary 1111 1110 10. This is also notated as FE80::/10.

The Unique Local Unicast address type is the IPv6 version of private addressing. These addresses can be routed the same as Aggregatable addresses but are only to be used on private networks. They are not permitted to be routed to the public Internet. Addresses in the Unique Local Unicast range always start with a binary 1111 1100 or 1111 1101. This is also notated as FC00::/8 and FD00::/8.

The Multicast address types perform the same as with IPv4. Addresses in the Link-Local Unicast range always start with a binary 1111 1111. This is also notated as FF00::/8.

The Anycast address type is new with IPv6 and replaces the broadcast addresses used with IPv4. An Anycast address uses the same format as the Aggregatable Global Unicast address type but is not only assigned to a single interface on a single device. The interfaces from a group of devices are assigned the same Anycast address. When a host uses this address for communications, the device that is closest to that host will respond.

Switching Types

Switches were initially introduced to provide higher-performance connectivity compared to hubs. This is because switches define multiple collision domains. Switches have always been able to process data at a faster rate than routers. The switching functionality is implemented in hardware, in Application Specific Integrated Circuits (ASIC), rather than in software, which is how routing has traditionally been implemented. However, switching was initially restricted to the examination of Layer 2 frames. The advent of more powerful ASICs allows switches to process Layer 3 packets and to process the contents of those packets at very high speeds.

The following sections examine the operation of traditional Layer 2 switching and Layer 3 switching.

Layer 2 Switching

The heart of a Layer 2 switch is its MAC address table, also known as its content-addressable memory (CAM) table because it resides in a device's content-addressable memory. This table contains a list of the MAC addresses that are reachable through each switch port. Recall that a physical MAC address uniquely identifies a device on a network, or more specifically, a device interface. When a switch is first powered up, its MAC address table is empty, as shown in Figure 1-19.

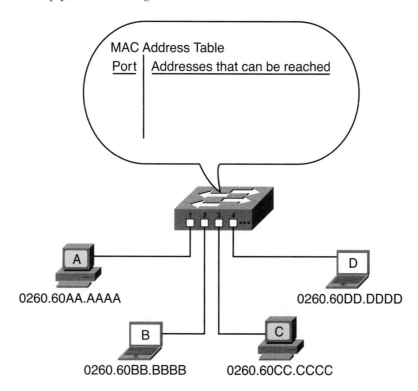

Figure 1-19 *MAC Address Table Is Initially Empty*

In this sample network, consider what happens when device A sends a frame destined for device D. The switch receives the frame on port 1 (from device A). Recall that a frame includes the MAC address of the source device and the MAC address of the destination device. The switch does not recognize the location of device D, so the switch must *flood* the frame out all the other ports, except the originating port. The switch sends the frame out of ports 2, 3, and 4. This means that devices B, C, and D all receive the frame. Only device D, however, recognizes its MAC address as the destination address in the frame. It is the only device on which the CPU is interrupted to further process the frame.

Note   Broadcast and multicast frames are, by default, flooded to all ports of a Layer 2 switch other than the incoming port. The same is true for unicast frames destined for any device not residing in the MAC address table.

In the meantime, the switch recognizes that device A can be reached on port 1 because the switch received a frame from device A on port 1. The switch puts the MAC address of device A in its MAC address table for port 1. This process is called *learning*. The switch is learning all the MAC addresses it can reach.

At some point, device D is likely to reply to device A. At that time, the switch receives a frame from device D on port 4. The switch records this information in its MAC address table as part of its learning process. This time, the switch knows the location of device A. The switch therefore forwards the frame only out of port 1. This process is called *filtering*. After the switch recognizes the necessary port, it sends the frames only through that port, rather than flooding them out of every port. This reduces the traffic on the other ports and interruptions that the other devices experience. Over time, the switch learns where all the devices are, and the MAC address table is fully populated, as shown in Figure 1-20.

The filtering process also allows a number of simultaneous conversations to occur between different devices. For example, if device A and device B want to communicate, the switch sends their data specifically between ports 1 and 2, leaving ports 3 and or 4 vacant. At the same time, devices C and D can communicate on ports 3 and 4 without interfering with the traffic on ports 1 and 2. Consequently, the network's overall through-put has increased dramatically.

The MAC address table is located in the switch's memory and has a finite size (depending on the specific switch used). If many devices are attached to the switch, the switch might not have the capacity for every one. If a device has not been utilized for a specified amount of time, it is removed (timed out) from the table. As a result, the most active devices are always in the table.

MAC addresses can also be statically configured in the MAC address table, and a maximum number of addresses allowed per port can be specified. One advantage of static addresses is that less flooding occurs, both when the switch first appears and because of addresses not being timed out of the MAC address table. However, this also means that if a device is moved, the switch configuration must be changed. A related feature available in some switches is the capability to *sticky-learn* addresses. The address is dynamically learned, as described earlier, but is then automatically entered as a static command in the switch configuration. However, by default, this configuration is not saved. You can ensure that only specific devices are permitted access by the network by limiting the number of addresses per port to one and statically configuring those addresses. This feature is particularly useful when addresses are sticky-learned.

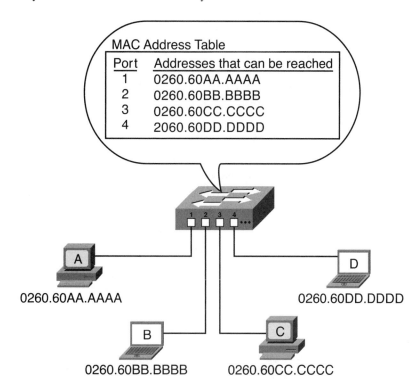

Figure 1-20 *Switch Learns Where All the Devices Are and Populates Its MAC Address Table*

Layer 3 Switching

A Layer 3 switch is actually a router with some of the functions implemented in hardware to improve performance. In other words, some of the OSI model network layer routing functions are performed in high-performance ASICs rather than in software.

The functions performed by routers (as described earlier in the "Routing" section) can be CPU intensive. Offloading the switching of the packet to hardware can result in a significant increase in performance.

A Layer 3 switch performs all the same functions as a router. The differences are in the physical implementation of the device rather than in the functions it performs. For functional purposes, the terms *router* and *Layer 3 switch* are synonymous.

Layer 4 switching is an extension of Layer 3 switching that includes examination of the contents of the Layer 3 packet. For example, the protocol number in the IP packet header indicates which transport layer protocol (for example, TCP or UDP) is being used. The port number in the TCP or UDP segment indicates the application being used (as described in the section "TCP/IP Transport Layer Protocols," earlier in this chapter). Switching based on the protocol and port numbers can ensure that certain types of traffic get higher priority on the network or take a specific path.

Spanning Tree Protocol

The following sections examine why the Spanning Tree Protocol is needed in Layer 2 networks. STP terminology and operation are then introduced.

Redundancy in Layer 2 Switched Networks

Redundancy in a network, as shown in Figure 1-21, is desirable so that communication can still occur if a link or device fails. For example, if switch X in this figure stopped functioning, devices A and B could still communicate through switch Y. However, in a switched network, redundancy can cause problems.

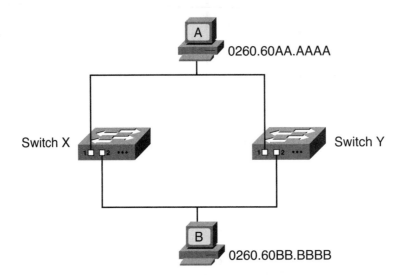

Figure 1-21 *STP Redundant Link Example*

The first type of problem occurs if a broadcast frame is sent on the network. For example, consider what happens when device A in Figure 1-21 sends an ARP request to find the MAC address of device B. The ARP request is sent as a broadcast. Both switch X and switch Y receive the broadcast. Let's focus on the broadcast received by switch X, on its port 1. Switch X floods the broadcast to all its other connected ports. In this case, it floods it to port 2. Device B recognizes the broadcast, but so does switch Y, on its port 2. Switch Y floods the broadcast to its port 1. This broadcast is received by switch X on its port 1, switch X floods it to its port 2, and so forth. The broadcast continues to loop around the network, consuming bandwidth and processing power. This situation is called a *broadcast storm*.

The second problem that can occur in redundant topologies is that devices can receive multiple copies of the same frame. For example, assume that neither of the switches in Figure 1-21 has located device B. When device A sends data destined for device B, switch X and switch Y both flood the data to the lower LAN. Device B receives two copies of the same frame. This could be problematic for device B, depending on how it is programmed to handle such situations.

The third difficulty that can occur in a redundant situation is within the switch itself. The MAC address table can change rapidly and contain inaccurate data. Again referring to Figure 1-21, consider what happens when neither switch has recognized the location of device A or B and device A sends data to device B. Each switch learns that device A is on its port 1, and each records this in its MAC address table. Because the switches do not yet know where device B is located, they flood the frame on their port 2. Each switch receives the frame from the other switch on its port 2. This frame has device A's MAC address in the source address field. Therefore, both switches now recognize that device A is on their port 2. As a result, the MAC address table is overwritten. The MAC address table now has incorrect information (device A is actually connected to port 1, not port 2, of both switches). Because the table changes rapidly, it might be considered unstable.

The obstacles mentioned here require a solution that would permit redundancy when necessary and disable the redundant network for regular traffic. STP does just that.

STP Terminology and Operation

The following sections introduce the IEEE 802.1D STP terminology and operation.

STP Terminology

STP terminology can best be explained by examining the operations of a sample network. Figure 1-22 illustrates this process.

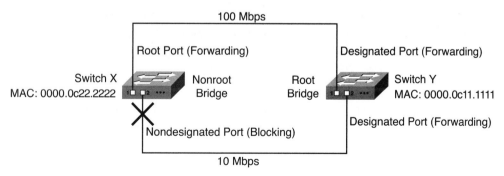

Figure 1-22   *STP Blocking Example*

Note   Notice that STP terminology refers to the devices as *bridges* rather than switches.

Within an STP network, one switch is elected as the *root bridge* because it is at the root (highest level) of the spanning tree. All other switches calculate their best path to the root bridge. Their alternative paths are implemented at the blocking state. These alternative paths are logically disabled from the perspective of regular traffic. But the switches still communicate with each other on these paths so that the alternative paths can be left unblocked in case an error occurs on the best path.

All switches running STP, which is turned on by default in Cisco switches, send out bridge protocol data units (BPDU). Switches running STP use BPDUs to exchange information with neighboring switches. One of the fields in the BPDU is the bridge identifier (ID). It comprises a 2-octet bridge priority and a 6-octet MAC address. STP uses the bridge ID to elect the root bridge. The switch with the lowest bridge ID is the root bridge. If all bridge priorities are left at their default values, the switch with the lowest MAC address becomes the root bridge. In Figure 1-22, switch Y is elected as the root bridge.

All the ports on the root bridge are called *designated ports*. They are all in the *forwarding* state, which means that they can send and receive data. The STP states are described in the next section.

On all *nonroot* bridges, one port becomes the *root port*, and it is always in the *forwarding* state. The root port is the one with the lowest cost to the root. The cost of each link is, by default, inversely proportional to the link's bandwidth, so the port with the fastest total path from the switch to the root bridge is selected as the root port on that switch. In Figure 1-22, port 1 on switch X is the root port for that switch because it is the fastest way to the root bridge.

Note If multiple ports on a switch have the same fastest total path costs to the root bridge, STP considers other BPDU fields. STP initially looks at the bridge IDs in the received BPDUs (the bridge IDs of the next switch in the path to the root bridge). The port that received the BPDU with the lowest bridge ID becomes the root port. If these bridge IDs are also equal, the port ID breaks the tie. The port with the lower port ID becomes the root port. The port ID field includes a port priority and a port index, which is the port number. Therefore, if the port priorities are the same (for example, if they are left at their default value), the lower port number becomes the root port.

Each LAN segment must have one designated port. It is located on the switch that has the lowest cost to the root bridge. If the costs are equal, the port on the switch with the lowest bridge ID is chosen and it is in the forwarding state. In Figure 1-22, the root bridge has designated ports on both segments, so additional ports are not required.

Note The root bridge sends configuration BPDUs on all its ports periodically—every 2 seconds, by default. These configuration BPDUs include STP timers. This ensures that all switches in the network use the same timers. On each LAN segment, the switch that has the designated port forwards the configuration BPDUs to the segment. Every switch in the network receives these BPDUs on its root port.

All ports on a LAN segment that are not root ports or designated ports are called *nondesignated* ports and transition to the blocking state. They do not send data, so the redundant topology is logically disabled. In Figure 1-22, port 2 on switch X is the non-designated port and is in the blocking state. Blocking ports do, however, listen for BPDUs.

If a designated port or a root bridge fails, the switches send topology change BPDUs and recalculate the spanning tree. The new spanning tree does not include the failed port or switch. The ports that were previously blocking might now be in the forwarding state. This is how STP supports the redundancy in a switched network.

STP States

Figure 1-23 illustrates the various STP port states.

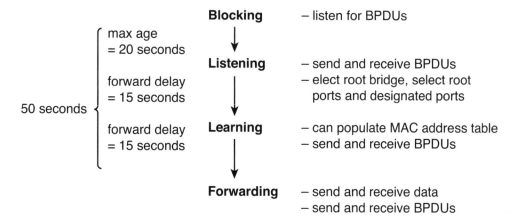

Figure 1-23 *STP Port States*

When a port is initially created, it is put in the blocking state, where it listens for BPDUs and then transitions to the listening state. A blocking port in an operational network can also transition to the listening state if it does not hear any BPDUs by the time the *max-age* timer expires (a default of 20 seconds). While in the listening state, the switch can send and receive BPDUs but not data. The root bridge and the various final states of all the ports are determined in this state.

If the port is chosen as the root port on a switch, or as a designated port on a segment, that port transitions to the learning state directly after the listening state. In the learning state, the port still cannot send data, but it can start to populate its MAC address table if any data is received. The length of time spent in each of the listening and learning states is dictated by the value of the *forward-delay* parameter, which is 15 seconds by default. After the learning state, the port transitions to the forwarding state, where it can operate normally. Alternatively, if in the listening state the port is not chosen as a root port or designated port, it becomes a nondesignated port and transitions back to the blocking state.

Note Do not confuse the STP learning state with the learning process that the switch goes through to populate its MAC address table. The STP learning state is a transitory state. Although a switch can learn MAC addresses from data frames received on its ports that are in the STP learning state, it does not forward those frames. In a stable network, switch ports are in either the forwarding or blocking state. Ports in the blocking state do not listen to data frames and therefore do not contribute to the switch's MAC address table. Ports in the forwarding state do, of course, listen to (and forward) data frames. Those frames populate the switch's MAC address table.

Several features and enhancements to STP are implemented on Cisco switches to reduce convergence time. That is the time it takes for all the switches in a network to agree on the network's topology after that topology has changed.

Rapid STP

Rapid STP (RSTP) is defined by IEEE 802.1w. RSTP incorporates many of the Cisco enhancements to STP, resulting in faster convergence. Switches in an RSTP environment converge quickly by communicating with each other. They determine which links can forward, rather than just wait for the timers to transition the ports among the various states. RSTP ports take on different roles than STP ports. The RSTP roles are

- Root
- Designated
- Alternate
- Backup
- Disabled

RSTP port states are also different from STP port states. The RSTP states are

- Discarding
- Learning
- Forwarding

RSTP is compatible with STP. For example, 802.1w alternate and backup port states correspond to the 802.1d blocking port state.

Virtual LANs

As noted earlier, a broadcast domain includes all devices that receive each other's broadcasts (and multicasts). All the devices connected to one router port are in the same broadcast domain. Routers block broadcasts (destined for all networks) and multicasts by default. Routers forward only unicast packets (destined for a specific device) and packets of a special type called *directed broadcasts*. Typically, a broadcast domain is thought of as being a physical wire, a LAN. But a broadcast domain can also be a VLAN, a logical construct that can include multiple physical LAN segments.

Figure 1-24 illustrates the VLAN concept. On the left side of the figure, three individual physical LANs are shown: Engineering, Accounting, and Marketing. These LANs contain workstations E1, E2, A1, A2, M1, and M2 and servers ES, AS, and MS. Rather than physical LANs, an enterprise can use VLANs, as shown on the right side of the figure. With VLANs, members of each department can be physically located anywhere, yet still be logically connected with their own workgroup. Therefore, in the VLAN configuration, all the devices attached to VLAN E (Engineering) share the same broadcast domain. The devices attached to VLAN A (Accounting) share a separate broadcast domain, and the devices attached to VLAN M (Marketing) share a third broadcast domain. Figure 1-24 also illustrates how VLANs can span multiple switches. The link between the two switches in the figure carries traffic from all three of the VLANs and is called a *trunk*.

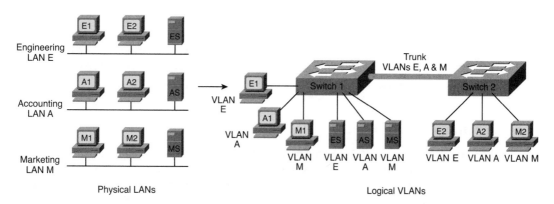

Figure 1-24   *VLAN Concept*

VLAN Membership

Static port membership means that the network administrator determines the relationship of a port to a VLAN regardless of the devices attached to it. This means that after the ports have been configured, the devices attaching to the switch must be plugged into the correct port. If they move, the switch must be reconfigured.

Alternatively, the VLAN membership can be configured dynamically. Some static configuration is still required, but it is on a separate device called a VLAN Membership Policy Server (VMPS). The VMPS could be a separate server, or it could be a higher-end switch that contains the VMPS information. VMPS information consists of a MAC address–to–VLAN map. As a result, ports are assigned to VLANs based on the MAC address of the device connected to the port. When a device is moved from one port to another (either on the same switch or another switch in the network), the switch dynamically assigns the new port to the proper VLAN for that device by consulting the VMPS.

Trunks

As mentioned earlier, a port that carries data from multiple VLANs is called a trunk. A trunk port can be on a switch, a router, or a server. A trunk port uses the protocol defined in IEEE 802.1Q.

The 802.1Q protocol is an IEEE standard protocol in which the trunking information is encoded within a Tag field inserted inside the frame header itself. Trunks using the 802.1Q protocol define a native VLAN. By default, traffic for the native VLAN is not tagged; it is carried across the trunk unchanged. Consequently, end-user stations that do not comprehend trunking can communicate with other devices directly over an 802.1Q trunk as long as they are on the native VLAN. The native VLAN must be defined as the same VLAN on both sides of the trunk. Within the Tag field, the 802.1Q VLAN ID field is 12 bits long, allowing up to 4096 VLANs to be defined. The Tag field also includes a 3-bit 802.1p user priority field. These bits are used as class of service (CoS) bits for QoS marking.

Note   Multiple switch ports can be logically combined so that they appear as one higher-performance port. Cisco accomplishes this with its EtherChannel technology, combining multiple Fast Ethernet, Gigabit Ethernet, or 10 Gigabit Ethernet links. Trunks can be implemented on both individual ports and on these EtherChannel ports.

STP and VLANs

Cisco developed per-VLAN Spanning Tree Plus (PVST+) so that switches can have one instance of STP running per VLAN, allowing redundant physical links within the network to be used for different VLANs and thus reducing the load on individual links. PVST+ is illustrated in Figure 1-25.

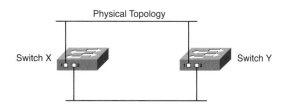

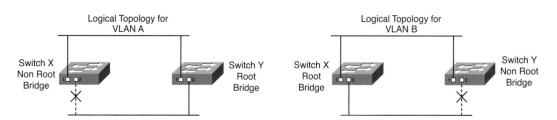

Figure 1-25 *PVST+ Redundant Link Example*

The top diagram in Figure 1-25 shows the physical topology of the network, with switches X and Y redundantly connected. In the lower-left diagram, switch Y has been selected as the root bridge for VLAN A, leaving port 2 on switch X in the blocking state. In contrast, the lower-right diagram shows that switch X has been selected as the root bridge for VLAN B, leaving port 2 on switch Y in the blocking state. With this configuration, traffic is shared across all links, with traffic for VLAN A traveling to the lower LAN on switch Y's port 2. The traffic for VLAN B traveling to the lower LAN goes out switch X's port 2.

Rapid per-VLAN Spanning Tree Plus (RPVST+) is a Cisco enhancement of RSTP that uses PVST+.

Multiple-Instance STP (MISTP) is an IEEE standard (802.1s) that uses RSTP and allows several VLANs to be grouped into a single spanning-tree instance. Each instance is independent of the others so that a link can forward for one group of VLANs while blocking for other VLANs. MISTP allows traffic to be shared across all the links in the network, but reduces the number of STP instances that would be required if PVST+ were implemented.

Inter-VLAN Routing

A Layer 3 device can be connected to a switched network in two ways: by using multiple physical interfaces or through a single interface configured as a trunk. These two connection methods are shown in Figure 1-26. The top diagram illustrates a router with three physical connections to the switch; each physical connection carries traffic from only one VLAN.

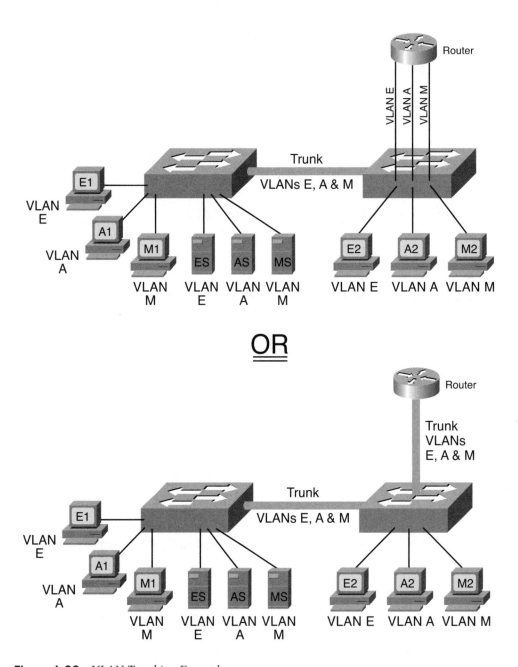

Figure 1-26 *VLAN Trunking Example*

The bottom diagram illustrates a router with one physical connection to the switch. The interfaces on the switch and the router have been configured as trunks. Multiple logical connections exist between the two devices. When a router is connected to a switch through a trunk, it is sometimes called a "router on a stick," because it has only one physical interface (a stick) to the switch. Each interface between the switch and the Layer 3 device, whether physical interfaces or logical interfaces within a trunk, is in a separate VLAN and is, therefore, in a separate subnet for IP networks.

Comprehensive Example

This section presents a comprehensive example that illustrates the encapsulation and decapsulation processes. It ties together many of the concepts covered in the remainder of this chapter. Figure 1-27 illustrates the network used in this example.

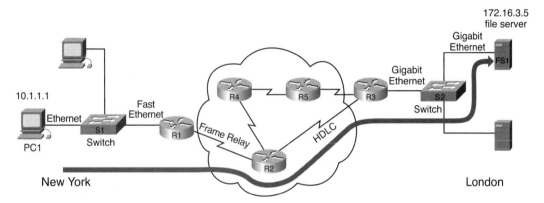

Figure 1-27   *PC1 in New York Is Sending FTP Data to FS1 in London*

In this network, PC1, located in New York, has an FTP connection with the file server FS1 in London. PC1 is transferring a file, using FTP, to FS1. The path between PC1 and FS1 goes through switch S1; Routers R1, R2, and R3; and switch S2, as illustrated by the thick line in the figure. The routers have communicated, using a routing protocol, to determine the best path between network 10.0.0.0 and network 172.16.0.0. PC1 has an IP address of 10.1.1.1, and FS1 has an IP address of 172.16.3.5. When PC1 first needed to send data to a device on another network, it sent an ARP request. Its default gateway, R1, replied with its own MAC address, which PC1 keeps in its memory.

FTP data is now being sent from PC1 to FS1. Figure 1-28 shows how this data flows within the devices in the network, and what the data looks like at each point within the network.

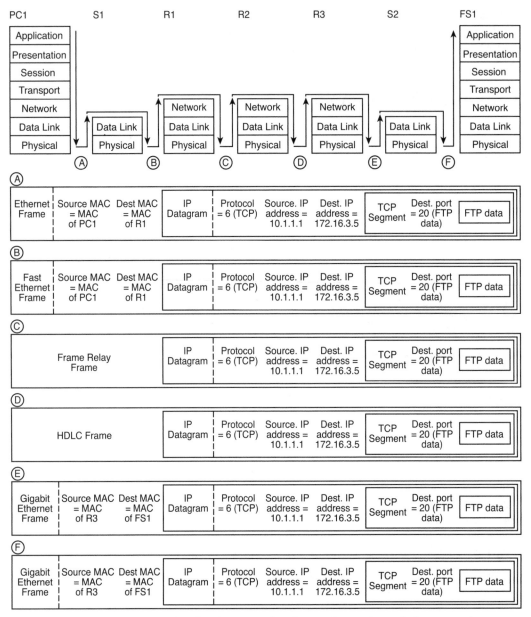

Figure 1-28   *Data Is Encapsulated and Decapsulated as It Flows Through the Network*

Starting at the left of Figure 1-28, PC1 prepares the data for transport across the network, and the resulting frame is shown as point A. PC1 encapsulates the FTP data in a TCP segment. The destination port field of the segment is set to 20, indicating that it contains FTP data. This TCP segment is then encapsulated in an IP datagram. The protocol number of the datagram is set to 6, indicating that it contains a TCP segment. The source IP address is set to PC1's address, 10.1.1.1, whereas the destination IP address is set to FS1's address, 172.16.3.5. The IP datagram is encapsulated in an Ethernet frame, with the source MAC address set to PC1's MAC address. The destination MAC address is set to R1's MAC address. PC1 then puts the frame on the Ethernet network, and the bits arrive at S1.

S1 receives the frame and reviews the destination MAC address, which is R1's MAC address. S1 looks in its MAC address table and confirms that this MAC address is on its Fast Ethernet port. Therefore, S1 encapsulates the IP datagram in a Fast Ethernet frame, as shown at point B in the figure. Notice that the source and destination MAC addresses have not changed in this new frame type. The datagram, segment, and data all remain untouched by the switch. S1 then puts the frame on the Fast Ethernet network, and the bits arrive at R1.

R1 receives the frame, and because it is destined for R1's MAC address, R1 decapsulates the frame to Layer 3. R1 reviews the destination IP address as 172.16.3.5 and compares it to its routing table. This network is accessible through R2 over a Frame Relay network. R1 encapsulates the IP datagram in a Frame Relay frame, as shown at point C in the figure. Notice that the datagram, segment, and data all remain untouched by the router, but the frame type has changed. R1 puts the frame on the Frame Relay network, and the bits arrive at R2.

R2 receives the frame and decapsulates it to Layer 3. R2 looks at the destination IP address 172.16.3.5 and compares it to its routing table. This network is accessible through R3, over an HDLC network. R2 encapsulates the IP datagram in an HDLC frame, as shown at point D in the figure. Notice that the datagram, segment, and data all remain untouched by the router, but the frame type has changed again. R2 then puts the frame on the HDLC network and the bits arrive at R3.

R3 receives the frame and decapsulates it to Layer 3. R3 reviews the destination IP address 172.16.3.5 and compares it to its routing table. This network is accessible through its Gigabit Ethernet interface, which is directly connected to that network. When R3 initially needed to send data to FS1, it sent an ARP request. FS1 replied with its own MAC address, which R3 keeps in its memory. R3 encapsulates the IP datagram in a Gigabit Ethernet frame, as shown at point E in the figure. The source MAC address is set to its own address, and the destination MAC address is set to FS1's address. Notice that the datagram, segment, and data all remain untouched by the router, but the frame type has changed. The bits arrive at S2.

S2 receives the frame and reviews the destination MAC address. It is FS1's MAC address. S2 looks in its MAC address table and identifies that this MAC address is on another one of its Gigabit Ethernet ports. Therefore, the IP datagram can reside in a Gigabit Ethernet frame, as shown at point F in the figure. Notice that the source and destination MAC addresses have not changed in this frame, and that the datagram, segment, and data all remain untouched by the switch. S2 then puts the frame on the other Gigabit Ethernet network, and the bits arrive at FS1. FS1 receives the frame, and because it is destined for FS1's MAC address, FS1 decapsulates the frame to Layer 3. FS1 looks at the destination IP address and determines that it is its own address. Therefore, FS1 decapsulates the segment and the FTP data. It sends it to its FTP application. The FTP data is now at its destination.

Summary

In this chapter, fundamental networking concepts were covered. These concepts form a solid foundation for understanding the remainder of this book. The following topics were explored:

- Introduction to networks

- Discussion of networking protocols and the OSI model, a key component of networking and the basis of modern protocol suites

- LANs and WANs

- Network devices, including hubs, switches, and routers

- Introduction to the TCP/IP suite and a discussion of the IP, TCP, and UDP protocols

- Routing, including an introduction to routing protocols

- Addressing, including MAC and IP addresses

- Layer 2 and Layer 3 switching

- Use and operation of STP in Layer 2 networks

- Concept and operation of VLANs

- Comprehensive example illustrating the encapsulation and decapsulation processes

Review Questions

Answer the following questions, and then refer to Appendix A for the answers.

1. Which of the OSI layers are considered "upper layers"?

2. Which of the OSI layers is responsible for routing?

3. Which of the LAN technologies has a maximum theoretical throughput of 100 Mbps?

4. Which WAN technology provides a point-to-point connection and typically runs either PPP or HDLC?

5. What transport layer protocol provides a connectionless, best-effort, unacknowledged transmission?

6. When using IPv6, how many bits are used by the address?

7. Name at least three of the routing protocols listed in this chapter.

8. List the private IPv4 address ranges.

9. Which of the IPv6 address types are used only on private networks?

10. When using the STP, which of the switches is considered the highest level when making forwarding decisions?

Chapter 2

Network Design Methodology

This chapter introduces a network design methodology and presents guidelines for building an effective network design solution. It includes the following sections:

- Understanding the Network Architectures for the Enterprise

- Identifying Design Requirements

- Identifying Customer Design Requirements

- Characterizing the Existing Network and Sites

- Using the Top-Down Approach to Network Design

A network design must meet the increasingly complex requirements of the organization that it supports. As a network designer, you must understand the needs of the organization and follow a methodology to help match needs to the network implementation. This chapter introduces principles and guidelines for building an effective network design.

The chapter begins with an overview of the Cisco Network Architectures for the Enterprise, which enables customers to build a more intelligent infrastructure. The chapter also describes how to gather customer requirements and identify business and technical constraints using the Cisco Lifecycle Services process. Because many customers build on an existing network, the chapter also presents methods of characterizing the existing network.

Understanding the Network Architectures for the Enterprise

In the current business climate, organizations are looking for techniques to enhance customer relationships, accommodate a mobile workforce, and increase productivity. In addition, companies are looking for ways to integrate emerging technologies such as wireless, virtualization, video, unified communications, and a vast number of application-level business solutions into their enterprise. These challenges create the need for a more flexible and dynamic network architecture.

Cisco has taken a holistic approach by creating three architectures that combine to create a network that addresses such challenges: Borderless Networks, Collaboration, and Data Center/Virtualization architectures.

Business Drivers for a New Network Framework

The following sections describe three business drivers that can impact network architecture:

- Business forces
- Technology-related forces
- IT challenges

Business Forces

Several business forces affect the strategic decisions for an enterprise network, including the following:

- **Return on Investment:** Companies seek to invest in their network infrastructure to improve productivity while positioning the company for future competitiveness. However, these investments must be justified and must eventually provide a return on investment. This requirement necessitates innovative solutions that allow technology to work within the business solution.

- **Regulation:** Another challenge facing companies is the existence of new industry regulations. Each industry has its own set of legal compliance requirements, for example, the Health Insurance Portability and Accountability Act (HIPAA) for the health insurance industry and the Restriction of Hazardous Substances (RoHS) directive for the restriction of hazardous waste. IT departments must find innovative solutions to ensure that companies remain in compliance with required regulations for its industry.

- **Competitiveness:** Companies have always competed to deliver products to the marketplace faster, provide unique differentiators to set themselves apart from their peers, and provide better customer service. However, to maintain their competitive edge, organizations must look for ways to integrate emerging technology into their business solutions.

Technology-Related Forces

Several technology-related forces affect the strategic decisions for the enterprise network, including the following:

- **Removal of borders:** The enterprise network must be able to provide connectivity among branch offices, teleworkers, mobile devices, customers, and partner networks. The removal of traditional network boundaries impacts productivity and transforms the way companies conduct business.

- **Virtualization:** Virtualization is one of the latest growing technologies affecting the IT industry. Although it is not a new concept, it has recently gained popularity, led by industry leaders like VMware. Virtualization offers the possibility of lower IT costs because of its ability to consolidate servers and other network components.

- **Growth of applications:** In the current business environment, intense competition and time-to-market pressures are prompting enterprises to seek new IT solutions that assist in quicker response time to market and customer demands. Consumers are demanding improved customer service, enhanced customization flexibility, and greater security, all at lower cost.

IT Challenges

Most network infrastructures are separated into three IT groups:

- **Data center:** Servers and storage networks
- **Network:** Routing, switching, security, and wireless WAN
- **Applications:** Voice and video

Each group has its own experience, budget, and challenges, which naturally create silos. However, for businesses to work more effectively, they must break down those silos and better leverage their experience in IT.

Cisco Network Architectures for the Enterprise

The Cisco Network Architectures for the Enterprise promotes a more effective use of networked resources. Table 2-1 lists some of the benefits.

Table 2-1   *Benefits of the Cisco Network Architectures for the Enterprise*

Benefit	Description
Functionality	Supports organizational requirements
Scalability	Supports growth and expansion of organizational tasks by separating functions and products into layers, a separation that makes it easier to grow the network
Availability	Provides necessary services reliably, anywhere, anytime
Performance	Provides desired responsiveness, throughput, and utilization on a per-application basis through the network infrastructure and services
Manageability	Provides control, performance monitoring, and fault detection
Efficiency	Through step-by-step network services growth, provides network services and infrastructure with reasonable operational costs and appropriate capital investment on a migration path to a more intelligent network

Cisco offers these benefits by recognizing the need for new and innovative business models and follows a holistic approach by creating three architectures that work together. Cisco Network Architectures for the Enterprise can be broken out into architectural approaches to three different markets: Borderless Networks, Collaboration, and Data Center/Virtualization.

These three approaches are described as follows and are shown in Figure 2-1:

■ **Borderless Networks:** Provide the foundation for connectivity across the enterprise network. Accelerate business transformation with an architecture-led approach that provides anyone, anything, anywhere, and anytime connectivity.

■ **Collaboration:** Maximizes personnel, team, and customer interactions within the organization to direct innovation.

■ **Data Center/Virtualization:** Transforms, optimizes, and protects the enterprise data center.

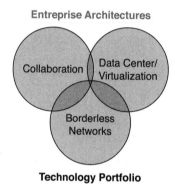

Figure 2-1 *Architectural Approaches*

Borderless Networks Architecture

The Cisco Borderless Networks Architecture provides a platform for the delivery of business solutions.

The current business environment requires agility, flexibility, and mobility. In addition, there is an increasing demand for direct interaction among partners, mobile employees, and customers. The response of businesses to these challenges has forced the elimination of traditional network boundaries.

Cisco Borderless Networks Architecture is a next-generation architecture solution that enables agile delivery of services and application when necessary. Cisco Borderless Networks Architecture enables limitless connectivity—securely, reliably, and seamlessly—as illustrated in Figure 2-2. The Cisco Borderless Networks Architecture serves as both a business and a technical architecture that ultimately optimizes both business and network performance.

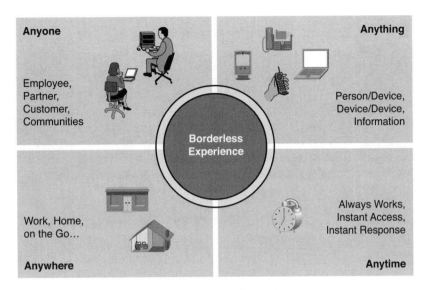

Figure 2-2 *Cisco Borderless Networks Architecture*

The Cisco Borderless Networks Architecture serves as the infrastructure for global collaboration, video, unified communication, and other critical business strategies. From a technical standpoint, system innovation, involving routing, switching, wireless, acceleration, and security, is required. Cisco is also introducing new technology, such as the Cisco Integrated Services Routers Generation 2 (ISR G2) to help deliver the Borderless Networks experience. This new approach allows decoupling of software and hardware, focusing on services.

Borderless Networks Architecture Approach

Figure 2-3 shows the Cisco Borderless Networks Architecture blueprint that consists of these four major building blocks:

■ **User Services:** These services include mobility, performance, and security. These elements are essential to providing the Borderless Networks experience.

■ **Network Services:** These services include resiliency and control. Cisco EnergyWise and Medianet provide key capabilities of the Cisco Borderless Networks Architecture, which is optimized for video, collaboration, and energy usage.

■ **Policy Control:** Policy control is applied to all users and devices across the Borderless Networks Architecture.

■ **Connection Management:** Connection management delivers secure access anytime, anywhere, regardless of how the network is accessed.

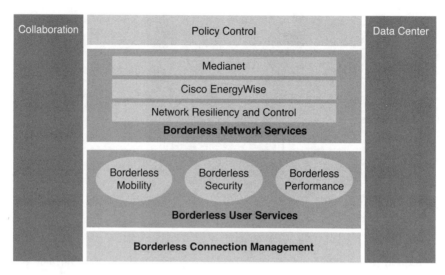

Figure 2-3 *Cisco Borderless Networks Architecture Blueprint*

Collaboration Architecture Approach

In the current business environment, companies must respond with a new generation of applications built for contemporary business requirements and deliver business value by making the most of the latest technologies. In response to the present environment, Cisco developed the Collaboration Architecture, as shown in Figure 2-4.

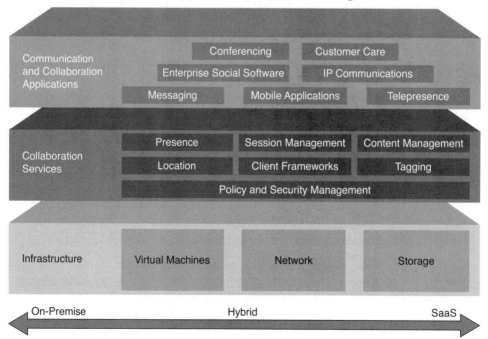

Figure 2-4 *Cisco Collaboration Architecture*

Technology has created a faster and more complex world that required organizations to change the way they operate. Globalization and new business models are breaking down traditional enterprise boundaries. In addition, there is growing demand for the enterprise to

- Expand business capabilities

- Operate more efficiently

- Improve real-time information access

- Enhance user interactions

The Cisco Collaboration Architecture will integrate collaboration into business processes at new and fundamental levels. It will also foster new models of people working together to achieve common goals within the extended enterprise. However, such applications require a next-generation architecture. In addition to its technical capabilities, the next-generation application architecture must

- Deliver new application and presentation models for the workspace

- Support collaboration across end-to-end business processes

- Support access at any time, anywhere, on any device, as well as take advantage of new technology opportunities

Data Center/Virtualization Architecture Approach

The IT industry is currently experiencing significant transformation. Innovative approaches addressing consolidation and virtualization are being developed, but they generally operate only within a single domain area: network, storage, or server. There is no single solution that pulls all of these areas together in a holistic integrated way.

The integration of the multiple platforms creates an area of overlap that challenges IT organizations. It adds complexity throughout the data center lifecycle.

Cisco has taken an architectural approach in solving the challenges faced by data centers. The Cisco Data Center/Virtualization Architecture technique is a next-generation architecture that is built upon Cisco Data Center 3.0 (see Figure 2-5).

Cisco Data Center 3.0 comprises a comprehensive portfolio of virtualization technologies and services that bring network, computing, storage, and virtualization platforms closer together to provide unparalleled flexibility, visibility, and policy enforcement within virtualized data centers.

This portfolio of virtualization technologies and services is listed in Table 2-2.

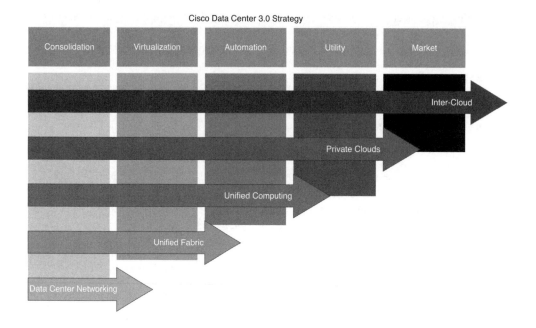

Figure 2-5 *Cisco Data Center/Virtualization Architecture*

Table 2-2 *Virtualization Technologies and Services*

Technology/Service	Function
Cisco Unified Computing System	Unifies network, computing, and virtualization resources into a single system that delivers end-to-end optimization for virtualized environments while retaining the ability to support traditional operating system and application stacks in physical environments
VN-Link technologies, including the Nexus 1000V virtual switch for VMware ESX	Delivers consistent per-virtual-machine visibility and policy control for SAN, LAN, and unified fabric
Virtual SAN, virtual device contexts, and unified fabric	Help converge multiple virtual networks to simplify and reduce data center infrastructure and total cost of ownership (TCO)
Flexible networking options	Support all server form factors and vendors, including options for integrated Ethernet and Fibre Channel switches for Dell, IBM, and HP blade servers, providing a consistent set of services across the data center to reduce operations complexity
Network-embedded virtualized application networking services	Allow consolidation of remote IT assets into virtualized data centers

Identifying Design Requirements

To design a network that meets customer needs, certain elements need to be identified. These include organizational goals and constraints. Technical goals and constraints must be identified as well. Cisco has formalized the lifecycle of a network into six phases: Prepare, Plan, Design, Implement, Operate, and Optimize (PPDIOO).

The following sections begin with an overview of PPDIOO. They also discuss how to assess the scope of the design project and how to complete the list of requirements for developing a comprehensive understanding of the needs of the customer. The sections then describe the process of determining which applications and network services already exist and which applications are planned, along with the associated organizational and technical goals and constraints using the Cisco PPDIOO approach.

Using the PPDIOO Approach for Networks

The Prepare, Plan, Design, Implement, Operate, and Optimize (PPDIOO) process reflects the phases of a standard network's lifecycle. As illustrated in Figure 2-6, The PPDIOO lifecycle phases are separate, yet closely related.

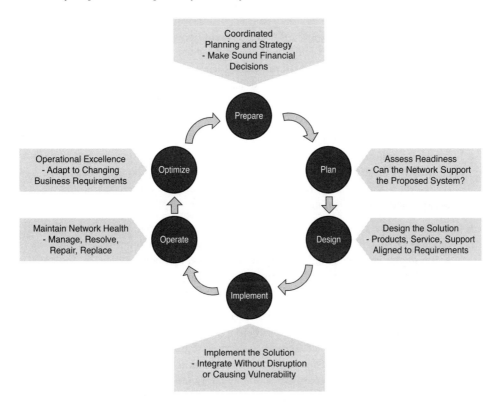

Figure 2-6 *PPDIOO Network Lifecycle Influences Design*

The following describes each PPDIOO phase:

- **Prepare phase:** This phase involves establishing the organizational (business) requirements, developing a network strategy, proposing a high-level conceptual architecture, and identifying technologies that can best support the architecture. Financial justification for the network strategy is established by assessing the business case for the proposed architecture.

- **Plan phase:** This phase involves identifying the network requirements, which are based on the goals for the network, where the network will be installed, who will require which network services, and so on. The Plan phase also involves assessing the sites where the network will be installed and any existing networks, and performing a gap analysis to determine whether the existing system infrastructure, sites, and operational environment can support the proposed system. A project plan helps manage the tasks, responsibilities, critical milestones, and resources required to implement the changes to the network. The project plan should align with the scope, cost, and resource parameters established in the original business requirements. The output of this phase is a set of network requirements.

- **Design phase:** The initial requirements determined in the Plan phase drive the network design specialists' activities. These specialists design the network according to those initial requirements, incorporating any additional data gathered during network analysis and network audit (when upgrading an existing network) and through discussion with managers and network users. The network design specification that is produced is a comprehensive detailed design that meets current business and technical requirements and incorporates specifications to support availability, reliability, security, scalability, and performance. This design specification provides the basis for the implementation activities.

- **Implement phase:** Implementation and verification begin after the design has been approved. The network and any additional components are built according to the design specifications, with the goal of integrating devices without disrupting the existing network or creating points of vulnerability.

- **Operate phase:** Operation is the final test of the design's appropriateness. The Operate phase involves maintaining network health through day-to-day operations, which might include maintaining high availability and reducing expenses. The fault detection and correction and performance monitoring that occur in daily operations provide initial data for the network lifecycle's Optimize phase.

- **Optimize phase:** This phase is based on proactive network management, the goal of which is to identify and resolve issues before problems arise and the organization is affected. Reactive fault detection and correction (troubleshooting) are necessary when proactive management cannot predict and mitigate the failures. In the PPDIOO process, the Optimize phase might lead to network redesign if too many network problems or errors arise, if performance does not meet expectations, or if new applications are identified to support organizational and technical requirements.

Benefits of the Lifecycle Approach

The network lifecycle approach lowers the total cost of network ownership by providing the following:

- Lowering the total cost of network ownership:
    - Identifying and validating technology requirements
    - Planning for infrastructure changes and resource requirements
    - Developing a sound network design aligned with technical requirements and business goals
    - Accelerating successful implementation
    - Improving the efficiency of the network and supporting staff
    - Reducing operating expenses by improving the efficiency of operation processes and tools
- Increasing network availability:
    - Assessing the state of the network's security and its ability to support the proposed design
    - Specifying the correct set of hardware and software releases and keeping them operational and current
    - Producing a sound operational design and validating network operation
    - Staging and testing the proposed system before deployment
    - Improving staff skills
    - Proactively monitoring the system and assessing availability trends and alerts
    - Proactively identifying security breaches and defining remediation plans
- Improving business agility:
    - Establishing business requirements and technology strategies
    - Preparing sites to support the system to be implemented
    - Integrating technical requirements and business goals into a detailed design and demonstrating that the network is functioning as specified
    - Expertly installing, configuring, and integrating system components
    - Continually enhancing performance
- Accelerating access to applications and services:
    - Assessing and improving operational preparedness to support current and planned network technologies and services

- Improving service-delivery efficiency and effectiveness by increasing availability, resource capacity, and performance

- Improving the availability, reliability, and stability of the network and the applications running on it

- Managing and resolving system problems and keeping software applications current

Design Methodology

When working in an environment that requires creative production on a tight schedule, such as designing an internetwork, using a methodology can be helpful. A methodology is a documented, systematic way of accomplishing something.

Following a design methodology can have many advantages:

- It ensures that steps are not missed when the process is followed.

- It provides a framework for the design process deliverables.

- It encourages consistency in the creative process, enabling network designers to set appropriate deadlines and maintain customer and manager satisfaction.

- It allows customers and managers to validate that the designers have analyzed and met their requirements.

The design methodology presented here includes three basic steps. Some of the design methodology steps are intrinsic to the PPDIOO Design phase, whereas other steps are related to other PPDIOO phases:

Step 1.   **Identify customer requirements.** Key decision makers identify the initial network requirements. Based on these requirements, a high-level conceptual architecture is proposed. This step is typically done within the PPDIOO Prepare phase.

Step 2.   **Characterize the existing network and sites.** The Plan phase involves characterizing sites, assessing any existing networks, and performing a gap analysis to determine whether the present infrastructure can support the proposed system. Characterization of the existing network and sites includes site and network audit and network analysis. During the network audit, the existing network is thoroughly checked for integrity and quality. During the network analysis, network behavior (traffic, congestion, and so on) is analyzed.

Step 3.   **Design the network topology and solutions.** The detailed design is developed and a design document is written. Decisions are made concerning network infrastructure, intelligent network services, network solutions, IP telephony, content networking, and other issues. A pilot or prototype network can also be built in to verify "proof of concept" of the design.

Identifying Customer Design Requirements

The process of gathering the design requirements from the customer consists of five steps that serve as goals for the designer. These steps involve discussions with customer staff members to gather the information and documentation necessary to begin the design process.

The process of identifying required information is not unidirectional. You might return to a step and make additional inquiries about issues as they arise during the design process.

The steps for data gathering are shown in Figure 2-7 and are detailed in the following sections.

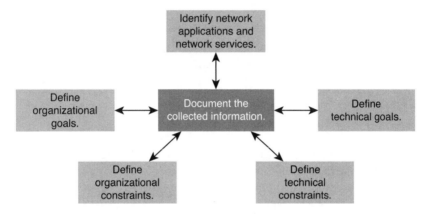

Figure 2-7   *Data-Gathering Steps*

Identifying Network Applications and Network Services

A critical step in data gathering is to determine the actual importance of the applications and which applications are planned for use. The use of a decision table can help to organize and categorize the solutions for the applications and services that are planned.

A decision table for identifying planned applications should list the following:

- Planned application types, such as email, collaboration (tools that aid group work), voice networking, web browsing, video on demand (VoD), database, file sharing and transfer, and computer-aided manufacturing

- Concrete applications that will be used (for example, Microsoft Outlook, Cisco Unified Meeting Place)

- The importance of certain applications as denoted with keywords such as *critical*, *important*, and *unimportant*

- Additional comments that are taken in the data-gathering process

Table 2-3 is an example of a completed planned network application table.

Table 2-3 *Planned Network Application Table*

Application Type	Application	Level of Importance	Comments
Collaboration	Cisco Unified MeetingPlace	Important	We need to be able to share presentations and applications during remote meetings.
Video browsing	Microsoft Internet Explorer, Opera, Netscape	Important	—
Videoconferencing	TelePresence	Critical	
Database	Oracle	Critical	All data storage will be based on Oracle.
Customer support	Customer applications	Critical	—

The planned infrastructure services table is similar to the planned applications table. It lists the following:

- Infrastructure services planned for the network

- Additional comments about those services

Table 2-4 shows an example of a completed planned infrastructure services table.

Table 2-4 *Planned Infrastructure Services Example*

Service	Comments
Security	Deploy security systematically, including firewalls, intrusion detection systems (IDS), and access control lists (ACL).
QoS	Direct priority to delay-sensitive voice traffic and other important traffic.
Network management	Utilize centralized management tools where appropriate and point product management as required.
High availability	Eliminate single points of failure and use redundant paths as needed.
Unified Communications	Focus on migrating the company from regular telephony.
Mobility	Commit to enhancing client laptop guest access and mobility of employee PCs.
Virtualization	Focus on the migration of physical servers to an ESX server.

Defining Organizational Goals

An effective network solution will support organizational processes. Every design project should begin by determining the organizational goals that are to be achieved. The criteria for success must be determined, and the consequences of a failure understood.

Network designers are often eager to start by analyzing the technical goals before considering the organizational goals and constraints. However, detailed attention to organizational goals and constraints is important for a project's success. In discussions about organizational goals, the designer obtains knowledge about the customer's expectations of the design's outcomes for the organization. Both short- and long-term goals should be identified. This organization-centered approach allows the network to become a strategic asset and competitive weapon for the customer and is important for the success of the project.

Preliminary research will enhance the positioning of the technologies and products to be used in the network. The analysis should include

- Organization's activities
- Products
- Processes
- Services
- Market
- Suppliers
- Competitive advantages
- Structure

This is an opportunity to determine what is important to the customer. A designer might ask the following questions to help determine organizational goals:

1. What are you trying to accomplish with this project?
2. What business challenges are you currently facing?
3. What are the consequences of not resolving these issues?
4. How would you measure or quantify success if you could provide solutions for the identified problems and issues?
5. What applications are most critical to your organization?
6. What is the major objective of this project?
7. What is driving the change?
8. Are there any government, safety, or legal mandates that you need to support?
9. What are your main concerns with the implementation of a new solution?
10. What technologies or services are needed to support your objectives?

11. What other technology projects and business initiatives will affect your group in the next two to five years?

12. What skill sets does your technical staff currently have?

13. What is your goal for return on investment (ROI)?

Organizational goals vary from organization to organization. The following are some typical goals that commercial organizations seek:

■ Increase the operation's generated revenue and profitability. A new design should reduce costs in certain segments and propel growth in others. The network designer and customer should discuss any expectations regarding new network's influence on revenue and profitability.

■ Improve data availability and interdepartmental communications to reduce development cycles and enhance productivity.

■ Facilitate customer support by providing additional services that can improve company reactions to customer needs and deliver better customer satisfaction.

■ Open the information infrastructure of the organization to all key constituencies (prospects, investors, customer's partners, suppliers, and employees). Build relationships and information accessibility to a new level as a basic for the network organizational model.

Note Similar, though not identical, goals are common to governmental, charitable, religious, and educational organizations. Most of these entities focus on using available resources effectively to attain the organization's goals and objectives. In not-for-profit organizations, key measures are typically stated in terms of cost containment, service quality, service expansion, and resource deployment.

Design requirements are typically stated in a Request for Proposal (RFP) or Request for Information (RFI) document from the enterprise. The first step in the design process should be to document the design requirements and gain enterprise certification and approval.

The following are examples of the types of data that can be gathered from common organizational goals:

■ **Increase competitiveness:** List competitive organizations and their advantages and weaknesses. Note possible improvements that might increase competitiveness or effectiveness.

■ **Reduce costs:** Reducing operational costs can result in increased profitability (even without a revenue increase) or increased services with the same revenue. List current expenses to help eliminate costs.

- **Improve customer support:** Customer support services help provide a competitive advantage. List current customer support services, including potential improvements.

- **Add new customer services:** List current customer services, and note future and desired (requested) services.

Table 2-5 shows an example of an organizational goals table for a sample corporation, Corporation X.

Table 2-5 *Corporation X's Organizational Goals*

Organizational Goal	Gathered Data (Current Situation)	Comments
Increase competitiveness	Corporation Y Corporation Z	Better products Reduced costs
Reduce cost	Repeating tasks: entering data multiple times and other time-consuming tasks	Single data-entry point Easy-to-learn applications Simple data exchange
Improve customer support	Order tracking and technical support done by individuals	Introduction of web-based order tracking and web-based tools for customer technical support
Add new customer services	Current services: telephone and fax orders, and telephone and fax confirmation	Secure web-based ordering Secure web-based confirmations

Identifying Organizational Constraints

When assessing organizational goals, it is important to analyze any constraints that might affect the network design. Some sample questions the designer might ask to help determine organizational constraints include the following:

1. What in your current processes is productive?

2. What in your current processes is not effective?

3. Which processes are labor-intensive?

4. What are the barriers for implementation in your organization?

5. What are your major concerns with the implementation of a new solution?

6. What financial and timing elements must be considered?

7. What projects already have budget approval?

8. Are other planned technology projects and business initiatives compatible with your current infrastructure and technology solutions?

9. Do you have a budget for technical development for your staff?

Typical constraints include the following:

- **Budget:** Reduced budgets often force network designers to implement affordable network design that includes compromises in availability of manageability, performance, and scalability. The budget includes equipment purchases, software licensing, maintenance agreements, staff training, and so on. The scope of the budget that is available to invest in a solid design must be acknowledged. It is also useful to know the areas that are able to be compromised for network performance to meet budgetary requirements.

- **Personnel:** The availability of existing trained personnel can be a design consideration. Organizations might not have the resources to train technicians. Additional constraints can be imposed if the organization is outsourcing network management. Trained technicians should verify that all elements are working in concert and are recognized on the network. Information regarding the number and availability of existing operations personnel and their experience and possible training requirements must be known.

- **Policies:** Organizations have different policies about protocols, standards, vendors, and applications. To design the network successfully, the designer must understand these. For example, the designer should determine customer policies related to single-vendor or multivendor platforms. An end-to-end, single-vendor solution might be a benefit, because compatibility issues do not restrain the network.

- **Schedule:** The new network design is often driven by the introduction of new network applications. The implementation time frames for new applications are often tightly connected. Therefore, they can influence the available time for network design. A product time frame should be discussed with the executive management of the organization and gain approval.

Table 2-6 shows an example of an organizational constraints table.

Table 2-6 *Organizational Constraints Example*

Organizational Constraint	Gathered Data	Comments
Budget	Amount of money to spend	Identify the amount that the organization will allocate for project.
Personnel	List available personnel and their expertise	Specify the number of networking engineers that will require additional training.
Policy	List preferred standards, protocols, vendors, and applications	Determine whether the organization plans to purchase equipment from the new vendor.
Scheduling	Specify time frames	Use tools for resource assignment, milestones, and critical path analysis.

Identifying Technical Goals

The technical goals of the project must also be determined before the design starts. Some sample questions the designer might ask to help determine technical goals include the following:

1. What are your technology priorities?

2. How does your technology budgeting process work?

3. What infrastructure issues exist or will exist, given your applications' introductions?

4. What skill sets does your technical staff need to acquire?

The following list describes some common technical goals:

- **Improve responsiveness and throughput of the network:** Responsiveness and throughput degrade as the number of users and applications increases. An additional consideration of network redesign might be to increase performance by upgrading link speed, partitioning the network, or both.

- **Simplify network management:** Simplify functions so that they are easy to use and understand.

- **Improve the security and reliability of mission-critical applications and data:** Increased internal and external threats to the enterprise network require the most up-to-date security rules and technologies to avoid disruptions to the operation.

- **Decrease expected downtime and related expenses:** When a network failure occurs, downtime must be minimal. The network must respond quickly to minimize related costs.

■ **Modernize outdated technologies:** The emergence of new network technologies and applications demands regular updates and the replacement of outdated equipment and technologies.

■ **Improve the scalability of the network:** Networks must be designed to provide upgrades and future growth.

Using a table helps the designer identify technical goals. The customer should determine the level of importance for each goal. One way of expressing the level of importance is with percentages. Specific technical goals are rated on a scale from 1 to 100, with the sum totaling 100. This scale provides direction for the designer when choosing equipment, protocols, features, and so on.

Table 2-7 shows an example of technical goals.

Table 2-7 *Technical Goals*

Technical Goals	Importance	Comments
Performance	20	Important at the central site, less important in branch offices.
Availability	25	Should be 99.9%.
Manageability	5	—
Security	15	Security for critical data transactions is extremely important.
Modernize	10	Implement IPv6 application.
Scalability	25	Scalability is critical.
Total	100	—

Note Performance is a general term that includes responsiveness, throughput, and resource utilization. The users of networked applications and their managers are usually most sensitive to responsiveness issues; speed is critical. The network system's managers often look to throughput as a measure of effectiveness in meeting the organization's needs. Executives who have capital budget responsibility tend to evaluate resource utilization as a measure of economic efficiency. It is important to consider the audience when presenting performance information.

Assessing Technical Constraints

Network designers might face various technical constraints during the design process. Some sample questions the designer might ask to help determine technical constraints include the following:

1. How do you determine your technology priorities?

2. Do you have a technology refresh process? If so, is that an obstacle or does it support the proposed project?

3. What urgent technical problems require immediate resolution or mitigation?

4. Do you have a technical development plan for your staff?

Good network design addresses constraints by identifying possible trade-offs, such as the following:

- **Existing equipment:** The network design process is usually progressive; legacy equipment must coexist with new equipment.

- **Bandwidth availability:** Insufficient bandwidth in parts of the network because of technical constraints must be resolved by other means.

- **Application compatibility:** If the new network is not being introduced at the same time as new applications, the design must provide compatibility with old applications.

Using a table can facilitate the process of gathering technical constraints. The designer identifies the technical constraints, notes the current situation, and provides the necessary changes required to mitigate the issues.

Table 2-8 shows an example of a technical constraints table.

Table 2-8   *Technical Constraints*

Technical Constraint	Gathered Data	Comments
Existing wiring	Copper cabling in backbone and uplinks	Replace existing copper cabling with fiber optics for uplinks and in the backbone.
Bandwidth availability	T1 WAN links	Upgrade speeds and consider another service provider that offers additional services.
Application compatibility	IPv6-based applications	Ensure that new network equipment supports IPv6.

Characterizing the Existing Network and Sites

The second step of the PPDIOO process is characterizing the existing network and sites. In many cases, a network already exists and the new design relies on restructuring and upgrading the existing network and sites. You should map the existing network topology and audit and measure network traffic using a variety of available tools. Even when a network does not exist, the sites that will be networked still should be examined.

Network designers face some great challenges that include determining the performance requirements in the appropriate amount of bandwidth needed to support data, voice, and video applications on a network. Inaccurate calculations can negatively affect services that are essential for maintaining customer satisfaction. A miscalculation to potentially increase costs can impact profitability. For these reasons, it is essential to perform an accurate characterization of the existing network.

The first step in characterizing the existing network and sites is to gather as much information as possible. This is typically done by following these steps:

Step 1.   Gather existing documentation for the network, and query the organization to discover any additional information (note that existing documentation might be inaccurate).

Step 2.   Perform a network audit that adds detail to the description of the network.

Step 3.   If possible, use traffic analysis information to augment organizational input when describing the application and protocols that are used on the network.

Note   Although traffic analysis is a good idea in principle, it is often too costly in terms of time and effort.

The following sections describe each of these steps and discuss the tools that are used.

Identifying Major Features of the Network

It is crucial to gather all pertinent network documentation. The designer can usually request additional data depending on the scope of the project. This information includes

- Site contact information (especially if remote deployments are planned)
- Existing network infrastructure (from physical diagrams and documents, and site surveys), including the following:
  - Locations and types of servers, including a list of supported network applications
  - Locations and types of network devices
  - Cabling that is currently in place, including network interface connection tables and worksheets

- Wiring closet locations

- Locations of telephone service demarcation points

- WAN speeds and locations of the WAN connection feeds

- Locations of power receptacles and availability of additional receptacles and power sources

  - Existing network infrastructure from logical topology diagrams, including the following:

    - Addressing scheme and routing protocols in use

    - VLAN number used

    - Infrastructure services supported, such as voice, storage, and wireless services

Sample Site Contact Information

Site contact information is important for projects involving remote deployments, especially for the coordination of equipment delivery and installations. The designer might have to conduct a physical site audit to obtain the necessary site information if the customer cannot provide all the necessary contact information.

The designer can also obtain additional information while at the site. For example, power availability can be determined by examining the existing wiring closets. Digital pictures taken by a remote site contact can assist in getting a quick sense of the remote environment. Table 2-9 illustrates a sample site contact form.

Table 2-9 *Sample Site Contact Form*

1. What is the site location/name?	
2. What is the site address?	
3. What is the shipping address?	
4. Who is the site contact?	Name: Title: Telephone: Mobile: Fax: Pager: Email: After-hours contact number:
5. Is this site owned and maintained by the customer?	Yes/No
6. Is this a staffed site?	Yes/No

Table 2-9   *Sample Site Contact Form*

7. What are the hours of operation?	
8. What are the building and room access procedures?	
9. Are there any special security/safety procedures?	Yes/No What are they?
10. Are there any union/labor requirements or procedures?	Yes/No What are they?
11. What are the locations of the equipment cabinets and racks?	Floor: Room: Position:

Sample High-Level Network Diagram

Figure 2-8 shows the high-level topology of a sample network, provided by a customer.

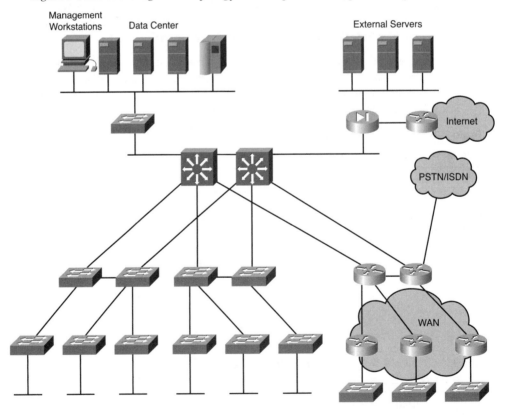

Figure 2-8   *Sample Customer-Provided High-Level Network Diagram*

If the customer provides you with a similar network topology diagram, it is important to understand that this is a high-level view of the network. Many questions remain about the expected functionality, including the following:

1. What is the IP addressing scheme?

2. What level of redundancy or high availability currently exists in the network?

3. What level of redundancy or high availability is required in the new network?

4. What are the details of the security design?

5. What types of link speeds and types are included in the network?

6. What network infrastructure services are in place, and what services are planned?

7. What is the planned topology (Layer 2 and Layer 3)?

8. How is connectivity provided to remote sites?

9. What network infrastructure services are in use, such as voice and video, and what is planned?

10. Are existing wireless devices in place, or are any wireless deployments planned?

11. What routing protocols are in use?

12. Are there any server farm or remote data center connectivity requirements?

13. What network management tools are in place?

It is important to obtain as much information as possible regarding the existing situation before commencing design.

Auditing the Existing Network

The auditing process begins with the consolidation of existing data about the network. You can gather up-to-date information from the current management software. If the organization has insufficient tools, you can choose to introduce additional software tools temporarily or even permanently, if they prove useful.

As Figure 2-9 shows, a number of different sources of information can be used in the audit process.

An audit provides details such as the following:

■ A list of network devices

■ Hardware specifications and versions

■ Software versions of network devices

■ Configurations of network devices

■ Output of various auditing tools to verify and augment the existing documentation

- Link, CPU, and memory utilization of network devices

- A list of unused ports, modules, and slots in network devices to determine whether the network is expandable

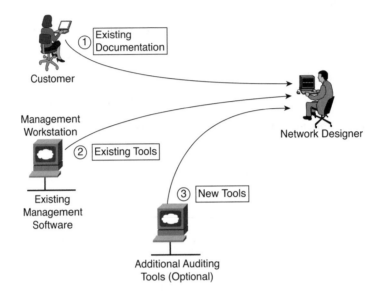

Figure 2-9   *Network Audit Information Sources*

The main objective of the assessment process is to supply as much internal information as possible. It should not require the purchase or installation of a large set of CPU-heavy auditing tools to collect configurations of network devices.

Figure 2-10 illustrates an example of automated assessment process information that is collected from the network management workstation. The system process should collect all information relevant to the redesign. Use the same process for all devices in the network that are affected by the design.

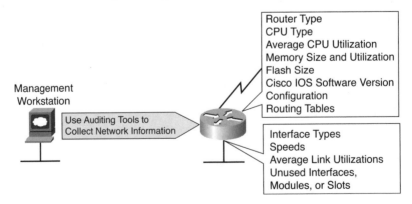

Figure 2-10   *Sample Information Collected During a Network Audit*

Using Tools for Auditing the Network

A number of quality network assessment tools are available. There are three basic categories for network assessment tools:

- Manual assessment:

    - Use monitoring commands on network development on small networks.

    - Use scripting tools to collect data on large networks.

- Use existing management and audit tools:

    - CiscoWorks, NetFlow, and NBAR.

    - Third-party tools, such as AirMagnet Survey PRO, BVS Yellowjacket 802.11 B/A/N/G, Dorado Software Redcell Engineering Editions, Netcordia NetMRI, neteXpose DNA, Pari Network Assessment Tool, and RISC Network Assessment Services.

- Use other tools, with a focus on areas such as VoIP, wireless, and security:

- Third-party tools such as AirMagnet VoFi Analyzer Pro, Ekahau Site Survey, GFI EventsManager, LANguard Network Security Scanner, NetIQ Vivinet Assessor, and neteXpose DNA.

Generally, a small network can be assessed without special tools. It can use monitoring commands on a small number of network devices to collect the relevant information. This can be partially automated by using scripting tools that execute monitoring commands automatically.

In large networks, a manual audit approach is extremely time-consuming and unreliable. In these situations, there are a number of special tools that can be used to collect the relevant information from the network devices. These include

- **Cisco Discovery Service:** This advanced web-service platform assists third-party network assessment tools to deliver detailed analysis and reporting on Cisco devices. Netformx DesignXpert Enterprise is an example.

- **Cisco tools:**

    - Use CiscoWorks to map the network and collect various types of information (such as network topology, hardware and software versions, and configurations).

    - NetFlow allows information gathering of every single flow in a network segment.

    - Network-Based Application Recognition (NBAR) is an intelligent classification engine.

- **Third-party tools:** For example, AirMagnet Survey PRO, BVS Yellowjacket 802.11 A.B/G/N, Dorado Software Redcell Engineering Editions, Netcordia NetMRI, neteXpose DNA, Pari Networks Assessment Tool, and RISC Network Assessment Services.

The following figures show example output from a number of available tools. Example 2-1 shows an example printout from Cisco IOS NetFlow.

Example 2-1   *Cisco IOS NetFlow* show ip cache flow *Output*

```
Router# show ip cache flow


IP packet size distribution (12718M total packets):
   1-32   64   96  128  160  192  224  256  288  320  352  384  416  448  480
   .000 .554 .042 .017 .015 .009 .009 .009 .013 .030 .006 .007 .005 .004 .004


   512  544  576 1024 1536 2048 2560 3072 3584 4096 4608
   .003 .007 .139 .019 .098 .000 .000 .000 .000 .000 .000


IP Flow Switching Cache, 4456448 bytes
  65509 active, 27 inactive, 820628747 added
  955454490 ager polls, 0 flow alloc failures
  Exporting flows to 1.1.15.1 (2057)
  820563238 flows exported in 34485239 udp datagrams, 0 failed
  last clearing of statistics 00:00:03


Protocol         Total  Flows   Packets Bytes  Packets Active(Sec) Idle(Sec)
--------         Flows  /Sec    /Flow  /Pkt   /Sec    /Flow    /Flow
TCP-Telnet      2656855    4.3      86    78   372.3      49.6     27.6
TCP-FTP         5900082    9.5       9    71    86.8      11.4     33.1
TCP-FTPD        3200453    5.1     193   461  1006.3      45.8     33.4
TCP-WWW       546778274  887.3      12   325 11170.8       8.0     32.3
TCP-SMTP       25536863   41.4      21   283   876.5      10.9     31.3
TCP-BGP           24520    0.0      28   216     1.1      26.2     39.0
TCP-other      49148540   79.7      47   338  3752.6      30.7     32.2
UDP-DNS       117240379  190.2       3   112   570.8       7.5     34.7
UDP-NTP         9378269   15.2       1    76    16.2       2.2     38.7
UDP-TFTP           8077    0.0       3    62     0.0       9.7     33.2
UDP-Frag          51161    0.0      14   322     1.2      11.0     39.4
ICMP           14837957   24.0       5   224   125.8      12.1     34.3
IP-other          77406    0.1      47   259     5.9      52.4     27.0
...
Total:        820563238 1331.7      15   304 20633.0       9.8     33.0
```

NBAR is mainly used for classification purposes for QoS. However, you can use it moderately to collect Layer 4 to Layer 7 information for network design. Example 2-2 shows an example output of the Cisco IOS NBAR **show ip nbar protocol-discovery** command.

Example 2-2 *NBAR* show ip nbar protocol-discovery *Output*

```
Router# show ip nbar protocol-discovery
FastEthernet0/0
            Input                    Output
            -----                    ------
Protocol    Packet Count             Packet Count
            Byte Count               Byte Count
            30sec Bit Rate (bps)     30sec Bit Rate (bps)
            30sec Max Bit Rate (bps) 30sec Max Bit Rate (bps)
----------- ------------------------ ------------------------
rtp            3272685                  3272685
               242050604                242050604
               768000                   768000
               2002000                  2002000
Gnutella       5133574                  5133574
               118779716                118779716
               383000                   383000
               987000                   987000
ftp            482183                   482183
               37606237                 37606237
               121000                   121000
               312000                   312000
http           144709                   144709
               32351383                 32351383
               105000                   105000
               269000                   269000
netbios        96606                    96606
               10627650                 10627650
               36000                    36000
               68000                    68000
<more>
```

As mentioned earlier, a number of third-party tools are available. Figure 2-11 shows a screen shot from the NetIQ Vivinet Assessor application showing a VoIP quality check.

Figure 2-12 shows a screen shot from the NetMRI appliance from Netcordia. The inventory results were expanded to show the "Cisco cat4506" devices, including IP addresses, device names, and operating system versions.

RSPAN with VACLs for Granular Traffic Analysis

Remote Switch Port Analyzer (RSPAN) selects network traffic sent to a network analyzer such as a SwitchProbe device or other remote monitoring (RMON) probe. With RSPAN, traffic can pass through one or more switches for analysis.

Figure 2-11   *NetIQ Vivinet Assessor*

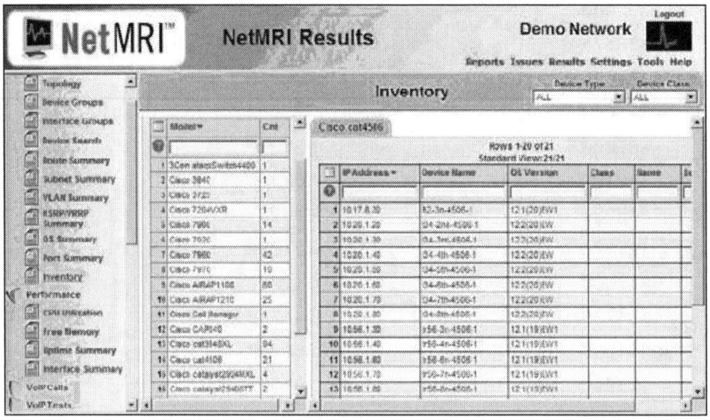

Figure 2-12   *Netcordia's NetMRI Appliance*

The RSPAN traffic from a selected source port or source VLANs is switched to an RSPAN VLAN and then forwarded to selected destination ports that are located in the RSPAN VLAN. By default, RSPAN always captures all traffic from the RSPAN source to the RSPAN destination, including control traffic, broadcast, and other frequently irrelevant traffic.

However, by combining RSPAN with a VLAN access control list (VACL) you can identify the exact traffic that needs to be captured. Only traffic matching the access control entries specified in the VACL are permitted to pass into the RSPAN VLAN and, by extension, to the RSPAN destination port.

Analyzing Network Traffic and Applications

Traffic analysis verifies the set of applications and protocols used in the network. It determines the applications' traffic patterns. It should reveal any additional applications or protocols running on the network. Each discovered application and protocol should be described in the following terms:

- Importance to the customer

- Quality of service (QoS)–related requirements

- Security requirements

- Scope: Describing the network to be used for the modules, applications, or protocols

Figure 2-13 illustrates an interactive approach.

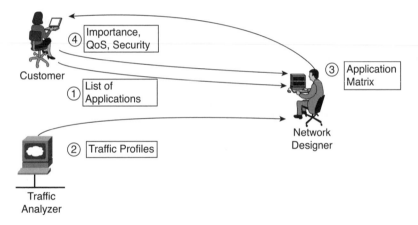

Figure 2-13   *Traffic Analysis Steps*

You can create a list of applications and protocols used in the network by applying the following steps:

Step 1.   Use customer input to list expected applications.

Step 2.   Utilize traffic analyzers to verify the customer's list of applications.

Step 3.   Present the customer with the new list of applications, and discuss discrepancies.

Step 4.   Generate the final list of applications and requirements (importance, QoS, security), as defined by the customer.

The following information was collected for a fictitious application to use as an example:

- **Name:** Application #8

- **Description:** Accounting software

- **Protocol:** Transmission Control Protocol (TCP) port 5151

- **Servers:** 2

- **Clients:** 50

- **Scope:** Campus

- **Importance:** High

- **Avg. rate:** 50 kbps with 10-second bursts to 1 megabit per second (Mbps)

Assume that a customer requirement concerns QoS on a WAN connection with limited bandwidth. In this case, the information collected is relevant because it describes the following:

- The application (TCP port 5151): This is required for performing classification.

- The importance of the application: This information is useful for evaluating how much bandwidth should be allocated to the application.

- The current bandwidth consumption according to the present QoS implementation.

Note   This information might not be relevant should the customer requirement concern a secure and resilient Internet connection. In that case, it might be necessary to gather additional information.

Using Tools for Analyzing Network Traffic

Tools implemented for traffic analysis range from manual identification of applications using Cisco IOS Software commands to dedicated software- or hardware-based analyzers. Analyzers capture live packets while the Simple Network Management Protocol (SNMP) gathers interface information.

Analysis tools include the following:

- Tools powered by Cisco Discovery Service, such as Netformx DesignXpert Enterprise.

- Cisco Network Services (CNS) NetFlow Collection Engine allows automatic information gathering of every single flow in the network segment.

- The Cisco Embedded Resource Manager (ERM) feature allows you to monitor internal system resource utilization for specific resources such as buffer, memory, and CPU. ERM monitors resource utilization from the perspective of various subsystems within the Cisco IOS Software, such as resource owners (RO) and resource users (RU). ERM allows you to configure threshold values for system resources.

- Use third-party hardware- or software-based products to analyze traffic in different subnets of the network. Examples include the following:

    - AirMagnet WiFi Analyzer PRO

    - VoFi Analyzer PRO

    - BVS Yellowjacket 802.11 A/B/G/N

    - Dorado Software Redcell Engineering Editions

    - Ekahau Site Survey

    - Netcordia NetMRI

    - NetIQ Vivinet Assessor

    - SolarWinds Orion

    - Pari Networks Assessment Tool

    - RISC Network Assessment Services

Reviewing Network Traffic Information

After the information has been gathered, it can be used to determine the health status of the network by comparing against the following guidelines:

- No shared Ethernet segments are saturated (no more than 40 percent network utilization).

- No WAN links are saturated (no more than 70 percent network utilization).

- The response time is generally less than 100 milliseconds (1/10 of a second).

- No segments have more than 20 percent broadcasts or multicasts.

- No segments have more than one cyclic redundancy check error per million bytes of data.

- On the Ethernet segments, less than 0.1 percent of the packets result in collisions.

- The Cisco routers are not overutilized (the 5-minute CPU utilization is no more than 75 percent).

Analyzing Network Health

Organizational input, network audit, and traffic analysis should provide enough information to identify possible problems in the existing network. You must convert the collected information into a concise summary report that identifies the possible drawbacks to the network. With this information, hardware and software upgrades can be proposed to support network requirements that were influenced by organizational requirements.

A summary report outlines the existing network results into a report that

■ Describes the required software features

■ Describes the potential problems in the existing network

■ Identifies the necessary actions to prepare the network for the implementation of required features

■ Influences the customer requirements

Figure 2-14 shows an example of a summary report problem statement.

• Requirement: Queuing in the WAN
• Identified problem:

    – Existing Cisco IOS Software version does not support new queuing technologies.
    – 15 out of 19 routers with older Cisco IOS Software are in the WAN.
    – 12 out of 15 routers do not have enough memory to upgrade to Cisco IOS Software Release 12.4 or later.
    – 5 out of 15 routers do not have enough flash memory to upgrade to Cisco IOS Software Release 12.4 or later.

Figure 2-14 *Summary Report Problem Statement*

The problems shown in Figure 2-14 are then paired with a list of recommendations that could resolve the highlighted issues. Figure 2-15 shows the list of recommendations for Figure 2-14.

• Recommended action:
    – 12 memory upgrades to 64 MB
    – 5 flash memory upgrades to 16 MB
• Options:
    – Replace hardware and software to support advanced queuing.
    – Find an alternative mechanism for that part of the network.
    – Find an alternative mechanism and use it instead of queuing.
    – Evaluate the consequences of not implementing the required feature in that part of the network.

Figure 2-15 *Summary Report Recommendations*

Summary report recommendations relate the existing network into the organizational requirements. A summary report can be utilized to recommend hardware and software to support the required features.

Creating a Draft Design Document

After thoroughly examining the existing network, the designer creates a draft design document. Figure 2-16 illustrates a draft design document's index (not yet fully developed), including the section that describes the existing network. The "Design Requirements" and "Existing Network Infrastructure" sections of the design document are closely relat-ed. They examine the existing network, which can result in changes to the "Design Requirements" section. Data from both sections directly influences the network's design.

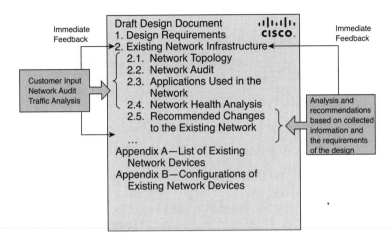

Figure 2-16   *Draft Design Document Index*

Typical draft documentation for an existing network should include the following items:

■ Logical (Layer 3) topology map or maps. Divide the topology into network modules if the network is too large to fit into one topology map.

■ Physical (Layer 1) topology map or maps.

■ The network audit results, including the types of traffic in the network, the traffic congestion points, the suboptimal traffic paths, and so on.

■ A summary section describing the major network services used in the existing net-work, such as Open Shortest Path First (OSPF), Border Gateway Protocol (BGP), and Internet Protocol Security (IPsec), with configurations of all network devices includ-ed as either a separate document or an appendix to the design document.

■ A summary description of applications and overlay services used in the network.

■ A summary description of issues that might affect the design or the established design requirements.

■ A list of existing network devices, with the platform and software versions.

■ Configurations of existing network devices.

Time Estimates for Performing Network Characterization

This section provides some guidelines to estimate how long it can take to characterize the network. The time required to characterize a network varies significantly, depending on the following factors:

- The experience of the network engineer

- The quality of documentation provided by the customer and the quality of the communication with the customer

- The size and complexity of network

- The efficiency of network management and discovery tools

- Whether the network devices are carefully managed through SNMP

- The amount of information needed for the scope of the project

Figure 2-17 provides a range of time estimates, in hours, for the characterization of networks in a variety of sizes. These estimates assume a highly skilled (Cisco Certified Internet Expert [CCIE] level) network engineer with efficient automated tools for network discovery and performance gathering, and a network in which the devices communicate with SNMP. The network characterization includes strategic evaluation and possible network redesign.

	Small Network 1-20 Switches/ Routers		Medium Network 20-200 Switches/ Routers		Large Network 200-800 Switches/ Routers		Very Large Network >800 Switches/ Routers	
a) Interview management team	4	4	8	8	12	12	16	16
b) Interview network team	4	4	6	6	8	12	24	24
c) Review documentation	4	4	6	6	8	12	16	16
d) Set up network discovery tool	4	4	6	6	8	8	16	16
e) Resolve SNMP access and similar problems	4	4	8	16	16	48	80	160
f) Allow tools to gather data	Variable		Variable		Variable		Variable	
g) Analyze captured data	4	8	16	16	24	24	40	40
h) Prepare high-level Layer 3 diagrams	4	4	4	8	8	16	16	32
i) Prepare report stating conclusions	16	16	32	32	48	48	80	80
j) Incremental effort to prepare network diagrams	Not Included		Not Included		Not Included		Not Included	
Total estimated manpower, in hours	44 - 48		86 - 98		132 - 180		288 - 384	

Figure 2-17 *Network Characterization Estimates (in Hours)*

Figure 2-17 illustrates the stages of network characterization. The following steps include a more detailed process:

Step 1.   Interview the management team to gather goals and constraints.

Step 2.   Interview the network team, and gather goals, constraints, documentation, and diagrams.

Step 3.   Review documentation and diagrams, and clarify items with the site team.

Step 4.   Set up the network discovery tool, which typically involves using automated discovery or entering a device list or IP address range into the tool. Verify that the tool has found most routers and switches, and start to collect performance data.

Step 5.   Resolve SNMP access and similar problems if devices have not been managed carefully in the past.

Step 6.   Allow the discovery tool to gather data. This process typically does not required oversight by the network engineer. The time for this step will vary depending on network, and should include seasonal or cyclical factors. Generally one week of data is sufficient.

Step 7.   Analyze the captured data. Minimizing the time required is dependent on using efficient tools.

Step 8.   Prepare high-level (Layer 3) diagrams of the proposed network.

Step 9.   Prepare the report of conclusions and recommendations.

Note   If the customer cannot supply detailed network diagrams, the preparation for this must be added to the time estimates.

Consequently, network characterization typically takes from one to many weeks of effort, depending on the size and complexity of the network and the other factors mentioned at the beginning of this section.

Using the Top-Down Approach to Network Design

After the organizational requirements and audit documentation from the existing network have been gathered, the network solution is ready to be designed, the implementation is ready to be planned, and optionally a network prototype is ready to be built.

The following sections provide you with the knowledge that is needed to apply an appropriate network design methodology using a modular top-down approach.

These sections begin with an explanation of how to assess the scope of the design project and how to complete the list of requirements. After gathering all customer requirements and putting them into decision tables, key and missing information will be identified. It is important to reassess the scope of the project to ensure a comprehensive understanding of the network requirements.

Top-Down Approach to Network Design

Designing an enterprise network is a complex project. Top-down design facilitates the process by dividing it into smaller and more manageable steps. This section describes the top-down network design approach.

Figure 2-18 shows the OSI layers to start with when designing based on the top-down approach.

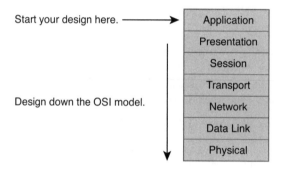

Figure 2-18   *Top-Down Design Method*

Top-down design clarifies the design goals and initiates the design from the perspective of the required applications and network solutions such as IP telephony and content networking. The top-down approach adapts the physical infrastructure to the needs of the network solution.

When you deploy a bottom-up approach by selecting network devices and technologies first, the network might not meet the needs of the organization. With a bottom-up approach, the risk of redesigning the network is very high.

To complete a top-down design, the following tasks must be completed:

- Analyze the requirements and applications of the organization.

- Complete the design from the top of the OSI reference model to the bottom:

  - Define requirements at the upper OSI layers (application, presentation, and session).

  - Specify the infrastructure that is required in the lower OSI layers (transport, network, data link, and physical).

- Gather additional data on the network as it can influence the logical and physical design. Adapt the design to the new data as required.

Top-Down Design Example

The organization in the example shown in Figure 2-19 requires a data network that is capable of supporting IP telephony, which allows the organization to avoid the costs of having two separate networks. The organization needs VoIP as the driving application. IP routing and QoS are needed at the transport and network layers. Cisco Unified Communications Manager addresses the application need for call routing.

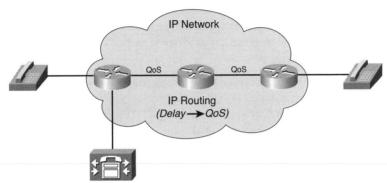

Cisco Unified Communications Manager

Figure 2-19   *Top-Down Voice Design Example*

The resulting network design includes IP-enabled routers (and other devices not shown in the figure) so that IP routing can take place in the network. To implement IP telephony, the network designer must manage the delay in the IP network with specific QoS mechanisms.

Cisco Unified Communications Manager is placed inside the network to manage and monitor IP telephone calls.

Note   Cisco Unified Communications Manager is a server-based application that establishes and maintains signaling and control for IP telephone sessions.

Decision Tables in Network Design

Decision tables are used for making systematic decisions when there are multiple solutions or options to a network issue. Decision tables simplify the selection of the most appropriate option and assist in determining the type of specific network building blocks (topology, routing protocols, security, and so on).

Basic guidelines for creating a network design decision table are included in the following steps:

Step 1.   Decide which network building block (the physical topology, routing protocol, security implementation, and so on) requires decisions.

Step 2. Collect possible options for a given situation. Be certain to include the best practice options to maximize value from the decision table.

Step 3. Create a table to include solutions and given requirements. Add the parameters or properties of specific options.

Step 4. Match the given requirements with the specific properties of the options.

Step 5. Select the most appropriate option. If all requirements are treated equally, choose the option with the most matches. If some requirements are considered more important than others, implement a weighting system. Each of the requirements is assigned a weight that is proportional to its importance in the decision-making process.

Table 2-10 is an example of a decision table for selecting a routing protocol based on multiple criteria. In this instance, several routing protocols are considered as possible options: Enhanced Interior Gateway Routing Protocol (EIGRP), Open Shortest Path First (OSPF), and Border Gateway Protocol (BGP).

Table 2-10 *Sample Decision Table for Routing Protocol Selection*

Option Parameters	EIGRP	OSPF	BGP	Required Network Parameters
Size of network	Large	Large	Very Large	Large
Enterprise-focused	Yes	Yes	No	Yes
Use of VLSM	Yes	Yes	Yes	Yes
Supports Cisco routers	Yes	Yes	Yes	Yes
Supports multiple vendors	No	Yes	Yes	Yes
Network support staff knowledge	Good	Fair	Poor	Good

For this example, the protocol chosen should meet the following requirements:

■ It should support a large network (100 or more routers). All three protocols support large networks with high-speed convergence and the use of variable-length subnet masks (VLSM).

■ It needs to support only Cisco equipment. EIGRP, OSPF, and BGP can all support Cisco equipment.

■ The network staff should have knowledge of the chosen protocol to troubleshoot the network.

■ The protocol should work well in the enterprise. Because BGP was designed to support interconnecting networks of autonomous systems, it is not optimized for use in the enterprise.

Note All requirements in this example have the same level of importance, so no weights are used.

Based on the stated requirements, EIGRP is the routing protocol of choice in this example.

Assessing the Scope of the Network Design Project

In assessing the scope of a network design, it must be determined whether the design is for a new network or a modification of an entire network, a single segment or module, a set of LANs, a WAN, or a remote access network. In a review of the design, the network designer can determine whether the design addresses a single function or all the OSI model layers.

Table 2-11 shows a sample design scope assessment.

The OSI reference model is important in the design phase. The network designer should review the project scope from the protocol layer perspective and decide whether the design is necessary at the network layer or whether other layers are involved.

Table 2-11   *Design Scope Assessment Example*

Scope of Design	Comments
Entire network	The headquarters office needs a backbone redesign. All branch office LANs will be upgraded to Fast Ethernet technology.
Network layer	Introduction of private IP addresses requires a new addressing plan. Certain LANs need segmentation. Routing must support the new addressing plan and provide greater reliability and redundancy.
Data link layer	The CO backbone and some branch offices require redundancy with redundant equipment and links. They also require a campus wireless RF site survey to enable mobility deployment and equipment scope.

Using Structured Design Principles

The output of the design should be a model of the complete system. To achieve this type of design output, the top-down approach is highly recommended. Rather than focusing on the network components, technologies, or protocols, target the systematic process that takes into account the business goals, technical objectives, and existing and future network services and applications. This systematic approach requires structured design practices, such as logical, physical, and layered models.

Network infrastructure and user and network services are tightly connected; they are bound to the same logical and physical models. Both the network infrastructure and user and network services components are logically subdivided under the Cisco Borderless Networks Architecture. Use the top-down approach during all design phases.

Structured top-down design practices focus on dividing the design task into related, less complex components. The following steps describe the process:

Step 1.   Identify the applications that will be needed to support the requirements of the customer.

Step 2.   Identify the logical connectivity requirements of the applications, with a focus on the necessary network solutions and the supporting network services. Examples of the infrastructure services include

- Voice

- Content networking

- Storage networking

- Availability

- Management

- Security

- QoS and IP multicast

Step 3.   Split the network functionality to develop the network infrastructure and hierarchy requirements.

Step 4.   Design each structured element separately but in relation to other elements. Network infrastructure and infrastructure services design are tightly connected, because they are bound to the same logical, physical, and layered models.

Logical Structure

After identifying the connectivity requirements, the designer works on each of the functional module's details. The network infrastructure and infrastructure services are composed of logical structures. Each of these structures (such as addressing, routing protocols, QoS, and security) must be designed separately but in close relation to other structures, with a goal of creating one homogeneous network.

Some logical structures are more closely related than others. Network infrastructure elements are associated more closely to each other than to infrastructure services. For example, physical topology and the addressing of design are often very closely related.

Physical Structure

There are several approaches to physically structuring a network module. The most common method is a three-layer hierarchical structure:

- Core

- Distribution

- Access

In this approach, three separate, yet related, physical structures are developed instead of a single, large network. This results in meaningful and functional homogeneous elements within each layer. Selecting the functionality and required technologies is easier when it is applied to separate structured network elements than to the complex network.

Network Design Tools

Several types of tools can be used to ease the task of designing a complex modern network. They include the following:

- **Network-modeling tools:** These tools are helpful when there are too many or large requirements. These tools model both simple and complex networks. The program processes the information that is provided and returns a proposed configuration. You can then modify the configuration and reprocess it to add redundant links, support additional sites, and so on.

- **Strategic analysis tools:** Strategic analysis or what-if tools help designers and other people who are working on the design (engineers, technologists, and business and marketing professionals) develop network and service plans, including detailed technical and business analyses. These tools attempt to calculate the effects of specific network components through simulated scenarios.

- **Decision tables:** As discussed earlier, decision tables are manual tools. They help designers to choose specific network characteristics from multiple options that are based on required parameters.

- **Simulation and verification tools or services:** These tools or services are used to verify the acquired design, thereby reducing the need for a pilot network implementation.

Figure 2-20 illustrates how the initial requirements information is processed with network design tools to produce a network design.

To verify a network design that was produced with the help of network-modeling tools, strategic analysis tools, and decision tables, either use simulation and test tools or build a pilot or prototype network. The pilot or prototype network also creates a proof of concept that confirms the appropriateness of the design implementation plan.

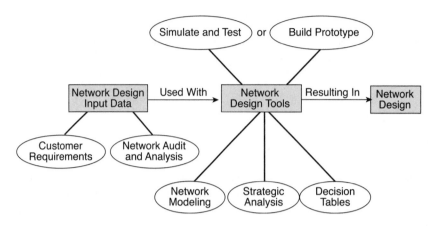

Figure 2-20   *Using Network Design Tools*

Testing the Design

After a design is complete, you should verify it. The design can be tested in an existing or live network (pilot) or in a prototype network that will not affect the existing network.

A prototype network is usually established for new network designs or additions to existing networks. A pilot network is normally used to verify designs that are implemented on an existing network infrastructure.

A successful design implementation in either a pilot or a prototype network serves as a proof of concept, in preparation for complete implementation.

A prototype or pilot implementation can have one of two results:

■ **Success:** This result is usually enough to prove the design concept.

■ **Failure:** This result is normally used to correct the design. The prototype or pilot phase is then repeated. In the case of small deviations, the design can be corrected and tested in the prototype or pilot network immediately.

Figure 2-21 is a sample topology subset of a planned network. The highlighted areas indicate the parts of the network involved in a redesign. This part of the topology is implemented first in a prototype to verify the design, and then a pilot is developed with live data to further test the design.

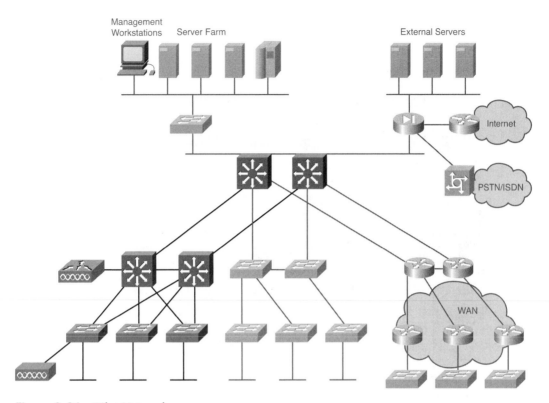

Figure 2-21   *Pilot Network*

Planning an Implementation

When the design is completed in the Prepare, Plan, Design, Implement, Operate, and Optimize (PPDIOO) process, the next step is to develop the implementation and migration plan in as much detail as possible.

The more detailed the implementation plan documentation, the less knowledgeable the network engineer needs to be to implement the design. While very complex steps usually require the designer to carry out the implementation, other staff members can complete well-documented detailed steps without the direct involvement of the designer.

When implementing a design, the possibility of failure must be considered, even after a successful pilot or prototype network test. You need to test at every step and have a procedure to revert to the original setup in case there is a problem.

Implementation of network design consists of several phases such as hardware installation, system configuration, and production launches. Each phase consists of several steps, and each step should contain the following:

- Description of the step
- References to design documents

- Detailed implementation guidelines

- Detailed rollback guidelines in case of failure

- Estimated time necessary for implementation

Figure 2-22 illustrates a sample implementation plan summary.

	Date Time	Description	Implementation Details	Complete
Phase 3	01/02/2010	Install campus hardware	Section 6.2.3	✓
Step 1		Connect switches	Section 6.2.3.1	✓
Step 2		Install routers	Section 6.2.3.2	✓
Step 3		Complete cabling	Section 6.2.3.3	✓
Step 4		Verify data link layer	Section 6.2.3.4	✓
Phase 4	01/03/2010	Configure campus hardware	Section 6.2.4	
Step 1		Configure VLANs		
Step 2		Configure IP addressing	Section 6.2.4.1	
Step 3		Configure routing	Section 6.2.4.2	
Step 4		Verify connectivity	Section 6.2.4.3	
Phase 5	01/05/2010	Launch campus updates into production	Section 6.2.4.4 Section 6.2.5	
Step 1	...	Complete connections to existing network	Section 6.2.5.1	
Step 2		Verify connectivity	Section 6.2.5.2	

Figure 2-22   *IDS and IPS Operational Differences*

In Figure 2-22, each step of the implementation phase is briefly described, with references to the implementation plan for further details. The concise implementation plan section should describe precisely what needs to be accomplished.

Figure 2-23 provides a detailed description of an implementation step. It describes the configuration of EIGRP on 50 routers in the network and lists the two major components of the step (in the per-router configuration procedure).

Documenting the Design

A design document lists the design requirements, documents the existing network and the network design, identifies the proof-of-concept strategy and results, and details the implementation plan. The final design document structure should be similar to the one shown in Figure 2-24.

• Section 6.2.7.3, "Configure routing protocols in the
WAN network module":
– Number of routers involved is 50.
– Use template from section 4.2.3, "EIGRP details."
– Per router configuration:
  • Use **passive-interface** command on all nonbackbone LANs. (See
    section 4.2.3, "EIGRP details")
  • Use summarization according to the design. (See section 4.2.3,
    "EIGRP details," and section 4.2.2, "Addressing details")
– Estimated time is 10 minutes per router.
– Roll-back procedure: Remove EIGRP configuration on all
  routers.

Figure 2-23   *Sample Detailed Design Implementation Step*

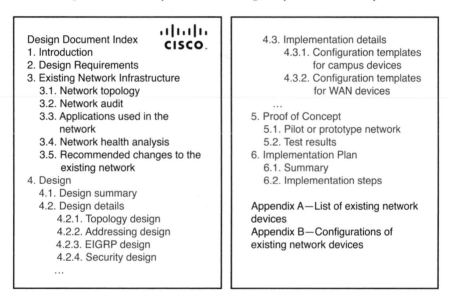

Figure 2-24   *Sample Design Document*

The final design document structure should include the following:

■ **Introduction:** This section presents the main reasons leading to the network design or
redesign.

■ **Design requirements:** This section identifies organizational requirements and
design goals.

■ **Existing network infrastructure:** This section describes an existing network and is
used only for a network redesign.

■ **Design:** This section identifies design and implementation details. The details include
the topology, addressing, and security. Provide implementation details such as configuration templates and exact configurations of network devices.

- **Proof of concept:** This section describes pilot or prototype network verification and test results.

- **Implementation plan:** This section provides the implementation details for technical staff members to carry out tasks without requiring the presence of the designer.

- **Appendixes:** These include lists and optional configurations of existing network devices (for network redesign).

Summary

In this chapter, you learned about the principles of network design, with a focus on the following topics:

- Cisco Network Architectures for the Enterprise is the framework for implementing intelligent networks. It maps business requirements to network requirements.

- The PPDIOO network lifecycle approach reflects the lifecycle phases of a standard network. This approach includes the following tasks:

  - Identifying customer requirements

  - Characterizing the existing network and sites

  - Designing the network topology and solutions

- The result of network characterization is a summary report describing the health of the network.

- After the design phase begins, a modular top-down approach facilitates the network design process.

References

For additional information, refer to these resources:

Cisco Borderless Networks Architecture, at www.cisco.com/go/borderless.

Cisco Collaboration Architecture, at www.cisco.com/go/collaboration.

Cisco Data Center, at www.cisco.com/go/datacenter.

Oppenheimer, P. *Top-Down Network Design, Third Edition*. Indianapolis, Indiana: Cisco Press, 2004.

Review Questions

Answer the following questions, and refer to Appendix A for the answers.

1. What are the top business drivers that can impact the network architecture?

2. What are some of the benefits provided by the Cisco Network Architectures?

3. Match the PPDIOO network lifecycle phases with their correct descriptions.

   Phases:

   a. Prepare phase

   b. Plan phase

   c. Design phase

   d. Implement phase

   e. Operate phase

   f. Optimize phase

   1. The network is built and verified based on design requirements.

   2. The network requirements, where the network will be installed, and who will require network services are identified.

   3. Includes the identification and resolving of network problems, proactively.

   4. A design is proposed based on the initial network requirements along with additional data.

   5. The organizational requirements, development of network strategy, and proposed high-level conceptual architecture are completed.

   6. Includes the maintenance of the network and day-to-day activities.

4. What are the three basic steps of the design methodology when using the PPDIOO lifecycle framework?

5. What steps are involved in identifying customer design requirements?

6. List some common organizational constraints.

7. List some site contact information that would be important for projects involving remote deployments when equipment delivery and installations must be coordinated.

8. Which command can be used to display NBAR protocol discovery information on a Cisco router?

   a. show ip nbar protocol-discovery

   b. show processes cpu

   c. show memory utilization

   d. show version

9. Which command displays packet size distribution and activity by protocol on a Cisco router?

   a. show ip nbar protocol-discovery

   b. show ip interface

   c. show version

   d. show ip cache flow

10. What are the layers in the three-layer hierarchical structure?

   a. Core, distribution, and desktop

   b. Core, distribution, and access

   c. Core, routing, and access

   d. Backbone, routing, and access

Chapter 3

Structuring and Modularizing the Network

This chapter introduces a modular hierarchical approach to network design, the Cisco Enterprise Architecture. This chapter includes the following sections:

- Network Hierarchy

- Using a Modular Approach to Network Design

- Services Within Modular Networks

- Network Management Protocols and Features

The traditional approach to building a network has been to follow the hierarchical core-distribution-access layered model. To further enhance the design process, Cisco has created the Network Architectures for the Enterprise. The Cisco Network Architectures for the Enterprise consists of five modules. The modules represent focused views of the Borderless Network, Collaboration, and Data Center/Virtualization architectures. Each module targets a specific segment of the network and consists of a distinct network infrastructure and services. Some network applications extend between the modules.

This chapter describes a basic network hierarchy and discusses the Cisco modular approach to designing an enterprise network.

Designing the Network Hierarchy

The hierarchical network structure is composed of the access, distribution, and core layers. Each layer has its own functions that are used to develop a hierarchical network design. The hierarchical model historically was used as the sole method for designing enterprise LAN and WAN data networks. Currently, the hierarchical model also serves as a major component for more advanced modular designs.

The following sections describe the hierarchical model and application of a modular approach to the design of complex networks. They also describe the benefits of the hierarchical model, the efficiencies that are gained by demarcating (layering) functions, and the responsibilities within an overall network design.

Introducing the Hierarchical Network Model

The hierarchical network model provides a modular view of a network. It is important to have a modular view to design and build a deterministic scalable network. This section describes the layers of the hierarchical network model.

The hierarchical network model provides a modular framework that allows flexibility in network design and facilitates ease of implementation and troubleshooting. The hierarchical model divides networks or their modular blocks into three layers—access, distribution, and core layers—as shown in Figure 3-1.

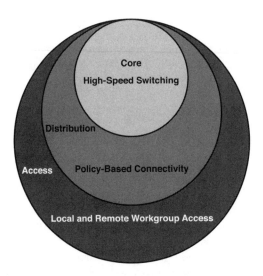

Figure 3-1 *Hierarchical Model Layers*

As shown in Figure 3-1, the hierarchical network design model consists of three layers:

■ **Access layer:** The first tier or edge of the campus. It is the place where end devices (such as PCs, printers, cameras, and so on) attach to the wired portion of the campus network. The access layer is also the place where devices that extend the network out one more level are attached. Two prime examples of devices that extend network connectivity out one more layer from the actual campus access switch are IP phones and wireless access points (AP). The access layer is one of the most feature-rich parts of the campus network, because of the wide variety of devices that can connect to it and the various services and dynamic configuration mechanisms that are necessary to this layer. When viewing the overall campus design, the access switch provides the majority of these access layer services and is the key element in enabling multiple campus services.

- **Distribution layer:** In the campus design, this layer has a unique role in that it acts as a services and control boundary between the access and the core. Both access and the core are dedicated special-purpose layers. The distribution layer, however, serves multiple purposes. It is an aggregation point for all the access switches, and it also acts as an integral member of the access-distribution block, providing connectivity and policy services for traffic flows within the access-distribution block. In addition, the distribution layer is an element in the core of the network and participates in the core routing design. Its third role is to provide the aggregation, policy control, and isolation demarcation point between the campus distribution building block and the rest of the network. In providing all these functions, the distribution layer participates in both the access layer and the core.

- **Core layer:** In some ways, this layer is the simplest, yet most critical, part of the campus. It provides a limited set of services and is designed to be highly available and operate in an always-on mode. In the current business environment, the core of the network must operate as a nonstop service. The core campus is the backbone that binds together all the elements of the campus architecture. It is that part of the network that provides connectivity between the end devices, computing, and data storage services that are located within the data center, and other areas and services within the network. The core of the network should avoid implementing any complex policy services, and it should not have any directly attached user/server connections. Also, the core should possess the minimal control plane configuration, combined with highly available devices that are configured with the correct amount of physical redundancy to provide nonstop services capability.

Each hierarchical layer focuses on specific functions, thereby allowing the network designer to choose the right systems and features based on their function within the model. This approach helps provide more accurate capacity planning and minimize total costs. Figure 3-2 illustrates a sample network showing the mapping to the hierarchical model's three layers.

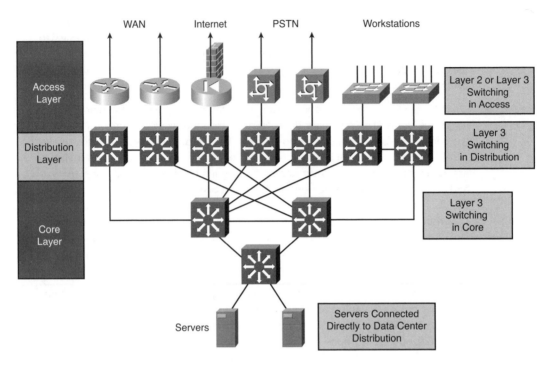

Figure 3-2 *Example Hierarchical Model Network*

The hierarchical layers do not have to be implemented as distinct physical entities; they are defined to aid in successful network design and to represent functionality that must exist within a network. The actual manner in which the layers are implemented depends on the needs of the network you are designing. Each layer can be implemented in routers or switches, represented by physical media, or combined in a single device. A particular layer can be omitted, but hierarchy should be maintained for optimum performance. The following sections detail the functionality of the three layers and the devices used to implement them.

Describing Access Layer Functionality

The purpose of the access layer is to meet the functions of end-device connectivity. This is accomplished by granting user access and providing (through specific applications) security, quality of service (QoS), and access policies to network resources.

The access layer has these characteristics:

- It supports the connectivity of any end devices to the wired portion of the campus network. These end devices can also extend the network out one more level (IP phones and wireless APs are key examples of this). The access layer also provides connectivity for the unique requirements of the data center.

- In the campus environment, the access layer incorporates shared, switched, or subnetted LAN access devices with ports. These are available to workstations and servers.

- In the WAN environment, the access layer provides remote users or sites with access to the campus network through a wide-area technology such as Frame Relay, Multiprotocol Label Switching (MPLS), DSL, or coaxial cable.

- Access is granted only to authenticated users or devices.

- It provides QoS and policy application using application recognition services such as QoS marking, policing, queuing, deep packet inspection, Network-Based Application Recognition (NBAR), and others.

Access can be provided to end devices as part of two scenarios:

- **Using Layer 2 switching (typical campus):** The access layer aggregates end-user-switched 10/100 ports and provides Fast Ethernet, Fast EtherChannel (FEC), and Gigabit Ethernet uplinks to the distribution layer. VLANs can be used to reduce the size of the broadcast domain across the access layer and allow each VLAN to supports its own spanning tree. Although applying one VLAN per switch is recommended, using a separate VLAN for data and another VLAN for voices will satisfy the connectivity requirements for workstation and IP phones. Transportation between the access layer switches and the distribution layer switches is based on a Layer 2 trunking system, typically using IEEE 802.1Q. A Layer 3 distribution switch can also provide the inter-VLAN communication for the access layer.

- **Using Layer 3 switching (typical WAN):** Access routing provides entry to remote office environments as well as the Internet. This is accomplished by using wide-area technologies that are combined with features such as route propagation, packet filtering, authentication, and so on.

Campus Access Layer Connectivity

In Figure 3-3, the campus access layer aggregates end users and provides uplinks to the distribution layer. The access switches are dual-attached to the distribution switches for high availability. A best practice is to implement one data VLAN per access switch to support one IP subnet and to connect the access switch through a Layer 3 link to the distribution switches. However, when deploying voice, Cisco recommends that two VLANs be enabled at the access layer: a native VLAN for data traffic and a voice VLAN. If multiple VLANs are implemented on an access switch, the connection to the distribution layer is typically 802.1q trunking with separation of per-VLAN spanning tree on each uplink for load balance and redundancy.

For spanning-tree support, Rapid Spanning Tree Protocol (RSTP) is a recommended best practice in the enterprise. RSTP is an evolution of the Spanning Tree Protocol (STP) (the IEEE 802.1D standard) and provides faster spanning-tree convergence after a topology change.

You can provide access to end devices as part
of two scenarios:

• Using Layer 2 switching (typical campus)
• Using Layer 3 switching (routed)

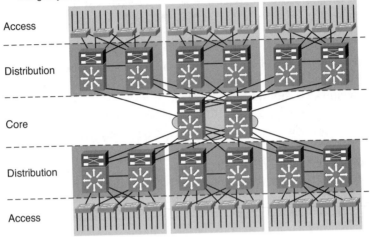

Figure 3-3 *Access Layer Connectivity*

Note When RSTP cannot be implemented, STP with the UplinkFast, PortFast, and
BackboneFast features should be implemented to provide equivalent convergence
improvements.

The access layer can be a feature-rich environment supporting convergence, high availability, security, QoS, and IP multicast. Some intelligent network services found at the
access layer include QoS trust boundary, broadcast suppression, DHCP snooping, and
Internet Group Management Protocol (IGMP) snooping.

Describing Distribution Layer Functionality

The distribution layer aggregates the wiring closets and uses a combination of Layer 2 and
Layer 3 switching to segment workgroups and isolate network problems, preventing them
from impacting the core layer. It is used to terminate access layer VLANs from access
layer switches. The distribution layer is also applied to enforce policy within the network.

The distribution layer is where routing and packet manipulation are performed, and it can
be a routing boundary between the access and core layers. The distribution layer connects network services to the access layer and implements policies regarding QoS, security, traffic loading, and routing.

The distribution layer allows the core layer to connect diverse sites while maintaining high performance. To further improve routing protocol performance, the distribution layer summarizes routes from the access layer. For some networks, the distribution layer offers a default route to access layer routers. It runs dynamic routing protocols when communicating with core routers.

In short, the distribution layer is the layer that provides policy-based connectivity. In terms of IP routing, the distribution layer represents a redistribution point between routing domains or the demarcation between static and dynamic routing protocols. The distribution layer can also be the point at which tasks such as controlled routing decisions and filtering occur.

As shown in Figure 3-4, the typical hierarchical campus design uses distribution blocks in a combination of Layer 2, Layer 3, and Layer 4 protocols and services to provide optimal convergence, scalability, security, and manageability.

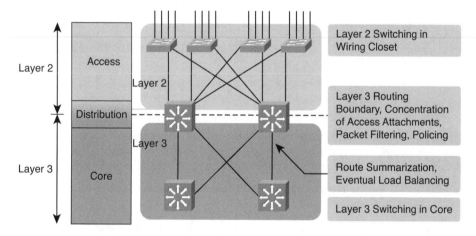

Figure 3-4 *Traditional Campus Network Distribution Layer Example*

The distribution layer in a routed campus network has these characteristics:

■   The access switch is configured as a Layer 2 switch that forwards traffic on high-speed trunk ports to the distribution switches.

■   The distribution switches are configured to support Layer 2 switching on their downstream access switch trunks.

■   The distribution switches are configured to support Layer 3 switching on their upstream ports toward the core of the network.

■   Route summarization is configured on interfaces toward the core layer.

As shown in Figure 3-5, in a routed campus network, the distribution layer is highly redundant, both toward the access layer and toward the core layer.

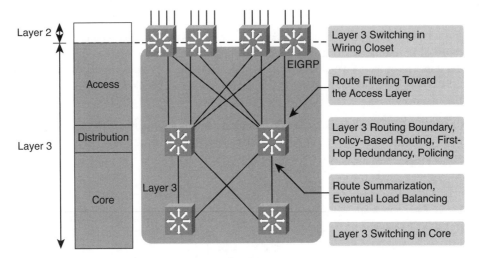

Figure 3-5 *Routed Campus Network Distribution Layer Example*

The distribution layer in a routed campus network has these characteristics:

■ Layer 3 switching is used toward the access layer and on the access layer.

■ Layer 3 switching is performed in the distribution layer and extended toward the core layer.

■ Route filtering is configured on interfaces toward the access layer to eliminate unnecessary route advertisements.

■ Route summarization is configured on interfaces toward the core layer.

Virtual Switches

Today, redundancy plays a major role in network design. Designers must look for ways to eliminate single points of failure throughout the networks. To provide redundancy, physical loops are sometimes introduced into the network. Fortunately, protocols such as STP are used to provide loop-free networks.

Although STP solves the looping problem, it comes at a cost: Some interfaces must be placed in blocking mode. This eliminates the ability to have all the interfaces forwarding and load balancing across the multiple chassis.

To answer this challenge, Cisco has created the Virtual Switching System (VSS). With the introduction of the virtual switch concept, the distribution switch pair can now be configured to run as a single logical switch. By converting the redundant physical distribution switches into a single logical switch, a significant change is made to the topology of the network. Using an access switch configured with two uplinks to two distribution switches requires a control protocol to determine which of the uplinks to use. Now the access switch has a single Multichassis EtherChannel (MEC) upstream link (using two or more physical links, one to each physical switch) that is connected to a single virtual distribution switch. Figure 3-6 illustrates this model.

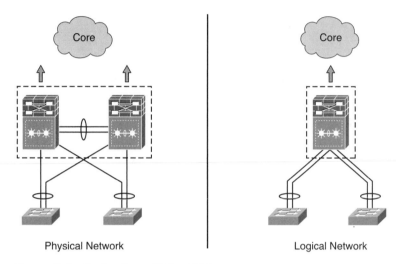

Figure 3-6 *Redundancy Using VSS*

Describing Core Layer Functionality

The core layer is a high-speed backbone that is designed to switch packets as fast as possible. Because the core layer is critical for connectivity, it must provide a high level of redundancy and must adapt to changes very quickly. A full mesh is strongly suggested. A well-connected partial mesh with multiple paths from each device is effectively a design requirement. The core layer should not perform any packet manipulation that would slow the switching of packets, such as checking access lists and filtering.

Core devices are most reliable when they can accommodate failures by rerouting traffic and respond quickly to changes in the network topology. Core devices must be able to implement scalable protocols and technologies, alternate paths, and load balancing.

Figure 3-7 shows an example of a Layer 3 switched campus core.

The typical packet flow between Layer 2 access switches follow these steps:

Step 1.   A packet is Layer 2–switched toward the distribution switch.

Step 2.   The distribution switch performs Layer 3 switching toward a core interface.

Step 3.   The packet is Layer 3–switched across the enterprise core.

Step 4.   The receiving distribution switch performs Layer 3 switching toward an access LAN.

Step 5.   The packet is Layer 2–switched across the access LAN to the destination host.

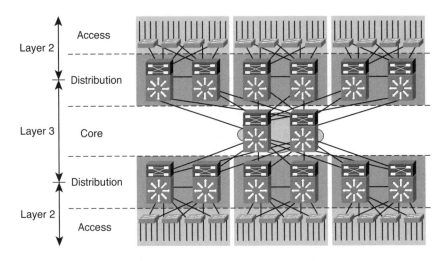

Figure 3-7   *Traditional Campus Network Core Layer Example*

Figure 3-8 shows an example of Layer 3 switching across the entire network.

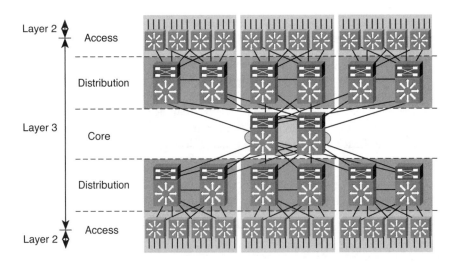

Figure 3-8   *Routed Campus Network Core Layer Example*

A typical packet flow between Layer 3 access switches follow these steps:

Step 1.   A packet is Layer 3–switched toward the distribution switch.

Step 2.   The distribution switch performs Layer 3 switching toward a core interface.

Step 3.   The packet is Layer 3–switched across the enterprise core.

Step 4.   The receiving distribution switch performs Layer 3 switching toward an access LAN.

Step 5.   The packet is Layer 3–switched across the access LAN to the destination host.

The three-tier architecture that was previously defined is traditionally used for a larger enterprise campus. For a small and medium-sized business (SMB), the three-tier architecture might be excessive. An alternative would be to use a two-tier architecture, in which the distribution and the core layer are combined. With this option, an SMB can reduce costs because both distribution and core functions are performed by the same switch. In a collapsed core, the switches would provide direct connections for the access layer switches, server farm, and edge modules.

One disadvantage with two-tier architecture is scalability. As a small campus begins to scale, the three-tier architecture should become a consideration.

Figure 3-9 shows an example of Layer 3 switching with a collapsed core.

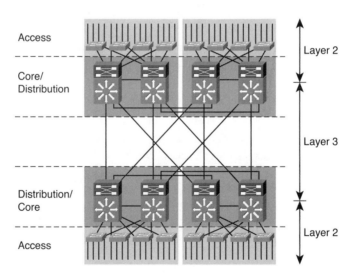

Figure 3-9   *Traditional Campus Network Collapsed Core Example*

A typical packet flow between Layer 2 access switches follow these steps:

Step 1. A packet is Layer 2–switched toward the distribution/core switch.

Step 2. The distribution/core switch performs Layer 3 switching.

Step 3. The receiving distribution/core switch performs Layer 3 switching toward an access LAN.

Step 4. The packet is Layer 2–switched across the access LAN to the destination host.

Figure 3-10 shows an example of Layer 3 switching with a collapsed core.

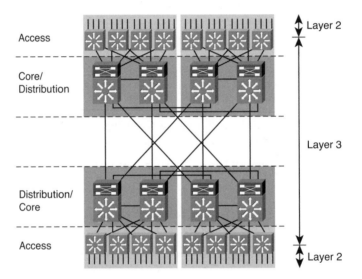

Figure 3-10 *Routed Campus Network Collapsed Core Example*

A typical packet flow between Layer 3 access switches follow these steps:

Step 1. A packet is Layer 3–switched toward the distribution/core switch.

Step 2. The distribution/core switch performs Layer 3 switching.

Step 3. The receiving distribution/core switch performs Layer 3 switching toward an access LAN.

Step 4. The packet is Layer 3–switched across the access LAN to the destination host.

Using a Modular Approach in Network Design

Cisco Borderless Networks Architecture provides an enterprise-wide framework that integrates the entire network, including campus, data center, WAN, branches, and teleworkers, to provide seamless connectivity anytime and anywhere. The Cisco Network

Architectures for the Enterprise separates the enterprise network into functional areas that are referred to as modules. The Cisco Network Architectures for the Enterprise includes several modules representing focused views of the Borderless Networks Architecture that target each place in the network. The modularity that is built into these architectures allows flexibility in network design and facilitates implementation and troubleshooting.

This section describes the modules of the Cisco Network Architectures for the Enterprise with an emphasis on the Borderless Networks design considerations.

As shown in Figure 3-11, the Cisco Network Architectures for the Enterprise separates the enterprise network into functional areas that are referred to as *modules.*

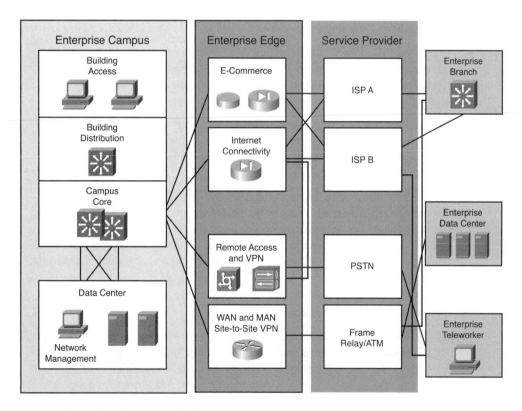

Figure 3-11   *Cisco Network Architectures for the Enterprise—Functional Areas*

The Cisco Network Architectures for the Enterprise consists of several functional areas and modules representing focused views of Borderless Networks Architecture that target each place in the network. The areas and modules in the Cisco Network Architectures for the Enterprise include the following:

■ **Enterprise Campus Functional Area:** Combines a core infrastructure of intelligent switching and routing with tightly integrated productivity-enhancing technologies including Cisco Unified Communications, mobility, and advanced security. The architecture provides the enterprise with high availability through a resilient multilayer design, redundant hardware and software features, and automatic procedures for reconfiguring network paths when failures occur. Multicast provides optimized bandwidth consumption, and quality of service (QoS) prevents oversubscription to ensure that real-time traffic, such as voice and video, or critical data is not dropped or delayed. Integrated security protects against and mitigates the impact of worms, viruses, and other attacks on the network, even at the switch-port level. Cisco enterprise-wide architecture extends authentication support using standards such as IEEE 802.1x and Extensible Authentication Protocol (EAP). It also provides the flexibility to add IP Security (IPsec) and Multiprotocol Label Switching Virtual Private Networks (MPLS VPN), identity and access management, and VLANs to compartmentalize access. These additions help improve performance and security while also decreasing costs.

- **Enterprise Edge Functional Area:** Offers connectivity to voice, video, and data services outside the enterprise. This area enables the enterprise to use Internet and partner resources and provide resources for its customers. QoS, service levels, and security are the main issues in the enterprise edge module.

- **Service Provider Functional Area:** Provides connectivity to other locations through the use of a service provider (SP) network. These locations include branch offices, customer locations, the public Internet, and the public switched telephone network (PSTN).

- **Remote Functional Area:** Provides the connectivity to the branch locations often through the use of a service provider network (and functional area). It is in this functional area where not only branches connect to the enterprise campus systems but also teleworkers. In some situations, all or part of the data center is also located at a remote location. It is in these situations where this location is considered part of the remote functional area.

Use these guidelines to create an enterprise network:

Step 1.   Divide the network into functional areas, where the enterprise campus module includes all devices in connections within the main campus. This is where the enterprise edge modules cover all communication with remote locations from the perspective of the enterprise campus, and where the remote modules include remote branches, teleworkers, and the remote data center.

Step 2.   Define clear boundaries between the enterprise campus, the enterprise edge, and the remote modules.

Note   Depending on the network, an enterprise can have multiple campus locations. A location that might be a remote branch from the perspective of a central campus location might globally use the Enterprise Campus Architecture.

Describing the Enterprise Campus Functional Area

The campus site is a large location that often serves as the corporate headquarters or a major office. Regional offices, SOHOs, and mobile workers might need to connect to the central campus for information. The enterprise campus functional area includes the campus infrastructure module and, typically, the data center (server farm) module.

Enterprise Campus Infrastructure Module

Using the hierarchical network model that was discussed in the previous chapter, the enterprise campus infrastructure module includes the following components:

- Building access layer

- Building distribution layer

- Campus core layer

These components are illustrated in Figure 3-12.

The campus infrastructure module connects devices within a campus to the data center and enterprise edge modules. A single building in a campus infrastructure design will contain a building access layer and a building distribution layer. To scale from a building model to a campus infrastructure, a backbone or campus core layer between buildings is added. The campus backbone also provides campus infrastructure module connectivity to the edge distribution and data center modules.

Note   The access, distribution, and core layers can appear in any module of the Cisco Network Architecture for the Enterprise.

Data Center Module

The data center module typically supports network management services for the enterprise, including monitoring, logging, troubleshooting, and other common management features from end to end.

The data center module usually contains internal email and corporate servers that provide application, file, print, and Domain Name System (DNS) services to internal users. Access to these servers is vital, so it is best that they are connected to two switches, enabling complete redundancy and load sharing. Moreover, the data center module switches are cross-connected within campus core layer switches, enabling high reliability and availability for all servers in a data center module.

The network management system can perform system logging, network monitoring, and general configuration management functions. For management purposes, an out-of-band connection (a network on which no production traffic travels) to all network components is recommended. For locations where an out-of-band network is impossible, the network management system uses the production network.

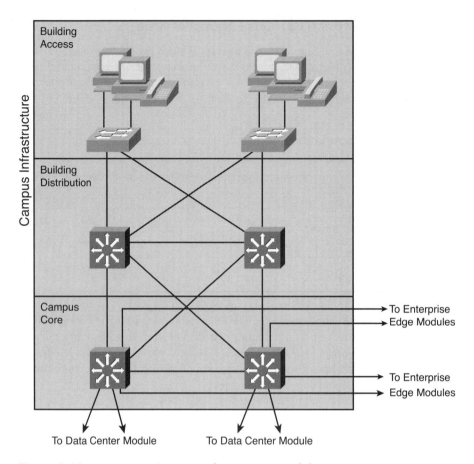

Figure 3-12   *Enterprise Campus Infrastructure Module*

Network management systems can provide configuration management for most devices in the network through the use of two primary technologies:

■   Cisco IOS routers can be configured as dedicated terminal servers and can provide a dedicated management network segment. The terminal server provides a reverse Telnet function to the console ports on the Cisco devices to route the enterprise. This technique is normally used as a backup method or for specific situations that require such technology.

■   More extensive management features (software changes, content updates, log and alarm aggregation, and the Simple Network Management Protocol [SNMP] management) are provided through the dedicated management network segment.

Note   These data center attributes also apply to remote data center modules.

Describing the Enterprise Edge Area

The enterprise edge infrastructure modules aggregate the connectivity from various elements outside the campus and route the traffic into the campus core layer. The enterprise edge modules perform security functions to secure enterprise resources when connecting across public networks and the Internet.

The enterprise edge modules can include

- E-commerce

- Internet connectivity

- Remote access and VPN

- WAN and MAN and Site-to-site VPN

These modules connect to the campus backbone either directly or through an edge distribution module. The enterprise edge modules use various services and WAN technologies as needed to provide connectivity. These services and technologies are typically provisioned from service providers.

Figure 3-13 illustrates the enterprise edge modules.

Use these guidelines to create the enterprise edge modules:

Step 1.   Determine the connections from the corporate network into the Internet, and assign them to the Internet connectivity module. The Internet connectivity module should have security to prevent any unauthorized access from the Internet to the internal network. The public web servers are located in this module or the e-commerce module

Step 2.   Create the e-commerce module (for business-to-business or business-to-customer scenarios) when customers or partners require Internet access to business applications and database servers. Deploy a high-security policy that allows customer access to predefined servers and services and restricts all other operations.

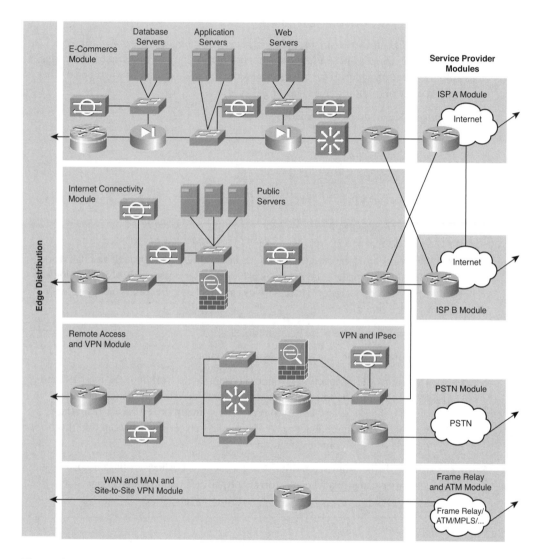

Figure 3-13   *Enterprise Edge Modules*

Step 3.   Design the remote access and VPN module if the enterprise requires VPN connections or dial-in for accessing the internal network from the outside world. Implement a security policy. Users should not be able to access the internal network directly without authentication and authorization. The VPN sessions use the connectivity from the Internet connectivity module.

Step 4.   Determine which part of the edge is used exclusively for permanent connections to remote enterprise locations (branch offices), and assign it to the WAN and MAN and site-to-site VPN modules. All WAN devices that support Frame Relay, ATM, MPLS, cable, leased lines, SONET or Synchronous Digital Hierarchy (SDH), and so on are located here.

E-Commerce Module

All e-commerce transactions pass through a series of intelligent services that provide scalability, security, and high availability within the overall e-commerce network design. To build a successful e-commerce solution, enterprises need these network devices:

■ **Web servers:** Acts as the primary user interface for e-commerce navigation.

■ **Application servers:** Host the various applications.

■ **Database servers:** Contain the application and transaction information that is the heart of the e-commerce business implementation.

■ **Firewall or firewall routers:** Govern communication and provide security between the various users of the system.

■ **Network intrusion prevention system (NIPS) appliances:** Provide monitoring of key network segments in the module to detect and respond to attacks against the network.

■ **Multilayer switch with IPS modules:** Provides traffic transport and integrated security monitoring.

Internet Connectivity Module

The Internet connectivity module provides internal users with connection to Internet services such as HTTP, FTP, Simple Mail Transfer Protocol (SMTP), and DNS. It also provides Internet users with access to information that is published on the public servers of an enterprise. This module can accept VPN traffic from remote users and forward it to the remote access and VPN module, where VPN termination takes place. The Internet connectivity module does not service e-commerce applications. The major components of the Internet connectivity module include

■ **SMTP mail servers:** Act as relays between the Internet and the intranet mail servers.

■ **DNS servers:** Serve as the authoritative external DNS servers for the enterprise and relay interface requests to the Internet.

- **Public servers (FTP and HTTP):** Provide public information about the organization. Each server on the public servers segment has host intrusion detection systems (IDS) to monitor against any rogue activity at the operating system level, in addition to activity in common server applications, including HTTP, FTP, and SMTP.

- **Firewall or firewall routers:** Provide network-level protection of resources, stateful filtering of traffic, and VPN termination for remote sites and users.

- **Edge routers:** Provide basic filtering and multilayer connectivity to the Internet.

WAN and MAN and Site-to-Site VPN Module

The WAN and MAN and site-to-site VPN module uses various WAN technologies, including site-to-site VPNs for routing traffic between remote sites and the central site. In addition to traditional media (leased lines and circuit-switched data link technologies, Frame Relay, and ATM), the WAN module can use more recent WAN and MAN technologies. These technologies include SONET and SDH, cable, DSL, MPLS, Metro Ethernet, wireless, and service provider VPNs. In addition to routing, access control, and QoS mechanisms, all Cisco devices that support these WAN technologies can be used in the WAN module. Although security is not as critical when all links are enterprise owned, security should be considered in the network design.

Remote Access and VPN Module

The remote access and VPN module initiates and terminates remote access traffic as well as VPN traffic that is forwarded by the Internet connectivity module from remote users and remote sites. Major components of the remote access and VPN module include

- **Cisco ASA security appliances:** Terminate IPsec tunnels and authenticate individual remote users, and provide firewall and intrusion prevention services.

- **Firewalls or firewall routers:** Provide network-level protection of resources and stateful filtering of traffic, provide differentiated security for remote-access users, authenticate trusted remote sites, and provide connectivity using IPsec tunnels.

- **NIPS appliances:** Provide Layer 4 to Layer 7 monitoring of key network segments in the module.

- **Dial-in access concentrators:** Terminate dial-in connections and authenticate individual users. Note that this technology is outdated and rarely used in today's enterprise networks.

Describing the Service Provider Area

The service provider modules included in this area represent the service provider infrastructure.

ISP Module

The ISP module represents connectivity to an ISP network. Enterprises can connect to the ISP for basic access to the Internet or can utilize the Internet to provide connectivity to remote enterprise locations.

Public Switched Telephone Network Module

The public switched telephone network (PSTN) module represents the dialup infrastructure for accessing the enterprise network using ISDN, analog, and wireless telephony (cellular) technologies. Enterprises can also use this module to back up existing WAN links. WAN backup connections are generally established on demand and are disconnected after an idle timeout.

Frame Relay and ATM Module

The Frame Relay and ATM module includes all WAN technologies for permanent connectivity with remote locations. Traditional Frame Relay and ATM are still frequently used; however, many modern technologies such as MPLS can fit into the same module. Table 3-1 illustrates various technologies currently used.

Table 3-1   *Permanent Connectivity WAN Options*

Technology	Description
Frame Relay	A connection-oriented, packet-switching technology that is designed to transmit data traffic efficiently at data rates of up to those provided by E3 and T3 connections. Its ability to connect multiple remote sites across a single physical connection reduces the number of point-to-point physical connections that are required to link sites together.
ATM	An alternative to Frame Relay and supports higher speeds. It is a high-performance, cell-oriented switching and multiplexing technology for carrying different types of traffic.
Leased lines	Provides the simplest permanent point-to-point connection between two remote locations. The carrier company reserves point-to-point links for its private use. Because the connection is exclusive, the carrier (service provider) can assure a given level of quality. The fee for the connection is a fixed monthly rate.
SONET and SDH	Standards for transmission over optical networks. Europe uses SDH; its equivalent, SONET, is used in North America.
Cable technology	Uses existing coaxial cable television (CATV) cables. This technology, when it is coupled with cable modems, provides much greater bandwidth than telephone lines and can provide extremely fast access to the Internet or enterprise network.

Table 3-1   *Permanent Connectivity WAN Options*

Technology	Description
DSL	A modern technology that uses existing twisted-pair telephone lines to transport high-bandwidth communication, such as voice, data, and video. DSL is sometimes referred to as "last-mile" technology because it is used only for connections from a telephone switching station (service provider) to a home or office, not between switching stations. DSL is used mostly by telecommuters to access enterprise networks. However, many more companies are migrating from traditional Frame Relay to DSL technology using VPNs because of its cost efficiency.
Wireless bridging technology	Another modern technology for interconnecting remote LANs. The point-to-point signal transmissions take place through the air over a terrestrial radio or microwave platform rather than through copper or fiber cables. This bridged wireless service does not require satellite feeds or local phone service. An advantage of bridged wireless is its ability to connect with users in remote areas without the need for laying down new cables. However, this technology is limited to shorter distances, and performance can be degraded by weather conditions.

Describing the Remote Area

The following sections describe the components and functions for the enterprise remote modules. The three modules supporting remote enterprise locations are as follows:

- Enterprise branch

- Enterprise data center

- Enterprise teleworker

Enterprise Branch Module

The enterprise branch module extends the enterprise by providing each location with resilient network architecture with integrated security, Cisco Unified Communications, and wireless mobility. Using the Borderless Networks concepts and connectivity from remote offices should be seamless, as if on the campus.

The branch office generally accommodates employees who have a compelling reason to be located away from the central site, such as a regional sales office. Branch office users must be able to connect to the central site to access company information. The branch office is sometimes called the remote site, remote office, or sales office.

Branch offices can benefit from services such as

- High-speed Internet access

- VPN connectivity to corporate intranets

- Telecommuting capabilities for work-at-home employees

- Videoconferencing

- Economical PSTN-quality voice and fax calls over the managed IP networks

The enterprise branch module typically uses a simplified version of the enterprise campus network infrastructure.

Enterprise Data Center Module

The remote enterprise data center module has a similar architecture to the campus data center discussed in the enterprise campus infrastructure section. With the data center network architecture, the network evolves into a platform that enhances the application, server, and storage solutions. This evolved data center equips organizations to manage increased security and cost, as well as regulatory requirements, while providing the ability to respond quickly to changing business environments.

The enterprise data center module can include the following components:

- **Networked infrastructure:** Gigabit or 10 Gigabit Ethernet switching, InfiniBand, and storage switching and optical transport

- **Interactive services:** Storage fabric services, computer services, security services, and application optimization services

- **Management:** Cisco Fabric Manager (element and network management) and Cisco VFrame (server and service provisioning)

The remote enterprise data center module also requires highly available WAN connectivity with business continuance capabilities to integrate it with the rest of the Cisco Network Architectures for the Enterprise.

Note The enterprise data center or data center module in the campus can leverage the WAN connectivity of the campus core, but the remote enterprise data center must implement its own WAN connectivity.

Enterprise Teleworker Module

The enterprise teleworker module provides users in geographically dispersed locations, such as home offices or hotels, highly secure access to central-site applications and network services.

The enterprise teleworker module uses Cisco Virtual Office to support teleworker and employees at remote locations. Cisco Virtual Office improves productivity, security, and business resiliency, while accounting for enterprise needs for lower operational costs.

The Cisco Virtual Office solution consists of the remote-site presence and the head-end presence. The remote-site presence consists of equipment that resides at the end-user premises. This includes a small Integrated Services Router (ISR) and a Cisco Unified IP Phone. The head end, which is traditionally the central office, is responsible for aggregating and terminating the secure tunnels from each remote site. The head end is also responsible for implementing the necessary polices for configurations, security, and quality of service.

The management capabilities at the head end are accomplished through a zero-touch deployment model. With this technology, configurations of remote-site equipment are automatically kept up to date and in compliance with corporate polices. When deployed, the router is programmed to automatically "call home" to the management servers at the head end to check for any relevant updates in configuration or software. These updates are then "pushed" to the devices without any need for human intervention on the remote site.

Supporting Services on Borderless Networks

Businesses that operate large enterprise networks seek an enterprise-wide infrastructure and services to provide a solid foundation for business and collaborative applications. In the following sections, network infrastructure services such as security, high availability, and collaboration services are presented with respect to the Borderless Networks Architecture.

Explaining the Role of Borderless Network Services

Borderless Network services support network-wide requirements for the application and provide a common set of capabilities to ensure the functionality of the applications. These services are the pillar in which collaborative applications are achieved. These services are delivered by infrastructure components such as

- Routers
- Switches
- Security
- Wireless
- Cisco Wide Area Application Services (WAAS)

Each module in the Network Architectures for the Enterprise is responsible for activating the appropriate services that are combined for end-to-end borderless communication.

By implementing network services, the overall network environment is capable of providing support for the most persistent application requirements, including security, high availability, reliability, flexibility, responsiveness, and compliance.

There are several key pillars of functionality that Borderless Network services deliver. Table 3-2 provides a detailed explanation of the functions.

Table 3-2 *Key Functions of Borderless Network Services*

Function	Benefit	Product
Mobility	Increases accuracy, speed, and efficiency when integrating mobility services, wireless technology, and network applications such as Cisco Unified Communications into the organization's IT infrastructure. When enabling business mobility in a converged environment, the challenge is to design, build, and operate a mobility solution that is in alignment with the business requirements and that can scale with the evolving business environment.	Cisco Motion is a new practical approach to resolve challenges experienced when enabling business mobility. Cisco Motion can provide the following: • Converge disparate networks • Manage the increasing quantity and diversity of mobile devices • Deliver device-to-network integration and security • Create an open platform for the development of mobility applications
Security	Implements a unified access policy with Cisco Identity Based Network Services (Cisco IBNS), providing visibility into network operations and lowering operating costs while reducing risk.	Cisco TrustSec provides the following: • Builds security and intelligence into the network with policy-based access control • Identity-aware networking • Data confidentiality and integrity Because these networks will have no borders, Cisco TrustSec helps secure borderless networks with confidence, consistency, and efficiency.
Performance	Offers key systems that are designed to enhance the performance, reliability, and resilience of business-critical applications on the network. Uses innovative technologies that are embedded in Cisco routing and switching solutions. These solutions are designed to increase network uptime and availability, while simplifying operations and ensuring a consistent customer experience.	—

Table 3-2   *Key Functions of Borderless Network Services*

Function	Benefit	Product
IP communication	Offers a complete suite of solutions and endpoints that provide reliable and advanced communications capabilities no matter where staff might be working. Organizations of all sizes and types can manage voice, video, mobility, and presence services among IP endpoints, media-processing devices, VoIP gateways, mobile devices, and multimedia applications.	—

Borderless Network services map application and collaboration requirements to the resources that they require from the network.

Mobility Considerations

Mobility is a service of the Borderless Networks Architecture that supports mobile clients that are connecting to the enterprise network. Mobile clients do not have a physical connection to the network, because wireless LANs (WLAN) replace the Layer 1 transmission medium of a traditional wired network (usually Category 5E or 6 cable) with radio transmission through the air. WLANs are designed for a local network. They are intended for in-building wireless networks, line-of-sight outdoor bridging applications, or a combination of both.

The Cisco Unified Wireless Network addresses the WLAN security, deployment, management, and control issues that are facing enterprises in a cost-effective manner. Users should securely access the network from any WLAN location. Employees are authenticated through IEEE 802.1x and Extensible Authentication Protocol (EAP). All information sent and received on the WLAN is encrypted. The WLANs support newer standards like IEEE 802.11n, as well as IEEE 802.11a/b/g and enterprise wireless mesh for indoor and outdoor locations.

WLANs have the following problems that are not found in wired networks:

■   Connectivity issues in WLANs can be caused by coverage problems, RF transmission multipath distortion, and interference from other wireless services or other WLANs.

■   Privacy issues are possible because RF signals can reach outside the facility.

WLANs can be connected to traditional LANs. To ensure successful implementation of wireless applications, the enterprise infrastructure and its configuration must be considered.

As shown in Figure 3-14, there are four components of a centralized WLAN deployment:

■   **End devices:** PCs and other end devices use radio waves to connect to wireless access points.

- **Wireless access points:** These shared devices function like a hub for the wireless end devices. Wireless access points are implemented in the access layer of the enterprise infrastructure.

- **Existing routed and switched wired network:** The wireless access points connect to the enterprise network.

- **WLAN controller:** Provides management and support for wireless services such as roaming. The WLAN controller is typically implemented in the core layer of the enterprise network.

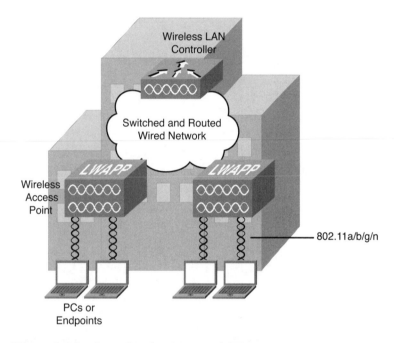

Figure 3-14 *Centralized WLAN Model Components*

Note This is a brief introduction to wireless design considerations. More details are covered in Chapter 10, "Identifying Design Considerations for Basic Wireless Networking."

Security Infrastructure Services

Security is an infrastructure service that increases the integrity of the network by protecting its resources and users from internal and external threats. It is crucial to have a complete understanding of the threats that are involved. Too often, network security deployments are configured incorrectly, too focused on security devices, or lack the appropriate threat-response options.

The Cisco Security Architecture for the Enterprise (SAFE) Blueprint consists of design blueprints based on the Cisco-validated designs. They are proven to be the best security practices that provide design guidelines for building secure and reliable network infrastructures. The Cisco SAFE Blueprint implements defense in depth by strategically positioning Cisco products and capabilities across the network and leverage cross-platform network intelligence and collaboration.

Security should be evaluated and applied on a module-by-module basis within the Cisco Network Architectures for the Enterprise. This is illustrated in Figure 3-15.

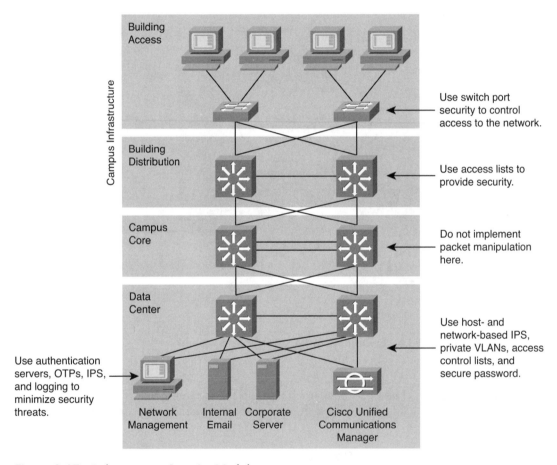

Figure 3-15   *Infrastructure Security Modules*

The Cisco SAFE Blueprint provides the design and implementation guidelines for building secure and reliable network infrastructures that are resilient to both well-known and new forms of attacks.

The following are some security considerations for each module that are recommended practice:

- **Building access layer:** Controls access at the port level with respect to the data link layer information (for example, MAC addresses). The building access layer is the first line of defense in the network against threats that are generated by devices that connect to them. This section discusses the various security measures used for securing the campus access layer, including the following:

  - Securing the endpoints using endpoint security software

  - Securing the access infrastructure and protecting network services, including DHCP, Address Resolution Protocol (ARP), and IP spoofing protection

  - Protecting against inadvertent loops using Cisco IOS Network Foundation Protection (NFP) best practices and Catalyst Integrated Security Features (CISF)

- **Building distribution layer:** Performs packet filtering to keep unnecessary traffic from the campus core layer. Packet filtering at the building distribution layer is a security function, because it prevents undesired access to other modules. Given that switches in this layer are usually Layer 3–aware multilayer switches, the building distribution layer is often the first location that can filter based on network layer information. This layer also protects the endpoints using network-based intrusion prevention and protects the infrastructure using NFP best practices.

- **Campus core layer:** Switches packets as quickly as possible. The campus core layer should not perform any security functions, because it would slow packet switching. The primary role of security in the enterprise core module is to protect the core itself, not to apply policy to mitigate transit threats that are traversing through the core.

The core switches are secured by following NFP infrastructure baseline security principles. This includes restricting and controlling administrative device access, securing the routing infrastructure, and protecting the management and control planes.

The following are the key areas of NFP baseline security best practice that are applicable to securing the enterprise core:

- **Infrastructure device access:** Implement dedicated management interfaces to the out-of-band (OOB) management network, limit the accessible ports, restrict the permitted communicators and the permitted methods of access, present legal notification, authenticate and authorize access using authentication, authorization, and accounting (AAA), log and account for all access, and protect locally stored sensitive data (such as local passwords) from viewing and copying.

- **Routing infrastructure:** Authenticate routing neighbors, implement route filtering, use default passive interfaces, and log neighbor changes.

- **Device resiliency and survivability:** Disable unnecessary services, filter and rate-limit control-plane traffic, and implement redundancy.

■ **Data center module:** Provides application services to end users and devices. Given the high degree of access that most employees have to these servers, the data center modules often become the primary target of internally originated attacks. Use host- and network-based intrusion prevention systems (IPS), private VLANs, and access control to provide a much more comprehensive response to attacks. Onboard intrusion detection systems (IDS) within multilayer switches can inspect traffic flows on the data center module.

The data center module typically includes a network management system that securely manages all devices and hosts within the enterprise architecture. Syslog provides important information regarding security violations and configuration changes by login security-related events (authentication and so on). Other servers, including a AAA security server, can work in combination with the one-time password (OTP) server to provide a very high level of security to all local and remote users. AAA and OTP authentication reduces the likelihood of a successful password attack.

Several reasons exist for strong protection of the enterprise campus infrastructure. There are security functions within each individual element of the enterprise campus. When setting up security infrastructure services, consider the following:

■ Relying on the security that has been established at the enterprise edge fails as soon as security there is compromised. Several layers of security increase the protection of the enterprise campus, which is usually where the most strategic assets reside.

■ If the enterprise allows visitors into its buildings, potential attackers can gain physical access to devices in the enterprise campus. Relying on physical security is not enough.

■ External access often does not stop at the enterprise edge. Applications require at least an indirect access to the enterprise campus resources, which requires strong security.

Designing Security to Protect Against External Threats

Security solutions must be designed in a layered and independent way. To accomplish this, the design must

■ Establish several layers of protection

■ Ensure that the security functions at one layer on one network module do not rely on the security function in other layers or modules

When designing security in an enterprise network, the enterprise edge is identified as the first line of defense to stop potential attacks from the outside. The enterprise edge is like a wall with small doors and strong "guards" that efficiently control access. This is illustrated in Figure 3-16.

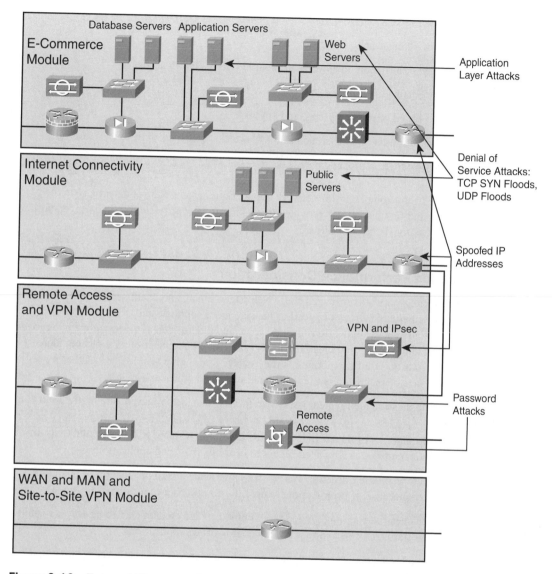

Figure 3-16 *External Threats to the Enterprise Edge*

There are several methods of possible attack on the enterprise from the outside, including the following:

- IP spoofing
- Password attacks

- Denial of service (DoS), distributed denial of service (DDoS)

- Spyware, malware, and adware

- Network intrusion, takeover, and unauthorized network access

- Junk email and viruses

- Web-based phishing, viruses, and spyware

- Application-layer attacks such as XML attacks, cross-site scripting (XSS), and so on

- Identity theft, fraud, and data leakage

Because of the complexity of network applications, access control must be extremely granular and flexible yet still provide strong security. Security should be balanced with ease of use for the network users.

Application Performance Considerations

Traditionally, networks managed static web pages, email, and client/server traffic. Modern enterprise networks, however, need to manage more sophisticated types of network applications. These applications include voice and video, such as videoconferencing, corporate training, audio and video broadcasts, and so on. Applications are placing increasing demands on IT infrastructures as they evolve into highly visible services that represent the face of the business to internal and external audiences.

Several application deployment issues can face IT managers today, including the following:

- Consolidation of data centers, in some cases, has resulted in lower productivity from remote employees who need access to centrally managed applications.

- A new web-based ordering system can experience a high proportion of abandoned orders because of poor responsiveness during the checkout process.

- A business partner might need more immediate and secure electronic access to shipment status information that is held in back-office applications.

- A purchasing application might need to log orders over a certain value for compliance purposes.

- IT organizations face new challenges in providing LAN-like response times across the corporate WAN.

It is no longer sufficient to add more bandwidth as needs grow. Evolving network applications require that the modern network be application-aware to provide optimal support.

A new role for the network is emerging. It must be a provider of application infrastructure services that extend the value of applications. Networks must improve delivery of content to users and other applications and offload infrastructure functions that burden today's development and operations teams.

Resolving Application Issues with Cisco Application Network Services

The network, in conjunction with Cisco Application Network Services (ANS), can play a critical role in resolving application-related issues, using these features:

- Wide-area application services in the branch office that compress, cache, and optimize content for remote users so that they experience LAN-like responsiveness

- Optimization of web streams that are being sent to portals, which reduces latency, suppresses unnecessary reloading of web objects, and offloads low-level tasks from the web server

- Security and remote connectivity services that can automatically validate a partner's request, route it to the appropriate back-office application, and encrypt and prioritize the response

- Application messaging services that can intercept and interpret purchase orders, locate the dollar amount, and log large orders to a database according to business policy rules

Cisco ANS Components

Some of the components used by Cisco ANS are shown in Table 3-3.

Table 3-3 *Cisco ANS Components*

Component	Benefits
Cisco Wide Area Application Engine (WAE)	Cisco WAE appliances are products that provide global LAN-like access to enterprise applications and data.
Cisco Wide Area Application Services (WAAS)	Cisco WAAS software gives remote offices LAN-like access to centrally hosted applications, servers, storage, and multimedia.
Cisco 2600/3600/3700 Series Content Engine Module	Cisco Content Engine Modules can be deployed in the data center or branch offices to optimize WAN bandwidth, accelerate deployment of mission-critical web applications, add web content security, and deliver live and on-demand business video.
Cisco Application Control Engine (ACE)	Cisco ACE is a state-of-the-art virtualized load balancer and application delivery solution that includes server load balancing, content switching, server offloading, and application optimization.
Policy-based routing (PBR)	PBR allows IT organizations to configure their network devices (a router or a Layer 3–to–Layer 7 switch) to selectively route traffic to the next hop, based on the classification of the traffic. WAAS administrators can use PBR to transparently integrate a WAE into their existing branch office network and data centers. PBR can be used to establish a route that goes through a WAE for some or all packets, based on the defined policies.

Table 3-3   *Cisco ANS Components*

Component	Benefits
Cisco Catalyst 6500 Series Content Switching Module (CSM)	This is a line card for the Cisco Catalyst 6500 Series switches that enhances the experience and response for client traffic to endpoints such as groups of servers, caches, firewalls, Secure Socket Layer (SSL) devices, or VPN termination devices. In addition, fault-tolerant Cisco CSM configurations maintain *full* state information and provide the true hitless failover that is required for mission-critical applications.
Cisco CSS Series Content Services Switches (CSS)	CSS Series switches provide robust application delivery (Layer 4 to Layer 7) services for Internet and intranet data centers. CSS Series switches introduce an intelligent, distributed architecture that improves application and site availability and transaction integrity.

Note   This is a brief introduction to Cisco ANS considerations.

IP Communications

IP communications is one example of the applications of Cisco Collaboration architecture. IP communications offer a complete suite of solutions and endpoints that provide reliable and advanced communications capabilities no matter where staff might be working. Organizations of all sizes and types can manage voice, video, mobility, and presence services between IP endpoints, media-processing devices, VoIP gateways, mobile devices, and multimedia applications.

The Cisco IP Communications solution provides an organization with the following:

■ Enhanced productivity and reduced communications delays with presence awareness. When using awareness capabilities, colleague, partner, or customer presence is available at a glance.

■ Efficiently run voice, data, and video communications over a single, converged network.

■ A wide array of Cisco IP endpoints that are designed to meet diverse communications needs.

■ Optimized operational efficiency with an integrated set of network management products that are designed to provide a single view into the entire Cisco Unified Communications solution.

Voice Transport

An IP phone is a device that relies heavily on the network infrastructure and services. To ensure successful implementation of a voice application, the enterprise infrastructure and its configuration must be considered.

Voice is a very general term; it is divided into these two implementations:

- **VoIP:** VoIP allows voice-enabled routers to convert analog voice into IP packets or packetized digital voice channels and route those packets between locations. Users do not often notice that VoIP is implemented in the network. They use their traditional telephones connected to a PBC. However, the private branch exchange (PBX) is not connected to the public switched telephone network (PSTN) or to another PBX, but rather to a voice-enabled router that is an entry point to VoIP. Voice-enabled routers can also terminate Cisco IP Phones by using Session Initiation Protocol (SIP) for call control and signaling.

- **IP telephony:** IP telephony is a voice implementation where traditional telephones are replaced with IP phones and a server (Cisco Unified Communications Manager [CUCM]) for call control and signaling. The IP phone performs voice-to-IP conversion. Connection to the PSTN requires a voice-enabled router or other gateway in the enterprise edge functional area, where calls are forwarded to the PSTN.

There are four main voice-specific components of the IP telephone network that are illustrated in Figure 3-17.

The main voice-specific components include

- **IP phones:** IP phones support calls in an IP telephony network. They perform voice-to-IP (and vice versa) coding and compression using special hardware. IP phones offer services such as user directory lookups and Internet access for stock quotes. The telephones are active network devices and require power for their operation. A network connection or an external power supply provides the power for the IP phone.

- **Switches with inline power:** Switches with inline power enable a modular wiring-closet infrastructure to provide centralized power for Cisco IP telephone networks. These switches are similar to traditional switches, with an option to provide power to the LAN ports where IP phones are connected. In addition, they perform some basic QoS mechanisms, such as packet classification, which is a baseline for prioritizing voice through the network.

- **Call-processing manager:** CUCM provides central call control and configuration management for IP phones. CUCM provides the core functionality to initialize IP telephone devices and perform call setup and routing of calls throughout the network. CUCM supports clustering, which provides a distributed scalable and highly available IP telephone model.

■ **Voice gateway:** Voice gateways, also called voice-enabled routers or switches, provide voice services such as voice-to-IP coding and compression, PSTN access, IP packet routing, backup call processing, and voice services. Backup call processing allows voice gateways to take over call processing in case the primary call-processing manager fails. Typically, voice gateways support a subset of call-processing functionality that is supported by CUCM.

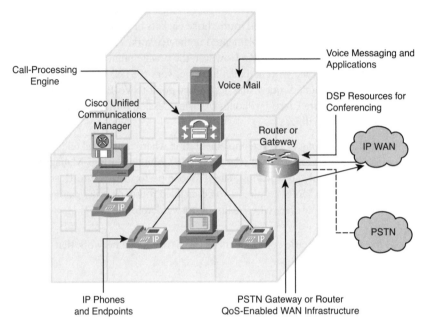

Figure 3-17   *VoIP Components*

Enterprises that want to deploy voice infrastructure services on their networks face new design challenges. They need to deploy a delay-sensitive overlay service from end to end, through all enterprise network modules.

A modular approach is shown in Figure 3-18.

The modular approach is recommended to simplify design, implementation, and troubleshooting. Each module and layer of the enterprise network should be evaluated before proceeding. The following points provide details for layers and modules:

■ **Building the access layer:** IP phones and user computers attach to Layer 2 switches. Switches provide power and packet classification, which is essential for proper voice packet manipulation through the network.

■ **Building the distribution layer:** This layer performs packet reclassification if the building access layer is unable to perform packet classification. It concentrates building access switches (wiring closets) and provides redundant uplinks to the campus core layer.

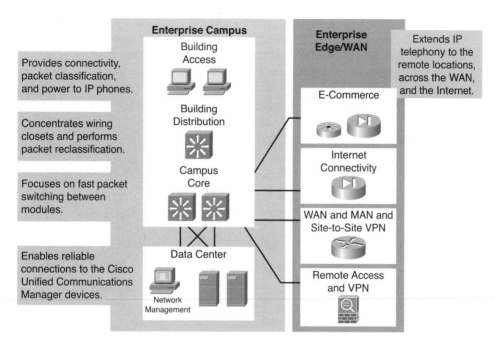

Figure 3-18   *Voice Network Modular Design Approach*

- **Campus core layer:** This layer forms the core of the network. All enterprise network modules are attached to it. Virtually all traffic between application servers and clients traverses the campus core layer. With the advent of wire-speed Layer 3 gigabit-switching devices, LAN backbones have migrated to switched gigabit architectures that combine all the benefits of routing with wire-speed packet forwarding.

- **Data center module:** This module includes multilayer switches and Cisco Unified Communications Manager (CUCM) devices. Because CUCM equipment is the heart of IP telephony, redundant links and redundant CUCM devices are essential for providing high availability.

- **Enterprise edge functional area:** The enterprise edge functional area, with its modules (for example, WAN and metropolitan-area network [MAN] and site-to-site Virtual Private Network [VPN] module(s)), can extend IP telephony from the enterprise campus to remote locations, the PSTN, and the Internet.

IP telephony requires modifications to the enterprise network infrastructure in terms of performance, capacity, and availability. It is an end-to-end solution, with clients (IP phones) located in the building access layer and CUCM devices located in the data center module.

Figure 3-19 shows a voice network solution within the Cisco Network Architectures for the Enterprise. It depicts how to modularize the solution on a module-by-module basis.

After the call is initiated on an IP phone in the campus, the call setup transmits to the CUCM in the server farm. At that point, an end-to-end session between two IP phones in one or more locations is established. CUCM is involved in only the call setup.

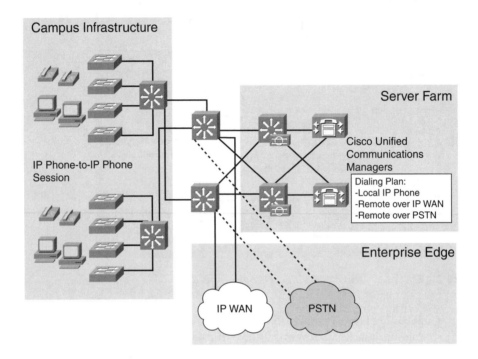

Figure 3-19   *Voice Network Solution Example*

Three scenarios for IP call routing are possible, as follows:

■   Calls that are destined for remote locations traverse the enterprise edge through the WAN and MAN modules or the remote access and VPN modules.

■   Calls that are destined for the PSTN are routed over the enterprise edge through the remote access and VPN modules.

■   Calls between IP phones traverse the server farm module and building access, building distribution, and campus core layers. Call setup uses all of these modules. Speech transport employs only the building access and building distribution layers and, in some cases, the campus core layer.

When designing IP telephony, the existing data infrastructure in each enterprise network module needs to be evaluated to determine upgrade requirements for the IP telephony solution. Follow these guidelines when designing the data infrastructure to support voice:

Step 1.   If required for the converging environment, provide infrastructure for additional bandwidth, consistent performance, or higher availability. Links and devices should have sufficient capacity for voice traffic. Links with high peak or busy-hour use might require an upgrade. The target devices for additional inspection and potential upgrades are those with high CPU use, high backplane use, high memory use, queuing drops, or buffer misses.

Step 2.   Review the redundancy capabilities in all network modules to ensure that they can meet the available goals for the current network design (or new design) that are recommended for IP telephony.

Step 3.   Evaluate device characteristics, including the chassis, module, and software inventory. This assessment will prove useful in determining IP telephony feature capabilities in the existing environment.

Step 4.   Evaluate overall network capacity and the impact of IP telephony on a module-by-module basis. This activity ensures that the network meets capacity requirements and that there will be no adverse impact on the existing network and application requirements.

High-Availability Network Services

Enterprise networks carry mission-critical information. Organizations need to protect this information with internetworking platforms that offer a sufficient level of resilience and high availability.

Redundant network designs meet some of the requirements for network high availability by duplicating network links and interconnectivity devices. Redundancy eliminates the possibility of having a single point of failure on the network. The goal is to duplicate required components whose failure could disable critical applications.

Because redundancy is expensive to deploy and maintain, redundant topologies need to be implemented with care. Be sure to select a level of redundancy that matches the requirements for availability and affordability.

Before selecting redundant design solutions, first analyze the business and technical goals to establish the availability that is required. Make sure that critical applications, systems, internetworking devices, and links can be identified. Analyze the tolerance for risk and the consequences of not implementing redundancy. Discuss the trade-offs of redundancy versus cost and simplicity versus complexity. Redundancy adds complexity to the network topology and to network addressing and routing.

The following redundancies can be implemented in networking:

■   Device redundancy, including card and port redundancy

■   Redundant physical connections to workstations and servers

- Route redundancy

- Link redundancy

Note   High availability is not ensured end to end simply by making the backbone redundant. If communications on a local segment are disrupted for any reason, the information will not reach the backbone. In other words, end-to-end high availability is possible only when redundancy is deployed throughout the network.

The common approach in designing route redundancy is to implement partial redundancy (a partial mesh instead of a full mesh and backup links to the alternate concentrator), protecting only the most vital points of the network, such as the links between the layers and concentration devices.

Full-Mesh Versus Partial-Mesh Redundancy

The full-mesh design forms any-to-any connectivity and is ideal for connecting a reasonably small number of devices. However, as the network topology grows, the number of links that are required to maintain a full mesh expand dramatically.

The partial-mesh network is similar to the full-mesh network but with some of the links removed. The partial-mesh backbone is appropriate for a campus network. The traffic predominantly travels into one centralized data center module.

When multilayer switching is deployed in the building access layer, as shown in Figure 3-20, Layer 2 switching (data link switching) is normally used between the building access switch and the workstations. Multilayer switching is used between the building access and building distribution switches.

The backup links can use different technologies, as in the scenario that is illustrated in Figure 3-21, where a Frame Relay circuit is used in parallel with a backup IPsec circuit. The primary requirement is to have sufficient capacity to meet critical needs.

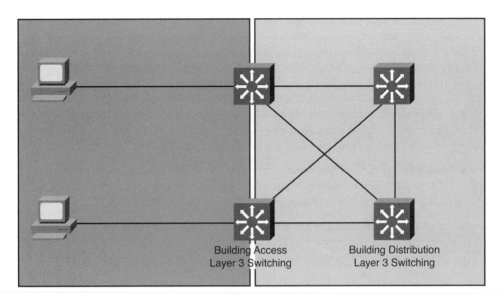

Figure 3-20 *Campus Infrastructure Redundancy Example*

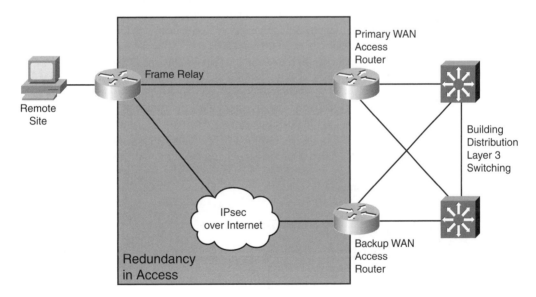

Figure 3-21 *Enterprise Edge Redundancy Example*

Because WAN links are often critical pieces of the internetwork, redundant media are often deployed in WAN environments. Backup links can be provisioned so that they are always on or so that they become active only when a primary link goes down or becomes congested.

Because of the high cost, most network designers do not often implement a completely redundant network. Instead, network designers implement partially redundant internetworks. When network designers think about improving reliability on critical workstations and servers, the solution often depends on the workstation hardware and operating system software in use. These are some common attachment methods:

- **Single attachment:** Used when a workstation needs to find an alternate router dynamically (by means of a routing protocol, ARP, Route Discovery Protocol [RDP], Hot Standby Router Protocol [HSRP], or Gateway Load Balancing Protocol [GLBP]).

- **Attachment through a redundant transceiver:** Physical redundancy with a redundant transceiver attachment is suitable in environments where the workstation hardware or software does not support redundant attachment options.

- **Attachment through a redundant network interface card (NIC):** Some environments (for example, most UNIX servers) support redundant attachment through dual NICs (primary and backup) that the device driver presents as a single interface to the operating system.

- **Fast EtherChannel (FEC) and Gigabit EtherChannel (GEC) port bundles:** Use port bundles to group multiple Fast or Gigabit Ethernet ports into a single logical transmission path between a switch and a router, a host, or another switch. STP regards a channel as one link. A switch can distribute frames across the ports in an EtherChannel according to the source and/or destination IP addresses or MAC addresses. If a port within an EtherChannel fails, traffic that was previously carried over the failed port will switch to the remaining ports within the EtherChannel.

Figure 3-22 presents the case where redundancy is provided by installing an additional interface card in the server. The device driver presents the configured NICs as a single interface (one IP address) to the operating system. The two NICs might use a common MAC address, or they might use two distinct MAC addresses and rely on gratuitous ARP to provide proper IP–to–MAC address mapping on switches when the backup interface card is activated. With a redundant NIC, a VLAN is needed between the two access switches to support single IP on the two server links.

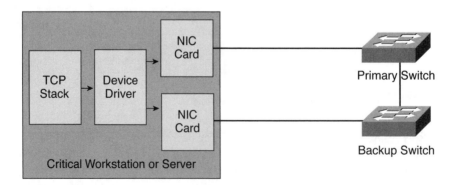

Figure 3-22 *Redundant NIC Example*

> **Note**   The workstation sends gratuitous ARP messages to update ARP and the forwarding tables on attached neighboring nodes (for example, Layer 2 switches).

Identifying Network Management Protocols and Features

Network administrators need tools for monitoring the functionality of network devices, connections, and services. Simple Network Management Protocol (SNMP) has become the standard for network management solutions, along with Remote Monitoring (RMON) and Management Information Base (MIB). Each managed device in the network has several variables that quantify the state of the device. By reading these values, managed devices can be monitored and controlled.

The following sections introduce management protocols. They describe the differences between SNMP versions 1, 2, and 3. The sections also describe the role of MIBs in SNMP and RMON. They introduce Cisco Discovery Protocol and explains its benefits and limitations. In addition, these sections describe methods for gathering network statistics, messages, and alerts by using network flow (NetFlow) and syslog.

Network Management Overview

Figure 3-23 illustrates a generic network management overview.

Network management is an important aspect of modern networks. It is supported with these elements:

- **Network management systems (NMS):** An NMS executes applications that monitor and control managed devices. An NMS provides the bulk of the processing and memory resources that are required for network management.

- **Network management protocols and standards:** These protocols and standards facilitate the exchange of management information between the NMS and managed devices. The key network management protocols and standards are as follows:

  - SNMP is, as its name implies, a Simple Network Management Protocol. An SNMP agent stores data that is specific to the managed device in a MIB.

  - A Management Information Base (MIB) is a detailed definition of the information on a network device that is accessible through a network management protocol like SNMP.

  - Remote Network Monitoring (RMON) is an extension to the standard MIB. RMON provides remote monitoring capability through the collection of network traffic data on remote links. The RMON agent resides on a managed device and collects specific groups of statistics, which an NMS can retrieve and use for long-term trend analysis.

- **Managed devices:** These devices are monitored and controlled by the NMS.

■ **Management agents:** These typically reside on managed devices and include SNMP agents and RMON agents.

■ **Management information:** This information is commonly stored in MIBs.

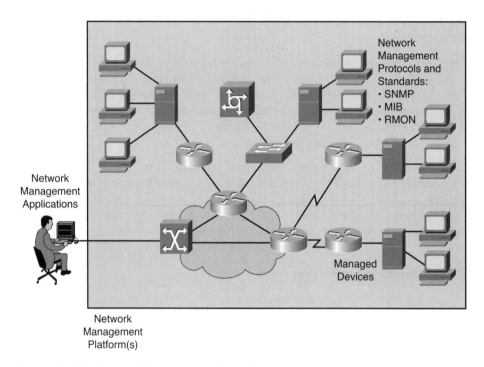

Figure 3-23 *Network Management Overview*

> **Note** References to the ISO network management model may be encountered. It defines five functional areas of network management: Fault management, Configuration management, Accounting management, Performance management, and Security management (FCAPS). These functional areas and the FCAPS model are rarely implemented as a single enterprise-wide network management system. A typical enterprise comprises various network infrastructure and service elements that are managed by element-specific network management systems. Information on specific management systems for technologies such as voice, security, and wireless is provided in later chapters.

SNMP

SNMP has become the standard for network management. It is a simple solution that requires little code to implement and thus enables vendors to easily build SNMP agents for their products. Therefore, SNMP is often the foundation of a network management architecture.

SNMP defines how management information is exchanged between network management applications and management agents. A network management application periodically polls the SNMP agents that reside on managed devices by querying the device for data. The periodic SNMP polling has the disadvantage of a delay between the time that an event occurs and the time that it is noticed by the NMS. There is a trade-off between polling frequency and bandwidth usage.

A network management application can display the information in a GUI on the network manager.

SNMP uses the User Datagram Protocol (UDP) transport mechanism of IP to retrieve and send management information, such as MIB variables.

SNMP management agents that reside on managed devices perform the following:

■ Collect and store information about the device and its operation

■ Respond to managerial requests

■ Generate traps to inform the manager of certain events

SNMP traps are sent by management agents to the network management system when certain events occur. Trap-directed notification can result in substantial savings of network and agent resources by eliminating the need for some SNMP polling requests.

The management agent collects data and stores it locally in the MIB. Community strings control access to the MIB. To view or set MIB variables, the user must specify the appropriate community string for read or write access.

SNMP Message Types

The initial version of the SNMP standard (SNMP version 1, or SNMPv1) is defined in RFC 1157. There are five basic SNMP messages that the network manager uses to transfer data from agents that reside on managed devices; these are illustrated in Figure 3-24.

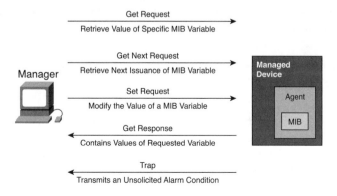

Figure 3-24 *SNMPv1 Message Types*

The five basic SNMP messages are

- **GET request:** Used to request the value of a specific MIB variable from the agent.

- **GET NEXT request:** Used after the initial GET request to retrieve the next object instance from a table or a list.

- **SET request:** Used to set a MIB variable on an agent.

- **GET response:** Used by an agent to respond to a GET request or GET NEXT request from a manager.

- **Trap:** Used by an agent to transmit an unsolicited alarm to the manager. An agent sends a trap message when a certain condition occurs, such as a change in the state of a device, a device or component failure, or an agent initialization or restart.

SNMP Version 2

SNMP version 2 (SNMPv2) provides improved performance and manager-to-manager communications as compared to SNMPv1. SNMPv2 was introduced with RFC 1441, but members of the Internet Engineering Task Force (IETF) subcommittee could not agree on the security and administrative sections of the SNMPv2 specification. There were several attempts to achieve acceptance of SNMPv2 through the release of experimental modified versions.

Community-based SNMPv2 (SNMPv2c), which is defined in RFC 1901, is the most common implementation. SNMPv2c deploys the administrative framework that is defined in SNMPv1, which uses read/write community strings for administrative access.

SNMPv2 introduces two new message types:

- **GET BULK request:** This message type reduces repetitive requests and replies and improves performance when retrieving large amounts of data (for example, tables).

- **Inform Request:** These messages alert an SNMP manager to specific conditions. Unlike SNMP trap messages, which are unconfirmed, the NMS acknowledges an Inform Request by sending an Inform Response message back to the requesting device.

SNMPv2 adds new data types with 64-bit counters, because 32-bit counters were quickly outmoded by fast network interfaces.

> **Note**   Neither SNMPv1 nor SNMPv2 offers security features. Specifically, SNMPv1 and SNMPv2 can neither authenticate the source of a management message nor provide encryption. Because of the lack of security features, many SNMPv1 and SNMPv2 implementations are limited to a read-only capability, reducing their utility to that of a network monitor.

SNMP Version 3

To correct the security deficiencies of SNMPv1 and SNMPv2, SNMP version 3 (SNMPv3) was developed. SNMPv3 is the latest SNMP version to become a full standard. It is described in RFCs 3410 through 3415. SNMPv3 adds methods to ensure the secure transmission of critical data between managed devices.

SNMPv3 provides secure access to devices by a combination of authenticating and encrypting packets over the network. There are many security features provided by SNMPv3, including the following:

- **Message integrity:** Ensures that a packet has not been tampered with in transit

- **Authentication:** Determines that the message is from a valid source

- **Encryption:** Scrambles the contents of a packet, which prevents it from being seen by an unauthorized source

There are also many benefits to using SNMPv3, including the following:

- Data can be collected securely from SNMP devices without fear of the data being tampered with or corrupted.

- Confidential information (SNMP Set command packets that change router configuration) can be encrypted to prevent the contents from being exposed on the network.

SNMPv3 provides both security models and security levels. A security model is an authentication strategy that is set up for a user and the group in which the user resides. A security level is the permitted level of security within a security model. A combination of a security model and a security level will determine which security mechanism is used when processing an SNMP packet. Table 3-4 illustrates SNMP security models and levels.

SNMPv3 introduces three levels of security:

- **NoAuthNoPriv:** This level uses a username match for authentication, and no privacy (encryption) is provided.

- **AuthNoPriv:** Authentication is based on Hashed Message Authentication Code (HMAC) with Message Digest 5 (HMAC-MD5) or HMAC with Secure Hash Algorithm (HMAC-SHA). No encryption is provided.

- **AuthPriv:** In addition to authentication, SNMPv3 provides authentication that is based on the HMAC-MD5 or HMAC-SHA algorithm. It provides Data Encryption Standard (DES) 56-bit encryption in addition to authentication that is based on the CBC-DES (DES-56) standard. It also supports Triple DES (3DES), a mode of the DES encryption algorithm that encrypts data three times, and Advanced Encryption Standard (AES), a very strong encryption standard adopted by the U.S. government.

Table 3-4 *SNMP Security Models and Levels*

Model	Level	Authentication	Encryption	Description
SNMPv1	NoAuthNoPriv	Community String	No	Uses a community string match for authentication
SNMPv2c	NoAuthNoPriv	Community String	No	Uses a community string match for authentication
SNMPv3	NoAuthNoPriv	Username	No	Uses a username match for authentication
SNMPv3	AuthNoPriv	MD5 or SHA	No	Provides authentication based on the HMAC-MD5 or HMAC-SHA algorithm
SNMPv3	AuthPriv	MD5 or SHA	Yes	Provides authentication based on the HMAC-MD5 or HMAC-SHA algorithm. Provides DES, 3DES, or AES encryption algorithms.

The following are details concerning SNMPv3 objects:

■ Each user belongs to a group.

■ A group defines the access policy for a set of users.

■ An access policy defines which SNMP objects can be accessed for reading, writing, and creating.

■ A group determines the list of notifications that its users can receive.

■ A group also defines the security model and security level for its users.

MIB Characteristics

A MIB stores management information for the local agent on the managed device. Each object in a MIB has a unique identifier that network management applications use to identify and retrieve the value of a specific object. The MIB structure is a tree-like structure. Similar objects are grouped under the same branch of the MIB tree. For example, various interface counters are grouped under the interfaces branch of the MIB tree. Standard MIBs are defined in various RFCs. For example, RFC 1213 defines the TCP/IP MIB. In addition to standard MIBs, there are private and vendor-specific MIB definitions. Vendors can obtain their own branch for the definition of their private MIB subtree and can create custom-managed objects under that branch.

• Standard managed objects:
   – Interfaces
   – Buffers
   – Memory
   – Standard protocols
• Private extensions to MIB-II:
   – 1.3.6.1.4.1.9
     or
   – iso.org.dod.internet.private.enter-
    prise.cisco
• Definitions available at
  http://www.cisco.com/public/mibs

• Private managed objects:
   – Small, medium, large, and huge buffers
   – Primary and secondary memory
   – Proprietary protocols

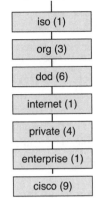

Figure 3-25 *Cisco Router MIB*

Cisco has defined private MIBs to support its definition of managed objects. A Cisco router MIB uses both standard and private managed objects, as shown in Figure 3-25.

A Cisco router has a number of standard managed objects that are defined in the standard section of the MIB tree; these include the following:

■ Interfaces

■ Buffers

■ Memory

■ Standard protocols

The router has private managed objects that have been introduced by Cisco in the private section of the MIB tree, such as these:

■ Small, medium, large, and huge buffers

■ Primary and secondary memory

■ Proprietary protocols

To use the private definitions of managed objects, the administrator must import the private definitions into the NMS. This process is useful for operators, because the resulting outputs are descriptive variable names.

Cisco maintains its private MIB definitions under the Cisco MIB subtree (1.3.6.1.4.1.9). Further information can be obtained for the Cisco MIB definitions that Cisco devices support at www.cisco.com/public/mibs.

MIB Variable Retrieval

If the network manager wants to retrieve the number of errors on the first interface, starting with interface number 0, the valid range for interface numbers is 0 through "maximum ports minus 1." Therefore, as shown in Figure 3-26, the manager creates the SNMP GET request message with reference to the MIB variable 1.3.6.1.2.1.2.2.1.20.0, which represents outgoing errors on interface 0. The agent creates the SNMP GET response message as a response to the request of the manager. The referenced variable is included in the response. In the example, the agent returns 11, indicating that there were 11 outgoing errors on that interface.

— Base format to retrieve the number of errors on an interface

iso	org	dod	internet	mgmt	mib	interface	ifTable	ifEntry	ifOutErrors
1	3	6	1	2	1	2	2	1	20

— Specific format to retrieve the number of errors on first interface

iso	org	dod	internet	mgmt	mib	interface	ifTable	ifEntry	ifOutErrors	Instance
1	3	6	1	2	1	2	2	1	20	0

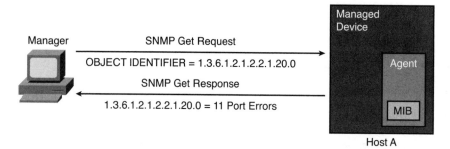

Figure 3-26   *MIB Variable Retrieval Example*

Monitoring networks using SNMP requires that the NMS poll each managed device on a periodic basis to determine its status. Frequent polling of many devices or MIB variables on a device across a network to a central NMS can result in performance issues. Performance issues include congestion on slower links or at the NMS connection or overwhelming NMS resources that prevent it from adequately processing all the collected data. Therefore, these important polling guidelines should be followed:

Step 1.   Restrict polling to only those MIB variables necessary for analysis.

Step 2.   Increase polling intervals (reduce the number of polls per period) over low-bandwidth links.

Step 3.   For larger networks, consider the deployment of management domains or a distributed model for deploying NMS. Management domains permit polling to be more local to the managed devices. This reduces overall management traffic across the network, as well as reduces the potential for one failed device or link to cut off management visibility to the remaining network. Aggregated management data can still be centralized. This model is particularly appropriate for networks that already have separate administrative domains or where large campuses or portions of the network are separated by slower WAN links.

Step 4.   Analyze and use the data collected. Do not collect data if it is not analyzed.

Step 5.   Leverage nonpolling mechanisms, such as SNMP traps, RMON, and syslog.

Using RMON

Using RMON, the managed device itself collects and stores MIB data. RMON can set performance or error thresholds and report only if the threshold is breached, which helps to reduce management traffic. RMON provides effective network fault diagnosis, performance tuning, and planning for network upgrades. RMON version 1 (RMON1) works on the data link layer data and provides the aggregate LAN traffic, statistics, and analysis for remote LAN segments.

RMON agents must look at every frame on the network. Therefore, RMON agents can cause performance problems on a managed device that has insufficient processing power and memory. The agents can reside in routers, switches, and dedicated RMON probes. Because packet processing can become resource-intensive, and the amount of data that the RMON agent collects can be very large, network managers often deploy dedicated RMON probes instead of enabling RMON agents on routers and switches. The RMON1 agents gather nine groups of statistics (ten with Token Ring). The agents then forward this information to a manager upon request, commonly through SNMP. Table 3-5 illustrates the RMON1 groups.

Table 3-5   *RMON1 Groups*

Group	Function
Statistics	Contains statistics such as packets sent, bytes sent, broadcast packets, multicast packets, cyclic redundancy check (CRC) errors, runts, giants, fragments, jabbers, collisions, and so on for each monitored interface on the device
History	Stores periodic statistical samples for later retrieval
Alarm	Sets specific thresholds for managed objects and to trigger an event upon crossing the threshold (which requires an events group)
Host	Contains statistics that are associated with each host that is discovered on the network

Table 3-5   *RMON1 Groups*

Group	Function
hostTopN	Contains statistics for hosts that top a list for a specific observed variable
hostTopN Filters	Contains rules for data packet filters, which generate events or are stored locally in a packet capture group
Matrix	Contains statistics for conversations between sets of addresses
Packet capture	Contains data packets that match rules that were set in the filters group
Events	Controls the generation and notification of events from this device
Token Ring	Outdated

RMON1 provides visibility into only the data link and physical layers. Performance and fault analyses of the higher layers still require other capture and decode tools. Because of the limitations of RMON1, RMON version 2 (RMON2) was developed to extend functionality to upper-layer protocols. RMON2 provides complete network visibility from the network layer to the application layer; this is shown in Figure 3-27.

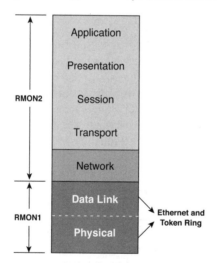

Figure 3-27   *RMON1 and RMON2 Layers*

RMON2 is not a replacement for RMON1, but an extension of it. RMON2 extends RMON1 by adding nine more groups that provide visibility to the upper layers.

The visibility of upper-layer protocols enables the network manager to monitor any upper-layer protocol traffic for any device or subnet, in addition to the data link layer traffic. RMON2 also provides end-to-end views of network conversations per protocol.

Table 3-6 illustrates the new groups that RMON2 supports.

Table 3-6 *Groups Supported by RMON2*

Group	Function
Protocol directory	Provides the list of protocols that the device supports
Protocol distribution	Contains the traffic statistics for each supported protocol
Address mapping	Contains network layer–to–MAC layer address mappings
Network layer host	Contains statistics for the network layer traffic to or from each host
Network layer matrix	Contains network layer traffic statistics for conversations between pairs of hosts
Application layer host	Contains statistics for the application layer traffic to or from each host
Application layer matrix	Contains application layer traffic statistics for conversations between pairs of hosts
User history collection	Contains periodic samples of user-specified variables
Probe configuration	Provides a standard way to remotely configure probe parameters such as trap destination and out-of-band management

RMON2 collects statistics beyond the data link layer of a specific segment. Network managers can view conversations at the network and application layers, including traffic that is generated by a specific host or even a specific application on the host.

NetFlow Characteristics

NetFlow answers the questions of what, when, where, and how traffic is flowing in the network. The NetFlow data can be exported using UDP or Stream Control Transmission Protocol (SCTP) to network management applications that further process the information. The data can be utilized in display tables and graphs for accounting and billing purposes as an aid for network planning. The infrastructure for NetFlow is shown in Figure 3-28.

The key components of NetFlow are the NetFlow cache or data source that stores IP flow information and the NetFlow export or transport mechanism that sends NetFlow data to a network management collector, such as the NetFlow Collection Engine.

NetFlow-collected data serves as the base for a set of applications that include network traffic accounting, usage-based network billing, network planning, and network monitoring. It also provides the measurement base for QoS applications. NetFlow captures the traffic classification, or precedence, that is associated with each network flow and enables differentiated charging based on QoS.

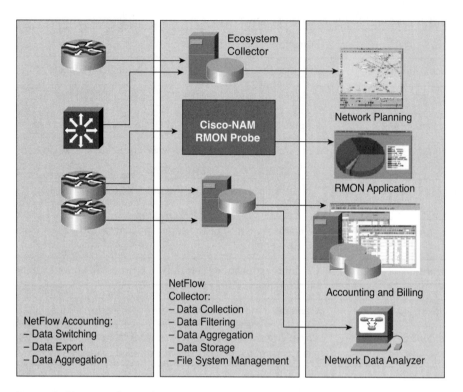

Figure 3-28   *NetFlow Infrastructure*

A network flow is defined as a unidirectional sequence of packets between source and destination endpoints. Flow endpoints are identified by IP address and transport layer application port numbers. NetFlow also identifies the flows by IP protocol type, type of service (ToS), and the input interface identifier. Expired flows are grouped together into "NetFlow export" datagrams for export from the NetFlow-enabled device. The NetFlow export must be configured to a FlowCollector, which is a device that provides NetFlow export data filtering and aggregation capabilities.

A flow record is maintained within the NetFlow cache for each active flow. Each flow record in the NetFlow cache contains fields that can later be exported to a collection device, such as the NetFlow Collection Engine.

Non-NetFlow-enabled switching manages incoming packets independently, with separate serial tasks for switching, security, services, and traffic measurements that are applied to each packet. NetFlow-enabled switching applies security such as access control list (ACL) processing to only the first packet of a flow. Information from the first packet is used to build an entry in the NetFlow cache. Subsequent packets in the flow are processed through a single streamlined task that manages switching, services, and data collection concurrently. Multilayer switches support multilayer NetFlow.

NetFlow services capitalize on the "flow" nature of traffic in the network to accomplish these tasks:

■ Provide detailed data collection with minimal impact on router performance

■ Process larger ACLs efficiently for packet-filtering and security services

The main NetFlow focus has always been IP flow information, but is now changing with the Cisco implementation of a generic export transport format. The Cisco IOS Software flexible and extensible export format (NetFlow version 9) is now in the Internet Engineering Task Force (IETF) RFC 3954, which is an information-only standards track in the IP Flow Information Export (IPFIX) working group. The new generic data transport capability within Cisco routers (IPFIX export) can be used to transport any performance information from a router or switch. This information includes

■ Layer 2 information

■ New security detection and identification information

■ IPv6

■ Multicast

■ Multiprotocol Label Switching (MPLS)

■ Border Gateway Protocol (BGP) information

NetFlow Versus RMON Information Gathering

NetFlow can be configured on individual interfaces, which allows more selectivity than RMON. NetFlow collects more detailed information on the traffic that passes through interfaces, including these types of information:

■ Source and destination interface numbers

■ Source and destination IP addresses

■ TCP/UDP source port and destination ports

■ Number of bytes and packets in the flow

■ Source and destination autonomous system (AS) numbers

■ IP type of service (ToS)

Compared to a solution that uses SNMP with RMON MIB, NetFlow offers these benefits:

■ Greater detail about collected data, including data time stamping

■ Data collection that is customized according to interface

■ Greater scalability for a large number of interfaces, without the limitation of RMON in the size of its memory table

■ A much lower performance impact than that of RMON, without a requirement for external probes

Applications Using NetFlow

A number of different applications can take advantage of NetFlow functionality. Table 3-7 displays some of the key applications.

Table 3-7 *Key Applications Provided by NetFlow*

Application	Function	Benefit
Accounting and billing	NetFlow data provides fine-grained metering for highly flexible and detailed resource utilization accounting.	Service providers can use this information to migrate away from single-fee, flat-rate billing to more flexible charging mechanisms that are based on time of day, bandwidth usage, application usage, QoS, and so on. Enterprises can use the information for departmental cost recovery or cost allocation for resource utilization.
Network planning and analysis	NetFlow data provides key information for sophisticated network architecture tools that are used to optimize strategic planning (for example, which devices to peer with, backbone upgrade planning, routing policy planning) and tactical network engineering decisions (such as adding resources to routers or upgrading link capacity).	This optimization has the benefit of minimizing the total cost of network operations while maximizing network performance, capacity, and reliability.
Network and security monitoring	NetFlow data provides extensive, almost real-time, network monitoring. Flow-based analysis techniques can be used to visualize traffic patterns that are associated with individual routers and switches on a network-wide basis and that provide aggregate traffic or application-based views.	This analysis provides network managers with proactive problem detection, efficient troubleshooting, and rapid problem resolution.
Application monitoring and profiling	NetFlow data enables network managers to gain a detailed, time-based view of application usage over the network.	Content and service providers can use this information to plan and allocate network and application resources, such as web server sizing and location, to meet customer demands.

Table 3-7 *Key Applications Provided by NetFlow*

Application	Function	Benefit
User monitoring and profiling	NetFlow data identifies customer and user network utilization and resource application.	Network managers can use this information to plan efficiently; to allocate access, backbone, and application resources; and to detect and resolve potential security and policy violations.
NetFlow data warehousing and mining	NetFlow data can be warehoused for later retrieval and analysis.	NetFlow data enables service providers to create a wider range of offered services. For example, the service provider can easily determine the traffic characteristics and provide new services to users, such as VoIP, which requires a QoS adjustment.

Cisco Discovery Protocol Features

Cisco Discovery Protocol is a (CDP) Cisco-proprietary protocol that enables the discovery of Cisco devices and their connectivity on the network. Cisco Discovery Protocol version 2 is the most recent release of the protocol and provides more intelligent device-tracking features.

CDP is a media- and protocol-independent protocol that is enabled by default on each supported interface of a Cisco device, such as routers, access servers, and switches. The physical media must support Subnetwork Access Protocol (SNAP) encapsulation.

CDP runs over the data link layer, which enables two systems that support different network layer protocols to communicate. Table 3-8 lists some of the information that Cisco devices exchange in the CDP packet.

CDP is a "hello-based" protocol. All Cisco devices that run CDP periodically advertise their attributes to their neighbors by using a multicast address. CDP packets advertise a hold time value in seconds, which indicates the length of time to retain the packet before discarding it. Cisco devices send CDP packets with a hold time value that is not 0 after an interface is enabled. A hold time value of 0 is sent immediately before an interface is idled. Sending a CDP packet with a hold time value of 0 allows a network device to quickly discover a lost neighbor.

By default, all Cisco devices receive Cisco Discovery Protocol packets and cache the information in the packet. The cached information is then available to an NMS using SNMP.

Table 3-8 *Information Included in the Cisco Discovery Protocol Packet*

Term	Definition
Device ID	The name of the neighbor device and either the MAC address or the serial number of this device
Local interface	The local interface that is connected to the discovered neighbor
Hold time	The remaining amount of time (in seconds) that the current device will hold the CDP advertisement from a sending router before discarding it
Capability	The type of device that is discovered (R: Router, T: Trans Bridge, B: Source Route Bridge, S: Switch, H: Host, I: IGMP, r: Repeater)
Platform	The product number of the device
Port ID	The port number on the discovered neighbor
Address	Identification of all the network layer protocol addresses that have been configured on the interface (or on the box, in the case of protocols that are configured globally, such as IP, Internetwork Packet Exchange [IPX], and DECnet)

Note Cisco devices never forward a CDP packet. CDP can be disabled on an interface or globally on a device.

If any information changes from the last received packet, the device caches the new information and discards the previous information, even if its hold-time value has not yet expired.

For security reasons, SNMP access should be blocked to CDP data (or any other data) from outside the network and from subnets other than the management station subnet.

Note Do not run CDP in these places:

■ On links that you do not want to be discovered, such as Internet connections

■ On links that do not go to Cisco devices

Syslog Features

The system message and error-reporting service (syslog) is an essential component of any network operating system. The system message service reports system state information to a network manager. The architecture used by syslog is shown in Figure 3-29.

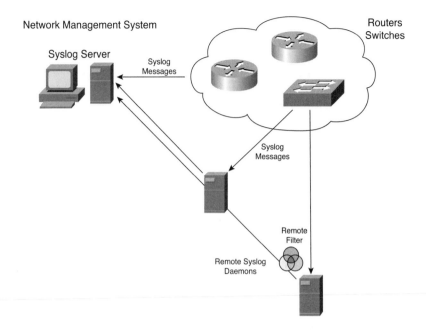

Figure 3-29 *Syslog Architecture*

Cisco devices produce syslog messages as a result of network events. Every syslog message contains a severity level and a facility. Many networking devices support syslog, including routers, switches, application servers, firewalls, and other network appliances.

Syslog defines the levels that are listed in Figure 3-30. The smaller numerical levels are the more critical syslog alarms. Syslog facilities are service identifiers that are used to recognize and categorize system state data for error and event message reporting. Cisco IOS Software has more than 500 facilities. The most common facilities are shown in Figure 3-30.

- Devices produce syslog messages.
- Syslog messages contain level and facility.
- Common syslog facilities:
  - IP
  - Open Shortest Path First (OSPF) protocol
  - SYS operating system
  - IP Security (IPsec)
  - Route Switch Processor (RSP)
  - Interface (IF)

- Syslog levels:
  - Emergency (level 0, highest level)
  - Alert (level 1)
  - Critical (level 2)
  - Error (level 3)
  - Warning (level 4)
  - Notice (level 5)
  - Informational (level 6)
  - Debugging (level 7)

Figure 3-30 *Syslog Facilities and Levels*

Other facilities include Cisco Discovery Protocol, Spanning Tree Protocol (STP), multicast, IP Security (IPsec), TCP, BGP, RADIUS, Telnet, and those facilities that are related to QoS services.

Example 3-1 shows samples of syslog messages that Cisco IOS Software produces. The most common messages are link up and link down messages and messages that a device produces when it exits from configuration mode.

Example 3-1 *Syslog Message Example*

```
20:11:31: %SYS-5- CONFIG I: Configured from console by console


20:11:57: %LINK-5-CHANGED: Interface FastEthernet0/0, changed state to administra-
tively down
20:11:58: %LINEPROTO-5-UPDOWN: Line protocol on Interface FastEthernet0/0, changed
state to down


20:12:04: %LINK-3-UPDOWN: Interface FastEthernet0/0, changed state to up
20:12:06: %LINEPROTO-5-UPDOWN: Line protocol on Interface FastEthernet0/0, changed
state to up
20:13:53: %SEC-6-IPACCESSLOGP: list internet-inbound denied udp 66.56.16.77(1029) -
> 63.78.199.4(161), 1 packet
20:14:26: %MLS-5-MLSENABLED:IP Multilayer switching is enabled
20:14:26: %MLS-5-NDEDISABLED: Netflow  Data Export disabled
20:14:26: %SYS-5-MOD_OK:Module 1 is online
20:15:47: %SYS-5-MOD_OK:Module 3 is online
20:15:42: %SYS-5-MOD_OK:Module 6 is online
20:16:27: %PAGP-5-PORTTOSTP:Port 3/1 joined bridge port 3/1
20:16:28: %PAGP-5-PORTTOSTP:Port 3/2 joined bridge port 3/2
```

If ACL logging is configured, the device generates syslog messages when packets match a parameter condition. ACL logging can be useful to detect packets that are denied access based on the security policy that is set by an ACL. System log messages can contain up to 80 characters and a percent sign (%), which follows the optional sequence number or time-stamp information, if configured. Messages are displayed in this format:

```
seq no:timestamp: %facility-severity-MNEMONIC:description
```

A sequence number appears on the syslog message if the **service sequence-numbers** global configuration command is configured. The time stamp shows the date and time of the message or event if the **service timestamps log [datetime | log]** global configuration command is configured.

The time stamp can have one of three formats:

1. mm/dd hh:mm:ss

2. hh:mm:ss (short uptime)

3. d h (long uptime)

Syslog messages are sent by default to console sessions. However, there are new features that provide more flexible and secure transporting of messages. The following are examples of two new features:

- **Reliable Delivery and Filtering for Syslog:** This feature allows a device to be customized for receipt of syslog messages. It provides reliable and secure delivery for syslog messages using Blocks Extensible Exchange Protocol (BEEP).

- **VPN Routing and Forwarding (VRF) Aware System Message Logging (Syslog):** This feature allows a router to send system logging (syslog) messages to a syslog server host that is connected through a VPN VRF interface.

To send syslog messages to the NMS, the device must be configured to send syslog messages to the address of the NMS that is running the syslog server function.

Network devices can be configured to send syslog messages directly to the NMS or to a remote network host on which a distributed syslog server is installed. Cisco Syslog Analyzer conserves bandwidth on WAN links, because the remote analyzer usually applies different filters and sends only the predefined subset of all syslog messages that it receives. The analyzer filters and periodically forwards messages to the central NMS. For example, an inexpensive product such as the syslog-ng application from BalaBit Software can be used to split off ACL logging data from normal router or switch syslog entries. This ensures that the ACL logging does not overwhelm a syslog reporting tool.

Note Cisco Syslog Analyzer is a CiscoWorks Resource Manager Essentials (CiscoWorks RME) application that supports a distributed syslog server architecture for localized collection, filtering, aggregation, and forwarding of syslog data to a central syslog server, allowing further processing and analysis. Syslog Analyzer also supports reporting functions in automatically parsing the log data into predefined or custom formats for ease of use and readability.

Upon receiving a syslog message, the NMS applies filters to remove unwanted syslog messages. Action filters can be applied to perform actions that are based on the received syslog message, such as paging or emailing the network manager.

Syslog data can consume considerable amounts of network bandwidth and can require a very large storage capacity. The required capacity is based on the number of devices sending syslog messages, the syslog facility and severity levels set for each, and any error conditions that can trigger excessive log messages. Therefore, it is important to enable logging only for network facilities of particular interest and to set the appropriate severity level to provide sufficient, but not excessive, detail. If the collected data is not analyzed, do not collect it. Syslog data should be selectively filtered and aggregated for distributed or centralized syslog servers to receive information based on the requirements.

Syslog messages from transit network devices can provide insight into and context for security events that might not be available from other sources. Within the context of a security incident, administrators can use syslog messages to understand communication relationships, timing, and in some cases, the attacker's motives and/or tools. These events should be considered complementary and be used in conjunction with other forms of network monitoring that might already be in place.

Summary

The Cisco Network Architectures for the Enterprise is a modular hierarchical approach to network design. The modularity that is built into the model facilitates network implementation and troubleshooting. The following are the key points should be taken from this chapter:

■ The hierarchical network structure is comprised of the access, distribution, and core layers.

■ Cisco Network Architectures for the Enterprise provides a modular hierarchical approach for providing network infrastructure and services to all places in the network.

■ Borderless Networks services provide intelligence to the network infrastructure, supporting application awareness within the network.

■ Network management protocols support the exchange of management information between the network management system and managed devices.

References

For additional information, refer to these resources:

Cisco, Inc. Enterprise Architecture Solution portal at www.cisco.com/en/US/netsol/index.html.

Oppenheimer, P. *Top-Down Network Design (Third Edition)*. Indianapolis, Indiana: Cisco Press, May 2004.

Cisco, Inc. Cisco Internetwork Design Guide, "Internetworking Design Basics," at www.cisco.com/en/US/docs/internetworking/design/guide/nd2002.html.

Cisco, Inc. NetFlow Services Solutions Guide, at www.cisco.com/en/US/products/sw/netmgtsw/ps1964/products_implementation_design _guide09186a00800d6a11.html.

Review Questions

Answer the following questions, and then refer to Appendix A for the answers.

1. Describe the role of each layer in the hierarchical network model.

2. What are three roles of the hierarchical model's core layer?

   a. Provide fast and efficient data transport

   b. Provide maximum availability and reliability

   c. Provide access to the corporate network through some wide-area technology

   d. Implement security policies

   e. Delineate broadcast domains

   f. Implement scalable routing protocols

3. What is a benefit of using the Virtual Switching System (VSS)?

4. What are the major functional areas in the Cisco Network Architectures for the Enterprise?

5. The Enterprise Edge functional area includes which modules?

6. Indicate which types of devices would be found in each of these modules (note that some devices are found in more than one module).

Modules:

- E-commerce module

- Internet Connectivity module

- Remote Access and VPN module

Devices:

- Web servers

- SMTP mail servers

- Firewalls or firewall routers

- Network intrusion prevention system (NIPS) appliances

- DNS servers

- ASA security appliances

- Public FTP servers

7. What types of redundancies can be implemented in networking?

8. What is a Cisco WAE appliance?

9. What are the RMON1 groups?

10. What are the syslog severity levels?

Chapter 4

Designing Basic Campus and Data Center Networks

This chapter introduces general campus switching and data center design considerations. It includes the following sections:

- Describing Campus Design Considerations

- Designing the Campus Infrastructure Module

- Describing Enterprise Data Center Considerations

- Describing Enterprise Network Virtualization Tools

The availability of multigigabit campus switches enables organizations to build high-performance, highly reliable networks. When a systematic network design approach is followed, performance, reliability, and manageability can be achieved. This chapter describes a hierarchical campus network design approach called "multilayer design." Multilayer design is modular, so organizations can increase their network capacity as needed. A multilayer campus design is based on a known campus topology, which aids in troubleshooting.

This chapter examines network infrastructure design for two locations in the network that use the multilayer campus design: the enterprise campus and the enterprise data center. The chapter first introduces general campus switching design considerations. It also describes the switching modularity and scalability options that are appropriate for situations ranging from building-sized networks to large campus networks and design considerations for the enterprise data center.

Describing Campus Design Considerations

The multilayer approach to campus network design combines data link layer switching with multilayer switching to achieve robust, highly available campus networks. The following sections describe general campus network considerations that will be analyzed and considered in campus design.

These sections provide an overview of the general technologies that are implemented in campus design. The network topology options and network configuration parameters of the network devices must be identified to be utilized effectively in the network design.

Campus Design Factors

The enterprise campus network is the foundation for enabling business applications, enhancing productivity, and providing a multitude of services to end users in an enterprise campus. An enterprise campus can be one or several physical buildings where the resources for a company are centrally located. The three broad categories that factor into enterprise campus design decisions are

- Network application characteristics

- Infrastructure device characteristics

- Environmental characteristics such as geography and wiring

If organizational requirements, supporting network services, and applications have been defined in the network characterization phase, the next step in the network lifecycle is to design an enterprise campus infrastructure that supports these requirements.

The characteristics of the infrastructure devices will also influence the design. Network designers need to consider trade-offs between data link layer switching in the access layer (based on MAC address) and multilayer switching (based on network layer address, transport layer, and application awareness). Most enterprise campus infrastructures use a combination of data link switching the access layer and multilayer switching in the distribution and core layers. High availability and high throughput are requirements throughout the infrastructure.

The physical environment of the building or buildings will influence the design, as will the number, distribution, and distance between the network nodes (that is, end users, hosts, network devices). Other factors include space; power; and heating, ventilation, and air conditioning (HVAC) support for the network equipment. Cabling to connect network nodes is one of the biggest long-term investments in network deployment. Therefore, the selection of the transmission media depends on the required bandwidth and distances, as well as emerging technologies that might be deployed over the same infrastructure in the future.

Network Application Characteristics and Considerations

Network applications can be categorized into the following four types:

- Peer-peer

- Client–local server

- Client–data center

- Client–enterprise edge server

These different categories are discussed in further detail in the following sections.

Peer-Peer Applications

From the network designer's perspective, peer-peer applications include applications in which the majority of network traffic passes from one network edge device to another through the organization's network. This is shown in Figure 4-1.

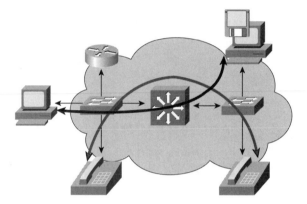

Figure 4-1   *Peer-Peer Applications*

Typical peer-peer applications include the following:

- **Instant messaging:** Two peers establish communication between two end systems. When the connection is established, the conversation is direct.

- **IP phone calls:** Two peers establish communication with the help of an IP telephony manager. The conversation occurs directly between the two peers when the connection is established. The network requirements of IP phone calls are strict because of the need for quality of service (QoS) treatment to minimize delay and variation in delay (jitter).

- **File sharing:** Some operating systems or applications require direct access to data on other workstations.

- **Videoconference systems:** Videoconferencing is similar to IP telephony. However, the network requirements are usually higher, particularly when related to bandwidth consumption and QoS requirements.

Client–Local Server Applications

Historically, clients and servers that were attached to a network device in a single LAN segment followed the 80/20 workgroup rule for client/server applications. This rule indicates that 80 percent of the traffic is local to the LAN segment and 20 percent leaves the segment.

With increased traffic on the corporate network and a relatively fixed location for users, an organization might split the network into several isolated segments with distributed servers for each specialized application. This is shown in Figure 4-2. Department administrators manage and control the servers. In this model, most department traffic occurs in the same segment, but some data exchange travels to the campus core.

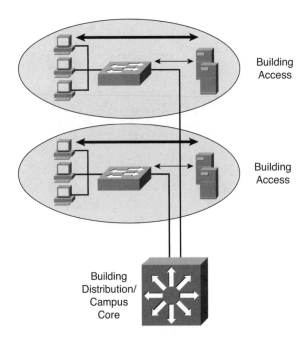

Figure 4-2 *Client–Local Server*

For traffic that is infrequently passing to another segment, the overall bandwidth requirement is not as crucial. For example, Internet access would pass through a common segment, which requires less performance than traffic to the local segment servers.

Client–Data Center Applications

Network bandwidth used to be costly but is now relatively inexpensive. Switch delay is insignificant with high-performance Layer 3 switches, so locating servers centrally rather than in the workgroup is now technically feasible. It reduces support costs.

In a large organization, the application traffic can cross more than one wiring closet or LAN to access applications in a data center. Client–data center applications apply the

20/80 rule, as shown in Figure 4-3. Only 20 percent of the traffic remains on the local LAN segment, and 80 percent leaves the segment to reach centralized servers, the Internet, and so on. Client–data center applications include the following:

■ Organizational mail servers

■ Common file servers

■ Common database servers for organizational applications

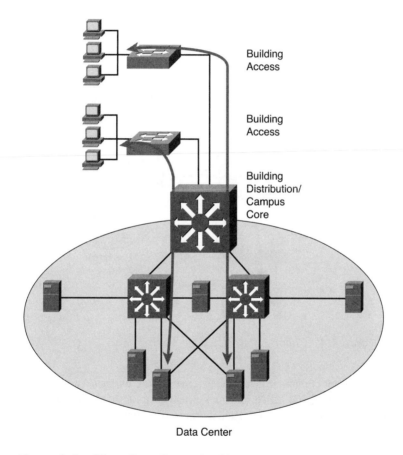

Data Center

Figure 4-3 *Client–Data Center Application*

Large organizations require users to have fast, reliable, and controlled access to critical applications. Servers are usually placed in a common data center to fulfill these demands and keep administrative costs low. The use of data centers requires a network infrastructure that is highly resilient and redundant and that provides adequate throughput. Typically, high-end LAN switches with the fastest LAN technologies, such as Gigabit Ethernet or 10 Gigabit Ethernet, are being deployed.

Client–Enterprise Edge Applications

As shown in Figure 4-4, client–enterprise edge applications use servers on the enterprise edge to exchange data between the organization and its public servers. Examples of these applications include external mail servers and public web servers.

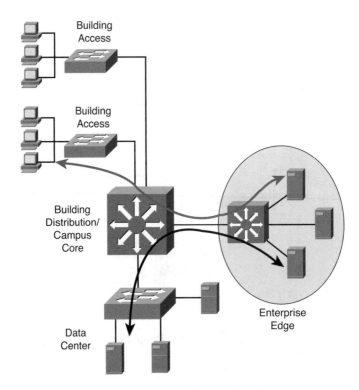

Figure 4-4 *Client–Enterprise Edge Application*

The most important communication issues between the campus network and the enterprise edge are security and high availability. An application that is installed on the enterprise edge can be crucial to organizational process flow. Outages can result in increased process cost.

The organizations that support their partnerships through e-commerce applications also place their e-commerce servers in the enterprise edge. Communication with the servers that are located on the campus network is vital because of two-way data replication. As a result, high redundancy and resiliency of the network are important requirements for these applications.

Application Requirements

Table 4-1 lists the types of application communication and compares their requirements with respect to some important network parameters. The following sections discuss these parameters.

The different network requirements are described as follows:

- **Connectivity type:** Today, most organizations use LAN switching instead of shared LAN cables at the data link layer for increased throughput and responsiveness. This offers greater utilization to satisfy the requirements of new organizational applications.

- **Total required throughput:** The required throughput varies by application. An application that exchanges data between users in the workgroup does not usually require a high-capacity network infrastructure. Organizational-level applications normally require a high-capacity link to the servers, which are usually located in the data center. Applications found on servers in the enterprise edge are not usually high consumers of bandwidth compared to the applications in the data center.

- **High availability:** A function of the application and the entire network between a client workstation and a server that is located in the network. Although network availability is mainly determined by the network design, the mean time between failures of individual components is a factor. Adding redundancy in the building distribution and the campus core layers is highly desirable.

- **Total network costs:** Depending on the application and the resulting network infrastructure, the total network costs will vary. The costs will be lower in a peer-to-peer environment and higher in a network designed with redundancy in the data center module and in the campus core and building distribution layers.

Table 4-1 *Application Requirements*

	Peer-Peer	Client–Local Servers	Client–Data Center	Client–Enterprise Edge Servers
Connectivity type	Switched	Switched	Switched	Switched
Total required throughput	Medium to high	Medium	High	Medium
High availability	Low to high	Medium	High	High
Total network costs	Low to medium	Medium	High	Medium

Environmental Characteristics and Considerations

The environment of a campus, including the location of the network nodes and the distances between the nodes, influences the network topology. When designing a campus network, the location of network nodes and the distances between the nodes must be determined. The scope of a new design is determined by the number of buildings involved. If there are multiple buildings, the interconnect of local and distant buildings must be determined, as required.

For a new design or network upgrades, the cost of the medium (including installation costs) must be evaluated along with the available budget. Technical characteristics such as signal attenuation and EMI must also be evaluated. Three major options exist for media:

- Copper-based media
- Optical fiber
- Wireless radio

Note   For network upgrades, new network media may not be included in the scope of the design project.

Intrabuilding Structure

An intrabuilding campus network structure provides connectivity for all end nodes located in the same building and gives them access to the network resources.

User workstations are usually attached, through twisted-pair copper wiring to the building access switches in the floor wiring closets. Wireless LANs (WLAN) can also be used to provide intrabuilding connectivity, enabling users to establish and maintain a wireless network connection throughout or between buildings, without the limitations of wires or cables.

Note   More discussions of WLAN are covered in Chapter 10, "Identifying Design Considerations for Basic Wireless Networking."

Access layer switches in wiring closets are normally connected to the building distribution switches over optical fiber. Optical fiber provides better transmission performance and less sensitivity to environmental disturbances than copper. Depending on the connectivity requirements to resources in other parts of the campus, the building distribution switches can be connected to campus core switches.

Interbuilding Structure

As shown in Figure 4-5, an interbuilding network structure provides connectivity between the central switches of the individual campus buildings. These buildings are usually in close proximity, typically only a few hundred meters to a few kilometers apart.

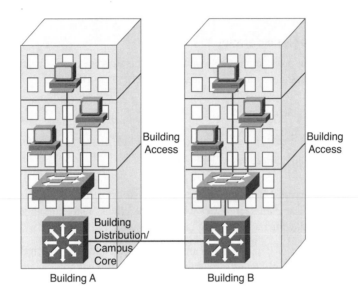

Figure 4-5 *Interbuilding Network Structure*

Normally, the end users in all the campus buildings need to use the common servers, so the demand for high-speed connectivity between the buildings is high. Within a campus, companies can deploy their own physical transmission media. To provide high throughput without excessive interference from environmental conditions, the appropriate media must be deployed. This requirement typically narrows the recommended choice to optical fiber.

Distant Remote Building Structure

To implement connectivity over distances that exceed a few kilometers (but that are still within a metropolitan area), the physical media is the most important factor that the network designer should consider.

Some companies deploy their own physical transmission media, such as fiber, microwave, or copper lines. Some organizations do not own physical transmission media to connect to all remote locations. They use connectivity options from public service providers to connect the locations, such as traditional WAN links or Metro Ethernet. The risk of downtime should be considered as service-level agreements (SLA) are available through service providers. Using unreliable and slowly repaired fiber, even if inexpensive, is not desirable for mission-critical applications. Speed and the cost of the network infrastructure depend heavily on the connectivity choice.

Note Additional discussion of connecting remote locations is covered in Chapter 5, "Designing Remote Connectivity."

Transmission Media Considerations

Transmission media provide physical connectivity between network devices. The most common physical transmission media used in modern networks are

- Twisted-pair cables (copper)

- Optical cables (fiber)

- Wireless (satellite, microwave, IEEE 802.11)

A network designer must be aware of the characteristics of each of the physical transmission media types. These characteristics will influence the available maximum distance and transmission speed, which are the main factors in cabling.

Deciding which type of cable to use is an important consideration when deploying or upgrading a network. Cabling infrastructure, which usually has an expected life of 10 years or more, represents a long-term investment.

Copper

The characteristics of copper twisted-pair cable depend on the quality of the material that is used. Twisted-pair cabling is widely used to interconnect workstations, servers, or other devices from their network interface card (NIC) to the building access or building distribution switches. Category 5e or greater twisted-pair cabling is recommended for speeds of 100 Mbps. Category 6 is recommended for Gigabit Ethernet. Because of the possibility of signal attenuation in the wires, the available cable length is usually limited to 100 meters.

A frequent consideration in cabling design is EMI. Because of high susceptibility to interference, twisted-pair cabling is not suitable for environments that are exposed to electromagnetic influences. Similarly, twisted-pair cabling is not appropriate for environments that can be affected by the interference that is introduced by the cabling itself.

Note EMI is also associated with some security issues, particularly eavesdropping, if a hacker gains access to the cabling infrastructure.

Distances longer than 100 meters might require Cisco Long-Reach Ethernet (Cisco LRE). Optical cable is also utilized, especially when immunity to EMI is required. Optical cable is used between buildings for electrical isolation, to avoid shock hazards and grounding problems.

Optical Fiber

The two main types of optical cable are multimode (MM) and single-mode (SM). Multimode fiber is optical fiber that carries multiple light waves or modes concurrently, each at a slightly different reflection angle within the optical fiber core. Because modes tend to disperse over longer lengths (modal dispersion), MM fiber transmission is used for relatively short distances. Typically, LEDs are used with MM fiber. The standard diameter of an MM fiber is 50 or 62.5 micrometers.

Single-mode (also known as monomode) fiber is optical fiber that carries a single wave (or laser) of light. Lasers are typically used with SM fiber. The standard diameter of an SM fiber core is between 2 and 10 micrometers. Single-mode fiber limits dispersion and loss of light and allows higher transmission speeds, but it is more expensive than multi-mode fiber.

Both MM and SM cables have lower loss of signal than copper cable. Therefore, optical cables allow longer distances between devices. Optical fiber cable has precise production and installation requirements. It costs more than twisted-pair cable.

Optical fiber requires a precise technique for cable coupling. Even a small deviation from the ideal position of optical connectors can result in either a loss of signal or a large number of frame losses. In environments where the cable does not consist of a single fiber run from point to point, the loss of signal at splices occurs very easily. Careful attention is imperative during optical fiber installation, because of the high sensitivity of the traffic to coupling misalignment and bend radius.

Wireless

Wireless LAN technology can either replace a traditional wired network or extend its reach and capabilities. In-building wireless LAN equipment consists of PC client adapters and access points, which perform functions that are similar to wired networking hubs. Access points are distributed throughout a building to expand range and functionality for wireless clients. Wireless bridges and access points can also be used for interbuilding connectivity and outdoor wireless client access. The majority of wireless clients support speeds of up to 54 Mbps using IEEE 802.1g in the 2.4-GHz band over a range of approximately 100 feet. However, with the new IEEE 802.11n standard, clients will be able to support speeds of up to 300 Mbps.

Note   The IEEE 802.11b standard supports speeds of up to 11 Mbps in the 2.4-GHz band; the IEEE 802.11a and 802.11g standards support speeds of up to 54 Mbps in the 5-GHz and 2.4-GHz bands, respectively; and the IEEE 802.11n standard supports speeds of up to 300 Mbps in both the 2.4- and 5-GHz bands.

The inherent nature of wireless networking is that it does not require wires or lines to accommodate data, voice, and video transport. The system will carry information across geographical areas that are otherwise prohibitive to connect.

Note   Wireless issues, including security and interference, are discussed in Chapter 10.

Campus Transmission Media Comparison

Table 4-2 presents the critical parameters that influence network transmission medium selection.

Table 4-2   *Campus Transmission Media Comparison*

	Copper Twisted-Pair	Multimode Fiber	Single-Mode Fiber	Wireless
Bandwidth	Up to 10 Gbps	Up to 10 Gbps	Up to 10 Gbps or higher	Up to 300 Mbps*
Distance	Up to 100 m	Up to 2 km (Fast Ethernet) Up to 550 m (Gigabit Ethernet) Up to 300 m (10 Gigabit Ethernet)	Up to 80 km (Fast Ethernet) Up to 100 km (Gigabit Ethernet) Up to 80 km (10 Gigabit Ethernet) Up to 10 km (100 Gigabit Ethernet)	Up to 500 m at 1 Mbps
Price	Inexpensive	Moderate	Moderate to Expensive	Moderate

The initial cabling decision should be based on these primary considerations:

- **Bandwidth:** The required bandwidth in a particular segment of the network or the connection speed between the nodes inside or outside the building.

- **Distance:** Consider the distances from the network devices (workstations, servers, printers, IP phones, and so on) to network nodes and between the network nodes. The distances supported with fiber will vary depending on whether it is supporting Fast Ethernet or Gigabit Ethernet, the type of fiber, and the fiber interface that is used.

Note   The wireless throughput is significantly less than its maximum data rate because of the half-duplex nature of radio frequency (RF) technology.

- Price: Although the cost of the medium is a clear factor, you must also consider the cost of installation.

Additional cabling decision criteria include

■ **Deployment area:** Consider whether the wiring is required for the wiring closet only (where users access the network) or for internode or even interbuilding connections.

■ **EMI:** The EMI requirements can influence the selection of the media.

Transmission Media Cabling Example

Figure 4-6 illustrates a typical campus network structure. The distances shown in the figure are for a sample network. The maximum distance that is supported varies depending on the fiber interface used. End devices, such as workstations, Cisco IP Phones, and printers, are located no more than 100 meters away from the LAN switch. Twisted-pair wiring can easily manage the required distance and speed while offering a reasonable price/performance ratio.

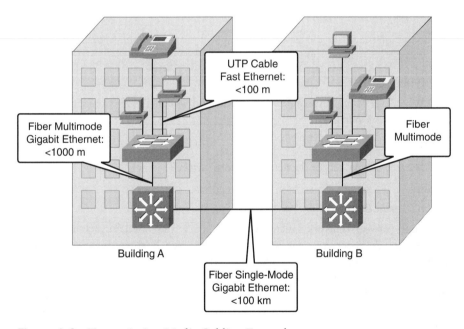

Figure 4-6   *Transmission Media Cabling Example*

Infrastructure Device Characteristics and Considerations

To select the appropriate type of infrastructure devices, you should understand the network topology and user needs. Network end devices are commonly connected using switched technology rather than using a shared media segment. Switched technology provides dedicated network bandwidth for each device on the network. It also supports multiple simultaneous frame flows (data link switching) and performs packet switching, as well as several functions at Layer 3 and at higher OSI layers (multilayer switching).

Switched networks can support network infrastructure services, such as QoS, security, and management. A shared media segment does not have the capability to support these features of the network.

One functional difference between data link layer and multilayer switching is the type of information inside the frame that is used to determine the correct output interface. Data link layer switching forwards frames that are based on data link layer information (MAC address). Multilayer switching forwards frames that are based on network layer information (IP address). Multilayer switching is hardware-based switching and routing integrated into a single platform.

To determine which LAN switch and features to deploy at each layer in the network, the following questions should be considered:

Infrastructure service capabilities (QoS, including policies, and so on):

1.   What network services does the organization require?

Size of the network segments:

2.   Based on the traffic characteristics, how will the network be segmented? How many end devices will be connected?

Convergence time:

3.   What level of high availability is required, and what is the maximum time for possible network outages?

Cost:

4.   What is the budget for the network infrastructure?

Quality of Service (QoS)

A campus network transports many types of applications and data, including high-quality video and delay-sensitive data such as real-time voice. Bandwidth-intensive applications stretch network capabilities and resources, but they can also enhance many business processes. Networks must provide secure, predictable, measurable, and (sometimes) guaranteed services. Achieving the required QoS by managed delay, delay variation (jitter), bandwidth, and packet loss parameters on a network can be the key to a successful end-to-end business solution. QoS is the set of techniques that are used to manage network resources.

Bandwidth demand on the network can exceed the available bandwidth. Most networks or individual network elements are oversubscribed. The sum of the bandwidth of all ports on a switch where end devices are connected is usually greater than that of the uplink port. When the ports are fully used, congestion on the uplink port is unavoidable. Within the enterprise campus, QoS is most often required on uplinks for traffic between the building access layer and the building distribution layer, or between the building distribution layer and the campus core layer.

A network operator configures bandwidth management with QoS mechanisms on the building access, building distribution, or campus core switches, depending on traffic flow and oversubscription of the uplinks.

QoS, as implemented on LAN switches, can be categorized into these four areas:

■ **Classification and marking:** Packet classification features allow the partitioning of traffic into multiple priority or class of service (CoS) levels. These features inspect the information in the frame and network header and determine the priority of the frame. *Marking* is the term given to the process of changing the priority level (or CoS) setting of a frame or packet.

■ **Scheduling:** Scheduling is the process that determines the order in which queues are serviced. CoS is utilized on data link layer switches to assist in the queuing process. Based on network, transport, and higher-layer information, multilayer switches can also provide QoS scheduling. Layer 3 IP QoS queue selection uses the IP Differentiated Services Code Point (DSCP) or IP precedence field of the IP packet.

■ **Congestion management:** Often, a network interface is congested (even at higher speeds, transient congestion is observed). Thus, queuing techniques are necessary to ensure that the critical application receives the necessary forwarding treatment. For example, real-time applications such as VoIP and stock trading might need to be forwarded with the lowest latency and jitter.

■ **Policing and shaping:** Policing is the process of reducing a stream of data to a predetermined rate or level. Unlike traffic shaping, where the frames can be stored in small buffers for a short period, policing drops the frame or lowers the priority of the frame that is out of the profile.

When configuring QoS features, select the specific network traffic, prioritize it according to its relative importance, and use congestion-management techniques to provide preferential treatment.

Designing the Campus Infrastructure Module

A campus network is constructed using campus infrastructure modules. The following sections discuss designing the campus infrastructure using Layer 2 and multilayer switching in the building access, building distribution, and campus core layers. These sections also introduce data center module design, for which dual homing and redundancy are required.

Design Considerations for the Campus Network

Each individual module of the enterprise campus has different requirements. As shown in Table 4-3, options must be considered for future expansion of the campus network. Adding new workstations to the network should not result in either high additional costs or performance degradation.

Table 4-3 *Campus Design Considerations*

	Building Access	Building Distribution	Campus Core	Data Center
Technology	Layer 2 or 3 switched	Layer 3 switched	Layer 3 switched	Layer 3 switched
Scalability	High	Medium	Low	Medium
High Availability	Medium	Medium	High	High
Performance	Medium	Medium	High	High
Cost per Port	Low	Medium	High	High

End users might not require high performance and high availability, but these features are crucial in the campus core layer and data center module.

With expanded performance and availability, the price per port also reflects an increase. The campus core layer and data center module require a guarantee of higher throughput so that they can manage all traffic flows without introducing additional delays or drops to the network traffic.

The following engineering and architectural principles are critical for the successful implementation of the enterprise campus:

■ **Hierarchy:** This provides a higher degree of stability, flexibility, and manageability for the individual pieces of the campus and the campus as a whole.

■ **Modularity:** The modules of the system are the building blocks that are assembled into the larger campus.

■ **Resiliency:** Systems must also be designed to resist failure under abnormal conditions.

■ **Flexibility:** This ability to modify portions of the network, add new services, or increase capacity without going through a major complete equipment upgrade is a key consideration for designing an effective campus network.

Design Considerations for the Building Access Layer

When implementing the building access layer for the campus, consider the following questions:

1. How many users or host ports are currently required in the wiring closet, and how many will it require in the future? Should the switches utilize a fixed or modular configuration?

2. How many ports are available for end-user connectivity at the walls of the buildings?

3. How many access switches are not located in wiring closets?

4. What cabling is currently available in the wiring closet, and what cabling options exist for uplink connectivity?

5. What Layer 2 performance is needed for the node?

6. What level of redundancy is needed?

7. What is the required link capacity to the building distribution switches?

8. How will VLANs and Spanning Tree Protocol (STP) be deployed? Will there be a single VLAN or several VLANs per access switch? Will the VLANs on the switch be unique or spread across multiple switches?

9. Are additional features, such as port security, multicast traffic management, QoS, and traffic classification based on ports, needed on the access switches?

Managing VLANs and STP

As a best practice, limit VLANs to a single closet whenever possible.

For the most deterministic and highly available network topology, the requirement to support STP or Rapid STP (RSTP) convergence should be used when needed to prevent loops. In general, use Rapid per-VLAN Spanning Tree Plus (RPVST+) when STP is required.

Under soft failure conditions where keepalives (bridge protocol data units [BPDU]) or routing protocol hellos) are lost, Layer 2 environments fail open, forwarding traffic with unknown destinations on all ports and causing potential broadcast storms. On the other hand, Layer 3 environments fail closed, dropping routing neighbor relationships, breaking connectivity, and isolating the soft failed devices. STP redundancy uses only one of two links, while routed redundancy uses both.

Several varieties of STP are commonly used in the enterprise campus:

■ STP is the original 802.1D version.

■ Common Spanning Tree (CST) assumes one spanning-tree instance for the entire bridged network, regardless of the number of VLANs.

■ Per VLAN Spanning Tree Plus (PVST+) is a Cisco enhancement of STP to apply per VLAN with IEEE 802.1Q trunking and CST.

■ RSTP, or IEEE 802.1w, is an evolution of STP that provides faster convergence of STP.

■ RPVST+ is the Cisco enhancement of RSTP using PVST+.

Note   When Cisco documentation refers to implementing RSTP, it is referring to the Cisco RSTP implementation, or RPVST+.

The Cisco RSTP implementation is far superior to IEEE 802.1D and even PVST+ from a convergence perspective. It greatly improves the restoration times for any VLAN that requires a topology convergence because of uplink issues. It also improves convergence time over BackboneFast for any indirect link failures.

Note If a network includes other vendor switches, you should isolate the different STP domains with Layer 3 routing or use a standards-based STP implementation to avoid STP compatibility issues.

Even if the recommended design does not depend on STP to resolve link or node failure events, STP is required to protect against user-side loops. There are many ways that a loop can be introduced on the user-facing access layer ports. Wiring mistakes, misconfigured end stations, or malicious users can create a loop. STP is required to ensure a loop-free topology and to protect the rest of the network from problems created in the access layer.

Note Some security personnel have recommended disabling STP at the network edge (access layer). This practice is not recommended, because the risk of lost connectivity without STP is far greater than any STP information that might be revealed.

Cisco STP Toolkit

The Cisco STP Toolkit provides tools to better manage STP when RSTP is not available. The options include

- **PortFast:** Used for ports to which end-user stations or servers are directly connected. When PortFast is enabled, there is no delay in passing traffic. The switch immediately puts the port in the STP forwarding state, skipping the listening and learning states. Two additional measures that prevent potential STP loops are associated with the PortFast feature:

  - **BPDU Guard:** PortFast transitions the port into the STP forwarding state immediately on linkup. Because the port still participates in STP, the potential for an STP loop exists if some device attached to that port also runs STP. The BPDU Guard feature enforces the STP domain borders and keeps the active topology predictable. If the port receives a BPDU, the port is transitioned into *errdisable state* (meaning that it was disabled because of an error) and an error message is reported.

  - **BPDU Filtering:** This feature blocks PortFast-enabled, nontrunk ports from transmitting BPDUs. STP does not run on these ports. BPDU filtering is not recommended, because it effectively disables STP at the edge and can lead to STP loops.

Note Although BPDU filtering is supported, it is recommended that it not be used as it effectively disables STP at the edge of the network and can lead to STP loops.

- **UplinkFast:** If the link on a switch to the root switch goes down and the blocked link is directly connected to the same switch, UplinkFast enables the switch to put a redundant port (path) into the forwarding state immediately. This typically results in convergence times of 3 to 5 seconds after a link failure.

- **BackboneFast:** If a link on the way to the root switch fails but is not directly connected to the same switch (in other words, it is an indirect failure), BackboneFast reduces the convergence time by max_age (which is 20 seconds by default), from 50 seconds to approximately 30 seconds. When this feature is used, it must be enabled on all switches in the STP domain.

- **STP Loop Guard:** When one of the blocking ports in a physically redundant topology stops receiving BPDUs, STP usually creates a potential loop by moving the port to the forwarding state. With the STP Loop Guard feature enabled, and if a blocking port no longer receives BPDUs, that port is moved into the STP loop-inconsistent blocking state instead of the listening/learning/forwarding state. This feature avoids loops in the network that result from unidirectional or other software failures.

- **RootGuard:** This feature prevents external switches from becoming the root. RootGuard should be enabled on all ports where the root bridge should not appear; this feature ensures that the port on which RootGuard is enabled is the designated port. If a superior BPDU (a BPDU with a lower bridge ID than that of the current root bridge) is received on a RootGuard-enabled port, the port is placed in a root-inconsistent state—the equivalent of the listening state.

- **BPDU Skew Detection:** This feature allows the switch to keep track of late-arriving BPDUs (by default, BPDUs are sent every 2 seconds) and to notify the administrator through syslog messages. Skew detection generates a report for every port on which a BPDU has arrived late (this is known as skewed arrival). Report messages are rate-limited (one message every 60 seconds) to protect the CPU.

- **Unidirectional Link Detection (UDLD):** A unidirectional link occurs whenever traffic transmitted by the local switch over a link is received by the neighbor but traffic transmitted from the neighbor is not received by the local device. If the STP process that runs on the switch with a blocking port stops receiving BPDUs from its upstream (designated) switch on that port, STP eventually ages out the STP information for this port and moves it to the forwarding state. If the link is unidirectional, this action would create an STP loop. UDLD is a Layer 2 protocol that works with the Layer 1 mechanisms to determine a link's physical status. If the port does not see its own device/port ID in the incoming UDLD packets for a specific duration, the link is considered unidirectional from the Layer 2 perspective. After UDLD detects the unidirectional link, the respective port is disabled and an error message is generated.

Note   PortFast, Loop Guard, RootGuard, and BPDU Guard are also supported for RPVST+.

Managing Trunks Between Switches

Trunks are typically deployed on the interconnection between the building access and building distribution layers. There are several best practices to implement with regard to trunks:

- When configuring switch-to-switch interconnections to carry multiple VLANs, set Dynamic Trunking Protocol (DTP) to on (**trunk**) with non-negotiate (**nonegotiate**) to disable support for DTP protocol negotiation.

- Manually prune unused VLANs from trunked interfaces to avoid broadcast propagation; automatic pruning should not be used.

- VLAN Trunking Protocol (VTP) transparent mode should be used because there is little need for a shared common VLAN database in hierarchical networks. Using VTP transparent mode will decrease the potential for operational errors.

- Trunking should be disabled on host ports (access), because host devices will not need to negotiate trunk status. This practice speeds up PortFast and is also a VLAN-hopping security measure.

Managing Default PAgP Settings

When connecting a Cisco IOS Software device to a Cisco Catalyst operating system device, make sure that the Port Aggregation Protocol (PAgP) settings that are used for establishing EtherChannels are coordinated. The defaults are different for a Cisco IOS device and a Catalyst Operating System device. As a best practice, Catalyst Operating System devices should have PAgP set to off when connecting to a Cisco IOS Software device if EtherChannels are not configured. If EtherChannel/PAgP is used, set both sides of the interconnect to desirable.

Note   The IEEE defined an industry-standard 802.3ad, a control protocol for link aggregation called Link Aggregate Control Protocol (LACP).

Consider Implementing Routing in the Building Access Layer

A routing protocol like Enhanced Interior Gateway Routing Protocol (EIGRP), when properly tuned, can achieve better convergence results than designs that rely on STP to resolve convergence events.

Note   Routing in the access layer is not as widely deployed in the field; this is mainly because of budgetary restrictions. Typically, the Layer 2 and Layer 3 boundary is between the access and distribution layers.

Design Considerations for the Building Distribution Layer

When implementing the building distribution layer, consider the following questions:

1. What is the required speed for the uplinks to the building core switches?

2. What cabling is currently available in the wiring closet, and what cabling options exist for uplink connectivity?

3. How many devices will each building distribution switch handle?

4. What type and level of redundancy are required? How many uplinks are needed?

5. As network services are introduced, can the network continue to deliver high performance for all its applications, such as video on demand (VoD), IP multicast, or IP telephony?

The network designer must pay special attention to the following network characteristics:

■   **Performance:** Building distribution switches should provide wire-speed performance on all ports. This feature is important because of building access layer aggregation as well as high-speed connectivity of the core switches.

■   **Redundancy:** Redundant building distribution layer switches and redundant connections to the core should be implemented. Using equal-cost redundant connections to the core supports fast convergence and avoids routing black holes. Network bandwidth and capacity should be engineered to withstand node or link failure.

When redundant switches cannot be implemented in the campus core and building distribution layers, redundant supervisors and the Stateful Switchover (SSO) and Cisco Nonstop Forwarding (NSF) technologies can provide significant resiliency improvements. These technologies result in one to three seconds of outage on a failover, which is less than the time needed to replace a supervisor and recover its configuration. Depending on the switch platform, full-image, In-Service Software Upgrade (ISSU) technology might be available so that the complete Cisco IOS Software image can be upgraded without taking the switch or network out of service, maximizing network availability.

■   **Infrastructure services:** Building distribution switches should not only support fast multilayer switching but should also incorporate network services such as high availability, QoS, security, and policy enforcement. The expansion or reconfiguration of the building distribution devices should be easy and efficient. These devices must support the required management features.

Best Practices in the Distribution Layer

When implementing the building distribution layer for the campus, the following recommendations should be followed for optimal convergence:

■   **Use first-hop redundancy protocols:** Convergence around a link or node failure in the Layer 2 and Layer 3 distribution boundary model depends on the default gateway redundancy and failover. Hot Standby Router Protocol (HSRP) or Gateway Load Balancing Protocol (GLBP) can be configured to achieve subsecond convergence and avoid routing black holes, if implementing Layer 2 between the access and distribution switches. In a mixed vendor environment, the Virtual Router Redundancy Protocol (VRRP) is an open standard first-hop redundancy protocol option.

■ **Deploy Layer 3 routing protocols from the distribution switches to the core switches:** Routing protocols from the building distribution switches to the core switches can support fast deterministic convergence for the distribution layer across redundant links.

■ **If required, connect distribution nodes to support Layer 2 VLANs spanning multiple access layer switches:** In a less-than-optimal design, where VLANs span multiple access layer switches, the distribution nodes must be linked by a Layer 2 connection, or the access switches must be connected through trunks. Otherwise, packets can be lost, and multiple convergence events can occur for a single interswitch link issue.

Using First-Hop Redundancy Protocols

The building distribution switch typically provides first-hop redundancy for default gateway redundancy using HSRP, GLBP, or VRRP. Default gateway redundancy is an important component in convergence in a hierarchical network design. This is illustrated in Figure 4-7. The redundancy allows a network to recover from the failure of the device that is acting as the default gateway for end nodes on a physical segment. Uplink tracking should also be implemented with a first-hop redundancy protocol.

Note   HSRP or GLBP timers can be reliably tuned to achieve 800 ms or better convergence for link or node failure in the Layer 2 and Layer 3 boundary in the building distribution layer.

In Cisco deployments, HSRP is typically used as the default gateway redundancy protocol. VRRP is an Internet Engineering Task Force (IETF) standards-based method of providing default gateway redundancy. More deployments are starting to utilize GLBP, because load balancing is more easily achieved on the uplinks from the access layer to the distribution layer, as well as first-hop redundancy and failure protection.

Note   A first-hop redundancy protocol only needs to be implemented if Layer 2 is implemented between the access switch and the distribution switch. If Layer 3 is implemented at the access switch, the default gateway is your access switch.

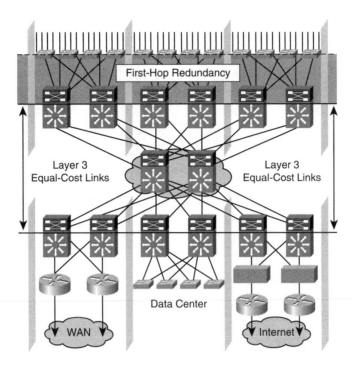

Figure 4-7   *First-Hop Redundancy Protocol Example*

Deploying Layer 3 Routing Protocols

Convergence based on the up or down state of a point-to-point physical link is faster than timer-based nondeterministic convergence. Instead of indirect neighbor or route loss detection using hellos and dead timers, physical link loss indicates that a path is unusable. All traffic is rerouted to the alternative equal-cost path.

For optimum distribution layer–to–core layer convergence, build redundant triangles, not squares, to take advantage of equal-cost redundant paths for the best deterministic convergence. Figure 4-8 illustrates the difference.

Layer 3 Distribution Interconnection

In the topology shown in Figure 4-9, the distribution layer interconnection is a Layer 3 point-to-point link. No VLANs span between access layer switches across the distribution switches. From an STP perspective, both access layer uplinks are forwarding, so the only convergence dependencies are the default gateway and return path route selection across the distribution-to-distribution link.

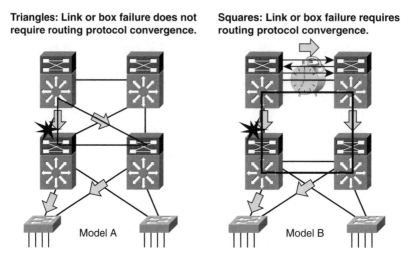

Figure 4-8 *Redundant Triangles Versus Redundant Squares*

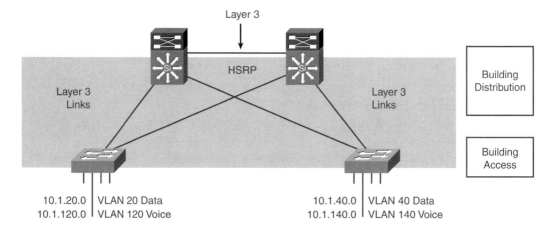

Figure 4-9 *Layer 3 Distribution Interconnection*

Layer 2 Distribution Interconnection

In the design shown in Figure 4-10, if VLANs must be supported between multiple distribution layer switches, STP will affect the network convergence. This design is more complex than the Layer 3 interconnection of the distribution switches. The STP convergence process will be initiated for uplink failures and recoveries.

The following steps should be taken to improve this suboptimal design:

■ Use RPVST+ as the version of STP.

■ Provide a Layer 2 link between the two distribution switches to avoid unexpected traffic paths and multiple convergence events.

■ If load balancing VLANs across uplinks, be sure to place the HSRP primary and the STP primary on the same distribution layer switch. The HSRP and RPVST+ root should be colocated on the same distribution switches to avoid using the interdistribution link for transit.

■ If multiple VLANs are implemented at the access layer, implement trunking between the access and distribution layers.

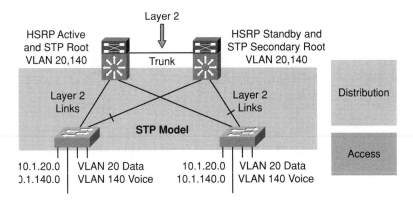

Figure 4-10 *Layer 2 Distribution Interconnection*

Using the Virtual Switching System at the Distribution Layer

In the topology shown in Figure 4-11, a distribution switch pair running the Virtual Switching System (VSS) can now be configured to run as a single logical switch. Rather than using an access switch configured with two uplinks to two distribution switches and needing a control protocol to determine which of the uplinks to use, now the access switch has a single Multichassis EtherChannel (MEC) upstream link connected to a single distribution switch.

Traffic is load-balanced per flow, rather than per client or per subnet. If one of the uplinks fails, the EtherChannel automatically redistributes all traffic to the remaining links in the uplink bundle, rather than waiting for STP, HSRP, or any other protocol to converge. The unification of the distribution switches is provided by a special-purpose EtherChannel bundle called Virtual Switch Link (VSL).

The following is a list of VSS best practices:

■ Use VSS to reduce configuration errors and eliminate first-hop redundancy protocols (FHRP) such as HSRP, GLBP, and VRRP.

■ Set the PAgP and Link Aggregation Control Protocol (LACP) timer settings to default values and use the normal UniDirectional Link Detection (UDLD) to monitor link integrity.

- Do not enable Loop Guard in a VSS-enabled campus network.

- Always bundle the link numbers in the VSL port channels in a power of 2 (for example, 2, 4, and 8) to optimize the traffic flow for load sharing.

- Trunks at both ends of the interfaces should be configured using the desirable-desirable or auto-desirable option in a VSS-enabled design.

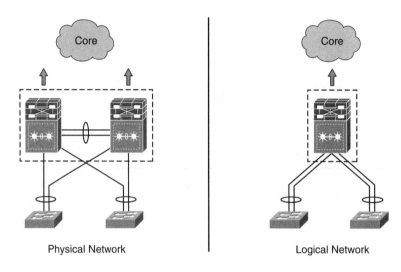

Figure 4-11 *Distribution Layer Redundancy with VSS*

Campus Core Design Considerations

Low price per port and high port density can govern access wiring closet environments, but high performance and high availability influence the design for the campus core layer.

Using core switches reduces the number of connections between the building distribution switches and simplifies the integration of the data center and enterprise edge modules. Campus core switches are primarily focused on wire-speed forwarding on all interfaces and are differentiated by the level of performance achieved per port rather than by high port densities.

As a recommended practice, a dedicated campus core layer should be deployed to connect three or more buildings in the enterprise campus, or four or more pairs of building distribution switches in a very large campus. The campus core helps make scaling the network easier. With a campus core, new building distribution switches would need connectivity only to the core, rather than full-mesh connectivity to all the distribution switches.

Note Not all campus implementations will need a campus core. As will be discussed layer in this chapter, the core and distribution layers can be combined at the distribution layer for a smaller campus.

When you implement a campus core layer, the issues to consider in a campus core layer design include

- The performance required in the campus core network, as well as the number of high-capacity ports for building distribution layer aggregation and connection to the data center or enterprise edge modules.

- The need for high availability and redundancy. Deploy at least two separate switches ideally located in different buildings. Core switches are typically multilayer switches.

Another campus core consideration is enterprise edge and WAN connectivity. For many organizations, the campus core provides these through edge distribution switches connected to the core.

Typically, the campus core switches should deliver high-performance, multilayer switching solutions for the enterprise campus and should address requirements for the following:

- Gigabit density

- Data and voice integration

- LAN, WAN, and metropolitan-area network (MAN) convergence

- Scalability

- High availability

- Intelligent multilayer switching in the campus core and to the building distribution and data center environments

For a large campus, the most flexible and scalable campus core layer consists of dual multilayer switches, as illustrated in Figure 4-12.

Multilayer switched campus core layers have several best-practice features:

- **Reduced multilayer switch peering (routing adjacencies):** Each multilayer building distribution switch connects to only two multilayer campus core switches, using a redundant triangle configuration. This implementation simplifies any-to-any connectivity between building distribution and campus core switches and is scalable to an arbitrarily large size. It also supports redundancy and load sharing.

- **Topology with no spanning-tree loops:** There is no STP activity in the campus core or on the building distribution links to the campus core layer, because all the links are Layer 3 (routed) links. Arbitrary topologies are supported by the routing protocol used in the campus core layer. Because the core is routed, it also provides multicast and broadcast control.

- **Improved network infrastructure services support:** Multilayer campus core switches provide better support for intelligent network services than data link layer core switches can support.

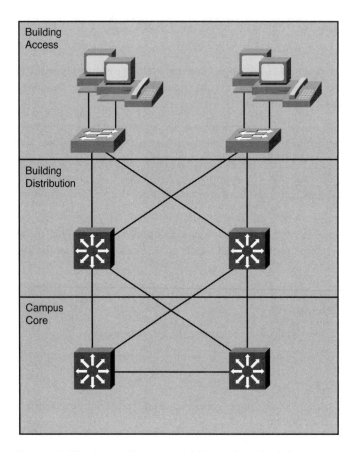

Figure 4-12 *Large Campus Multilayer-Switched Campus Core Design*

This design maintains two equal-cost paths to every destination network. Recovery from any link failure is fast and load sharing is possible, which results in higher throughput in the campus core layer.

Multilayer switches are more sophisticated devices for high-speed packet routing. The switches can support Layer 3 and higher functions in the hardware, although the hardware might not support all features.

Note   If a selected feature, such as security or QoS, is not supported in hardware, the switch must perform the function in software, which may dramatically reduce the data transfer rate.

Small and Medium Campus Design Options

A small campus or large branch network might have fewer than 200 end devices. The network servers and workstations might be connected to the same wiring closet. Switches in small campus network designs might not require high-end switching performance or much scaling capability.

In many cases, the campus core and building distribution layers can be combined into a single layer, as illustrated on the left of Figure 4-13. A low-end multilayer switch provides routing services closer to the end user when multiple VLANs exist. For a very small office, one low-end multilayer switch can support the LAN access requirements for the entire office.

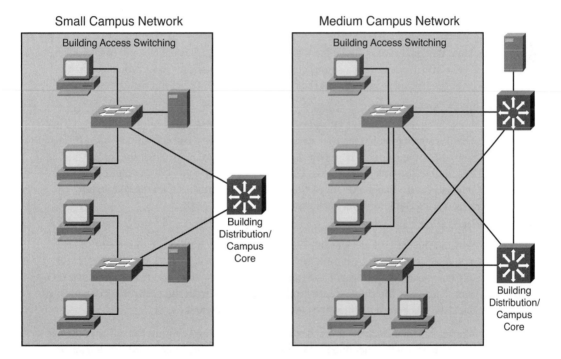

Figure 4-13 *Small and Medium Campus Collapsed Core*

For a medium-sized campus with 200 to 1000 end devices, the network infrastructure typically consists of building access layer switches with uplinks to building distribution multilayer switches that can support the performance requirements of a medium-sized campus network. If redundancy is required, redundant multilayer switches can attach to the building access switches. They provide full link redundancy, as illustrated on the right side of Figure 4-13.

> **Note**   Additional discussions of branch and teleworker infrastructure considerations are covered in Chapter 5.

Edge Distribution at the Campus Core

The edge distribution switches filter and route traffic into the campus core. Multilayer switches are the key devices that aggregate edge connectivity and provide advanced services. In the edge distribution module, the speed of switching is not as important as security. The edge distribution module isolates and controls access to devices that are located in the enterprise edge and enterprise WAN modules. The enterprise edge servers are closer to the external users and, therefore, introduce a higher risk to the internal campus. To protect the core from threats, the switches in the edge distribution module must protect the campus from the following attacks:

■ **Unauthorized access:** The edge distribution must verify each user and user rights before traffic passes to the campus core. Filtering mechanisms must provide control over specific edge subnets and their ability to reach areas within the campus.

■ **IP spoofing:** IP spoofing is a hacker technique for impersonating the identity of another user by using the IP address of that user. Denial of service (DoS) attacks use the IP-spoofing technique to generate requests to the servers, with the stolen IP address as the source. The server does not respond to the original source but does respond to the stolen IP address. DoS attacks are difficult to detect and defend against. A significant amount of this type of traffic makes the attacked server unavailable and interrupts business.

■ **Network reconnaissance:** Sending packets into the network and collecting responses from the network devices implement network reconnaissance (discovery). These responses provide basic information about the internal network topology. Network intruders use this approach to learn about network devices and the services that they run. Therefore, filtering potential traffic that results from the network reconnaissance mechanisms before it enters the enterprise network can be crucial.

■ **Packet sniffers:** Packet sniffers, devices that monitor and capture the traffic in the network, represent another threat. Packets that belong to the same broadcast domain are vulnerable to capture by packet sniffers, especially if the packets are broadcast or multicast. Multilayer switches can make it harder for a packet sniffer attack to be effective.

The edge distribution devices provide the last line of defense for all external traffic that is destined for the campus infrastructure module. In terms of overall functionality, the campus edge distribution switches are similar to the building distribution layer. Both use access control to filter traffic, although the edge distribution switches can rely on the other enterprise and WAN modules to provide additional security. Both modules use multilayer switching to achieve high performance. The edge distribution module can provide additional security functions because its performance requirements might not be as high.

When the enterprise includes a significant data center rather than a simple server farm, remote connectivity and performance requirements are more stringent. Edge distribution switches can be located in the data center, giving remote users easier access to corporate resources. Appropriate security concerns need to be addressed in this module.

Describing Enterprise Data Center Considerations

The multilayer approach to campus network design generally applies to the network infrastructure, network services, and applications in the enterprise data center. The following sections describe general enterprise data center considerations that should be considered in the enterprise design. These sections also provide an overview of the general technologies and models that are used in the enterprise data center design. Detailed data center design is not covered in this book.

Describing the Enterprise Data Center Architectures

Figure 4-14 shows how data centers have changed in the last two decades.

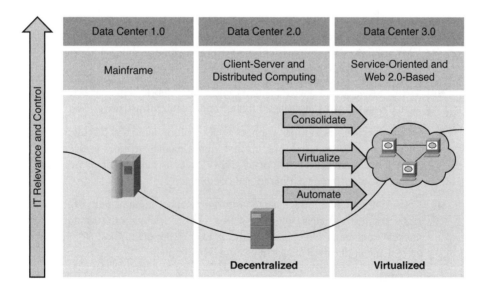

Figure 4-14 *Evolution of Data Center "Architectures"*

At first, data centers were monolithic and centralized, employing mainframes and terminals that the users employed to perform their work on the mainframe. The mainframes are still utilized in the finance sector because they are an advantageous solution in terms of availability, resilience, and service-level agreements (SLA).

The second era emphasized client/server and distributed computing with applications designed so that the user could apply client software to access an application. Also, services were distributed because of poor computing ability and high link cost. Mainframes were too expensive to serve as an alternate solution.

Currently, with communication infrastructure being relatively cheaper, and an increase in computing capacities, data centers are being consolidated. Consolidation resolves the long-term expense issue of the distributed approach. The new solution utilizes equipment virtualization, resulting in a much higher utilization of servers than in the distributed approach. The new solution also brings a significantly higher return on investment (ROI) and lower total cost of ownership (TCO).

Cisco Enterprise Data Center Architecture Framework

Cisco Data Center 3.0 includes a comprehensive portfolio of virtualization technologies and services that bring network, compute/storage, and virtualization platforms closer together. These technologies and services provide unparalleled flexibility, visibility, and policy enforcement within virtualized data centers. The following are the three main components of the data center architectures:

- **Virtualization:**

  - Cisco VN-Link technologies, including the Nexus 1000V virtual switch for VMware ESX, deliver consistent per-virtual-machine visibility and policy control for SAN, LAN, and unified fabric.

  - Virtual SAN, virtual device contents, and unified fabric help converge multiple virtual networks to simplify and reduce data center infrastructure and TCO.

  - Flexible networking options support all server form factors and vendors, including options for integrated Ethernet and Fibre Channel switches for Dell, IBM, and HP blade servers. These options provide a consistent set of services across the data center to reduce operational complexity.

  - Cisco Unified Computing System unifies network, compute, and virtualization resources into a single system that delivers end-to-end optimization for virtualized environments, while retaining the ability to support traditional operating system and application stacks in physical environments.

- **Unified fabric:**

  - There are two primary approaches to deploying a unified data center fabric: Fibre Channel over Ethernet (FCoE) and Internet Small Computer Systems Interface (iSCSI). Both are supported on the unified fabric, which provides a reliable 10 Gigabit Ethernet foundation.

  - Unified fabric lossless operation also improves the performance of iSCSI that is supported by both Cisco Catalyst and Cisco Nexus Series switches. In addition, the Cisco MDS series of storage switches has hardware and software features that are specifically designed to support iSCSI.

- The Cisco Nexus family of switches was designed to support unified fabric. Currently, the Cisco Nexus 5000 and Nexus 4000 support Data Center Bridging (DCB) and FCoE, while support on the Nexus 7000 is forthcoming, as is FCoE support on the Cisco MDS family.

- Special host adapters, called *converged network adapters*, are required to support FCoE. Hardware adapters are available from Emulex and QLogic, while a software stack is available for certain Intel 10 Gigabit Ethernet network interfaces.

- FCoE is supported on VMware ESX vSphere and higher.

- **Unified computing:** The Cisco Unified Computing System is a next-generation data center platform that accomplishes the following:

  - Unites computing, networking, storage access, and virtualization into a cohesive system

  - Integrates a low-latency, lossless 10 Gigabit Ethernet unified network fabric with enterprise-class, x86-architecture servers

  - Increases IT staff productivity and business agility through just-in-time provisioning and mobility support

  - Provides a standards-based unified network fabric that is supported by a partner ecosystem of industry leaders

  - Offers Cisco VN-Link virtualization support

  - Offers Cisco Extended Memory Technology

As shown in Figure 4-15, starting with the top layer of components, virtual machines (VM) are one of the key components of the Cisco Data Center 3.0. VMs are entities that are running an application within the client operating system, which is further virtualized and running on common hardware.

The logical server personality is defined using management software. The logical server personality defines the properties of the server, which include the following:

- Amount of memory

- Percent of total computing power

- Number of network interface cards (NIC)

- Boot image

The network hardware serves as consolidated connectivity, such as the Cisco Nexus 5000 line of products. FCoE is one of the key technologies that provide fabric unification.

VLANs and virtual storage-area networks (VSAN) provide virtualized LAN and SAN connectivity, separating physical networks and equipment into virtual entities.

On the lowest layers, there is virtualized hardware. Storage devices can be virtualized into storage pools, and network devices are virtualized using device contexts.

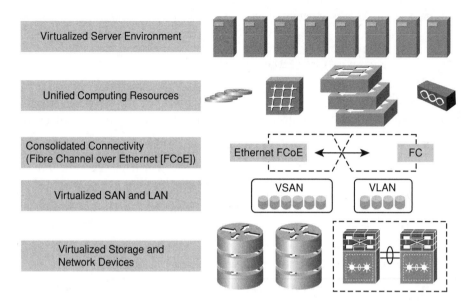

Figure 4-15 *Data Center 3.0 Component Layout*

Server Challenges

Along with facilities and network equipment, servers are also a key factor in the data centers and can present certain challenges. A high number of servers consume a lot of energy, and energy efficiency is very important. Rack servers are more cost-effective. They provide high performance but consume space and energy, which can be costly. Additional efficiency efforts need to be considered because of these cost factors. Blade servers provide similar computing power, but on a smaller-space footprint, with smaller cabling and powering requirements.

On both types of servers, software virtualization is used to increase server utilization. It requires fewer physical servers and provides more availability. For managing servers, solutions range from manufacturer-specific (for example, Integrated Lights Out [iLO]) to virtualization-specific (for example, VMware Infrastructure Client). These products ease the management overhead required to manage a large quantity of servers.

Data Center Facility Aspects

The data center facility has multiple aspects that need to be properly addressed when the facility is being planned, designed, and built.

The architectural and mechanical faculty specifications define

- Available space
- Amount of load a floor can bear

- Available power capacity for data center deployment

- Available cooling capacity

- Cabling infrastructure type and management

In addition, the facility must also meet certain environmental conditions. The type of data center devices defines the operating temperature and humidity levels that must be maintained.

Physical security is vital. The data center typically houses data that should not be available to third parties. Access to the premises must be well controlled. Protection of equipment and data from certain disasters should be employed as well. This includes fire protection and alarm systems. Facility capacities are limited and need to be properly designed. Companies must also address regulatory issues, enable business resilience, and comply with environmental requirements. Data centers need to implement an infrastructure that can protect and recover applications, communications, and information and provide uninterrupted access.

When it comes to building a reliable data center and maximizing an investment, the design must be considered early in the building development process. The design should encompass coordinated efforts that cut across several areas of expertise, including telecommunications, power, architectural, and HVAC.

Each of the components of the data center and it supporting systems must be planned, designed, and implemented to work together to ensure reliable access while supporting future requirements. Neglecting any aspect of the design can render the data center vulnerable to costly failures, early obsolescence, and intolerable levels of availability. There is no substitute for careful planning and following the guidelines for data center physical design.

Space

The space aspect involves the physical footprint of the data center. This includes

- How to size the data center

- Where to locate servers within a multipurpose building

- How to make it adaptable for future needs and growth

- How to construct the data center to effectively protect the valuable equipment inside

The data center space defines the number of racks that can be used and the equipment that can be installed. These are not the only parameters to consider. Another equally important parameter is the floor loading capability, which determines which and how much equipment can be installed in a certain rack. The weight of the rack is also a consideration. Correct placement and need for future equipment must be carefully analyzed so that data center physical infrastructure and support are deployed optimally.

Sometimes neglected, the size of the data center has a great influence on cost, lifespan, and flexibility. It is essential to determine the proper size of the data center. Although it can prove challenging, this task should be done correctly. It must take into account several variables, including

- The number of people supporting the data center

- The number and type of servers, storage, and networking gear utilized

- The size of nonserver/storage/network areas, which depends on how passive infrastructure is deployed

Be aware that a data center that is too small will not adequately meet server, storage, and network requirements and will inhibit productivity and generate additional costs for upgrades or expansions. Alternatively, an extensive data center is a waste of money from the initial construction to the perspective of ongoing operational expenses.

Properly sized data center facilities also take into account the placement of equipment. If properly selected, the data center facility can grow when needed. Otherwise, costly upgrades or relocations must be performed.

Considerations for cabinets and racks include

- Loading, which determines what and how many devices can be installed

- Weight of the rack and equipment installed

- Heat produced by the equipment installed

- Power consumed by the equipment installed

Power

The power in the data center facility is used to power servers, storage, network equipment, lighting, and cooling devices (a major part). Some power is "lost" upon conversion.

The variability of usage is hard to predict when determining power requirements for the equipment in the data center. The server environment's power usage is dependent on the computing load. The harder that the processor of the server works, the greater the power draw from the AC supply. This, of course, determines the heat output that needs to be dissipated.

Power requirements are based on the desired reliability. It can include two or more power feeds from the utility, an uninterruptible power supply (UPS), multiple circuits to systems and equipment, and on-site generators. It takes careful planning to determine power requirements.

Estimating power needs involves analysis of the power required for existing and anticipated devices. Power requirements must also be estimated for all support equipment, such as UPSs, generators, conditioning electronics, HVAC, lighting, and so on. The power estimation must be created to accommodate required redundancy and future growth.

The facility electrical system must power data center equipment such as servers, storage, and network equipment. It must also insulate the equipment against surges, utility power failures, and other potential electrical problems (thus addressing the redundancy requirements).

Physically, the power system must accommodate electrical infrastructure elements such as power distribution units (PDU), circuit breaker panels, electrical conduits, wiring, and so on.

Cooling

Environmental conditions such as temperature and humidity must be controlled. They are considered by deploying probes to measure temperature fluctuations, data center hot spots, and relative humidity, and by using smoke detectors.

Overheating is an equipment issue with high-density computing. Some factors include

- More heat overall.

- Hot spots.

- High heat and humidity threaten equipment life spans.

- Computing power and memory requirements demand more power and generate more heat.

- Data center demand for space-saving servers (density=heat). 3 kilowatts (kW) per chassis is not a problem for one chassis, but five or six chassis/racks = 20 kW.

- Humidity levels affect static electricity and condensation; maintaining a 40 to 55 percent relative humidity level is recommended.

The facilities must have proper airflow to reduce the amount of heat generated by concentrated equipment. Adequate cooling equipment must be used for flexible cooling. Additionally, the cabinets and racks should be arranged in an alternating pattern to create "hot" and "cold" aisles. In the cold aisle, equipment racks are arranged face to face. In the hot aisle, the equipment racks are arranged back to back. Perforated tiles in the raised floor of the cold aisles allow cold air to be drawn into the face of the equipment. The cold air is washed over the equipment and is expelled out the back into the hot aisle. In the hot aisle, there are no perforated tiles. This prevents the hot air from mingling with the cold air.

Not every active piece of equipment exhausts heat out the back. Other considerations for cooling include

- Increase airflow by blocking unnecessary air escapes and/or increasing the height of the raised floor.

- Spread equipment out over unused portions of the raised floor if space permits.

- Use open racks instead of cabinets when security is not a concern, or use cabinets with mesh fronts and backs.

- Use perforated tiles with larger openings.

Here is some helpful conversion information: One watt = 3.41214 British Thermal Units (BTU). This value is a generally used value for converting electrical values to BTUs and vice versa. Many manufacturers publish kW, kilovolt ampere (kVA), and BTU ratings in their equipment specifications. Sometimes, dividing the BTU value by 3.413 does not equal the published wattage. It is recommended that you use information provided by the manufacturer. If data is unavailable, the previous formula can be helpful.

Although the blade server deployment optimizes the computing/heat ratio, the heat produced actually increases since the blade servers are space optimized. It allows more servers to be deployed in a single rack. High-density equipment produces a lot of heat. In addition, the increasing computing and memory power of a single server results in higher heat production. Thus, the blade server deployment results in more heat being produced, which requires proper cooling capacity and proper data center design. The solutions that address the increasing heat requirements must be considered when blade servers are deployed within the data center. The design must also take into consideration the cooling that is required for the current sizing of the data center servers as well as anticipated growth. It should also take into account future heat production. If cooling is not properly addressed and designed, the result is a shortened equipment life span.

The cooling solution can address the increasing heat by following these recommendations:

■ Increase the space between the racks/rows.

■ Increase the number of HVAC units.

■ Increase the airflow through the devices.

■ Utilize new technologies, such as water-cooled racks.

Cabling

The data center's cabling, the passive infrastructure, is equally important for proper data center operation. A structured and well-organized physical hierarchy aids the data center operation. The electrical infrastructure is crucial for keeping server, storage, and network devices up and running. The physical network cabling, which runs and terminates between devices, dictates if and how these devices communicate with one another and the outside world.

The cabling infrastructure also governs the physical connector and media type of the connector. Two options are widely used today: copper and fiber optics–based cabling.

Fiber optics are less susceptible to external interferences and offer greater distances while copper is ubiquitous and less costly. The cabling must be abundant to provide ample connectivity and employ various media types to accommodate different connectivity requirements. It must remain well organized for the passive infrastructure to be easy to maintain. (No one wants a data center where the cables run across the floor, creating a health and safety hazard.) Typically, the cabling needs to be deployed in tight spaces, terminating at various devices.

Cabling usability and simplicity are affected by

- Media selection

- Number of connections provided

- Type of cabling termination organizers

These parameters must be addressed during the initial facility design. Server, storage, network components, and all employed technologies must be evaluated.

Proper cabling infrastructure design can prevent the following issues from occurring:

- Improper cooling because of restricted airflow

- Hard-to-implement troubleshooting

- Unplanned dependencies resulting in more downtime upon single component replacement

- Downtimes because of accidental disconnects

For example, with under-floor cabling, airflow is restricted by power and data cables. Raised flooring is a difficult environment in which to manage cables because cable changes mean lifting floor panels and potentially having to move equipment racks.

The solution is a cable management system consisting of integrated channels located above the rack for connectivity. Cables should be located in the front or rear of the rack for easy access. Typically, cabling is located in the front of the rack in service provider environments. Remember that when data center cabling is deployed, the space constraints and presence of operating devices (namely, servers, storage, and networking gear) make cabling infrastructure reconfiguration difficult. Thus, scalable cabling is crucial for proper data center operation and lifespan. Conversely, poorly designed cabling will incur downtime because of reconfiguration or expansion requirements that were not considered by the original cabling infrastructure. Cable management is a major topic in its own right. Working with the facilities team that installs and maintains the data center cabling allows a better understanding of potential complications with a new or reconfigured environment in the data center.

Enterprise Data Center Infrastructure

Figure 4-16 shows a typical large enterprise data center design. The design follows the Cisco multilayer infrastructure architecture, including core, aggregation (or distribution), and access layers.

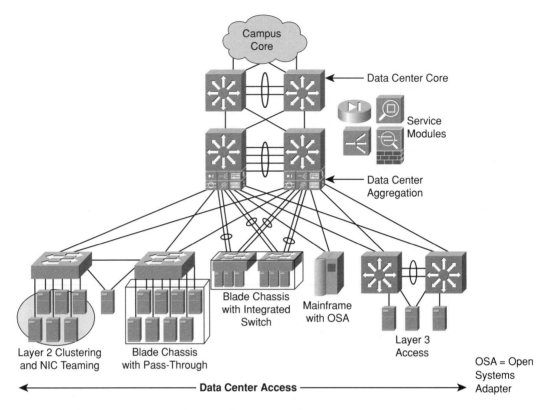

Figure 4-16 *Enterprise Data Center Infrastructure Overview*

The data center infrastructure must provide port density and Layer 2 and Layer 3 connectivity for servers at the access layer. At the same time, the infrastructure must also support security services that are provided by access control lists (ACL), firewalls, and intrusion prevention systems (IPS) at the data center aggregation layer. The data center infrastructure must support server farm services, such as content switching, caching, and Secure Socket Layer (SSL) offloading, while integrating with multitier server farms, mainframes, and mainframe services (such as TN3270, load balancing, and SSL offloading). Network devices are often deployed in redundant pairs to avoid a single point of failure.

Data Center Access Layer

The data center access layer provides Layer 2, Layer 3, and mainframe connectivity. The design of the access layer varies depending on whether Layer 2 or Layer 3 access is used. The access layer in the data center is typically built at Layer 2, which allows more efficient sharing of service devices across multiple servers. It also allows the use of Layer 2 clustering, which requires the servers to be Layer 2 adjacent. With Layer 2 access, the default gateway for the servers can be configured at the access layer or the aggregation layer.

With a dual-homing NIC, a VLAN or trunk between the two access switches is required to support the single IP address on the two server links to two separate switches. The default gateway is implemented at the access layer as well.

Although Layer 2 at the aggregation layer is tolerated for legacy designs, new designs try to contain Layer 2 to the access layer. With Layer 2 at the aggregation layer, there are physical loops in the topology that must be managed by STP. Rapid per-VLAN Spanning Tree Plus (RPVST+) is a recommended best practice to ensure a logically loop-free topology over the physical topology.

A mix of both Layer 2 and Layer 3 access models with one rack unit (1RU) and modular platforms permits a flexible solution and allows application environments to be optimally positioned.

Data Center Aggregation Layer

The aggregation layer (distribution layer) collects the uplinks from the access layer to the data center core. This layer is the critical point for control and application services. Security and application service devices (such as load-balancing devices, SSL offloading devices, firewalls, and IPS devices) are often deployed as a module in the aggregation layer. This design lowers TCO and reduces complexity by reducing the number of components needed to configure and manage.

The aggregation layer typically provides Layer 3 connectivity from the data center to the core. Depending on the requirements and the design, the boundary between Layer 2 and Layer 3 at the aggregation layer can be in the multilayer switches, the firewalls, or the content-switching devices in the aggregation layer. The aggregation layer might also need to support a large STP processing load depending on the data center applications.

Data Center Core Layer

Implementing a data center core is a best practice for large data centers. It initially prevents disruption to the data center environment if a core has to be introduced at a later date. Consider the following drivers when determining whether a core solution is appropriate:

- **10 Gigabit Ethernet density:** Without a data center core, will there be enough 10 Gigabit Ethernet ports on the campus core switch pair to support both the campus distribution and the data center aggregation modules?

- **Administrative domains and policies:** Separate cores help to isolate campus distribution layers from data center aggregation layers for troubleshooting, administration, and implementation of polices (such as QoS, ACLs, troubleshooting, and maintenance).

- **Anticipation of future development:** The impact that can result from implementing a separate data center core layer at a future date can make it worthwhile to install the core layer at the beginning.

The data center typically connects to the campus core using Layer 3 links. The data center network is summarized depending on the data center applications, and the core injects a default route into the data center network.

Key core characteristics include

- Distributed forwarding architecture

- Low-latency switching

- 10 Gigabit Ethernet scalability

- Scalable IP multicast support

Describing Enterprise Network Virtualization Tools

As the demand has grown for IT departments to cut costs while improving efficiency, virtualization has become a critical element in today's enterprise network. With virtualization technologies, businesses can enable a single physical device or resource to act like multiple versions of itself. Virtualization can also enable multiple physical devices to act as one single logical device.

Virtualization is a crucial element of the Cisco Network Architectures for the Enterprise. The use of virtualization enhances agility and improves network efficiency, reducing both capital expenses and operational expenses.

The following sections discuss the common network and device technologies and their benefits. In addition, key considerations for network virtualization design are covered.

Virtualization Challenges

Network designers face many challenges that drive the need for virtualization. The following represents a few of these drivers:

- There is a need to reduce the growing operational cost of housing, powering, and cooling the devices in the data center, while at the same time increasing productivity. In today's rapidly growing data centers, this challenge directly impacts the profitability of the business.

- There is a need to provide access for different users to the same physical network, while keeping users logically separate to the degree that they have no visibility into other groups. This requirement has challenged network managers for many years.

- The ability to provide flexible connectivity options while keeping user groups closed is vital in today's campus networks.

- There is a need to reduce the number of physical devices that are performing individual tasks.

- There is a need to eliminate underutilized hardware that yields poor price/performance ratios.

What Is Virtualization?

Virtualization is a general term used to represent a variety of different technologies. The common theme among these technologies is the ability to abstract logical components from hardware (for example, operating systems and applications) or networks (for example, LANs and SANs) and run them in a virtual environment.

There are a number of advantages to using virtualization:

■ It consolidates many low-performance devices into a few high-performance devices. This provides a more efficient utilization of hardware, which increases the price/performance ratio.

■ It provides flexibility that makes it easier to add, reassign, or repurpose resources in the system.

■ It provides better use of computing resources, higher server densities, and seamless server migrations.

■ It separates users that are accessing the same physical network into groups with visibility into only their assigned logical network.

■ It provides distinct security policies to different departments.

Types of Virtualization

Two different types of virtualization technologies are used in enterprise networks today:

■ **Network virtualization:** Refers to the creation of logical isolated network partitions that are overlaid on a common physical infrastructure. Each partition is logically isolated from the others. Each partition must behave and appear as a fully dedicated network to provide privacy, security, and an independent set of policies, service levels, and even routing decisions. Here are examples of network virtualization technologies:

   ■ **VLAN:** Virtual local-area network

   ■ **VSAN:** Virtual storage-area network

   ■ **VPN:** Virtual Private Network

   ■ **VRF:** Virtual Routing and Forwarding

■ **Device virtualization:** Enables a single physical device to act like multiple versions of itself. Device virtualization allows logical devices to run independently of each other on a single physical server. This is possible through the creation (in software) of virtual device hardware that can function like the physical hardware. In addition, device virtualization provides the ability to combine multiple physical devices into one logical unit. Here are some examples:

   ■ Server virtualization

   ■ Cisco Adaptive Security Appliance (ASA) firewall context

- Cisco Application Control Engine (ACE) context

- Virtual Switching System (VSS)

Virtualization Technologies

The following are examples of network virtualization:

- **Virtual Switching System (VSS):** A network system virtualization technology that pools multiple Cisco Catalyst 6500 Series switches into one virtual switch, increasing operational efficiency, boosting nonstop communications, and scaling system bandwidth capacity to 1.4 Tbps. At the initial phase, a VSS will allow two physical Cisco Catalyst 6500 Series switches to operate as a single logical virtual switch, which is called a Virtual Switching System.

- **Virtual Routing and Forwarding (VRF):** A routing virtualization technology that creates multiple logical Layer 3 routing and forwarding instances that coexist within a single physical router. VRF plays a major role in VPN technologies like Multiprotocol Label Switching (MPLS). Routing information is visible only within each instance, allowing duplicate IP addressing schemes.

- **Virtual PortChannel (vPC):** vPCs combine two Cisco Nexus 7000 Series switches or two Cisco Nexus 5000 Series switches in such a way that they represent themselves as a single logical switch to neighboring devices, to allow these neighboring devices to create an EtherChannel link to virtual logical switch.

The following are examples of device virtualization:

- **Device context:** Enables the ability to partition a single appliance into multiple virtual devices, known as a context. Each context is an independent device with its own policy, interfaces, and administrators. Multiple contexts are similar to multiple standalone devices. Many of the same features available on the physical device are also supported in a virtualized context. The following represents some of the Cisco devices that support the use of context:

  - Cisco ASA

  - Cisco Intrusion Prevention System (IPS)

  - Cisco ACE

  - Cisco Nexus 7000 - Virtual Device Contexts (VDC)

- **Server virtualization:** A technique that allows the abstraction of server resources to provide flexibility and optimize usage on a standardized infrastructure. As a result, data center applications are no longer bound to specific hardware resources. This makes the application unaware of the underlying hardware, yet able to view the CPUs, memory, and network infrastructure as shared resource pools available through virtualization. The following represent some examples of server virtualization:

- VMware ESX Server

- Citrix XenServer

- Microsoft Hyper-V

Network Virtualization Design Considerations

A scalable solution is needed for keeping groups of users totally separate and centralizing services and security policies, while still preserving the high-availability, security, and scalability benefits of the campus design. To address this solution, the network design needs to effectively address these issues:

- **Access control:** Ensures that legitimate users and devices are recognized, classified, and authorized for entry to their assigned portions of the network. Security at the access layer is vital for protecting the campus LAN from external threats, whether they are inadvertent or malicious and whether they are presented by a user or harbored by an infected device. With the delivery of wireless and mobile access to the campus LAN, user authentication and other security measures take an increased importance.

- **Path isolation:** Refers to the creation of independent logical traffic paths over a shared physical network infrastructure. Path isolation ensures that the substantiated user or device is mapped to the correct secure set of available resources (in effect, the correct VPN). The main goal when segmenting the network is to preserve and improve the scalability, resiliency, and security services that are available in a nonsegmented network.

- **Services edge:** Helps ensure that the right services are accessible to the legitimate set or sets of users and devices with centralized policy enforcement. Sometimes a need arises for members of different closed user groups to communicate with each other or share network resources, typically in a limited fashion. For example, traffic from the red group can go in the blue group, but it must go through a firewall, or the communication is limited to certain hours of the day. In such cases, the network must have a central point of policy enforcement.

A highly effective way to address policy enforcement in the campus LAN is to integrate firewall services into the distribution layer.

Summary

When developing the enterprise campus and the enterprise data center designs, organization and network requirements must be analyzed. Consider the projected traffic pattern, technology performance constraints, and network reliability. The level of redundancy must also be considered along with methods to support the redundancy strategy.

The requirements can vary for different-sized campuses or data centers. The sites and the existing network must be characterized, the planned network technology must be identified, and the location of the end devices at the sites must be determined.

The enterprise campus design has an access layer and a distribution layer and can also include a core layer, depending on the size of the campus. A data center (server farm) module can be implemented to support small- to medium-sized server requirements. A separate enterprise data center can be implemented with larger-sized server requirements. The enterprise data center design has an access layer and an aggregation layer and can also include a core layer, depending on the size of the data center.

The designs should use components that support the current requirements and are adaptable to include future technologies.

References

For additional information, refer to these resources:

Cisco, Inc. Enterprise Campus 3.0 Architecture: Overview and Framework, at www.cisco.com/en/US/docs/solutions/Enterprise/Campus/campover.html.

Cisco, Inc. Introduction to Data Center Switching, at www.cisco.com/en/US/netsol/ns668/index.html.

Cisco, Inc. Design Zone for Data Centers, at www.cisco.com/en/US/netsol/ns743/networking_solutions_program_home.html.

Cisco, Inc. Network Virtualization for the Campus, at www.cisco.com/en/US/solutions/collateral/ns340/ns517/ns431/ns658/net_implementation_white_paper0900aecd804a17c9.html.

Review Questions

Answer the following questions, and then refer to Appendix A for the answers.

1. What is the difference between the 80/20 rule and the 20/80 rule?

2. Which parts of the enterprise campus typically have both high-availability and high-performance requirements?

3. A link between the building distribution and campus core is oversubscribed, but it carries mission-critical data along with Internet traffic. How would you ensure that the mission-critical applications are not adversely affected by the bandwidth limitations?

4. A corporate network is spread over four floors. Each floor has a Layer 2 switch and more than one VLAN. One connection from each floor leads to the basement, where all WAN connections are terminated and all servers are located. Traffic between VLANs is essential. What type of device should be used in the basement?

5. What are the recommended best practices related to managing VLANs and STP in the building access layer?

6. What functions does the building distribution layer provide?

7. As a recommended practice, when should a dedicated campus core layer be deployed?

8. What is the function of the edge distribution module?

9. What is the purpose of the data center aggregation layer?

10. When determining whether to implement a core layer within a data center design, what factors should you consider?]

Chapter 5

Designing Remote Connectivity

This chapter discusses wide-area network technologies and design and includes the following sections:

- Identifying WAN Technology Considerations

- Designing the Enterprise WAN

- Designing the Enterprise Branch

Connectivity to remote locations such as the Internet, branches, offices, and teleworkers is provided through enterprise edge technologies and the enterprise WAN architecture. Infrastructure support is provided at the remote locations with enterprise branch architectures.

To connect to remote locations, WAN technologies and WAN transport media must be utilized when considering ownership, reliability, and backup issues. In addition, WAN remote access choices include cable and DSL technologies that are used with Virtual Private Networks (VPN). The enterprise branch is a remote location that is smaller than an enterprise campus and can use a simpler architecture.

Identifying WAN Technology Considerations

The enterprise edge connects campus resources to remote enterprise locations. It can include the WAN, Internet connectivity, remote access, and VPN modules. Many WAN technologies exist today, and new technologies are constantly emerging. The following sections explain the role of a WAN and the requirements necessary for achieving a reliable and efficient WAN design. They also describe the characteristics of the WAN technologies that are currently available.

Review of WAN Features

A WAN is a communications network that covers a relatively broad geographic area. Most often, a WAN uses the transmission facilities that are provided by service providers (carriers) such as telephone companies. WANs generally carry various traffic types, such as voice, data, and video. A network provider often charges user fees called *tariffs* for the services that are provided by the WAN. Therefore, WAN communication is often known as a service; some considerations include

- **Service-level agreements (SLA):** Networks carry application information between computers. If the applications are not available to network users, the network is failing to achieve its design objectives. Organizations need to define what level of service, such as bandwidth or allowed latency and loss, is acceptable for the applications that run across the WAN.

- **Cost of investment and usage:** WAN designs are always subject to budget limitations. Selecting the right type of WAN technology is critical in providing reliable services for end-user applications in a cost-effective and efficient manner.

The following are the objectives of an effective WAN design:

- A well-designed WAN must reflect the goals, characteristics, and policies of an organization.

- The selected technology should be sufficient for current and (to some extent) future application requirements.

- The associated costs of investment and usage should stay within the budget limitations.

Figure 5-1 illustrates ways that WAN technologies connect the enterprise network modules.

Typically, the intent is to provide these results:

- Connectivity between the enterprise edge modules and ISPs

- Connectivity between enterprise sites across the service provider and public switched telephone network (PSTN) carrier network

- Connectivity between enterprise sites across the ISP network

WAN connections can be point-to-point between two locations or a connection to a multipoint WAN service offering, such as a Frame Relay or Multiprotocol Label Switching (MPLS) network. An alternative to WAN connections is a service provider IP network that links the remote sites of an enterprise network. Complete cooperation at the IP layer between the enterprise edge and service provider network is required for this type of connection. DSL and cable are technologies that are frequently used for ISP access for teleworkers and very small offices. This type of network service provides no guarantee of the quality of sessions and is considered a "best effort."

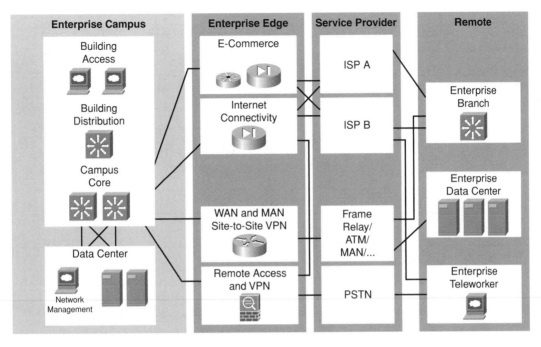

Figure 5-1   *Types of WAN Interconnections*

Comparison of WAN Transport Technologies

Table 5-1 reviews WAN technologies that are based on the main factors that influence technology selection. The table provides baseline information to help compare the performance and features that different technologies offer. The options that service providers offer usually limit technology decisions.

Table 5-1   *WAN Transport Technology Comparison*

Technology	Bandwidth	Latency and Jitter	Connect Time	Tariff	Initial Cost	Reliability
TDM	M	L	L	M	M	M
ISDN	L	M/H	M	M	L	M
Frame Relay	L	L	L	M	M	M
ATM	M/H	L	L	M	M	H
MPLS	M/H	L	L	M	M	H
Metro Ethernet	M/H	L	L	M	M	H
DSL	L/M**	M/H	L	L	L	M

Table 5-1   *WAN Transport Technology Comparison*

Technology	Bandwidth	Latency and Jitter	Connect Time	Tariff	Initial Cost	Reliability
Cable Modem	L/M**	M/H	L	L	M	L
Wireless	L/M	M/H	L	L	M	L
SONET/SDH	H	L	L	M	H	H
DWDM	H	L	L	M	H	H
Dark Fiber	H	L	L	M	H	H

*L=Low, M=Medium, H=High   **Unbalanced Transmit (Tx) and Receive (Rx)

Time-Division Multiplexing

Time-division multiplexing (TDM) reserves point-to-point connection bandwidth for transmissions indefinitely, rather than using bandwidth only as required. TDM is a type of digital multiplexing in which two or more channels are derived from a given data stream by interleaving pulses representing bits from different channels. For example, a North American T1 circuit is made up of 24 channels that run at 64 kbps, for a total of 1.536 Mbps. When framing overhead is included, the total reaches 1.544 Mbps. A T3 circuit is made up of 28 T1s or 672 channels; including overhead, a T3 circuit provides 44.736 Mbps. Corresponding European standards are the E1 standard, which supports 32 64-kbps channels for a total of 2.04 Mbps, and the E3 standard, which supports 480 64-kbps channels that provides 34.368 Mbps. A carrier can establish a connection in the TDM network by dedicating a channel with the use of TDM. By contrast, packet-switched networks traditionally offer the service provider more flexibility and use network bandwidth more efficiently than TDM networks because the network resources are shared dynamically. Subscribers using TDM are charged an amount based on their guaranteed use of the network.

ISDN Connectivity

Integrated Services Digital Network (ISDN) is a system of digital phone connections that has been available as a communications standard since 1984. This system allows voice and data to be transmitted simultaneously across the world using end-to-end digital connectivity. Connectivity over ISDN offers increased bandwidth, reduced call setup time, reduced latency, and lower signal-to-noise ratios than analog dialup. However, the industry is moving from broadband technologies such as DSL, cable, and public wireless to IP Security (IPsec) VPNs. ISDN presents an effective solution solely for remote-user applications, where broadband technologies are not available.

Analog modern dialup or plain old telephone service (POTS) provides data connectivity over the PSTN using analog modems. Dialup supports relatively low-speed connections, while broadband technologies such as DSL, cable, and public wireless are faster. Dialup point-to-point service is typically no longer a cost-effective solution for WAN connectivity. It is only cost-effective as a backup access solution for Internet connectivity in teleworker environments.

Frame Relay

Frame Relay is an example of a packet-switched technology for connecting devices on a WAN. Frame Relay has been deployed since the late 1980s. Frame Relay networks transfer data using one of two connection types:

- Permanent virtual circuits (PVC), which are permanent connections

- Switched virtual circuits (SVC), which are temporary connections that are created for each data transfer and are then terminated when the data transfer is complete (not a widely used connection)

Multiprotocol Label Switching

MPLS is a switching mechanism that uses labels (numbers) to forward packets. In a normal routed environment, frames pass from a source to a destination on a hop-by-hop basis. Transit routers evaluate the Layer 3 header of each frame and perform a route table lookup to determine the next hop toward the destination. However, MPLS enables devices to specify paths through the network. This is performed by using labels that are based on initial route lookup and classification of quality of service (QoS), as well as bandwidth needs of the applications, while taking into account Layer 2 attributes. MPLS labels can correspond to parameters such as a QoS value, a source address, or a Layer 2 circuit identifier. After a path has been established, packets that are destined to the same endpoint with the same requirements can be forwarded based on these labels, without a routing decision at every hop. Labels usually correspond to a Layer 3 destination address, which makes MPLS equal to destination-based routing. Label switching occurs regardless of the Layer 3 protocol. One of the strengths of MPLS is that it can be used to carry many kinds of traffic, including IP packets, as well as native ATM, SONET, and Ethernet frames. A designer's main objective is to minimize routing decisions and maximize switching use.

Metro Ethernet

Metro Ethernet uses Ethernet technology to deliver cost-effective, high-speed connectivity for metropolitan-area network (MAN) and WAN applications. Service providers have started to offer Metro Ethernet services to deliver converged voice, video, and data networking. Metro Ethernet provides a data-optimized connectivity solution for the MAN and WAN based on technology that is widely deployed within the enterprise LAN. Metro Ethernet supports high-performance networks in the metropolitan area, meeting the increasing need for faster data speeds and more stringent QoS requirements. Where traditional TDM access is rigid, complex, and costly to provision, Metro Ethernet services provide scalable bandwidth in flexible increments, simplified management, and faster, lower-cost provisioning. This simple, easy-to-use technology appeals to customers who are already using Ethernet throughout their LANs.

DSL Technology

Digital subscriber line (DSL) is a technology that delivers high bandwidth over traditional telephone copper lines. The term *xDSL* covers a number of similar yet competing forms of DSL. Asymmetric DSL (ADSL) is the most common form of DSL, which utilizes frequencies that normally are not used by a voice telephone call—in particular, frequencies higher than normal human hearing. ADSL can be used only over short distances, typically less than 18,000 ft. The distinguishing characteristic of ADSL over other forms of DSL is that the volume of data flow is greater in one direction than the other; that is, it is asymmetric.

Figure 5-2 illustrates a typical ADSL service architecture.

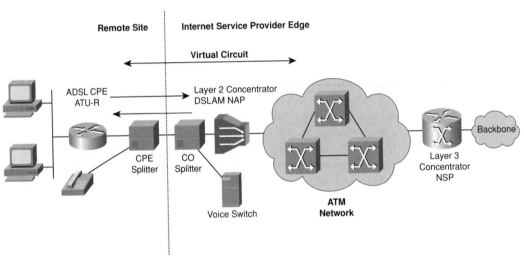

Figure 5-2   *ADSL Implementation Example*

The network consists of customer premises equipment (CPE), the network access provider (NAP), and the network service provider (NSP):

- The CPE refers to an end-user workstation, such as a PC, together with an ADSL modem or an ADSL transmission unit-remote (ATU-R).

- The NAP provides ADSL line termination by using DSL access multiplexers (DSLAM).

- The DSLAM forwards traffic to the local access concentrator, the NSP, which is used for Layer 3 termination.

An ADSL circuit connects an ADSL modem on each end of a twisted-pair telephone line. This setup creates three information channels:

- Medium-speed downstream channel

- Low-speed upstream channel

- Basic telephone service channel

Filters (splitters) split off the basic telephone service channel from the digital modem. This feature guarantees uninterrupted basic telephone service, even if ADSL fails.

Cable Technology

Cable is a technology for data transport that uses coaxial cable media over cable distribution systems. This technology is a good option for environments where cable television is widely deployed.

The Universal Broadband Router (uBR), also referred to as the cable modem termination system (CMTS), provides high-speed data connectivity and is deployed at the cable company head end. The uBR forwards data upstream to connect with either the PSTN or the Internet. The cable modem (also referred to as the cable access router) at the remote location supports voice, modem, and fax calls over the TCP/IP cable network. The uBR is designed to be installed at the head-end facility or distribution hub of a cable operator and to function as the CMTS for subscriber end devices. In general, cable operators install cable modems at the customer premises to support small businesses, branch offices, and corporate telecommuters.

Note The Data–over–Cable Service Interface Specifications (DOCSIS) protocol describes data-over-cable procedures that the equipment must support.

Wireless Technology

The term *wireless* describes telecommunications in which electromagnetic waves carry the signal. Common examples of wireless equipment include cellular phones, Global Positioning Systems (GPS), cordless computer peripherals, satellite television, and wireless LANs.

Wireless implementations include the following:

- **Bridged wireless:** Designed to connect two or more networks, typically located in different buildings at high data rates for data-intensive, line-of-sight applications. Building-to-building wireless connects two or more networks that are located in different buildings. A series of wireless bridges or routers can connect discrete distant sites into a single LAN and thus interconnect hard-to-wire sites, discontiguous floors, satellite offices, school or corporate campus settings, temporary networks, and warehouses.

■ **Mobile wireless:** Includes cellular applications and others. Mobile cellular wireless technologies are migrating to digital services on wireless. Second- and third-generation mobile phones are migrating to digital services that offer connectivity and higher speeds. There are three widely deployed mobile wireless technologies:

■ **Global System for Mobile Communications (GSM):** A GSM is a digital mobile radio that uses the Time Division Multiple Access (TDMA) technology, which allows eight simultaneous calls on the same RF in three bands: 900, 1800, and 1900 MHz. The transfer data rate is 9.6 kbps. A unique benefit of GSM is its international coverage, allowing the use of a GSM phones almost transparently while traveling abroad, without the need to change any settings or configuration parameters.

■ **General Packet Radio Service (GPRS):** A GPRS extends the capability of GSM speed and supports intermittent and bursty data transfer. Speeds that are offered the client are in the range of ISDN speeds (64 to 128 kbps).

■ **Universal Mobile Telecommunications Service (UMTS):** Also called third-generation (3G) broadband, UMTS provides packet-based transmission of text, digitized voice, video, and multimedia at data rates of up to 2 Mbps. UMTS offers a consistent set of services to mobile computer and phone users, no matter where they are located in the world.

■ **Wireless LAN:** Developed to meet the demand for LAN connections over the air. It is often used in intrabuilding connections. Wireless LANs have developed to cover a growing range of applications, such as guest access and voice over wireless. They support services such as advanced security and location of wireless devices.

SONET and SDH Technology

Circuit-based services architecture is the basis for SONET and Synchronous Digital Hierarchy (SDH). This technology uses TDM and delivers high-value services over an optical infrastructure. SONET or SDH provides high-speed, point-to-point connections that guarantee bandwidth, regardless of actual usage (for example, common bit rates are 155 and 622 Mbps, with a maximum of 10 Gbps). SONET or SDH rings offer proactive performance monitoring and automatic recovery ("self-healing") through an automatic protection switching (APS) mechanism.

Figure 5-3 illustrates a typical SONET/SDH implementation example.

SONET or SDH rings support two IP encapsulations for user interfaces: ATM or Packet over SONET/SDH (POS), which sends native IP packets directly over SONET or SDH frames. Optical Carrier (OC) rates are the digital hierarchies of the SONET standard. They support the following speeds:

■ OC-1 = 51.85 Mbps

■ OC-3 = 155.52 Mbps

■ OC-12 = 622.08 Mbps

- OC-24 = 1.244 Gbps

- OC-48 = 2.488 Gbps

- OC-192 = 9.962 Gbps

- OC-255 = 13.21 Gbps

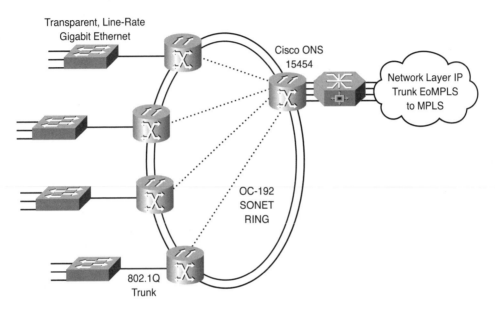

Figure 5-3   *SONET/SDH Example*

Note   SONET and SDH represent important differences in terminology. SONET is an ANSI specification. SDH is the SONET-equivalent specification that is proposed by the ITU. European carriers use SDH widely; Asian and Pacific Rim carriers commonly use SONET.

DWDM Technology

Dense wavelength division multiplexing (DWDM) improves the utilization of optical fiber. Multichannel signaling on a single strand of fiber increases its available bandwidth to the equivalent of several Gigabit Ethernet links. DWDM is a crucial component of optical networks. It maximizes the use of installed fiber cable and allows service providers to efficiently offer new services over the existing infrastructure. Flexible add-and-drop modules permit service providers to drop and insert individual channels along a route. An open architecture system allows various devices, including SONET terminals, ATM switches, and IP routers, to be connected.

Dark Fiber

Dark fiber refers to fiber-optic cables that are leased from the service provider, where the framing is provided by the enterprise. Dark fiber connection allows framing options other than SONET/SDH. The edge devices connect directly over the site-to-site dark fiber using other encapsulations, such as Gigabit Ethernet. To transmit data over long distances, regenerators are inserted into the link to maintain signal integrity and provide appropriate jitter control. Depending on the carrier and location, dark fiber is now available on the wholesale market for both metro and wide-area links at prices that were previously associated with leased-line rentals.

In terms of reliability, SONET/SDH networks offer advanced features over DWDM and dark fiber, such as automatic backup and repair mechanisms to cope with system failure. The failure of a single SONET/SDH link or network element does not lead to failure of the entire network.

WAN Link Categories

From the ownership perspective, WAN links are divided into three broad categories:

- **Private WAN:** Uses private transmission systems to connect distant LANs. The owner of a private WAN must buy, configure, and maintain the physical layer connectivity (copper, fiber, wireless, coaxial) and the terminal equipment that is required to connect locations. Thus, private WANs are expensive to build, labor-intensive to maintain, and difficult to reconfigure for constantly changing business needs. The advantages of using a private WAN include higher levels of security and transmission quality.

- **Leased WAN:** Uses dedicated bandwidth that is leased by an enterprise from a service provider with either private or leased terminal equipment. The provider provisions the circuit and is responsible for maintenance. Some examples include TDM and SONET circuits. The enterprise pays for the allocated bandwidth, whether or not it is used, and operating costs tend to be high.

- **Shared WAN:** Shares physical resources with many users. Carriers offer various circuit- or packet-switching transport networks, such as MPLS or Frame Relay, for user traffic. The provider provisions the circuit and is responsible for the maintenance. Linking LANs and private WANs into a shared network involves a compromise among cost, performance, and security.

There are fixed costs in a typical WAN environment:

- Equipment purchases, such as modems, CSUs and DSUs, and router interfaces

- Circuit and service provisioning

- Network management tools and platforms

Recurring costs include the service provider monthly circuit fees and the support and maintenance of the WAN, including any network management center personnel.

WAN Transport Technology Pricing and Contract Considerations

Historically, WAN transport costs include an access circuit charge and, for TDM, a distance-sensitive rate. Some carriers have dropped or reduced distance-based factors as TDM circuits have become a commodity.

Access circuits generally take 60 days or more to be provisioned by the service provider. The higher the bandwidth, the more lead time it can take. For Metro Ethernet, availability can be spotty and the lead times can be long. Construction fees can be required for the fiber access. Service and pricing options between carriers should be compared to reduce fees, depending on competition in the area.

Note   The details in this section are specific to the United States; pricing, timing, and contract details differ from country to country.

For Frame Relay and ATM, typical charges include a combination of an access circuit charge (per-PVC) and possibly per-bandwidth (committed information rate [CIR] or minimum information rate [MIR]) charges. Some carriers have simplified these rates by charging based on the access circuit and then setting the CIR or MIR to half that speed. This technique allows bursts to two times the guaranteed rate.

Frame Relay generally has been available at up to T3 speeds. In some cases, T3 is the size of trunks between Frame Relay switches, so the service providers do not want to offer T3 access circuits.

For MPLS VPN service, pricing is generally set to compete with Frame Relay and ATM. Some providers are encouraging customers to move to MPLS VPNs by offering lower prices for bandwidth than for Frame Relay and ATM. Other service providers price MPLS VPNs somewhat higher than Frame Relay or ATM because they are providing a routing service, which has value beyond bandwidth alone.

Tariffed commercial services are typically available at published rates and are subject to certain restrictions. Some carriers are moving toward unpublished rates, allowing more flexibility in options and charges.

In general, for a standard carrier package, the time that is needed to contract a WAN circuit is usually one month. If negotiating a service-level agreement (SLA), six months or more of discussions with the service provider, including the legal department, should be expected. Unless a very large customer is represented, it might not be possible to influence many changes in the SLA.

Contract periods usually last from one to five years. Because the telecommunications industry is changing rapidly, enterprises generally do not want to get locked into a long-term contract. Escape clauses that apply in the case of a merger or poor performance can help mitigate the business risks of long-term contracts.

For dark fiber, contract periods are generally 20 years in length. One key factor is the right of nonreversion, meaning that no matter what happens to the provider, the fiber belongs to the customer for 20 years. This way, the enterprise is protected in the case of situations such as a service provider merger, bankruptcy, and so on. The process to repair fiber cuts needs to be defined in the SLA.

WAN Design Requirements

When developing the WAN design by using the Prepare, Plan, Design, Implement, Operate, and Optimize (PPDIOO) methodology, continue the process of designing the topology and network solutions. This should be accomplished after taking the earlier steps of analyzing organizational requirements and characterizing the existing network.

To develop the WAN topology, consider the projected traffic patterns, technology performance constraints, and network reliability. The design document should describe a set of discrete functions that the enterprise edge modules perform. The document should also describe the expected level of service that is provided by each selected technology, based on the services that a service provider offers.

A network design should be adaptable to future technologies and should not include any design elements that limit the adoption of new technologies as they become available. This consideration needs to be balanced with the issue of cost-effectiveness throughout a network design and implementation. For example, many new internetworks are rapidly adopting VoIP. Network designs should support future VoIP without requiring a substantial upgrade by provisioning hardware and software that have options for expansion and upgradability.

Most users seek application availability in their networks. The chief components of application availability are response time, throughput, and reliability. Applications such as voice and video are negatively impacted by jitter and latency. Table 5-2 shows some examples of applications and their requirements.

Table 5-2   *Identifying Application Requirements*

Requirement	Data File Transfer	Data-Interactive Application	Real-Time Voice	Real-Time Video
Response time	Reasonable	Within a second	Round trip of less than 250 ms of delay with low jitter	Minimum delay and jitter
Throughput and packet loss tolerance	High/Medium	Low/Low	Low/Low	High/Medium
Downtime (high reliability has low downtime)	Reasonable; zero downtime for mission-critical applications	Low; zero downtime for mission-critical applications	Low; zero downtime for mission-critical applications	Minimum; zero downtime for mission-critical applications

Response Time

Response time is the time between a user request and a response from the host system. Users accept response times up to a certain limit, at which point user satisfaction declines. Applications in which a fast response time is considered critical include interactive online services, such as point-of-sale machines.

Response time is also a measure of usability for end users. They perceive the communication experience in terms of how quickly a screen updates or how much delay is present on a phone call. They view the network in terms of response time, not link utilization.

Note   Voice and video applications use the terms *delay* and *jitter* to express the responsiveness of the line and the variation of the delays.

Throughput

In data transmission, throughput is the amount of data that is moved successfully from one place to another in a given time period. Applications that put high-volume traffic onto the network have a high impact on throughput. In general, throughput-intensive applications involve file-transfer activities. Usually, throughput-intensive applications do not require short response times, so they can be scheduled when response time–sensitive traffic is low (for example, after normal work hours).

Note   Wireless throughput will be significantly less than the maximum data rate because of the half-duplex nature of RF technology.

Figure 5-4 illustrates response time and link utilization.

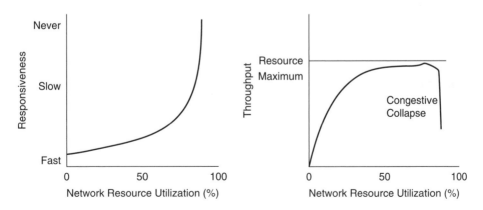

Figure 5-4   *Utilization/Throughput Correlation*

The response time increases with the offered traffic until it becomes unacceptable to the end user. Similarly, the link utilization increases with the offered traffic until the link becomes saturated. The goal of the designer is to determine the maximum offered traffic that is acceptable to both the end user and the network manager. Planning for a WAN capacity increase should begin early, usually when link utilization reaches 50 percent. Additional bandwidth purchases should start at 60 percent utilization. A link utilization of 75 percent typically means that increased WAN capacity is already urgently needed.

Packet Loss

BER is usually expressed as 10 to a negative power. For example, a transmission might have a BER of 10 to the minus 6 (10^{-6}), meaning that 1 out of 1,000,000 bits transmitted was in error. The BER indicates how frequently a packet or other data unit must be retransmitted because of an error. A BER that is too high might indicate that a slower data rate could improve the overall transmission time for a given amount of transmitted data. In other words, a slower data rate can reduce the BER, thereby lowering the number of packets that must be resent.

Note In telecommunication transmission, packet loss is expressed as a bit error rate (BER), which is the percentage of bits that have errors relative to the total number of bits received in a transmission.

Reliability

Although reliability is always important, some applications have requirements that exceed typical needs. Some organizations that require nearly 100 percent uptime for critical applications are

- Financial services
- Securities exchanges
- Emergency
- Police
- Military operations

These organizations require a high level of hardware and topological redundancy. Determining the cost of any downtime is essential to identify the relative importance of the reliability of the network.

QoS Considerations for Bandwidth Constraints

WAN links are typically much slower than LAN links. Transmitting data over a WAN is expensive. Therefore, using data compression, adjusting window sizes, or using a combination of queuing, access rate limits, and traffic shaping can optimize bandwidth usage and improve overall efficiency.

Cisco has developed QoS techniques to mitigate temporary congestion and provide preferential treatment for critical applications. QoS mechanisms, such as queuing, policing (limiting) of the access rate, and traffic shaping enable network operators to deploy and operate large-scale networks. These networks can efficiently manage both bandwidth-hungry applications, such as multimedia, and web traffic and mission-critical applications, such as host-based applications.

Figure 5-5 illustrates how the different technologies covered in this section fit together within the enterprise edge.

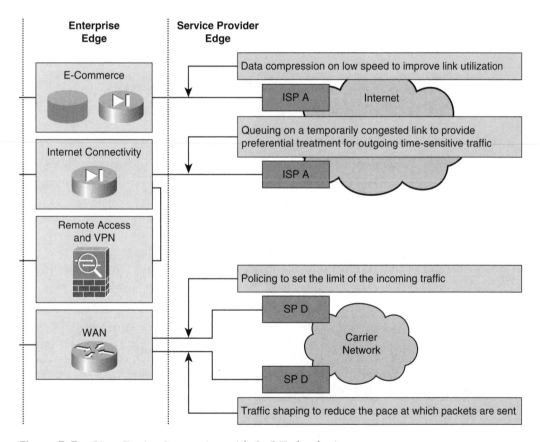

Figure 5-5   *Cisco Design Integration with QoS Technologies*

Classification

To provide priority to certain flows, the flow must first be identified and (if desired) marked. These two tasks are commonly referred to as just classification. The following represents features that support the classification process:

■   **Network-Based Application Recognition (NBAR):** Allows packets to be classified by matching on fields at the application layer. Prior to the introduction of NBAR, the most granular classification was Layer 4 TCP and User Datagram Protocol (UDP) port numbers.

■ **Committed access rate (CAR):** Used to set precedence that is based on extended access list classification. This allows considerable flexibility for precedence assignment, including assignment by application or user, by destination and source subnet, and so on.

Congestion Management

One of the ways that network elements manage an overflow of arriving traffic is to use a queuing algorithm. It sorts the traffic and then determines a method of prioritizing it onto an output link.

When positioning the role of queuing in networks, the primary issue is the duration of congestion. If WAN links are constantly congested, an organization either requires greater bandwidth or should use compression. Queuing is required only on congested WAN links.

Note   Queuing occurs at the outbound interface and is appropriate for cases where WAN links are occasionally congested.

There are two types of queues:

■ **Hardware queue:** Uses the first in, first out (FIFO) strategy, which is necessary for the interface drivers to transmit packets one by one. The hardware queue is sometimes referred to as the transmit queue, or TxQ.

■ **Software queue:** Schedules packets into the hardware queue based on the QoS requirements, custom queuing (CQ), priority queuing (PQ), and weighted fair queuing (WFQ).

Priority Queuing

PQ is useful for time-sensitive, mission-critical protocols. It establishes four interface output queues, each serving a different priority level.

Custom Queuing

CQ establishes up to 16 interface output queues. When the appropriate number of frames is transmitted from a queue, the transmission window size is reached and the next queue is checked. CQ is a much more equitable solution for mission-critical applications than PQ because it guarantees some level of service to all traffic.

Weighted Fair Queuing

WFQ manages problems inherent in the FIFO queuing method. WFQ ensures that different traffic flows are sorted into separate streams, or conversation sessions, and alternately dispatched. WFQ is the default in Cisco IOS Software for links at or below 2.048 Mbps. Faster links use a hardware FIFO default.

Class-Based Weighted Fair Queuing

Class-based weighted fair queuing (CBWFQ) extends the standard WFQ functionality to provide support for user-defined traffic classes. With CBWFQ, traffic classes are defined based on match criteria, including protocols, access control lists (ACL), and input interfaces. Packets that satisfy the match criteria for a class constitute the traffic for that class. A queue is reserved for each class, and traffic that belongs to a class is directed to the appropriate queue.

After a class has been defined according to its match criteria, characteristics can be assigned. To characterize a class, assign it bandwidth, weight, and maximum packet limit. The bandwidth that is assigned to a class is the guaranteed bandwidth that is delivered to the class during congestion.

To characterize a class, the queue limit for that class needs to be specified, which is the maximum number of packets that are allowed to accumulate in the queue for the class. Packets that belong to a class are subject to the bandwidth and queue limits that characterize the class.

Low Latency Queuing

Low latency queuing (LLQ) brings strict PQ to CBWFQ. Strict PQ allows delay-sensitive data such as voice to be dequeued and sent first (before packets in other queues are dequeued), which gives delay-sensitive preferential treatment over other traffic.

Without LLQ, CBWFQ provides WFQ that is based on defined classes with no strict priority queue available for real-time traffic. CBWFQ allows traffic classes to be defined and assigned characteristics. For example, the minimum bandwidth that is delivered to the class during congestion can be designated.

For CBWFQ, the weight for a packet that belongs to a specific class is derived from the bandwidth that is assigned to the class during configuration. Therefore, the bandwidth of a class determines the order in which packets are sent. All packets are serviced fairly based on weight. No class of packets can be granted strict priority. This scheme poses problems for voice traffic, which is largely intolerant of delay, and especially for voice traffic that is intolerant of variation in delay.

Traffic Shaping and Policing

Traffic shaping and traffic policing (also referred to as committed access rate [CAR]) are similar mechanisms. They inspect traffic and then take an action that is based on the characteristics of that traffic (usually the traffic is over or under a given rate). An example of traffic shaping is shown in Figure 5-6. Sometimes, the action is based on bits in the headers, such as the Differentiated Services Code Point (DSCP) or IP precedence.

Policing either discards the packet or modifies some aspect of it, such as its IP precedence. In this case, the policing agent determines that the packet meets given criteria. By comparison, traffic shaping adjusts the transmission rate of packets that match certain criteria. Traffic shaping holds packets in a buffer and releases them based on a preconfigured rate. It is available only on traffic that is leaving an interface.

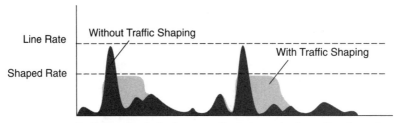

Traffic shaping limits the transmit rate to a value lower than line rate.

Figure 5-6 *Traffic Shaping Example*

An enterprise policy management scheme could deem that traffic generated by a particular resource such as voice should be considered "first-class" traffic so that it receives a top-priority marking. Other traffic, such as data, could drop to a lower-priority class.

Topologies that have higher-speed links that feed into lower-speed links (such as from a central site to a branch office) often experience bottlenecks at the remote end. Traffic shaping helps eliminate the bottleneck by throttling back traffic volume at the source. The most common use of traffic shaping in the enterprise is to smooth the flow of traffic across a single link toward a service provider transport network. This is done to ensure compliance with the traffic contract. This technique avoids service provider policing at the receiving end. Shaping reduces the bursty nature of the transmitted data. It is most useful when the contract rate is less than the line rate. Traffic shaping can also be used to respond to signaled congestion from the transport network when the traffic rates exceed the contract guarantee.

Link Efficiency

Currently, Cisco IOS Software offers several efficiency mechanisms: Link Fragmentation and Interleaving (LFI), Multilink PPP (MLP), and Real-Time Transport Protocol (RTP) header compression:

■ **Multilink PPP (MLP):** Can logically connect multiple links between two systems, as needed, to provide extra bandwidth. Remotely accessing resources through MLP allows an increase in overall throughput. This is done by logically aggregating the bandwidth of two or more physical communication links such as analog modems, ISDN, and other analog or digital links. MLP is based on Internet Engineering Task Force (IETF) standard RFC 1990.

PPP is commonly used to establish a direct connection between two nodes. It can connect computers using serial cable, phone lines, trunk lines, cellular telephones, specialized radio links, or fiber-optic links. Most ISPs use PPP for their customers' dialup access to the Internet. An encapsulated form of PPP, called PPP over Ethernet, or PPPoE, is commonly used in a similar role with DSL Internet service. PPP is frequently used as a Layer 2 protocol for connection over synchronous and asynchronous circuits.

- **Link Fragmentation and Interleaving (LFI):** Interactive traffic (Telnet, VoIP, and so on) is susceptible to increased latency and jitter when the network processes large packets (for example, LAN-to-LAN FTP transfers traversing a WAN link), especially as they are queued on slower links. The Cisco IOS LFI feature reduces delay and jitter on slower-speed links by breaking up large datagrams and interleaving low-delay traffic packets with the resulting smaller packets.

- **Real-Time Transport Protocol (RTP) header compression:** Increases efficiency for many of the newer VoIP or multimedia applications that take advantage of RTP, especially on slow links, by compressing the RTP/UDP/IP header from 40 bytes to 2 to 4 bytes.

Window Size

The window size specifies the maximum number of frames that are transmitted without receiving an acknowledgment. Acknowledgment procedures are particularly important in a protocol layer that provides reliability, such as hop-by-hop acknowledgment in a reliable link protocol or end-to-end acknowledgment in a transport protocol.

The current window is defined as the amount of data that can be sent by a protocol without acknowledgment, which is always less than or equal to the window size. This form of data acknowledgment provides a means in which the network is "self-clocked" so that data flows steadily between the two endpoints of the connection. For example, if the TCP window size is set to 8192, the sender must stop after sending 8192 bytes if no acknowledgment comes from the receiver. This value might be unacceptable for long WAN links with significant delays. In these cases, the window size can be adjusted to a higher value. Frequent retransmissions are a risk, however, because of links with high error rates, which reduce the throughput dramatically.

Note   Adjustable windows and equipment that can adapt to varying line conditions are strongly recommended.

Designing the Enterprise WAN

Many WAN technologies exist today, and new technologies are constantly emerging. In general, the most appropriate WAN selection results in high efficiency and leads to user satisfaction. The network designer should be aware of possible WAN design choices when considering enterprise requirements. The following sections describe the characteristics of WAN architectures.

Traditional WAN Designs

Each WAN design is based on application requirements, the geography, and the available service provider offerings. One of the main issues in traditional WAN connections is the selection of the appropriate physical WAN technology. Options include the following:

- **Leased lines:** Point-to-point connections that are reserved for transmissions rather than used only when transmission is required. The carrier establishes the connection to dedicate a physical wire or to delegate a channel using frequency division multiplexing (FDM) or time-division multiplexing (TDM). Usually, leased-line connections use synchronous transmission.

- **Circuit-switched networks:** This is a type of network that, for the duration of the connection, obtains and dedicates a physical path to a single connection between two endpoints in the network. Ordinary voice telephone service over the public switched telephone network (PSTN) is circuit switched. The telephone company reserves a specific physical path to the number being called for the duration of the call. During that time, no one else can use the physical lines that are involved. Examples of circuit-switched networks are asynchronous serial and ISDN.

- **Packet- and cell-switched networks:** These are carrier-created permanent virtual circuits (PVC) or switched virtual circuits (SVC) that deliver packets among different sites. Users share common carrier resources and can use different paths through the WAN. This option allows the carrier to use its infrastructure more efficiently than with leased point-to-point links. Examples of packet-switched networks are X.25, Frame Relay, and Switched Multimegabit Data Service (SMDS).

The three basic design approaches for packet-switched networks include star, fully meshed, and partially meshed topologies.

Star Topology

A star, or hub-and-spoke, topology features a single hub (central router) that provides access from remote networks into a core router. All communication between networks goes through the core router. The advantages of a star approach are simplified management and minimized tariff costs. However, the disadvantages are significant. Consider the following:

- The central router (hub) represents a single point of failure.

- The central router limits overall performance for access to centralized resources.

- The central router is a single pipe that manages all traffic that is intended either for the centralized resources or for the other regional routers.

- The topology is not scalable.

Fully Meshed Topology

In a fully meshed topology, each routing node on the periphery of a given packet-switching network has a direct path to every other node on the cloud. The key rationale for creating a fully meshed environment is to provide a high level of redundancy. It is not viable in large packet-switched networks. The following are key issues for a fully meshed topology:

- A large number of virtual circuits are required (one for every connection between routers).

- Problems are associated with the requirement for large numbers of packet and broadcast replications.

- Configuration is complex for routers without routing protocol multicast support in nonbroadcast environments.

Partially Meshed Topology

A partially meshed topology reduces the number of routers within a region that have direct connections to all other nodes in the region. All nodes are not connected to all other nodes. There are many forms of partially meshed topologies. In general, partially meshed approaches provide the best balance for regional topologies, based on the number of virtual circuits, redundancy, and performance.

Remote-Access Network Design

Remote access provides access primarily to users who are connecting to network resources from external locations, such as Internet hotspots, public access, and so on. The principal function is to provide access to internal resources and applications. Remote access is an important service for the Internet edge. With remote access enabled on the Internet edge, mobile workers, teleworkers, partners, and even external customers are able to access resources. To ensure that this service is available and secure, many important security design considerations must be taken into account.

When designing a remote-access network for teleworkers and traveling employees, the type of connection influences the technology selections. For example, the decision needs to be made whether to choose a data link or a network layer connection. The most suitable choice among a wide range of remote-access technologies can be made by analyzing the application requirements and service provider offerings.

Here is a summary of typical remote-access requirements:

- Data link layer WAN technology from remote sites to the enterprise edge network (consider investment and running costs)

- Low-volume data file transfer and interactive traffic, without any specific requirements regarding quality

■ The ability to access the same applications that are used in the office, both voice and data, from anywhere

Remote access to the enterprise network is typically provided over permanent or on-demand connections. The typical initial design options are as follows:

■ On-demand connections for traveling workers

■ Permanent connections for remote teleworkers through a dedicated circuit or a provisioned service

Remote-access technologies can include DSL, cable, and hotspot wireless services.

VPN Design

A VPN is defined as connectivity that is deployed on a shared infrastructure with the same policies, including security and performance, as a private network. The infrastructure that is used can be the Internet, an IP infrastructure, or any WAN infrastructure, such as a Frame Relay network or an ATM WAN.

The three types of VPNs are grouped according to their applications:

■ **Access VPN:** Provides entry to a corporate intranet over a shared infrastructure with the same policies as a private network. Remote-access connectivity is through ISDN, DSL, wireless, or cable technologies. Access VPNs enable businesses to outsource their dialup or other broadband remote-access connections without compromising their security policy. Access VPNs include two architectural options: client-initiated connections or connections that are initiated by a network access server (NAS). With client-initiated access VPNs, users establish an encrypted IP tunnel from their PCs across the shared network of a service provider to their corporate network. An alternate architecture for access VPNs defines the tunnels that are initiated from the NAS, where remote users dial in to the local service provider points of presence (POP) and the service provider initiates a secure, encrypted tunnel to the corporate network.

■ **Intranet VPN:** Links remote offices. The intranet VPN services are typically based on dedicated access that extends the basic remote-access VPN to other corporate offices across the Internet or across the IP backbone of the service provider. The main benefits of intranet VPNs are as follows:

   ■ Reduced WAN infrastructure needs

   ■ Lower ongoing leased-line or Frame Relay charges

   ■ Operational savings

■ **Extranet VPN:** An organization uses either the Internet or a service provider network to connect to its business partners. The security policy becomes very important at this point because the organization does not want a hacker to spoof any orders from a business partner.

> **Note**   VPNs that use the Internet have no performance guarantees.

Enterprise Versus Service Provider–Managed VPNs

Deploying a VPN can help ensure a business that its networks provide secure remote connectivity. The next step is to determine whether to design, build, and manage the network in house or to use a provider for service management. The following points represent technology that is used by the enterprise (in house) or a service provider to offer multiservice IP VPNs:

- Enterprise-managed VPN
  - IP Security (IPsec):
    - IPsec direct encapsulation
    - Cisco Easy VPN
    - Point-to-point Generic Routing Encapsulation (GRE) over IPsec
    - Dynamic Multipoint Virtual Private Network (DMVPN)
    - Virtual tunnel interface (VTI)
    - Layer 2 Tunneling Protocol version 3 (L2TPv3)
- Service provider
  - Multiprotocol Label Switching (MPLS)
  - Metro Ethernet
  - Virtual Private LAN Services (VPLS)

Enterprise Managed VPN: IPsec

The IPsec standard provides a method to manage authentication and data protection between multiple cryptographic peers that are engaging in secure data transfer. IPsec includes the Internet Security Association and Key Management Protocol (ISAKMP)/Oakley and two IPsec IP protocols: Encapsulating Security Payload (ESP) protocol and Authentication Header (AH).

IPsec uses symmetrical encryption algorithms for data protection. Symmetrical encryption algorithms are more efficient and easier to implement in hardware. These algorithms need a secure method of key exchange to ensure data protection. Internet Key Exchange (IKE) ISAKMP/Oakley protocols provide this capability.

This solution requires a standards-based way to secure data from eavesdropping and modification. IPsec provides such a method. IPsec provides a choice of transform sets so that a user can choose the strength of his data protection. IPsec also has several Hash-based Message Authentication Codes (HMAC) from which to choose. Each provides different levels of protection for attacks, such as man-in-the-middle packet replay (antireplay) and data integrity attacks.

IPsec Direct Encapsulation

IPsec provides a tunnel mode of operation that enables it to be used as a standalone connection method. This option is the most fundamental IPsec VPN design model; Figure 5-7 illustrates this model. IPsec direct encapsulation designs cannot transport IGP dynamic routing protocols or IP multicast traffic.

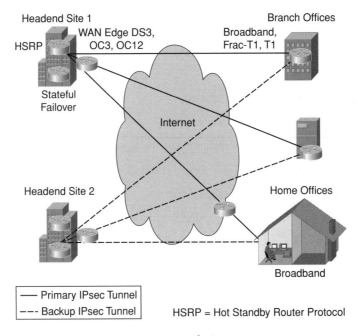

Figure 5-7   *IPsec Direct Encapsulation*

Each remote site initiates an IPsec tunnel to a predefined head end. Remotes can have static or dynamic IP addresses, while head ends must have static IP addresses.

Resiliency can be provided by IPsec stateful failover at the head-end locations. Branch routers can be configured with a list of head ends. If a connection cannot be established with the first head end, subsequent head ends are tried until a successful connection is made.

Cisco Easy VPN

Cable modems, xDSL routers, and other forms of broadband access provide high-performance connections to the Internet. Many applications also require the security of VPN connections that perform a high level of authentication and that encrypt the data between two particular endpoints. However, establishing a VPN connection between two routers can be complicated. Typically, it requires tedious coordination between network administrators to configure the VPN parameters of the two routers.

As Figure 5-8 illustrates, the Cisco Easy VPN Remote feature eliminates much of this tedious work by implementing the Cisco VPN Client protocol. This allows most VPN parameters to be defined at a Cisco Easy VPN Server. After the Cisco Easy VPN Server has been configured, a VPN connection can be created with minimal configuration on a Cisco Easy VPN Remote, such as a Cisco 800 Series router or a Cisco 1700 Series Modular Access Router.

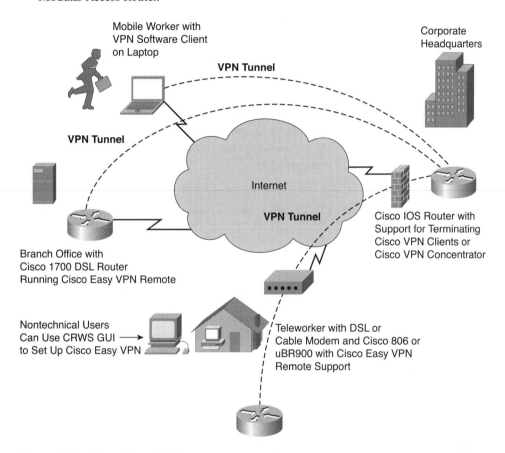

Figure 5-8 *Cisco Easy VPN*

Point-to-Point GRE over IPsec

IPsec can be deployed with point-to-point Generic Route Encapsulation (GRE), which is an IPsec-encrypted, point-to-point GRE tunnel that provides additional functionality. With the addition of point-to-point GRE to IPsec, dynamic interior gateway protocol (IGP) routing protocols and IP multicast traffic can be transported over the VPN tunnel.

GRE over IPsec designs offer the following advantages:

■ IP multicast and non-IP protocols are supported.

■ Dynamic IGP routing protocols over the VPN tunnel are supported.

- Quality of service (QoS) policies can be configured per point-to-point GRE over an IPsec tunnel (scalability might be an issue).

- Distribution of IPsec tunnels to head-end routers is deterministic, with routing metrics and convergence choosing the best path.

- All primary and secondary or backup point-to-point GRE over IPsec tunnels are preestablished. A new tunnel does not have to be established in the event of a failure scenario.

Each remote site is connected with a point-to-point GRE over IPsec tunnel to a predefined head end. Remotes can have static or dynamic IP addresses, while head ends must have static IP addresses.

Resiliency can be provided by configuring point-to-point GRE over IPsec tunnels to multiple head-end routers at one or more geographic hub locations. An IGP dynamic routing protocol is exchanged over the point-to-point GRE over IPsec tunnels. Primary tunnels are differentiated from secondary tunnels by configuring slightly different routing metrics.

IPsec DMVPN

Dynamic Multipoint VPN (DMVPN) is a Cisco IOS Software solution for building IPsec + GRE VPNs in an easy, dynamic, and scalable manner. DMVPN relies on two proven technologies:

- **Next-Hop Resolution Protocol (NHRP):** Creates a distributed (NHRP) mapping database of all the spoke tunnels to real (public interface) addresses

- **Multipoint GRE (mGRE) tunnel interface:** A single GRE interface to support multiple GRE and IPsec tunnels, which simplifies size and complexity of configuration

DMVPN offers configuration reduction and no-touch deployment. DMVPN also supports the following features:

- IP unicast, IP multicast, and dynamic routing protocols

- Remote peers with dynamically assigned addresses

- Spoke routers behind dynamic NAT and hub routers behind static NAT

- Dynamic spoke-to-spoke tunnels for scaling partially meshed or fully meshed VPNs

In addition, the following items are true about DMVPNs:

- Dynamic IGP routing protocols over the VPN tunnel are supported.

- QoS service policies can be configured per point-to-point GRE over IPsec tunnel (scalability might be an issue).

- Distribution of IPsec tunnels to head-end routers is deterministic, with routing metrics and convergence choosing the best path.

- All primary and secondary or backup GRE over IPsec tunnels are preestablished. A new tunnel does not have to be established in the event of a failure scenario.

Each remote site is connected with a point-to-point GRE tunnel interface to a predefined head end. The head-end routers use mGRE interfaces to dynamically accept new tunnel connections.

Resiliency can be provided by configuring DMVPN tunnels that are mapped to mGRE interfaces on multiple head-end routers at one or more geographic hub locations.

Remotes can have static or dynamic IP addresses, while head ends must have static IP addresses. An IGP dynamic routing protocol is exchanged over the DMVPN tunnels, and primary and secondary tunnels are differentiated by configuring slightly different routing metrics.

IPsec tunnel protection is generally used to map the cryptographic attributes to the tunnel that is originated by the remote router. Dead peer detection (DPD) can be enabled to the detect loss of a peer connection.

NHRP is configured on both the head-end and branch office routers, and is a requirement for using mGRE interfaces.

IPsec VTI Design

Virtual tunnel interface (VTI) design is one of the newest IPsec VPN design options available in Cisco IOS Software. VTI designs have a number of distinct advantages over other IPsec design options, including the ability to transport IGP dynamic routing protocols and IP multicast traffic without the addition of point-to-point GRE or mGRE headers.

In addition, VTI tunnels are assigned an interface so that tunnel-level features, such as a QoS service policy, can be enabled on each tunnel. This makes it possible to have per-VPN tunnel/destination QoS.

L2TPv3 Design

L2TPv3 offers a high-speed, transparent Layer 2–to–Layer 2 service over an IP backbone. L2TPv3 signaling is responsible for negotiating control plane parameters, session IDs, and cookies; for performing authentication; and for exchanging configuration parameters. L2TPv3 is also used to deliver hello messages and circuit status messages in a reliable manner. These messages are critical to support circuit interworking, such as the Local Management Interface (LMI), and to monitor the remote circuit status.

L2TPv3 supports the following Layer 2 payloads, which can be included in L2TP packets that are tunneled over the pseudowire:

- Frame Relay

- Ethernet

- IEEE 802.1q (VLAN)

- High-Level Data Link Control (HDLC)
- PPP

Service Provider–Managed VPNs: MPLS

Multiprotocol Label Switching (MPLS) enables enterprises and service providers to build next-generation intelligent networks that deliver a wide variety of advanced, value-added services over a single infrastructure. This economical solution can be integrated seamlessly over any existing infrastructure, such as IP, Frame Relay, ATM, or Ethernet. Subscribers with differing access links can be aggregated on an MPLS edge without changing their current environments, as MPLS is independent of access technologies.

Integration of MPLS application components, including Layer 3 VPNs, Layer 2 VPNs, traffic engineering, QoS, and IP version 6 (IPv6), enable the development of highly efficient, scalable, and secure networks that guarantee service-level agreements (SLA).

MPLS Layer 3 VPN Design

Cisco IOS MPLS Layer 3 VPN is the most widely deployed MPLS technology. MPLS Layer 3 VPNs use a peer-to-peer VPN model that leverages Border Gateway Protocol (BGP) to distribute VPN-related information. This peer-to-peer model allows enterprise subscribers to "outsource" routing information to service providers, resulting in significant cost savings and a reduction in operational complexity for enterprises.

With MPLS VPNs, networks are learned with an interior gateway protocol (IGP) routing protocol such as Open Shortest Path First (OSPF), Enhanced Interior Gateway Routing Protocol (EIGRP), or Routing Information Protocol version 2 (RIPv2), with static addresses that are configured by an administrator or with BGP from other internal routers. MPLS VPNs use an additional label to specify the VPN and the corresponding VPN destination network. This additional label allows overlapping addresses between VPNs.

With MPLS Layer 3 VPNs, service providers can offer value-added services like QoS and traffic engineering, enabling network convergence that encompasses voice, video, and data. MPLS Layer 3 VPNs can be deployed with a Cisco MPLS TE and Fast Reroute (FRR) to offer "tight SLAs." QoS-based offerings vary from two to five classes of services.

Service Provider–Managed VPNs: Metro Ethernet

Demand for bandwidth in the metropolitan-area network (MAN or metro) is exploding as a result of data-intensive applications, new business models that rely on the Internet, and population growth. Increasingly, service providers are meeting that demand with Metro Ethernet access services. These services are based on Ethernet, IP, and optical technologies such as dense wavelength division multiplexing (DWDM) or coarse wavelength division multiplexing (CWDM). Compared to fixed bandwidth facilities, Metro Ethernet access services provide more bandwidth, the ability to provision bandwidth in flexible increments, resiliency with Route Processor Redundancy (RPR), and better support for converged voice, video, and data services.

Today, more service providers are using Ethernet access to their backbone network, whether through SONET/SDH, MPLS, Frame Relay, or the Internet. Broadband connectivity is provided by an Ethernet hand-off to either a cable modem or DSL bridge. This provides the following benefits:

- **Service-enabling solution:** Layering value-added advanced services in addition to the network

- **More flexible architecture:**

  - Increasing port speeds without the need to dispatch a technician, and typically with no new customer premises equipment (CPE)

  - Evolving existing services (Frame Relay/ATM internetworking) to an IP-optimized solution

- **Seamless enterprise integration:** Ease of integration with typical LAN network equipment

Service Provider–Managed VPNs: VPLS

VPLS is a class of VPN that supports the connection of multiple sites in a single bridged domain over a managed IP/MPLS network. VPLS presents an Ethernet interface to customers. This interface simplifies the LAN/WAN boundary for service providers and customers and enables rapid and flexible service provisioning. This is illustrated in Figure 5-9. This occurs because the service bandwidth is not tied to the physical interface. All services in a VPLS appear to be on the same LAN, regardless of location.

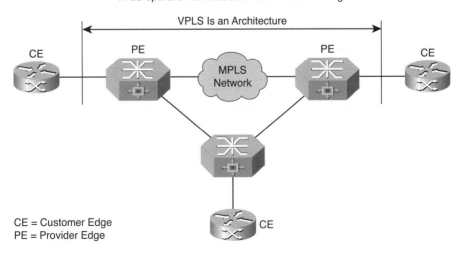

- VPLS defines an architecture that delivers Ethernet Service (EMS) over an MPLS network.
- VPLS operation emulates an IEEE Ethernet bridge.

VPLS Is an Architecture

CE = Customer Edge
PE = Provider Edge

Figure 5-9 *VPLS Design*

VPLS uses edge routers that can learn, bridge, and replicate on a VPN basis. These routers are connected by a full mesh of tunnels, enabling any-to-any connectivity.

VPLS supplies an architecture that provides Ethernet Multipoint Service (EMS) across geographically dispersed locations using MPLS as a transport. EMSs are attractive. They offer solutions to problems that many enterprise customers and service providers are seeking to address (for example, high-speed, secure, any-to-any forwarding at Layer 2). The requirement to forward frames at Layer 2 is important. Many new applications and services dictate that the service be transparent to upper-layer protocols (ULP) or can lack network layer addressing altogether (for example, NetBIOS Extended User Interface [NetBEUI]).

WAN Backup Strategy Design

WAN links are relatively unreliable compared to LAN links, and often are much slower than the LANs that they connect. The combination of uncertain reliability, lack of speed, and high importance makes the WAN link a good candidate for redundancy.

Each enterprise edge solution requires a WAN backup to provide high availability between sites. Branch offices should experience minimum downtime in the event of primary link failure. Backup connections can be established using either dialup or permanent connections.

The primary WAN backup options are as follows:

- **Dial backup routing:** Dial backup routing uses dialup services such as ISDN. The switched circuit provides the backup service for another type of circuit, such as point-to-point or Frame Relay. The router initiates the dial backup line based on object tracking parameters or when a failure is detected on the primary circuit. The dial backup line provides WAN connectivity until the primary circuit is restored and then terminates.

- **Permanent secondary WAN link:** The deployment of an additional permanent WAN link between each remote office and the central office (CO) makes the network more fault-tolerant. This capability offers two advantages:

  - **Backup link:** If a connection between any remote office and the CO fails, the backup link is used. The Reliable Static Routing Backup Using Object Tracking feature can ensure reliable backup in the case of several catastrophic events. If the connection to the main office is lost, the status of the tracked object changes from up to down. When the state of the tracked object changes to down, the routing table entry for the primary interface is removed. Traffic is then forwarded to the preconfigured destination from the secondary interface. This ability allows applications to proceed in the event of a WAN link failure and thus improves application availability.

    - **Increased bandwidth:** This additional bandwidth decreases response times when the router connected supports load balancing between two parallel links of equal cost. In this case, load balancing is performed automatically through routing protocol.

■ **IPsec:** Using an IPsec VPN, the WAN traffic can be directed back to the corporate headquarters through the Internet when a failure is detected.

In Figure 5-10, the connections between the central site enterprise edge and remote sites use permanent primary and secondary WAN links for redundancy. To increase the utilization of the backup link, a routing protocol such as EIGRP is used to support load balancing over unequal paths on either a per-packet or a per-destination basis.

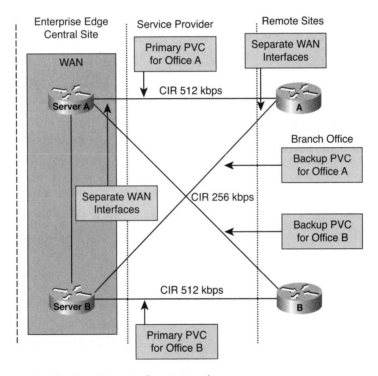

Figure 5-10 *WAN Backup Example*

Backup links should be provisioned so that they become active when a primary link fails or becomes congested. Backup links often use different technologies; for example, leased lines are used with backup IPsec VPNs.

Using the Internet as a WAN Backup

The Internet can be used as an alternate option for a failed WAN connection. This type of connection is considered "best effort" and guarantees no bandwidth. This topic describes a WAN backup design for use over the Internet.

When relying on the Internet to provide a backup for branch offices, the enterprise must cooperate fully with the ISP and announce its networks to gain connectivity. If a connection between any branch office and the CO fails, the backup IPsec tunnel is used. In addition, the Reliable Static Routing Backup Using Object Tracking feature can ensure reliable backup in the case of several failures.

Selecting the Enterprise WAN Architecture

After identifying the remote connectivity requirements and understanding traditional WAN designs, the WAN architecture is ready to be selected.

When selecting technologies, decision makers should consider the following factors:

- **Support for network growth:** Enterprises that anticipate significant growth should choose a technology that allows the network to grow with their business. Issues to be considered are the amount of time, cost, and effort that is involved in connecting new branches and remote offices. WAN technologies with high support for network growth make it possible to add new branches or remote offices with minimal configuration at existing sites. This minimizes costs and IT staff requirements for such changes. WAN technologies with lower support for network growth require significantly more time and cost to expand the network.

- **Appropriate availability:** Businesses that are heavily impacted by even the smallest disruption in network communications should consider availability to be a priority when choosing a connectivity technology. Highly available technologies provide inherent redundancy where no single point of failure exists in the network. Lower-availability technologies can still dynamically recover from a network disruption in a short time, but this minor disruption might be considered too costly for some businesses. Technologies that do not inherently provide high availability can be more accessible through redundancy in design by using products with redundant characteristics, such as multiple WAN connections, or by using backup power supplies.

- **Operational expenses:** Some WAN technologies can result in higher costs than others. A private-line technology such as Frame Relay or ATM, for example, typically results in higher carrier fees than a technology such as an IPsec-based IP VPN, which can take advantage of the public Internet to help reduce costs. It is important to note, however, that migrating to a particular technology for the sole purpose of reducing carrier fees, without considering network performance and QoS, can limit support for some advanced technologies such as voice and video.

- **Operational complexity:** Cisco MAN and WAN technologies have varying levels of inherent technical complexity, so the level of technical expertise that is required within the enterprise can also vary. In most cases, businesses can upgrade their MAN or WAN to take advantage of the expertise of the existing IT staff, requiring minimal training. When an enterprise chooses to maintain greater control over its network by taking on responsibilities that are usually reserved for a service provider, extensive IT training would be required to successfully deploy and manage a particular WAN technology.

- **Voice and video support:** Most Cisco MAN and WAN technologies support QoS, which helps enable advanced applications such as voice and video over the network. In cases where a WAN technology uses a service provider with a Cisco QoS–certified, multiservice IP VPN, an adequate level of QoS is assured to support voice and video traffic. In cases where the public Internet is used as the WAN connection, QoS cannot always be guaranteed. A high-broadband connection (greater than 786 kbps upstream) might be required for small offices, teleworkers, and remote Cisco Contact Center agents using voice and video communications.

- **Effort and equipment cost to migrate from private connectivity:** When an enterprise is taking the next step in upgrading its MAN or WAN, it is important to evaluate the short- and long-term costs and benefits. In many cases, a business can migrate from private connectivity to another technology with minimal investment in equipment, time, and IT staffing. In some instances, however, this transition can require a significant short-term investment, not only in new equipment but also in IT training. Such an investment can provide increased cost savings, lower operational expenditures, and increased productivity over the long term.

- **Network segmentation support:** Network segmentation allows enterprises to support a single network that is logically segmented. One advantage to network segmentation is the reduction of expenditures that are associated with equipment and maintenance, network administration, and network carrier charges, compared to separate physical networks. Another advantage is increased security because segmentation can ease the effort in isolating departments or limiting the access of partners on the corporate network.

Cisco Enterprise MAN and WAN Architecture

The Cisco Enterprise MAN and WAN Architecture employs a number of MAN and WAN technologies that are engineered and optimized to interoperate as a contiguous system.

The architecture provides the integrated QoS, network security, reliability, and manageability that are required for supporting various advanced business applications and services. These architectures offer a number of secure alternatives to traditional private WAN connectivity and help increase network scalability and reduce monthly carrier fees.

The Cisco Enterprise MAN and WAN Architecture technologies are compared in Table 5-3.

Table 5-3 *Cisco Enterprise WAN and MAN Architecture Comparison*

	Private WAN	ISP Service	Service Provider MPLS and IP VPN	Self-Deployed MPLS
Secure Transport	IPsec (optional)	IPsec (mandatory)	IPsec (mandatory)	IPsec (mandatory)
High Availability	Excellent	Good	Excellent	Excellent
Multicast	Good	Good	Good	Excellent

Table 5-3   *Cisco Enterprise WAN and MAN Architecture Comparison*

	Private WAN	ISP Service	Service Provider MPLS and IP VPN	Self-Deployed MPLS
Voice and Video Support	Excellent	Low	Excellent	Excellent
Scalable Network Growth	Moderate	Good	Excellent	Excellent
Easily Shared WAN Links	Moderate	Moderate	Moderate	Excellent
Operational Costs	High	Low	Moderate (depends on transport)	Moderate to High
Network Control	High	Moderate	Moderate	High
Effort to Migrate from Private to WAN	Low	Moderate	Moderate	High

Additional architectural technology information includes the following:

■ **Private WAN:** Private connectivity takes advantage of existing Frame Relay, ATM, or other connections. To provide an additional level of security when connecting sites, these technologies can be combined with strong encryption, such as Data Encryption Standard (DES), Triple Data Encryption Standard (3DES), and Advanced Encryption Standard (AES). It is ideally suited for an enterprise with moderate growth expectations and where relatively few new branches or remote offices will be deployed over the coming years. Businesses require secure, dedicated, and reliable connectivity for compliance with information privacy standards. However, this technology can result in relatively high recurring monthly carrier fees and is not the preferred technology for extending connectivity to teleworkers and remote call agents. An enterprise might choose encrypted private connectivity to network its larger branch offices, but it might opt for other technologies, such as an IPsec VPN, to connect remote users and smaller sites.

■ **ISP service (site-to-site and remote-access IPsec VPN):** These services take advantage of the ubiquity of public and private IP networks. The use of strong encryption standards (DES, 3DES, and AES) makes this WAN option more secure than traditional private connectivity. This option is also compliant with many of the new information security regulations imposed on government and industry groups, such as healthcare and finance. This technology, when implemented over the public Internet, is best suited for businesses that require basic data connectivity. However, if support for delay-sensitive, advance applications such as voice and video is required, an IPsec VPN should be implemented over a service provider private network where an adequate level of QoS is assured to support voice and video traffic. Relatively low carrier fees make this technology appropriate for businesses seeking to connect a high number of teleworkers, remote Cisco Contact Center agents, or small remote offices over a geographically dispersed area.

- **SP MPLS and IP VPN:** A network-based IP VPN is similar in many ways to private connectivity but with added flexibility, scalability, and reach. The any-to-any nature of an MPLS-enabled IP VPN (in other words, any branch can be networked to any branch), combined with its comprehensive QoS for voice and video traffic, suits the needs of many enterprises. This is especially true for businesses with high growth expectations, where many new branches and remote offices will be added over the next few years. The secure, reliable connectivity and relatively lower carrier fees that are inherent in this technology make a network-based IP VPN a good choice for businesses that want to use a managed service solution to connect branches, remote offices, teleworkers, and remote call agents.

- **Self-deployed MPLS:** Self-deployed MPLS is a network segmentation technique that allows enterprises to logically segment the network. Self-deployed MPLS is typically reserved for very large enterprises or a service provider that is willing to make a significant investment in network equipment and training. It is also used for those businesses that have an IT staff that is comfortable with a high degree of technical complexity. Further discussion of self-deployed MPLS is beyond the scope of this book.

Note   Cisco Wide Area Application Services (WAAS) is a comprehensive WAN optimization solution that accelerates applications over the WAN, delivers video to the branch office, and provides local hosting of branch-office IT services. Cisco WAAS allows IT departments to centralize applications and storage in the data center while maintaining LAN-like application performance. It also provides locally hosted IT services while reducing the branch-office device footprint.

Enterprises can use a combination of these architectures as needed to support their remote connectivity requirements.

Figure 5-11 shows an example implementation of three Cisco Enterprise MAN and WAN Architectures in a healthcare environment.

Selecting Enterprise WAN Components

After identifying the remote connectivity requirements and architecture, select the individual WAN components.

Hardware Selection

When selecting hardware, use the Cisco documentation to evaluate the WAN hardware components. Consider the following functions and features:

- Port densities
- Packet throughput

- Expandability capabilities

- Readiness to provide redundant connections

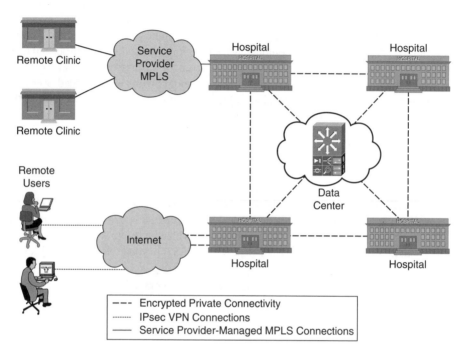

Figure 5-11 *Cisco WAN Architecture Example*

Hardware Selection: Cisco ISR G2

Cisco ISR G2s are part of the Borderless Networks within the Cisco Network Architectures for the Enterprise that enable business innovation and growth across all remote sites. The next-generation architecture delivers a new workspace experience by meeting the performance requirements for the next generation of WAN and network services. This architecture enables the cost-effective delivery of high-definition collaboration at the branch office and provides it secure transition to the next generation of cloud and virtualized network services.

Designed for optimal service delivery on a single platform, the new Cisco ISR G2 routers provide businesses with greater power to deliver a superior customer experience and deploy services "on demand" as business needs dictate, while reducing overall operating costs. A general layout of how each of the specific ISR G2 places within the enterprise is shown in Figure 5-12.

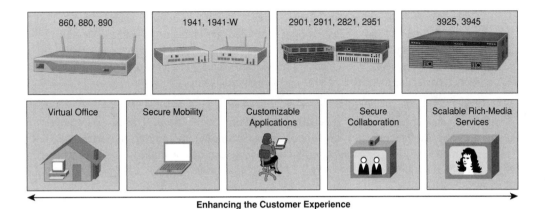

Figure 5-12 *Cisco ISR G2 Selections*

These innovations enable branch offices to do the following:

- Deliver next-generation WAN and network service requirements

- Become more productive through increased video-based collaboration and rich-media services

- Securely transition to cloud and virtualized network services

- Minimize energy consumption and costs to support corporate sustainability

- Enable small IT teams to scale services worldwide

Designing the Enterprise Branch

The Cisco Enterprise Branch Architecture takes into account services such as voice, data, video, and security that customers want to deploy at their endpoints, no matter how far away the endpoints are or how they are connected. Using Borderless Networks, the Cisco Enterprise Branch Architecture should provide seamless connectivity.

An effective network design for enterprise branches and teleworkers requires knowledge of the campus technologies.

Enterprise Branch Architecture

The Cisco Enterprise Branch Architecture takes into account the services that customers want to deploy at their endpoints, no matter how far away the endpoints are or how they are connected.

Customers are seeking opportunities to protect, optimize, and grow their businesses by increasing security and consolidating voice, video, and data onto a single IP network. Additional concerns include investing in applications that will improve productivity and operating efficiencies. These services provide customers with new opportunities to reduce costs, improve productivity, and safeguard information assets.

The Cisco Enterprise Branch Architecture is an integrated, flexible, and secure framework for extending headquarters applications in real time to remote sites. It uses the Cisco Network Architectures for the Enterprise framework but applies it to the smaller scale of a branch location. Common network components that can be implemented in the branch include the following:

- Routers that provide WAN edge connectivity
- Switches that provide the LAN infrastructure
- Security appliances that defend the branch devices
- Wireless access points for device mobility
- Call-processing and video equipment for IP telephony and video support
- End-user devices, including IP phones and computers

Enterprise Branch Design

Requirements vary for different-sized branch offices. For the branch design, the following questions should be asked:

1. How many branch locations need to be supported?
2. How many existing devices (users, hosts, and network infrastructure) will be supported at each location?
3. What amount of scalability should be supported? (How much growth is expected at each location?)
4. What are the high-availability requirements at each location?
5. Which level of security should be integrated in the design?
6. Should security be managed locally or through the corporate location?
7. Are there any requirements for local server farms or network areas that sit between the internal network and an external network (a demilitarized zone [DMZ])?
8. Should network management be supported locally or through the corporate location?
9. What wireless services are needed, and how will they affect the clients, network, and environment?
10. What is the approximate available budget?

The number of devices that are supported is limited by the physical number of ports available. In addition to the scalability considerations, the high-availability requirements point to various design models as well.

It is recommended that branch offices be categorized based on the number of users as follows:

- **Small office:** Up to 50 users, single-tier design

- **Medium office:** Between 50 and 100 users, dual-tier design

- **Large office:** Between 100 and 200 users, three-tier design

Using this classification, the design models are described in the following sections. High availability, scalability, and migration to advanced services requirements also influence the model to be adopted.

Note   The remote teleworker (branch of one) design model is also discussed in this section.

The Integrated Services Router (ISR) at the WAN edge provides various voice, security, and data services that are integrated with the LAN infrastructure. Depending on the edge router, the following interfaces are available to integrate with the LAN:

- Integrated interfaces (10/100/1000)

- High-speed WAN interface card (WIC) Ethernet 10/100 interfaces

- Network modules

- Embedded security

New Features on the ISR G2 Routers

The Cisco Integrated Services Router Second Generation (ISR G2) portfolio builds upon the market success of the first generation of ISRs with new features that deliver greater enhancements for service virtualization, video-ready capabilities, and operational excellence. The Cisco ISR G2 innovations deliver the following:

- Video-ready branch office for a superior customer experience with new services that transform the branch-office workspace such as

  - Media engines that enable business-grade video applications that are based on high-density, video-ready digital signal processors (DSP) that deliver the medianet high-definition experience

  - Bandwidth-optimized and scalable video services, including media-rich videoconferencing, video surveillance, video streaming, and digital signage

- High-performance (up to 8x), nonstop branch office experience to meet your future WAN and services requirements

- Cisco TelePresence capability to your midsize branch offices with T1/E1 links

- Service virtualization to deliver highly effective business innovation that achieves unparalleled service that includes

  - Cloud extensibility and services virtualization for mission-critical application survivability to remote sites

  - Broadest services offering to all branch-office sites, including security, unified communications, WAN optimization, application integration, and customizable virtual services

  - A revolutionary "on-demand" services delivery model that is enabled by the innovative Cisco Services Ready Engine (SRE)

Small Branch Office Design

Small branch office designs connect the access router with Layer 2 switch ports in one of three ways:

- **Integrated switching in the ISR or multiservice router:** This option has a lower port density and supports from 16 to 48 client devices on either a Cisco EtherSwitch network module or a Cisco EtherSwitch service module. This option provides a one-box solution that offers ease of management and uses the Cisco 3900 Series ISR or Cisco 2900 Series ISR for streamlined branch offices. Depending on the module, the integrated switch ports can provide power to end devices using Power over Ethernet (PoE).

- **Trunked network interface on the ISR to external switches or access points:** There is no link redundancy between the access switches or access points and the ISR. The access switches can provide power to end devices, including access points using PoE.

- **Logical EtherChannel interface between the ISR and access switches:** This approach uses a Cisco EtherSwitch module in the ISR to provide link redundancy to access layer switches. The access switches can provide power to end devices using PoE.

In all cases, the default gateway is on the ISR. The ISR provides Layer 3 services such as DHCP, firewall, and Network Address Translation (NAT).

If redundant access layer links and higher-bandwidth uplinks are required, only the second option, with higher-performance devices, can be used. The choice of the edge router also depends on the voice and Virtual Private Network (VPN) support that is needed.

The access switch supports Layer 2 services, and the Cisco ISR provides Layer 3 services. Typical access switches include the Cisco Catalyst 2960, 3560, and 3750 Series switches. To keep manageability simple, there are no loops in the topology.

Note   Although there are no Layer 2 loops in the planned design, spanning tree must be enabled and configured to protect the network from any accidental loops.

The recommended spanning-tree protocol is Rapid per-VLAN Spanning Tree Plus (RPVST+) for all Layer 2 deployments in a branch office environment. There is a default gateway for each VLAN configured in the topology. All the Layer 3 configurations are done on the ISR. The access switches must be configured with an IP address for management purposes.

Both the Cisco 2921 and 2951 ISRs support three integrated 10/100/1000 interfaces, which are Layer 3 native. Both the Cisco 2921 and 2951 ISRs support one slot for a network module. The Cisco 2921 and 2951 ISRs both support the 16-, 24-, and 48-port Cisco EtherSwitch network modules.

Medium Branch Office Design

The medium branch office topology is similar to the small office topology. One exception is that the WAN edge devices are larger, typically two Cisco 2921 or Cisco 2951 ISRs, and the access switches supporting LAN connectivity are external.

To scale up to 100 users, the following options are available:

- Use a higher-port-density external access switch.

- Use an ISR module that supports switched access ports that provide redundancy in the connection to the access switches through EtherChannel.

This design uses the integrated 10/100/1000 interfaces as Layer 3 trunks, providing the flexibility to use various access switches. The stackable Cisco Catalyst 3750 Series switch with an IP base image or an IP services image can be used as the access switch to support 24 or 48 users per switch. The IP base image feature set includes advanced quality of service (QoS), rate limiting, access control lists (ACL), and basic static and Routing Information Protocol (RIP) routing capability. The IP services image provides a richer set of enterprise-class features, including advanced hardware-based IP unicast and multicast routing.

An additional Advanced IP Services Software license is also available. This license is required for IP version 6 (IPv6) routing (Layer 3 switching).

With Cisco StackWise technology, customers can create a single, 32-Gbps switching unit with up to nine Cisco Catalyst 3750 Series switches. Cisco StackWise technology uses special stack-interconnect cables and stacking software. The stack behaves as a single switching unit that is managed by a master switch that is elected from one of the member switches. The master switch automatically creates and updates all the switching and optional routing tables. Support for the number of users needing PoE depends on the specific access switch that is used.

Large Branch Office Design

A large branch office design is like a small to medium campus design with 100 to 1000 users.

In addition to supporting more users, a large office might also need higher LAN switching capability if it is supporting a server farm or DMZ. Support for some of these services requires the use of appliance devices if higher throughput is required. To meet these requirements, a distribution layer is added to the small-office or medium-office topology by introducing a multilayer switch to provide the required LAN switching capabilities, port density, and flexibility to support additional appliances.

A stacked switch LAN topology is highly available, scalable, and manageable. High-availability requirements are met because link redundancy and device redundancy are built into the design. For high availability between the distribution and the edge layers, redundant links are used.

The port density of the stacked switches allows a number of access switches to be connected without compromising high availability. The distribution switches typically run the enhanced images, which support more features, including various routing protocols and advanced features, such as policy-based routing.

If Cisco Catalyst 3560 and 3750 Series switches are used at the access layers, other Layer 2 security features, such as DHCP snooping, Dynamic ARP Inspection (DAI), and IP Source Guard, can be enabled to provide additional security measures. The default gateways for all the VLANs at the access layer are configured on the distribution layer.

Enterprise Teleworker (Cisco Virtual Office Solution) Design

Another remote place in the enterprise network consists of the enterprise teleworkers. Organizations are constantly striving to reduce costs, improve employee productivity, and retain valued employees. These goals can be attained by providing employees with the ability to work from home with the same level of quality, function, performance, convenience, and security that is available in the office. With a work environment in the residence, employees can optimally manage their work schedules, allowing higher productivity (less affected by office distractions) and greater job satisfaction (flexibility in schedule). This transparent extension of the enterprise to employee homes is the objective of the Cisco Enterprise Teleworker (or Cisco Virtual Office solution) Architecture.

Occasional remote users have much lighter application requirements than part-time and full-time teleworkers. They can connect through a wireless hotspot or as a guest network at a hotel, allowing them to have little control over network resiliency and availability.

The situation of enterprise teleworkers that are operating as a Cisco Virtual Office can be differentiated from other forms of work-at-home or telecommuting scenarios. The difference is that the emphasis is on delivering seamless managed accessibility to the complete range of applications and services that are critical to the operational effectiveness of enterprises. The Cisco Enterprise Teleworker Architecture is part of the overall secure Cisco Network Architectures for the Enterprise infrastructure. The Cisco Enterprise

Teleworker Architecture gives companies the ability to integrate and securely manage their remote workers within the corporate network, while providing a high-quality end-user experience that supports a complete range of enterprise applications for the enterprise teleworker. The enterprise teleworker typically connects to an ISP through a DSL or cable modem and can use an analog dialup session to back up this connection.

The enterprise teleworker solution is implemented with a small ISR such as the Cisco 877, 878, and 888 Integrated Services Routers with integrated switch ports behind a broadband modem. The solution uses a transparent, always-on VPN tunnel back to the enterprise.

This architecture provides centralized management, where the customer can apply security policies, push configurations, and periodically test the connection through the broadband cloud and back to the corporate office. This allows the customer to see the latency, jitter, and packet loss that is being experienced at any given time. This solution can support advanced applications such as voice and video as part of the complete suite of enterprise services for the end user. For example, a teleworker can access the central-office IP telephone system from home, with comparable voice quality. The teleworker can also take advantage of higher-function IP telephony capabilities instead of using the public switched telephone network (PSTN).

An alternative solution is an unmanaged VPN approach, where the end user implements a software VPN from the PC across a generic broadband router, access point, or hub appliance. This alternate solution typically cannot support the level of feature integration, QoS, and managed support that is needed to deliver voice, video, multimedia, and traditional data to the end user in a reliable manner. The alternate solution is appropriate for occasional remote users, with their lighter application requirements.

New ISRs for Small Offices and Teleworkers

Cisco 860 and 880 Series ISRs deliver integrated services at broadband speeds to small offices and teleworkers or to service providers to deploy as part of their managed network services:

- Cisco 860 Series ISRs offer the following:

  - Concurrent broadband services for small offices and remote sites

  - Security features, including:

    - Stateful Inspection Firewall

    - IPsec VPNs (Triple Data Encryption Standard [3DES] or Advanced Encryption Standard [AES])

  - 4-port 10/100 Fast Ethernet managed switch with VLAN support

  - CON/AUX port for console or external modem

  - Secure IEEE 802.11g/n access-point option that is based on the IEEE 802.11n 2.0 standard

- Easy setup, deployment, and remote management capabilities through web-based tools and Cisco IOS Software

- Cisco 880 Series ISRs offer the following:

  - High performance for broadband access in small offices and small branch-office and teleworker sites

  - Collaborative services with secure analog, digital voice, and data communication

  - Business continuity and WAN diversity with redundant WAN links: Fast Ethernet, symmetric high-bit-rate DSL (G.shdsl), asymmetric DSL (ADSL) 2/2+, very-high-data-rate DSL 2 (VDSL2), third-generation (3G), and ISDN

  - Survivable Remote Site Telephony (SRST) voice continuity for enterprise small branch-office and teleworker sites

  - Enhanced security, including:

    - Firewall: With advanced application and control for email, instant messaging (IM), and HTTP traffic

    - Site-to-site, remote-access and dynamic VPN services: IPsec VPNs (3DES or AES), Dynamic Multipoint VPNs (DMVPN), Group Encrypted Transport VPNs (GET VPN) with onboard acceleration, and Secure Socket Layer (SSL) VPNs

    - Intrusion prevention system (IPS): An inline, deep-packet inspection feature that effectively mitigates a wide range of network attacks

    - Content filtering: A subscription-based integrated security solution that offers category-based reputation rating, keyword blocking, and protection against adware, malware, spyware, and URL blocking

  - Four-port 10/100 Fast Ethernet–managed switch with VLAN support; two ports support Power over Ethernet (PoE) for powering IP phones or external access points

  - Secure IEEE 802.11g/n access-point option based on draft 802.11n standard with support for autonomous or Cisco Unified WLAN architectures

  - CON/AUX port for console or external modem

  - One USB 1.1 port for security eToken credentials, booting from USB, and loading configuration

  - Easy setup, deployment, and remote-management capabilities through web-based tools and Cisco IOS Software

Summary

In this chapter, the following key points were covered on remote connectivity network design:

- Analyze network requirements:

    - Type of applications, traffic volume, and traffic pattern

    - Redundancy and backup needed

- Characterize the existing network and sites:

    - Technology used

    - Location of hosts, servers, terminals, and other end nodes

- Develop WAN and branch network design:

    - Select WAN and branch technology to support requirements

    - Select hardware and software components to support requirements

- Network application and connectivity requirements that influence the WAN design

- The Cisco Enterprise MAN and WAN Architecture provides integrated QoS, network security, reliability, and manageability:

    - On private WANs

    - On ISP service through site-to-site and remote-access VPNs

    - On service provider–managed IPO or MPLS VPNs

- The Cisco Enterprise Branch Architecture supports small, medium, large, and tele-worker locations.

References

For additional information, refer to these resources:

Cisco, Inc. Cisco product index for routers, at www.cisco.com/en/US/products/hw/routers/index.html.

Cisco, Inc. Cisco product index for switches, at www.cisco.com/en/US/products/hw/switches/index.html.

Cisco, Inc. Ethernet Access for Next Gen Metro and Wide Area Networks, at www.cisco.com/en/US/docs/solutions/Enterprise/WAN_and_MAN/Ethernet_Access_for_NG_MAN_WAN_V3.1_external.html.

Cisco, Inc. Enterprise Internet Edge Design Guide, at www.cisco.com/en/US/docs/solutions/Enterprise/Security/IE_DG.html.

Cisco, Inc. Cisco Integrated Services Routers, at www.cisco.com/en/US/products/ps10906/Products_Sub_Category_Home.htm.

Cisco, Inc. Cisco Internetworking Technology Handbook, at docwiki.cisco.com/wiki/Internetworking_Technology_Handbook.

Cisco, Inc. LAN Baseline Architecture Branch Office Network Reference Design Guide, at www.cisco.com/univercd/cc/td/doc/solution/designex.pdf.

Cisco, Inc. LAN Baseline Architecture Overview—Branch Office Network, at www.cisco.com/univercd/cc/td/doc/solution/lanovext.pdf.

Review Questions

Answer the following questions, and then refer to Appendix A for the answers.

1. What is the definition of a WAN?

2. Which of the WAN transport technologies reserves a point-to-point connection bandwidth indefinitely for transmissions?

3. Which device is used to provide ADSL line termination?

4. Which of SONET's optical carrier rates provides 622.08 Mbps?

5. Which feature is able to classify packets based on matching fields at the application layer?

6. Which WAN topology includes a single central hub with remote networks directly connected back to the central location?

7. Which Cisco IOS Software technology provides an easy, dynamic, and scalable IPsec and GRE VPN solution?

8. Which Layer 3 VPN technology leverages the Border Gateway Protocol to distribute VPN-related information?

9. Which service provider VPN technology presents itself as an Ethernet interface to customers and allows several remote sites to appear as if they are on the same LAN?

10. Which Cisco Enterprise MAN and WAN technology provides a comprehensive WAN optimization solution that accelerates applications over the WAN?

Chapter 6

Designing IP Addressing

This chapter discusses IP addressing design and includes the following sections:

- Designing IPv4 Addressing

- Designing IPv6 Addressing

An efficient IP addressing design is key for addressing and routing on an IP network. This chapter begins with an overview of IP addressing and general considerations for planning a network addressing scheme. It continues with a discussion of the specific considerations and migration strategies for IP version 4 (IPv4) and IP version 6 (IPv6).

Designing IPv4 Addressing

The following sections focus on IPv4 and discuss considerations regarding routing protocol choices that are related to IP addressing. An effective and efficient IPv4 addressing scheme is a critical component of the overall enterprise network design.

IPv4 Addressing

The following IPv4 concepts are prerequisite knowledge for this book:

- IP uses a 32-bit address to designate a host on a network and uses a 32-bit mask to identify the network portion of the address.

- IP classes were the original method used to allocate IP address ranges to organizations. IP classes utilized fixed-length fields for networks. Classless interdomain routing (CIDR) uses variable-length fields for networks that support a more efficient allocation of addresses than the original class-based method.

- Static addressing assigns a permanent address to a device. It is appropriate for network infrastructure devices such as routers that are permanently connected to the network.

■ Dynamic addressing assigns temporary IP addresses when devices connect to the network. DHCP is one way to dynamically assign addresses and also set TCP/IP stack configuration parameters, such as the subnet mask, default gateway, and Domain Name System (DNS) server. Dynamic addressing is typically employed by end users that connect to and disconnect from the network.

■ DNS is a mechanism to convert symbolic names into IP addresses.

■ Public addresses are used to reach a unique device that is connected to the public Internet.

■ Private addresses are nonpublic (not routable on the Internet) and are for internal use to designate a unique device within an organization.

■ Network Address Translation (NAT) and Port Address Translation (PAT) can be used to translate between public and private addresses. Static NAT is a one-to-one mapping of a private IP address to a public IP address. Dynamic NAT maps a private IP address to a public IP address from a group of public IP addresses. NAT overloading, or PAT, is a form of dynamic NAT that maps multiple private IP addresses to a single public IP address by using different ports.

Private and Public Addressing Guidelines

This section discusses guidelines for private and public addressing in the enterprise network.

As a recommended practice, public addresses should be used for required connectivity to the Internet and external organizations such as outside DNS servers and web servers, and private addresses should be used within the internal network. Use NAT and PAT as needed to translate between private internal addresses and public external addresses.

Private IP addresses are typically used throughout the enterprise network, except in the following places:

■ The Internet connectivity module, where public IP addresses are used for Internet connections and public accessible servers

■ The e-commerce module, where public IP addresses are used for the database, application, and web servers

■ The remote access and Virtual Private Network (VPN) module, where public IP addresses can be used for selected connections

Recommended Practices for NAT

The criteria for NAT deployment are accessibility to the public network and public visibility. Use NAT to translate in one of the following ways:

■ **One private address to one public address:** Used when servers from the internal network with private IP addresses must be visible from the public network. Defines the translation statically to translate from the public IP address to the server private IP address.

■ **Many private addresses to one public address:** Used for end systems that need access to the public network but do not need to be visible to the outside world.

■ **Combination:** Both techniques can be combined throughout the network.

Developing an Addressing Plan

The first step in an IP addressing plan design is to determine the size of the network, so the necessary number of IP addresses and subnets can be established. This section describes how to determine the size of a network for an IP addressing plan.

To determine the network size, answer these questions:

1. How many locations are in the network? Determine the number of locations and identify their type.

2. How many devices need addressing in each location? Determine the number of end systems, router interfaces, switches, firewall interfaces, and network devices per location.

3. What are the IP addressing requirements for individual locations? Collect information about which systems will use DHCP and which will use static addresses. In addition, obtain information on which systems can use private addresses instead of public addresses.

4. Which size subnet is appropriate? Make decisions that are based on the collected information about the number of networks and planned switch deployment to estimate appropriate subnet size. For example, if 48 port switches were being deployed in wiring closets with a single device per port, subnets of 64 addresses would be appropriate because 64 is the closest power-of-2 value that is higher than 48.

Figure 6-1 provides an example of general network topology.

To gather the correct information about network size and its relation to the IP addressing plan, it is necessary to understand a general picture of the network topology. General network topology information can assist in determining the number of locations, location types, and their correlations. This information is the foundation for gathering the data regarding network size and the individual location requirements that are related to the IP addressing plan. The information for the example in Figure 6-1 is shown in Table 6-1.

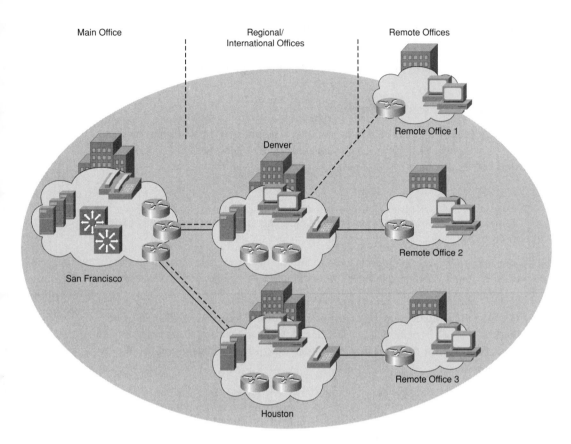

Figure 6-1   *General Network Topology Example*

Table 6-1   *Network Locations*

Location	Type	Comments
San Francisco	Main office	The central location where the majority of users are located
Denver	Regional office	Connects to the San Francisco main office
Houston	Regional office	Connects to the San Francisco main office
Remote Office 1	Remote office	Connects to the Denver regional office
Remote Office 2	Remote office	Connects to the Denver regional office
Remote Office 3	Remote office	Connects to the Houston regional office

The network size, in terms of the IP addressing plan, relates to the number of devices and interfaces that need an IP address. The overall network size can be determined by factoring in the following for each location:

■ Approximate number of workstations

■ Servers

■ Cisco IP Phones

■ Router interfaces

■ Switch management and Layer 3 interfaces

■ Firewall interfaces

■ Additional network devices

This estimate provides the minimum overall number of IP addresses that are necessary to address the network. All networks tend to grow, so it is recommended to keep a reserve of up to 20 percent for potential network expansion. A commonly suggested reserve is 20 percent for the main and regional offices and 10 percent for the remote offices. Carefully discuss the network growth issue with the organization to ensure an accurate estimate of the required resources. An example of an addressing plan for this figure is shown in Table 6-2.

Table 6-2 *IP Addressing Plan Example*

Location	Office Type	Work-stations	Servers	IP Phones	Router Interfaces	Switches	Firewall and Other Device Interfaces	Reserve, %	Total
San Francisco	Main	600	35	600	17	26	12	20	1290
Denver	Regional	210	7	210	10	4	0	20	441
Houston	Regional	155	5	155	10	4	0	20	329
Remote Office 1	Remote	12	1	12	2	1	0	10	28
Remote Office 2	Remote	15	1	15	3	1	0	10	35
Remote Office 3	Remote	8	1	8	3	1	0	10	21
Total	—	1000	50	1000	45	37	12	—	2144

Planning the IP Addressing Hierarchy

Based on the addressing needed per location, an IP addressing hierarchy can be planned.

Network designers implement the IP addressing hierarchy based on network size, geography, and topology. In large networks, a hierarchy within the IP addressing plan is mandatory for a stable network. A planned hierarchical IP addressing structure with extra capacity is a recommended practice for all sizes of networks because of the following considerations:

■ **Influence of IP addressing on routing:** An IP addressing plan influences the overall routing in the network. Features such as fixed-length subnet masking (FLSM) and variable-length subnet masking (VLSM), implemented with classful and classless routing protocols, influence the IP addressing plan and the choice of routing protocol. Before assigning IP addresses to devices and allocating blocks of IP addresses to various parts of the network, the criteria for an appropriate and effective IP addressing scheme should be considered. Routing stability, service availability, network scalability, and modularity are some of the key characteristics of every network that IP address allocation and deployment directly affect.

■ **Modular design and scalable solutions:** Whether building a new network or adding a new service to an existing infrastructure, a modular design delivers a long-term, scalable solution. IP addressing modularity allows aggregation of routing information on a hierarchical basis.

■ **Support for route aggregation:** To reduce routing overhead and improve the stability and scalability of routing, use route aggregation. To implement route aggregation, the network must be divided into contiguous IP address areas and the designer must have a solid understanding of the effects of IP address assignment on route aggregation (summarization) and hierarchical routing.

Design Consideration: Route Summarization Groups

Within the context of hierarchical addressing, the IP network addressing plan must include provisions for summarization at key points in the network.

When a router announces a route to a given subnet, the route is a summarization of all the individual addresses that reside on that subnet. The use of summarization to reduce the size of the routing table helps localize topology changes, a benefit that promotes network stability. The stability is enhanced because a reduced routing-table size means reduced bandwidth use. It also reduces memory use and the number of CPU cycles that are required to calculate the best path.

To reduce the routing overhead in a large network, a multilevel addressing hierarchy needs to be implemented. The depth of the hierarchy depends on the network size and the size of the upper-level summarization group. These are the levels of the hierarchy:

- **First level:** Represented by the locations within the network. Each location is typically a group of summarized subnets, which is known as a summarization group.

- **Second level:** Done within the first-level summarization group. A large location can be divided into smaller summarization groups that are represented by buildings or cities within a certain location. Not all first-level summarization groups require a second level of hierarchy.

- **Third level:** Can be performed within the second-level summarization group to minimize further potential routing overhead and instability. The floors within individual buildings can represent the third-level summarization group.

Based on the estimated counts per location, it is recommended to reserve a subnet consisting of a summarizable block of N numbers that are a power of 2. This block can start at any address that is a multiple of N. For example, to support 11 users with growth, a subnet of 16 numbers would be allocated in the address space, with a starting address that is a multiple of 16.

Address Blocks by Location

Based on the address counts from the previous example, an address block hierarchy can be designed; these address blocks are shown in Table 6-3 and detailed in this section. This example assumes that the design is to be easily summarized.

To determine the number of available host addresses on a subnet, use the formula $2^N - 2$, where N is the number of bits set to 0 (that is, the mask). Subtract 2 because a host cannot be represented with a host part of either all 0s or all 1s. The first IP address that is available for hosts can be determined in a particular network, for the host part, by setting the last bit (reading from right to left) to 1 and all others to 0. The last IP address available can be determined by setting the last bit in the host part to 0 and all other bits to 1.

For the main campus, allocate 2048 addresses based on an estimated count of 1290 addresses. This subnet is then further divided into smaller subnets that support floors or wiring closets.

For the Denver region, 512 + 32 + 64 addresses are needed to support the Denver campus and the two remote offices. So allocate 1024 addresses to the Denver region. This subnet will be further divided into smaller subnets that support buildings, floors, or wiring closets.

For the Houston region, 512 + 32 addresses are needed to support the Houston location and its remote office. So allocate 1024 addresses to the Houston region.

Because the largest remote office needs 64 addresses, and plenty of address space is available, allocate 64 addresses to each remote office.

Table 6-3 *Address Blocks by Location Example*

Location	Number of Addresses Required	Rounded Power of 2	Address Block
San Francisco Campus	1290	2048	172.16.0.0–172.16.7.255/21
Denver Region			
Denver Office 1	441	512	172.16.8.0–172.16.9.255/23
Remote Office 1	32	64	172.16.10.0/26
Remote Office 2	35	64	172.16.10.64/26
Denver Total	—	1024	172.16.8.0–172.16.13.255/23
Houston Region			
Houston Campus	329	512	172.16.12.0–172.16.13.255/23
Remote Office 3	32	64	172.16.14.0/26
Houston Total	—	1024	172.16.12.0–172.16.15.255/22

Finally, divide the 172.16.0.0/16 address space into these summarizable address ranges in the address block column.

Hierarchical IP Addressing Plan

Well-designed IP addressing, as illustrated in Figure 6-2, enables efficient aggregation of routing advertisements, which consumes less bandwidth and less router CPU and hides individual route flaps.

Route aggregation on border routers between contiguously addressed areas improves control over routing table growth. Route summarization (aggregation) should be implemented on the area borders. In a link failure, routing updates are not propagated to the rest of the network, but they stay in the area. This feature reduces routing overhead from bandwidth consumption and relieves routers from unnecessary routing table recalculation.

Note Efficient aggregation of routing advertisements narrows the scope of routing update propagation and significantly decreases the cumulative frequency of routing updates.

In contrast, poorly designed IP addressing in a network results in random assignment of IP addresses on an as-needed basis. This suboptimal practice provides no option to divide the network into contiguous address areas to implement route summarization. Some of the results of poorly designed IP addressing include

- **Additional bandwidth consumption as a result of excess routing traffic:** Because of individual route changes, routers need to send routing updates constantly. Thus, the routing traffic consumes more bandwidth than does a single summarized stable route.

- **Increased routing table recalculation:** Routing updates require routing table recalculation, which can affect router performance and the ability to forward traffic.

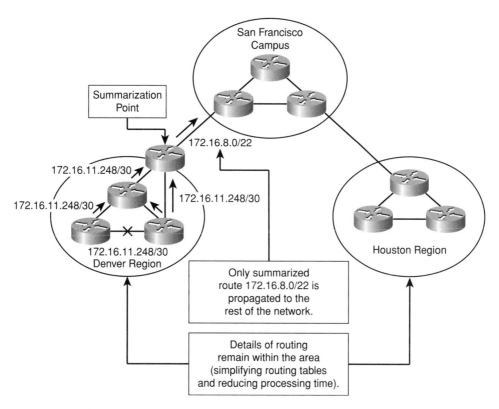

Figure 6-2   *Hierarchical IP Address Plan Example*

The typical enterprise network uses both static and dynamic address assignment methods. The static IP address assignment method is typically used for network infrastructure devices, within the data center modules, and in the modules of the enterprise edge and WAN (the e-commerce, Internet connectivity, remote access and VPN, and WAN modules). Static addresses are required for systems such as servers or network devices, where the IP address needs to be known at all times for general access or management.

The dynamic IP address assignment method is typically used to assign IP addresses to end-user devices, including workstations, Cisco IP Phones, and mobile devices.

DHCP is commonly used to assign IP addresses automatically and to set TCP/IP stack configuration. The DHCP server is allowed to send parameters (default gateway, DNS server, and so on) in addition to the IP address and the subnet mask.

When a host is started, its address-acquire process sends an IP address request by sending its physical hardware address to the network. The DHCP server intercepts the request and responds with the host IP address, subnet mask, and additional IP parameters.

DHCP Address Allocation Mechanisms

DHCP supports three possible address allocation mechanisms:

■ **Manual:** The network administrator assigns the IP address to a specific MAC address. DHCP is used to dispatch the assigned address to the host.

■ **Automatic:** The IP address is permanently assigned to a host.

■ **Dynamic:** The IP address is assigned to a host for a limited time or until the host explicitly releases the address. This is referred to as an address *lease*. This mechanism supports automatic address reuse when the host to which the address has been assigned no longer needs the address.

Recommended Practices for Name Resolution

Names are used to identify different hosts and resources on the network and to provide user-friendly interaction with computers. A name is much easier to remember than an IP address. Name resolution maps a name to an IP address.

Network hosts identify themselves to each other by using naming schemes. Each computer on the network can have an assigned name to provide easier communication. The IP network layer protocol uses IP addresses to transport datagrams, so a name used to identify a host must be mapped, or resolved, to an IP address. This process is called *name resolution*.

The process of resolving a host name to an IP address can be either of the following:

■ **Static:** With static name–to–IP address resolution, the administrative overhead and configuration are similar to a static address assignment strategy. The network administrator manually defines name–to–IP address resolutions in a special file on each device by entering the name and IP address pairs on a local host file, using either a graphical or text interface. Manual entries create additional work for the administrator, who must enter them on every host. Manual entries are often prone to errors and omissions.

■ **Dynamic:** The dynamic name–to–IP address resolution is very similar to the dynamic address assignment strategy. The administrator needs only to enter the local name–to–IP address resolutions on a local DNS server and does not need to repeat the task on every host. The server then performs the job of name–to–IP address resolution for the local devices. The dynamic name–to–IP address resolution method facilitates renumbering and renaming.

To resolve symbolic names to actual network addresses, devices need to comprehend the DNS server address. Queries on the name server are performed through resolver or name resolver programs, which are usually part of the end-user or host operating system. An application sends a query to a name resolver, which resolves the request with either the local database (HOSTS file) or the DNS server.

To enable DNS name resolution, the network administrator must set up the DNS server, enter information about host names and corresponding IP addresses, and configure the hosts to use the DNS server for name resolution.

Note DHCP can automatically send the default gateway and DNS server parameters to the end-user device in addition to the IP address and the subnet mask.

Figure 6-3 illustrates the steps of resolving an IP address using a DNS server. The steps are described as follows.

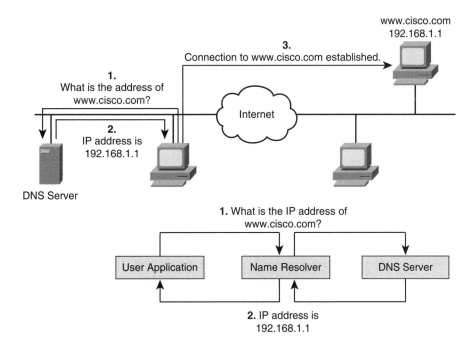

Figure 6-3 *DNS Name Resolution Example*

Step 1. A user wants to browse www.myweb.com. Because the host does not know the IP address of that site, it queries the DNS server.

Step 2. A server responds with the appropriate IP address for www.myweb.com.

Step 3. The host establishes a connection to the appropriate IP address (site).

Note   A fully qualified domain name (FQDN) is a complete domain name for a specific host on the Internet with the data necessary to convert it into a specific IP address. The FQDN consists of a host name and a domain name. For example, www.myweb.com is the FQDN on the Internet for the myweb web server. The host is "www," the domain is "myweb," and the top-level domain name is "com."

Locating DHCP and DNS Servers in the Network

DHCP and DNS servers can be implemented at multiple places in the network, depending on the service they support.

For the enterprise campus, DHCP and internal DNS servers should be located in the data center. These servers should be redundant. For remote locations, Cisco routers can provide DHCP and DNS at the enterprise edge. External DNS servers should be implemented in a redundant fashion. They should be colocated at two service provider facilities or with one DNS server located at the service provider facility and one in a demilitarized zone (DMZ) at the enterprise campus or remote data center.

IP Address Space Planning Road Map

IP address space planning requires careful consideration of many factors, which include

- Number of subnets currently needed

- Number of subnets needed for future use

- Number of hosts currently in the largest subnet

- Number of hosts needed for future use

It is a good practice to reserve some address space for the future. For example, if 125 hosts are on one subnet, a prefix of /25 (126 hosts) should be not be used. This is because it can create a serious negative impact on the network in the future. On the other hand, there is no needed to reserve too much space. The target is a trade-off between the cost of address space and allowing for future growth.

A topology network map needs to be created; this map should include where the NAT technology and summarization points that are planned will be located.

Finally, the IP address assignment and domain name resolution method for each segment of the network must be determined.

Designing IPv6 Addressing

The following sections cover IP version 6 (IPv6) address considerations and recommended practices in the campus network. An effective and efficient IPv6 addressing scheme is one of the main components of the overall enterprise network design.

IPv6 Addressing

IP version 6 (IPv6) was designed as a successor to IP version 4 (IPv4), to overcome IPv4 limitations. An IPv6 address is 128 bits long, providing a much larger address space than the address space in IPv4. It can provide approximately 3.40×10^{38} addresses.

IPv6 addresses are represented as a series of 16-bit fields that are presented as a hexadecimal number and separated by colons (:), in the format x:x:x:x:x:x:x:x. To shorten the writing of IPv6 addresses, a few techniques are available:

■ The leading 0s in a field are optional addresses.

■ IPv6 addresses often contain successive hexadecimal fields of 0s. To shorten IPv6 addresses, double colons (::) can be used to compress successive hexadecimal fields of 0s at the beginning, middle, or end of an IPv6 address (the double colons represent successive hexadecimal fields of 0s).

Note An IPv6 address can only use double colons once. Otherwise, the number of 0s to add will not be known.

For example, the IPv6 address 2031:**0000**:130F:**0000:0000:0**9C0:876A:130B can be written as the following: 2031:0:130F::9C0:876A:130B.

A single interface will have multiple IPv6 addresses of different types. IPv6 addresses contain a scope field that categorizes the types of applications suitable for the address.

Benefits of IPv6 Addressing

This section provides an overview of the benefits of IPv6 addressing.

The main benefits of IPv6 include

■ **Larger address space:** IPv6 increases the IP address size from 32 to 128 bits. This increase supports more addressing hierarchy levels, a much greater number of addressable nodes, and simpler address autoconfiguration.

■ **Globally unique IP addresses:** Every node can have a unique global IP address, which eliminates the need for Network Address Translation (NAT).

■ **Site multihoming:** IPv6 allows hosts to have multiple IPv6 addresses and allows networks to have multiple IPv6 prefixes. This multihoming ability facilitates connection to multiple ISPs without breaking the global routing table.

■ **Header format efficiency:** A fixed header size makes processing more efficient.

■ **Improved privacy and security:** With IPv6, IP Security (IPsec) support is a protocol requirement. In addition, IPv6 introduces optional security headers.

- **Flow-labeling capability:** A new capability enables packet labeling to belong to particular traffic flows, so the sender can request special handling, such as nondefault quality of service (QoS) or "real-time" service.

- **Increased mobility and multicast capabilities:** Mobile IPv6 allows an IPv6 node to change its location on an IPv6 network and maintain existing connections. With Mobile IPv6, the mobile node is always reachable through one permanent address. A connection is established with a specific permanent address assigned to the mobile node. Regardless of the amount of times that the mobile node changes locations and addresses, the connection remains intact.

IPv6 Address Types

Like IPv4, in IPv6, a single source can address datagrams to either one or many destinations at the same time. Here are some IPv6 address types:

- **Unicast (one-to-one):** The process is the same as IPv4. A single source sends data to a single destination. A packet that is sent to a unicast IPv6 address is delivered to the interface that is identified by that address. Various IPv6 unicast addresses are supported, including

  - Link-local address

  - Unique local address

  - Global aggregatable address

  - IPv4-compatible IPv6 address

> **Note**   IPv6 address scopes are discussed later in this chapter.

- Anycast (one-to-nearest): This is an identifier for a set of interfaces that typically belong to different nodes. A packet that is sent to an anycast address is delivered to the closest interface, as defined by the routing protocols in use. They are identified by the anycast address. In other words, receivers that share the same characteristics are assigned the same anycast address. A sender that is interested in contacting a receiver with those characteristics sends packets to the anycast address, and the routers deliver the packet to the receiver that is nearest to the sender.

Anycast addresses can be used for a service location. For example, an anycast address could be assigned to a set of replicated FTP servers. A user in China who wanted to retrieve a file would be directed to the Chinese server, and a user in Europe would be directed to the European server. Anycast addresses are allocated from the unicast address space. An anycast address cannot be used as the source address of an IPv6 packet. The node must be explicitly configured with which anycast address to recognize.

- **Multicast (one-to-many):** This is the same as IPv4, an address for a set of interfaces (in a given scope) that typically belong to different nodes. A packet that is sent to a multicast address is delivered to all the interfaces that the address identifies.

Note   IPv6 does not use the concept of broadcast addresses. Multicast addresses are used instead.

Link-Local Addresses

A link-local address is useful in the context of the local network. Its scope limits its relevance to only one link. A link-local address is an IPv6 unicast address that can be automatically configured on any interface by using the link-local prefix FE80::/10 (1111 1110 10) and the interface identifier. This is illustrated in Figure 6-4. Link-local addresses are used in the Neighbor Discovery Protocol and the stateless autoconfiguration process. Use link-local addresses to connect devices on the same local network without having to use globally unique addresses. Many routing protocols use link-local addresses. An IPv6 router must not forward packets to other links that have either link-local source or destination addresses.

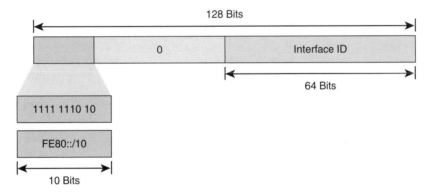

Figure 6-4   *IPv6 Link-Local Address*

Unique Local Address

A unique local address (defined in RFC 4193) is designed for use in local networks and is not routable in the global Internet. It is an IPv6 unicast address that is a substitute for a site-local address, and it uses the prefix FC00::/7 (1111 110). The eighth bit is always set to 0 and can be set to 1 in the future. The next 40 bits form the Global ID, a globally unique prefix that indicates the site. This is illustrated in Figure 6-5. This Global ID is allocated pseudorandomly to minimize the possibility of overlap with other sites.

The unique local address is more functional than the site-local address. This prefix is globally unique in a network where each site can commonly have more than one of these prefixes and can use them at the same time.

Global Aggregatable Address

A global aggregatable address is an IPv6 address from the global aggregatable unicast prefix. Global aggregatable unicast addresses enable aggregation of routing prefixes, which limits the number of routing table entries in the global routing table. Global aggregatable addresses are used on links that are aggregated upward through organizations, then to intermediate-level ISPs, and eventually to top-level ISPs. The structure is shown in Figure 6-6.

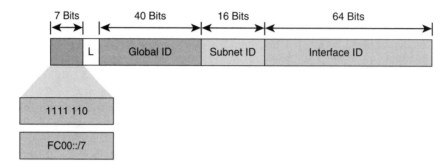

Figure 6-5 *IPv6 Unique Local Address*

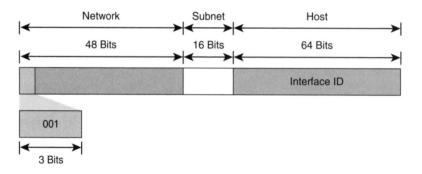

Figure 6-6 *IPv6 Global Aggregatable Address*

The structure is detailed as follows:

- A fixed prefix of 2000::/3 (001) indicates a global aggregatable IPv6 address.

- The IPv6 unicast space encompasses the entire IPv6 address range, with the exception of FF00::/8. Under RFC 4291, Internet Assigned Numbers Authority (IANA) unicast address assignments are currently limited to the IPv6 unicast address range of 2000::/3. IANA assignments from this block are registered in the IANA registry at www.iana.org/assignments/ipv6-unicast-address-assignments.

- Individual organizations use a 64-bit field for the host, with the interface ID used to identify interfaces on a link. The 64-bit field must be unique to the link.

IPv6 Address Assignment Strategies

As with IPv4, IPv6 presents two major address assignment strategies: static and dynamic (also called autoconfiguration). Static address assignment in IPv6 is the same as in IPv4: The administrator must manually configure the IPv6 address on every device in the network. IPv6 dynamic address assignment strategies include the following:

- **Link-local address:** The host configures its own link-local address autonomously, using identifiers for an interface and the link-local prefix FE80::/10.

- **Stateless autoconfiguration:** A router on the link advertises global prefixes and a willingness to function as a default router for the link, either periodically or at the request of the host. Hosts can automatically generate global IPv6 addresses without the need for either manual configuration or the help of a server, such as a DHCP server, using these router messages and their interface IDs.

- **Stateful using DHCPv6:** DHCPv6 is an updated version of DHCP for IPv4, which supports IPv6 addressing. DHCPv6 enables the network administrator to have more control than stateless autoconfiguration. It can be used to distribute other information, including the DNS server. DHCPv6 can be used for automatic domain name registration using a dynamic DNS server. DHCPv6 uses multicast addresses.

Identifying IPv6 Name Resolution

IPv6 and IPv4 static and dynamic name resolution is very similar. Two types of name resolution are available with IPv6:

- **Static name resolution:** Relies on manual entries in the local configuration files of the host.

- **Dynamic name resolution:** Uses a DNS server, which has built-in support for IPv6, usually with IPv4. An IPv6-aware application requests the IPv6 address of the destination host name (for example, www.myweb.com) from the DNS with a request for an A6 record (an address record for the IPv6 host, a new DNS feature). The name resolver, usually part of the operating system, queries for the address. The network administrator must set up the appropriate DNS server with IPv6 support. It must connect the DNS server to the IPv6 network with a valid IPv6 address. On the host side, the administrator must either enter valid DNS addresses manually or use DHCPv6.

A dual-stack host is aware of both IPv4 and IPv6 protocol stacks, with a new application programming interface (API). It supports both IPv4 and IPv6 addresses and DNS requests. A converted application can use both IPv4 and IPv6.

An IPv6- and IPv4-enabled application chooses which stack to use (the typical default is IPv6) and asks the DNS server for the destination host name address (www.myweb.com). After receiving the response from the DNS server, the application then requests the source host to connect to the destination host using IPv6.

Note   Microsoft Windows 7 and Windows Server 2008 fully support IPv6 and provide enhanced performance for IPv6 networking.

Making the Transition from IPv4 to IPv6

IPv4-to-IPv6 migration requires careful planning. Completing the transition from IPv4 to IPv6 can take several years because of the high cost of upgrading the equipment. During the transition, both IPv4 and IPv6 must coexist. To enable smooth and end-user-transparent communication between the IPv4 and IPv6 parts of a network, various solutions are available to the network administrator. Three primary mechanisms help with the transition from IPv4 to IPv6:

- **Dual-stack:** Both the IPv4 and the IPv6 stacks run on a system. This system can communicate with both IPv6 and IPv4 devices.

- **Tunneling:** IPv6 packets are encapsulated to traverse IPv4 networks and vice versa. Tunneling encapsulates packets of one type into packets of another type. In the case of a transition to IPv6, tunneling encapsulates IPv6 packets into IPv4 packets. By using overlay tunnels, isolated IPv6 networks can communicate without upgrading the IPv4 infrastructure between them. Both routers and hosts can use tunneling with one of these techniques:

  - **Manually configured:** The tunnel source and tunnel destination are manually configured with IPv4 and IPv6 addresses. Tunnels can be configured between border routers or between a border router and a host.

  - **Semiautomatic:** A tunnel broker uses a web-based service to semiautomatically create a tunnel. A tunnel broker is a server on the IPv4 network that receives tunnel requests from dual-stack clients, configures the tunnel on the tunnel server or router, and associates the tunnel from the client to a tunnel server or router. A simpler model combines tunnel broker and server on one device.

  - **Automatic:** These are the automatic mechanisms to achieve tunneling:

    - **IPv4-compatible:** The tunnel is constructed using an IPv4-compatible address (an IPv6 address that consists of 0s in the upper bits and an embedded IPv4 address in the last 32 bits). Because it does not scale, this mechanism is appropriate only for testing.

    - **6to4:** Each 6to4 site has a /48 prefix, which is the concatenation of 2002 and the IPv4 address of the edge router. The 2002::/16 range is a specially assigned address range for 6to4. When the edge router receives an IPv6 packet with a destination address in the 2002::/16 range, the router extracts the IPv4 address that is embedded in the IPv6 destination address and encapsulates the IPv6 packet in an IPv4 packet with the extracted IPv4 address of the destination edge router. The destination edge router deencapsulates the IPv6 packet from the received IPv4 packet and forwards the IPv6 packet to its final destination. To reach the native IPv6

Internet, a 6to4 relay router is needed that offers traffic forwarding to the IPv6 Internet.

- **6over4:** A router that is connected to a native IPv6 interface can be used, and with a 6over4-enabled interface, IPv6 traffic can be forwarded between 6over4 hosts and native IPv6. IPv6 multicast addresses are mapped into the IPv4 multicast addresses. IPv4 becomes a "virtual Ethernet" for IPv6. To achieve that result, an IPv4 multicast-enabled network is needed.

- **Translation:** This mechanism translates one protocol to the other to facilitate communication between the two networks. For legacy equipment that will not be upgraded to IPv6, and for some deployment scenarios, techniques that can connect IPv4-only nodes to IPv6-only nodes are available. Translation is basically an extension of NAT techniques. An IPv6 node behind a translation device has complete connectivity to other IPv6 nodes and offers NAT functionality to communicate with IPv4 devices. Possible solutions include the following:

  - **Application layer gateways (ALG):** ALGs use a dual-stack approach and enable a host in one domain to send data to another host in the other domain. This method requires that all application servers on a gateway run IPv6.

  - **API:** A specific module in the TCP/IP stack of a host can be installed for every host on the network. The module intercepts IP traffic through an API and converts it for the IPv6 counterpart.

  - **Translation techniques:** Techniques are available to translate IPv4 addresses to IPv6 addresses and vice versa. Translation can occur at the transport layer or on the network layer as with current NAT devices. The two main network translation solutions are Network Address Translation–Protocol Translation (NAT-PT) and Dual Stack Transition Mechanism (DSTM).

In addition, Cisco has designed the Cisco IPv6 Provider Edge Router over Multiprotocol Label Switching (MPLS) feature (Cisco 6PE), which supports smooth integration of IPv6 into MPLS networks. Because MPLS routers switch packets based on labels rather than address lookups, customers with an MPLS backbone can scale IPv6 traffic easily and do not need to make costly hardware upgrades.

Strategies for IPv6 Deployment

There are three main campus IPv6 deployment models:

- **Dual-stack model:** In this model, IPv4 and IPv6 coexist in the network. Devices have one IPv4 stack and one IPv6 stack.

- **Hybrid model:** The strategy of this model is to employ several independent transition mechanisms with the same deployment design goals. There are two main variations of the hybrid model:

    - **Hybrid model example 1 (HME1):** Provides hosts with access to IPv6 services, when the network infrastructure does not support IPv6 natively, by using a combination of a dual-stack mechanism and Intra-Site Automatic Tunnel Addressing Protocol (ISATAP) tunnels.

    - **Hybrid model example 2 (HME2):** Uses manual tunnels to connect two or more dual-stack areas through an IPv4 core network.

- **Service block model:** Offers unique capabilities to customers that are facing the challenge of providing access to IPv6 services within a short time period. The service block model uses a combination of ISATAP tunnels, manually configured tunnels, and dual-stack mechanisms.

Dual-Stack Model

As shown in Figure 6-7, the dual-stack node supports both IPv4 and IPv6 stacks. Applications can communicate with both IPv4 and IPv6 stacks. The IP version choice is based on name lookup and application preference. This mechanism is the most appropriate choice for the campus and access networks during the transition period and is the preferred technique for transition to IPv6. Operating systems use a dual-stack approach to support the maximum number of applications.

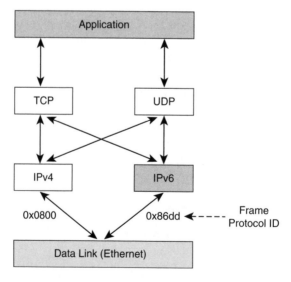

Figure 6-7   *Dual-Stack Model*

Some of the operating systems that support IPv6 dual-stack are

■   FreeBSD

■   Linux

■   Oracle Solaris (formerly Sun Solaris)

■   Mac OS

■   Microsoft Windows 2000, XP, Vista, and 7 operating systems

The dual-stack model has several advantages over the other models. The primary advantage is that the dual-stack model does not require tunneling within the network. The dual-stack model runs IPv4 and IPv6 independently. Both protocols have independent routing, high availability, QoS mechanisms, security, and multicast policies. When the dual-stack model is used, packets are forwarded without additional encapsulation overhead, which increases processing performance.

The only drawback of the dual-stack model is that an upgrade of existing network equipment is required if the equipment does not support the IPv6 protocol.

Hybrid Model

The key reason to use the hybrid model is flexibility. Any combination of transition mechanisms can be used to create the best solution for a given network environment. The hybrid model adapts to almost any existing network infrastructure. Transition mechanisms are based on multiple criteria (IPv6-capable hardware, number of hosts, location of IPv6 services, and so on).

The hybrid model uses three main transition mechanisms:

■   Dual-stack mechanism

■   ISATAP

■   Manually configured tunnel

Two specific examples describe this model:

■   Hybrid model example 1 (HME1) using ISATAP to connect dual-stack hosts through the IPv4 distribution layer to the core layer, plus dual-stack in the core layer and beyond

■   Hybrid model example 2 (HME2) using dual-stack in the access layer and distribution layer of each area, plus manually configured tunnels between them

HME1

The main idea behind HME1 is that dual-stack hosts located in the access layer can use IPv6 services when the distribution layer is not IPv6-capable. This is illustrated in Figure 6-8. Because there are no IPv6 services in the distribution layer, hosts from the access layer cannot reach IPv6 addresses and need to run an ISATAP tunnel to the core layer.

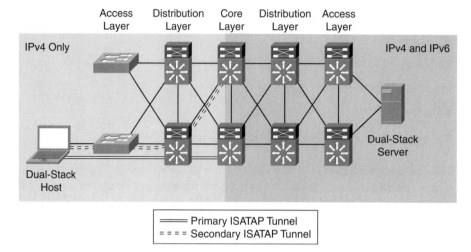

Figure 6-8 *HME1 Example*

There are two main solution requirements for using an HME1 strategy:

■ ISATAP support on the operating system of the dual-stack host

■ Dual-stack and ISATAP support on the core layer switches

There are alternatives to these two solutions that can be used to deploy the HME1 model. They include tunnel termination at the network layer as different from the core layer or the use of 6to4 tunnels instead of ISATAP if the access layer hosts run heterogeneous operating systems (Linux, FreeBSD, Oracle Solaris, or Mac OS).

The primary benefit of HME1 is that the existing network equipment can be leveraged without the need for upgrades, especially on the distribution layer switches. If the distribution layer switches currently provide acceptable IPv4 service and performance and are still within the depreciation window, HME1 can be a suitable choice.

It is important to understand the drawbacks of the hybrid model, specifically with HME1. They include

■ IPv6 multicast is not supported within ISATAP tunnels.

■ Terminating ISATAP tunnels in the core layer makes the core layer appear to be an access layer to the IPv6 traffic. Network administrators and network architects design the core layer to be highly optimized for the role it plays in the network. It is very often stable, simple, and fast. Adding a new level of intelligence to the core layer might not be acceptable.

As with any design that uses tunneling, there must be certain considerations. They should include

- Performance

- Management

- Security

- Scalability

- Availability

The use of tunnels is always a secondary recommendation compared to the dual-stack model design.

HME2

The aim of HME2 is to configure manual tunnels between dual-stack distribution layers through the core layer that do not have IPv6-capable equipment, or have limited IPv6 support with low performance. This is shown in Figure 6-9. Two tunnels from each switch are used for redundancy and load balancing. Routing and IP multicast on the tunnel are configured similarly to dual-stack mechanisms.

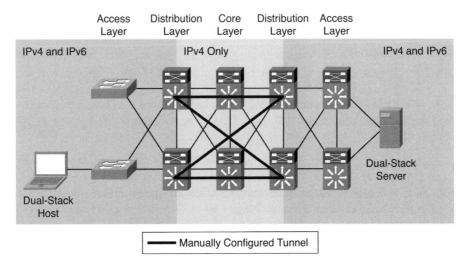

Figure 6-9 *HME2 Example*

This configuration should be considered for any nontraditional QoS configurations on the core that can impact tunneled or IPv6 traffic, because the QoS policies on the core do not have visibility into the tunneled IPv6 packets. Similar considerations apply to the security of the network core. If special security policies exist in the core layer, those policies need to be modified (if they are supported) to account for the tunneled traffic that is crossing the core.

HME2 is a good model to use if the campus core is being upgraded or has plans to be upgraded, and access to IPv6 services is required before the completion of the core upgrade.

Like most traffic in the campus, IPv6 should be forwarded as fast as possible. This is especially true when tunneling is used, because there is an additional processing step that is involved in the encapsulation and decapsulation of the IPv6 packets. Cisco Catalyst platforms such as the Cisco Catalyst 6500 Supervisor Engine 32 and the Cisco Catalyst 6500 Supervisor Engine 720 forward tunneled IPv6 traffic in hardware.

In many networks, HME2 is less applicable than HME1, but HME2 is nevertheless discussed in the model overview section as another option. As with any design that uses tunneling, considerations that must be accounted for include

■   Performance

■   Management (some static tunnels are difficult to manage)

■   Scalability

■   Availability

The use of tunnels is always a secondary recommendation to the dual-stack model (DSM) design.

Service Block Model

The service block model is significantly different compared to the other deployment models. Although the underlying concept of this model is not new, it does offer unique capabilities to customers who are facing the challenge of providing access to IPv6 services in a short time. The service block model can be deployed as an overlay network without causing any impact to the existing IPv4 network. This is shown in Figure 6-10.

A second helpful characteristic is that the service block solution is completely centralized. However, when the existing network becomes IPv6 capable, the service block model can become decentralized, because connections into the model change from tunnels to dual-stack. Therefore, after all network layers are IPv6 capable, the service block model can be removed or repurposed for other uses.

The primary advantage of the service block model implementation is its lesser impact on the existing network configuration. This model provides control over the IPv6 services deployment by using the following:

■   Per-VLAN tunnels can be configured through ISATAP to control the flow of connections and allow the measurement of IPv6 traffic use.

■   Access on a per-server or per-application basis can be controlled through access control lists (ACL) and routing policies at the service block model.

■   The service block model allows high availability of ISATAP and manually configured tunnels as well as all dual-stack connections.

■   Flexible options allow hosts to have access to the IPv6-enabled ISP connections. This is accomplished by allowing a segregated IPv6 connection strictly used for

IPv6-based Internet traffic or by providing links to the existing Internet edge connections that have both IPv4 and IPv6 ISP connections.

■ Implementation of the service block model does not disrupt the existing network infrastructure and services.

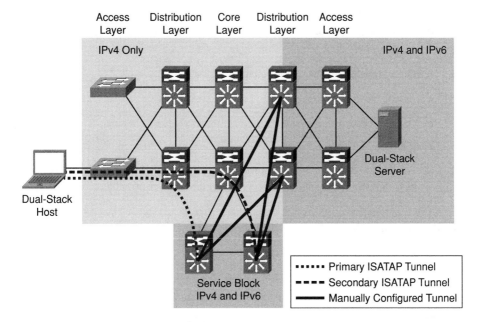

Figure 6-10 *Service Block Example*

The main drawback of the service block model is that the tunneling mechanisms are a primary way to provide access to the service, as with HME1 and HME2. It also necessitates the cost of additional equipment that is not required in HME1 and HME2.

Because of drawbacks associated with the hybrid model and the service block model, it is recommended that the dual-stack model be deployed whenever possible.

Summary

In this chapter, you learned about IPv4 and IPv6 addressing. The following topics were explored:

■ Key components of an IPv4 hierarchical addressing scheme include IP address structure, address classes, subnetting, and masking.

■ Well-designed hierarchical IPv4 addressing enables efficient aggregation of routing advertisements, which consumes less bandwidth and router CPU:

■ Dynamic IP address assignment is a recommended practice in the enterprise.

- Dynamic name resolution with a DNS server is a recommended practice in the enterprise.
- IPv6 was designed as a successor to IPv4, to overcome the limitations of IPv4:
  - The IPv6 address structure and address types support a much larger address space than IPv4.
  - IPv6 supports three unicast address types: link-local, unique local, and global aggregatable.
- There are three main IPv6 deployment models:
  - Dual-stack model
  - Hybrid model
  - Service block model
- Because of the drawbacks to using the hybrid and service block models, it is recommended that the dual-stack model be deployed whenever possible.

References

For additional information, refer to these resources:

Cisco, Inc. Cisco IOS IP Addressing Services Configuration Guide, Release 12.4, at www.cisco.com/en/US/docs/ios/ipaddr/configuration/guide/12_4/iad_12_4_book.html.

Welcher, Peter J. Chesapeake NetCraftsmen. Making Your Router Serve, at www.netcraftsmen.net/welcher/papers/dhcpdns.html.

Internet Assigned Numbers Authority. Internet Protocol version 6 Address Space, at www.iana.org/assignments/ipv6-address-space.

Internet FAQ Archives. RFC 3587, "IPv6 Global Unicast Address Format," at www.faqs.org/rfcs/rfc3587.html.

Cisco, Inc. Deploying IPv6 in Campus Networks, at www.cisco.com/en/US/solutions/ns340/ns414/ns742/ns815/landing_cIPv6.html.

Comer, Douglas E. and D. L. Stevens. *Internetworking with TCP/IP Volume 1: Principles, Protocols, and Architectures, 5th Edition*. Englewood Cliffs, New Jersey: Prentice-Hall, 2006.

Cisco, Inc. Cisco IP Version 6 Solutions, at www.cisco.com/univercd/cc/td/doc/cisintwk/intsolns/ipv6_sol/index.htm.

Cisco, Inc. Campus Network for High Availability Design Guide, at www.cisco.com/en/US/docs/solutions/Enterprise/Campus/HA_campus_DG/hacampusdg.html.

Review Questions

Answer the following questions, and then refer to Appendix A for the answers.

1. How many bits are used by an IPv4 address?

2. In which modules are private IP addresses not typically used?

3. What formula is used to determine the number of available hosts on a subnet?

4. What are the three possible address allocation mechanisms provided by DHCP?

5. What are the two ways that can be used to provide IP–to–host name lookup?

6. The IPv6 address 2003:0:4321::2:1 is the shortened version of what address?

7. What are the available IPv6 address types?

8. Which of the available IPv6 unicast address subtypes always has a prefix of FE80::/10?

9. Which of the available IPv4-to-IPv6 transition technologies runs a copy of both IPv4 and IPv6?

10. Which of the IPv6 transition models works by configuring manual tunnels between dual-stack distribution layers over an IPv4 core?

Chapter 7

Designing and Selecting Routing Protocols

This chapter discusses IP routing protocols and contains the following sections:

■ Reviewing Enterprise Routing Protocols

■ Designing a Routing Protocol Deployment

This chapter provides recommended practices for deploying routing protocols in the enterprise, based on network characteristics and customer requirements.

Reviewing Enterprise Routing Protocols

The following sections discuss the factors that help determine which routing protocol to use in an enterprise network that employs IP version 4 (IPv4) or IP version 6 (IPv6). The sections begin with a review of basic routing protocol concepts and fundamentals. They continue to discuss characteristics of enterprise routing protocols.

Reviewing Routing Protocol Fundamentals

The following sections review some routing protocol fundamentals.

Differentiating Between Distance Vector and Link-State Routing Protocols

There are two types of interior gateway protocols:

■ **Distance vector protocols:** Routing by rumor is the process where routing table maintenance decisions are made based on hearsay. Each router relies on its neighbor routers to maintain correct routing information. Each router passes only the results of local decisions to its neighbors. An example of a distance vector protocol is Routing Information Protocol (RIP) version 2 (RIPv2). Distance vector protocols are usually easy to implement and maintain. On the other hand, the process of routing by rumor means that network changes are propagated slowly from one router to the next, and global convergence is slow.

■ **Link-state protocols:** Each router floods information about itself (its link states) either to all other routers in the network or to a part of the network (area). Each router makes its own routing decision that is based on all received information by using the common Shortest Path First (SPF), or Dijkstra's, algorithm, which calculates the shortest path to any destination. IP link-state protocols include OSPF and Integrated Intermediate System–to–Intermediate System (IS-IS). These protocols offer several advantages when compared to distance vector protocols. One main advantage is convergence. As soon as a network topology change occurs, information regarding the change is sent to all routers in a given area. As soon as the network converges and all routers have the same information, routing updates stop, thus decreasing the overall routing overhead. Link-state protocols are usually more complex than vector protocols. They require more knowledge both for the initial implementation and daily maintenance.

Note   Enhanced Interior Gateway Routing Protocol (EIGRP) has characteristics of both distance vector and link-state protocols. Because of this, is it also referred to as a hybrid or advanced distance vector protocol.

Distance Vector Routing

Distance vector routing is called "routing by rumor" because routing table maintenance decisions are made locally and are based on hearsay from immediate neighbors. This is illustrated in Figure 7-1. Distance vector protocols periodically send complete routing tables to all connected neighbors. Because of the speed of loop detection timers, convergence is slow.

In large networks, the routing table can become enormous, which causes significant traffic on the links.

An example of a distance vector protocol is RIPv2, which is a standardized protocol that was developed from the RIPv1 protocol. These are the characteristics of RIPv2:

■ The metric for path selection is hop count.

■ The maximum allowable hop count is 15.

■ Routing updates are multicast.

■ RIPv2 permits variable-length subnet masking (VLSM) on the network, whereas RIPv1 does not permit VLSM.

Note   Pure distance vector protocols are typically not adequate for large enterprise network implementations.

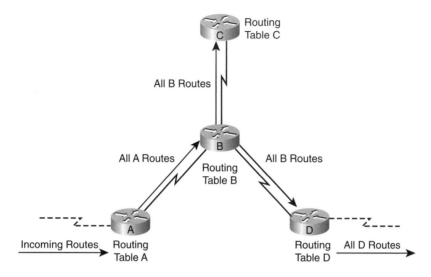

Figure 7-1   *Distance Vector (Routing by Rumor) Example*

Link-State Routing

The link-state protocols OSPF and Integrated IS-IS use implementations of the Hello protocol to establish neighbor relationships. Information that is shared through the neighbor relationship allows each router to understand a complete topology of the network. The SPF algorithm creates the shortest-path tree for all reachable destinations and thus selects the best routes.

With link-state protocols, the information regarding connected links (subnets on those links) on all routers is flooded throughout the network or to a specific area of the network. This is illustrated in Figure 7-2. Therefore, all routers in the network have detailed knowledge of the entire network, unlike routers using distance vector routing protocols, where routers receive knowledge of only the best routes from neighboring devices.

After the initial exchange of all link states, and upon reaching the FULL state of operation, almost no periodic updates are sent through the network. (However, in OSPF, synchronizing periodic updates still takes place every 30 minutes for each specific route. This is not at the same time for all routes. The method of staggering updates reduces the routing traffic volume.) Updates are triggered only when a change in a link state occurs (for example, when a link goes down or the bandwidth changes).

Most control packets used in link-state operations are sent through multicast. This type of propagation can cause problems when deploying link-state protocols in nonbroadcast multiaccess (NBMA) networks, such as with some Frame Relay and ATM topologies.

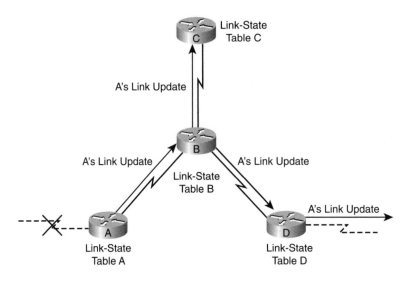

Figure 7-2   *Link-State Example*

Differentiating Between Interior and Exterior Routing Protocols

The Internet is based on the autonomous system (AS) concept. As a result, two types of routing protocols are required: interior and exterior routing protocols. An AS, otherwise known as a domain, is a collection of routers under a common administration, such as a company internal network or an ISP network.

Protocols are required for the following situations:

- Intra-AS (inside an AS) routing, which requires interior gateway protocols (IGP)

- Inter-AS (between autonomous systems) routing, which requires exterior gateway protocols (EGP). The only widely used EGP protocol is Border Gateway Protocol version 4 (BGP version 4 [BGP-4]).

Different types of protocols are needed for these reasons:

- Inter-AS connections require more options to manually select routing characteristics. EGPs should be able to implement various policies.

- The speed of convergence and finding of the shortest path to the destination are of crucial importance for intra-AS routing protocols.

Therefore, the routing metrics of EGP protocols include more parameters so that the administrator can influence routing path selection. Alternatively, IGPs tend to use less complicated metrics to ease and speed up the decisions on best routing paths.

Interior Versus Exterior Routing Protocols

Figure 7-3 shows three autonomous systems (domains). They are interconnected with interdomain links and BGP. IGPs (OSPF, IS-IS, and EIGRP) are implemented for intra-AS (intradomain) routing.

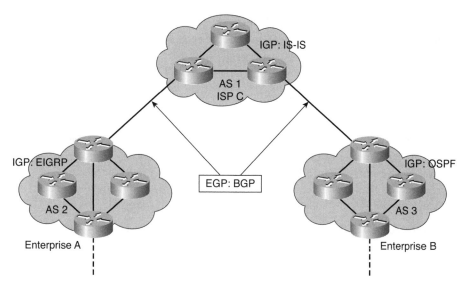

Figure 7-3   *Interior Versus Exterior Routing Protocol Example*

If autonomous systems need to communicate with each other, they require some form of interdomain routing among the networks. This can include static routes, used in simple cases, or more typically, EGP.

BGP is the dominant EGP in use. BGP is especially beneficial when an AS is connected to the Internet through multiple ISPs. This implementation of redundant connectivity for inter-AS connections is called *multihoming*. An administrator can apply specific policies when using BGP (for example, traffic exit points, return traffic path, and levels of quality of service [QoS]) to comply with the contract requirements from specific ISPs.

Note   IGPs are typically deployed within the enterprise. BGP is typically used to connect the enterprise to an ISP.

Differentiating Between Hierarchical and Flat Routing Protocols

Flat routing protocols propagate all routing information throughout the network, while hierarchical routing protocols divide large networks into smaller areas. Classful routing means that the protocol performs automatic summarization of network information only on major class network boundaries (Class A, B, or C). These protocols require fixed-length subnets.

Link-state protocols are hierarchical. Large networks are divided into multiple areas using link-state protocols such as OSPF and IS-IS. With route summarization configured, smaller routing updates are propagated among areas, resulting in higher scalability and a better fit for large networks. Link-state protocols are classless and support VLSM. The summarization on an arbitrary boundary within an IP address can be implemented.

EIGRP, by default, operates like a classful protocol and performs automatic summarization of network information only on major class network boundaries (Class A, B, or C). However, it also supports VLSM and manual summarization; with this support, it is possible to build a hierarchical network design using EIGRP.

Routing Protocol Convergence

Convergence occurs whenever the network topology changes and all routers in that network learn the impact of the new topology. Convergence is both collaborative and independent. The routers share information with each other but must independently calculate the impact of the topology change on their own routes. They develop an agreement with the new topology independently, so they are said to converge on this consensus.

Convergence properties include the speed of propagation of routing information and the calculation of optimal paths. The quicker the convergence, the better the routing protocol and the network design. The use of hierarchical addressing and summarization helps localize topology changes, a benefit that speeds convergence.

Network convergence, or propagation of routing information, occurs whenever a new routing protocol is started in the network. A network is not completely operable until it has converged, so routing protocols require short convergence times.

With a specific network topology, different routing protocols need various amounts of time to converge. Pure distance vector protocols are slower than link-state protocols, because they use periodic updates and a hold-down mechanism. Thus, when network convergence is of crucial importance in the design requirements, the fast-converging protocols should be used.

Link-state protocols converge much faster because they instantly propagate routing updates. Therefore, whenever a change in a link state occurs, a link-state update floods through the entire network, which results in fast convergence. There is no need to wait for the next periodic update.

EIGRP is a special case because it incorporates the distance vector principle of metric propagation (in other words, only the best information is sent to the neighbors). However, EIGRP has no periodic updates and does not implement the principle of holddown. EIGRP stores available backup routes in its topology table. If a certain lost destination has a backup route, the switchover to the best backup route is almost immediate and involves no action from other devices in the network. With proper EIGRP deployment, very fast convergence can be achieved.

Note   When all edge routers of a network converge, the complete network has also converged.

Routing Protocols for the Enterprise

The two recommended protocols for routing within the enterprise are EIGRP and OSPF. BGP is typically used to interconnect the enterprise to an ISP. The following sections discuss the characteristics of enterprise routing protocols.

EIGRP

EIGRP is a Cisco-proprietary protocol for IPv4 or IPv6 routing. EIGRP also supports legacy protocols of Internetwork Packet Exchange (IPX) and AppleTalk traffic. EIGRP was developed from IGRP, which is a pure distance vector protocol. EIGRP is a hybrid (or advanced distance vector) routing protocol, which is a distance vector protocol with additional link-state protocol features.

These are some additional EIGRP advantages:

■   Triggered updates (EIGRP has no periodic updates)

■   Use of a topology table to maintain all the routes that have been received from neighbors (not only the best ones)

■   Establishment of adjacencies with neighboring routers by using the Hello protocol

Other advantages of EIGRP are its support for VLSM and manual route summarization. These features allow EIGRP to create hierarchically structured large networks.

Routes are propagated in EIGRP in a distance vector approach, from neighbor to neighbor, and only the best routes are sent onward. A router that is running EIGRP does not have a complete view of a network, because it sees only the routes that it has received from its neighbors. In a pure link-state operation (for example, OSPF and IS-IS), all routers in the same area have identical information and, therefore, have a complete view of the area and its link states.

EIGRP by default uses minimum bandwidth and cumulative delay of the path in the metric calculation. This is a recommended practice, but EIGRP can be configured to also include worst reliability between source and destination, worst loading on a link between source and destination, and the smallest maximum transmission unit (MTU) in the metric calculation.

Note   Minimum bandwidth is the minimum from the routing update and the interface bandwidth. The bandwidth is known for LAN interfaces and is taken from the bandwidth command on serial interfaces. If the bandwidth is not specified on a serial interface, it is assumed to be the line rate of the configured interface.

One advantage of EIGRP is its fast-convergence Diffusing Update Algorithm (DUAL) route calculation mechanism. DUAL allows the insertion of backup routes (also known as feasible successors) into the EIGRP topology table, which are used in case of primary route failure. Because it is a local procedure, the switchover to the backup route is immediate and does not involve action in any other routers. There is, however, a requirement that must be met for a route to become available as a backup route (also called a feasible successor). It is required that the advertised distance (also called the reported distance [RD]) from the neighboring router be lower than the current feasible distance (FD) on the local router. This is called the feasibility condition.

EIGRP, by default, summarizes routes on the classful network boundaries. Autosummarization can be turned off and manual summarization can be incorporated. Manual summarization of subnet routes improves scalability and network performance because the routing protocol uses fewer resources.

Because EIGRP does not use periodic routing table updates, it uses less bandwidth, especially in large networks, where the number of routes becomes very large. EIGRP also uses a Hello protocol to establish and maintain adjacencies with its neighbors through multicast. If many neighbors are reachable over the same physical link, as is the case in NBMA networks, the Hello protocol might create significant routing traffic overhead. Therefore, the network must be designed appropriately so as to use all the EIGRP advantages. Fast convergence, good scalability, and support for unequal load balancing make EIGRP an excellent choice for an enterprise routing protocol.

EIGRP deployments primarily support IPv4 networks and can support IPv6. EIGRP also supports legacy network layer protocols through protocol-dependent modules (PDM), including IPX and AppleTalk. EIGRP is a Cisco-proprietary protocol and can pass protocol information with licensed devices only.

Open Shortest Path First

Open Shortest Path First (OSPF) is an open standard protocol for routing IPv4. It was developed in 1988 by the Internet Engineering Task Force (IETF) to replace RIP in larger, more diverse media networks.

OSPF was developed for large, scalable networks where RIP failed to satisfy requirements because of its inherent limitations. OSPF is superior to RIP in most aspects. OSPF has much faster convergence. It supports VLSM, manual summarization, and hierarchical structure. It better calculates the metric for best-path selection and it has no hop-count limitations. At inception, OSPF supported the largest networks.

In 1998, minor changes in OSPF version 2 (OSPFv2) addressed some of the problems of version 1 while maintaining complete backward compatibility.

The concept of multiple separate areas inside one domain (or AS) was implemented in OSPF to reduce the amount of routing traffic and to make networks more scalable. In OSPF, there must always be one backbone area, usually called Area 0, to which all other nonbackbone areas are attached. All nonbackbone areas must be directly attached to the backbone Area 0. A router is a member of an OSPF area when at least one of its interfaces operates in that area. Routers that reside on boundaries between the backbone and a non-backbone area are called Area Border Routers (ABR) and have at least one interface in each area. The boundary between the areas is created in the ABR itself.

If external routes are propagated into the OSPF AS, the router that redistributes those routes is called the Autonomous System Boundary Router (ASBR). Careful design and correct mapping of areas to the network topology are important, because manual summarization of routes can only be performed on ABRs and ASBRs.

Figure 7-4 illustrates an OSPF multiarea network.

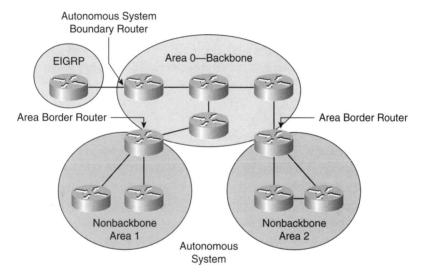

Figure 7-4   *OSPF Multiarea Network Example*

When traffic is sent from one nonbackbone area to another, it crosses the backbone area. For example, in Figure 7-4, the Area 1 ABR must forward Area 1 traffic into the backbone. The Area 2 ABR receives the traffic and forwards it to the appropriate destination inside Area 2.

OSPF is a link-state protocol, which is ideal for an enterprise network. OSPF achieves fast convergence times by using triggered link-state updates, which include one or more link-state advertisements (LSA). LSAs describe the state of links on specific routers and are propagated unchanged over one area. Therefore, all routers in the same area have identical topology tables, and each router has a complete view of all links and devices in the area. When LSAs cross into another area, the ABRs usually change them, depending on the type of LSA.

When the OSPF topology table is fully populated, the router applies the SPF algorithm to calculate the shortest paths to the destination networks. Triggered updates and metric calculations that are based on the cost of a specific link ensure a quick selection of the shortest path toward the destination.

Note On Cisco equipment, the OSPF link cost is a value that is inversely proportional to the bandwidth of the link.

A multiarea structure that is implemented in OSPF guarantees good scalability. However, strict area implementation rules require proper design so that scalability features such as manual summarization of routes on ABRs and ASBRs, stub areas, and not-so-stubby areas (NSSA) can be implemented. The stub and NSSA features for nonbackbone areas decrease the amount of LSA propagation from the backbone Area 0 into nonbackbone areas by replacing these advertised routes with default routes. This decrease allows low-end routers to run in the peripheral areas of the network. Fewer LSAs mean smaller OSPF topology tables, less OSPF memory usage, and lower CPU usage in stub area routers.

Because it is a classless protocol, OSPF supports the use of VLSM and achieves better utilization of IP address space. Fast convergence and good scalability also make OSPF an excellent choice for the enterprise routing protocol.

Border Gateway Protocol

Border Gateway Protocol (BGP) is a protocol that is representative of EGPs. It is primarily used to interconnect autonomous systems. Because the original EGP is obsolete, BGP is the only EGP in current use.

RFC 4271 (www.ietf.org/rfc/rfc4271.txt) defines a BGP version 4 (BGP-4) AS as "a set of routers under a single technical administration, using an IGP and common metrics to route packets within the autonomous system, and using an EGP to route packets to other autonomous systems."

At its core, BGP is a path vector protocol, which uses AS-path metrics as a basis for routing decisions. (For example, to get to network 10.10.10.0/24 if the path goes through ASs 1234 then 4321, this metric would be 1234, 4321.) BGP has a number of additional metric parameters, called path attributes, which allow administrators to influence routing decisions. Inter-AS routing involves considerable strategic routing policy decisions for ISPs to comply with peering and other types of agreements.

Figure 7-5 illustrates a BGP network example.

As shown in Figure 7-5, BGP is used to interconnect multiple autonomous systems. The AS is identified by a unique AS number that is used by the BGP routing updates. Because of the multiple connections between autonomous systems and the need for path manipulation, static routing is excluded. The connectivity of one AS to multiple ISP autonomous systems is called *multihoming*. The figure shows AS 65000 redundantly connected to three neighboring autonomous systems (65500, 65250, and 64500).

Note Private AS numbers in the range of 64512 to 65535 are used as an example only. ISPs use public AS numbers. Private AS numbers are used only for non-ISPs or in special cases.

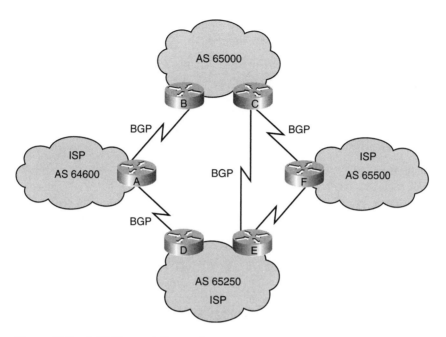

Figure 7-5 *BGP Network Example*

Use BGP for inter-AS routing in these situations:

■ If an AS has multiple connections to other autonomous systems

■ If an AS is a transit AS, meaning that it allows packets from other autonomous systems to transit themselves to reach another AS (which is a normal mode of operation for ISPs)

■ If the traffic flowing to or from the AS must be manipulated

The use of static routes is recommended for inter-AS routing if none of these requirements exists.

Note BGP implementation requires considerable knowledge. Improper implementations can cause great damage, especially when complete BGP Internet tables are exchanged between neighbors (in other words, more than 300,000 routes).

BGP that runs between routers of different autonomous systems is called External BGP (EBGP). BGP that runs between routers of the same AS is called Internal BGP (IBGP).

EBGP runs on routers that communicate between different ASs and by default must be directly connected. IBGP runs on all routers or on specific routers inside the AS. IBGP neighbors need not be directly connected, as long as they know how to reach each other.

Neighbor reachability information can be acquired either by using the IGP that is running in the AS or by using configured static routes.

IBGP is usually not the only protocol running in the AS. It is used merely to avoid redistribution of an entire Internet routing table into an IGP. The EBGP information is in transit autonomous systems where, for routing purposes, all Internet routes must be known on internal routers, which are transferred into IBGP and returned into EBGP. In this way, the redistribution into IGP (which could throttle IGP routing because of the amount of routing data) is avoided.

The primary use for IBGP is to carry EBGP (inter-AS) routes through the AS, because the EBGP tables are too large for an IGP to manage.

These are other useful implementations of IBGP:

- Policy-based routing (PBR) can be applied in internal autonomous systems with the help of BGP path attributes.

- QoS Policy Propagation on BGP (QPPB) uses IBGP to spread common QoS parameters (for example, class of service [CoS]) from one router to other routers in the network, which results in a synchronized QoS policy.

- In Multiprotocol Label Switching (MPLS) Virtual Private Networks (VPN), the multiprotocol version of BGP is used to carry MPLS VPN information. In that way, the successful implementation of a VPN with MPLS is possible.

IPv6 Routing

IPv6 routing types and protocols are generally similar to IPv4 routing protocols. They provide the same benefits, but have updated features that are related to IPv6 (for example, prefixes, multicast addresses, and so on).

There are two types of static routes for IPv6:

- Directly attached static routes that refer directly to outbound interfaces

- Recursive static routes that point to the next-hop IP address

RIP next generation (RIPng) is an adapted variation from the RIPv2 protocol, which is modified to advertise IPv6 prefixes. It is a distance vector protocol that is defined in RFC 2080. RIPng has many IPv4 features (15 hops, split horizon, and so on), and it is based on User Datagram Protocol (UDP) (port 521) and uses the FF02::9 multicast address. RIPng allows multiple RIPng routing processes to run on the same router (whereas RIP for IPv4 allows only one process per router).

OSPFv3 is a link-state routing protocol that was developed to support IPv6 prefixes and is defined in RFC 5340. It uses multicast addresses FF02::5 and FF02:6. OSPFv3 is based on OSPFv2 but has some differences, including new LSA types, and no authentication. OSPFv3 can run on a router that is already using OSPFv2, because OSPFv2 and OSPFv3 use separate SPF calculations and tables.

EIGRP version 6 (EIGRPv6) works much like EIGRP for IPv4. It is an advanced distance vector protocol that uses hello packets, DUAL algorithm for fast convergence, Real-Time Transport Protocol (RTP) as a transport, and multicast address FF02::A.

MP-BGP is an exterior protocol that is defined in RFC 4760 and contains a multiprotocol extension for BGPv4. It describes an Address Family Identifier (AFI) and some specific IPv6 extensions.

Selecting an Enterprise Routing Protocol

The selection of a routing protocol is based on the design goals and the physical topology of the network. Both EIGRP and OSPF are recommended practices for enterprise routing protocols.

When to Choose EIGRP

EIGRP, which is based on IGRP, is a hybrid (advanced distance vector) protocol that incorporates the best aspects of distance vector and link-state features (topology table, no periodic route propagation, and triggered updates). It is well suited to almost all enterprise environments, including LAN, point-to-point, and NBMA. In NBMA, split-horizon functionality can be disabled for EIGRP.

Note   EIGRP is a Cisco-proprietary protocol that is licensed to limited vendors.

When to Choose OSPF

OSPF is a standards-based link-state protocol, which is based on the SPF, or Dijkstra's, algorithm for best-path calculation. Initially, OSPF was designed for networks that consist of point-to-point links, but later it was successfully adapted for operation in LAN and NBMA environments. Because of the hierarchical design requirement, there are design considerations when using OSPF in larger networks. One backbone area is required, and it must attach all nonbackbone areas directly to that backbone area. Expansion of the backbone area can cause design issues, because the backbone area must remain contiguous.

Designing a Routing Protocol Deployment

The selection and implementation of a routing protocol are based on specific needs and topologies. The following sections describe scenarios where routing protocols are deployed based on different needs. The network characteristics and customer requirements, as well as the multiprotocol multivendor environment, are considered.

Applying Routing Protocols to a Hierarchical Network Structure

The choice of routing protocols is based on network design goals.

Routing in the Campus Core

The campus core provides high-speed data transmission between building distribution devices. The campus core is critical for connectivity and incorporates a high level of redundancy by using redundant links and load sharing between equal-cost paths. It must provide an immediate response in the event of a link failure and must adapt very quickly to change.

The campus core must converge and adapt to changes quickly to provide a seamless transport service. EIGRP and OSPF both acclimate to changes quickly and have short convergence times. Make the decision to use EIGRP or OSPF based on the underlying physical topology, IP addressing, equipment that is used, and possible issues that are related to the routing protocol in a particular situation.

There are a couple of disadvantages to each routing protocol in the campus core layer:

- OSPF imposes a strict hierarchical design. OSPF areas must map to the IP addressing plan, which might be impossible to accomplish.

- EIGRP restricts vendor selection because it is a Cisco-proprietary protocol. To overcome this restriction, multiple routing protocols with careful redistribution can be used.

Note Using static routing in the campus core is not an option, because static routing requires administrative intervention for changes and link failures.

Routing in the Building Distribution Layer

The building distribution layer is the intermediate point between the campus core and the building access layer. The physical media, IP addressing, and choice of routing protocols that are used in the campus core and building access layers affect the routing protocol choice in the building distribution layer.

As a recommended practice, use the same routing protocol in all three layers of the enterprise campus. If multiple routing protocols must be implemented, redistribution between the routing protocols should be implemented in the distribution layer.

For example, if EIGRP is the campus core routing protocol and RIP is the building access routing protocol for legacy support, use both routing protocols on the building distribution devices and apply redistribution with filtering to provide connectivity.

Recommended routing protocols in the building distribution layer include EIGRP and OSPF.

Routing in the Enterprise Edge Functional Area

The enterprise edge functional area provides access to network resources for local and remote users. The underlying physical topology, IP addressing, and the equipment that is deployed direct the choice of routing protocol. The routing protocols in the enterprise edge modules are typically OSPF, EIGRP, BGP, and static routing. Routing protocols that are running in the enterprise edge module are referred to as "edge routing" protocols.

There are advantages and disadvantages to each routing protocol in the enterprise edge:

- EIGRP offers the administrator more influence on routing and is suitable for NBMA environments, where there is a split-horizon issue (for example, Frame Relay or ATM multipoint interfaces). When equipment from multiple vendors is part of the overall design, the use of EIGRP is restricted.

- The limitations of using OSPF as an enterprise edge routing protocol involve its high memory and processing power requirements, which can impact older routers, as well as its strict hierarchical design. Use OSPF in environments such as LAN, NBMA, and dialup. OSPF also requires significant configuration expertise.

Note   The high memory and processing power requirements of using OSPF can be avoided with the use of summarization and careful area planning.

Routing in the Remote-Access and VPN and Internet Connectivity Modules

A remote-access and VPN module is used to provide connectivity to corporate networks for remote users through dialup and dedicated IP Security (IPsec) VPNs across the Internet. For most IPsec VPN environments, static routing can be used.

For connectivity to the Internet, either static routes or BGP should be used. The decision should be based on redundancy requirements and multiple exit points. Static routes present less overhead than BGP routing and are used when only a single exit point exists. However, use BGP when there are multiple exit points and when multihoming is desired.

Advanced routing features such as redistribution, filtering, and summarization allow multiple routing protocols to coexist and provide greater scalability. Proper design is needed, or routing issues will be introduced.

Route Redistribution

Redistribution between different routing protocols refers to passing routing knowledge from one protocol to another. There are several scenarios in which multiple protocols are used in a single network:

- When migrating from an older interior gateway protocol (IGP) to a new IGP. Multiple redistribution points can exist until the new protocol has displaced the old one entirely (in the entire network).

- Some departments might not want to upgrade their routers, or they might not implement a sufficiently strict filtering policy. In these cases, redistribution between those protocols is needed.

- In a mixed-vendor environment, a Cisco protocol can be used on the Cisco portion of the network, and then use redistribution with a standard protocol to communicate with outside devices.

Redistribution occurs on routing protocols and domain boundaries on a router with interfaces that participate in multiple routing protocols and routing domains. Redistribution of routes is necessary in these situations:

■ Multiple routing protocols are used in the network (for example, RIPv2, EIGRP, and OSPF).

■ Multiple routing domains are used in the network (for example, two EIGRP routing processes).

Redistribution is often applied between the campus core and enterprise edge protocols. Redistribution is possible in two ways:

■ **One-way route redistribution:** Routing information is redistributed from one routing protocol or domain to another but not vice versa. When this type of redistribution occurs, static or default routes are required in the opposite direction to provide connectivity.

■ **Two-way redistribution:** Routing information is redistributed from one routing protocol or domain to another and vice versa. Static or default routes are not needed because all routing information is passed between two entities.

Note Two-way redistribution should not be implemented without route filtering. Without filtering, routes redistributed from one routing protocol into another will end up being redistributed back into the source routing protocol as new routes, possibly causing routing problems.

Route Redistribution Planning

When deciding where and how to use route redistribution, these three things should be determined:

■ Routing protocols and domains to be used in the network

■ Routing protocols and domain boundaries (boundary routers)

■ Directions of route redistribution (one- or two-way redistribution)

If the design of route redistribution is not formulated carefully, suboptimal routing and routing loops can be introduced into the network. These problems occur when routes are redistributed back into a network that has redundant paths between dissimilar routing protocols or domains. The solution to this problem is achieved through route filtering.

Redistribution occurs on routing protocol and domain boundaries. Therefore, redistribution is also necessary in the building distribution layer when multiple routing protocols or routing domains exist.

Figure 7-6 shows some potential redistribution points in an enterprise network. Some remote sites need connectivity only to the data center module, so one-way redistribution can be performed to inject routes from remote sites into the campus core. If a routed access layer exists, it can be configured so that the enterprise IGP will propagate only the default route down to the building access layer. The building access layer advertises its own subnets to the building distribution layer.

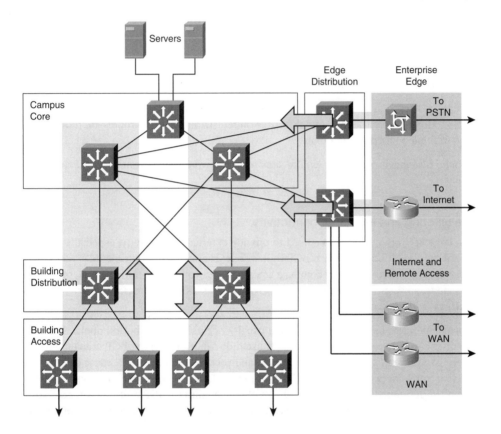

Figure 7-6   *Route Redistribution Planning Example*

The other demand in this figure is connectivity to remote sites. If connectivity is needed between remote sites, either two-way redistribution is required to provide connectivity or else appropriate static routes need to be configured in the core layer.

Remote-Access and VPN and Internet Connectivity Module Route Redistribution

Redistribution might also be necessary in the remote-access and VPN and Internet connectivity modules. For the remote-access module and VPN module with static routing, redistribution takes static routes and injects them into the campus core routing protocol. In the opposite direction, default routing provides connectivity for remote users.

For the Internet connectivity module with only one exit point, the exit point is the default route for Internet traffic and is propagated through the campus core routing protocol. When multiple exit points exist toward multiple ISPs for route redundancy, use BGP to provide Internet connectivity and redistribution.

Route Filtering

Route filtering prevents the advertisement of certain routes through the routing domain. Filtering can occur on the routing domain boundary where redistribution occurs. It can also occur in the routing domain to isolate some parts of the network from other parts of the network. Route filtering can also be employed to limit routing traffic from external domains that might be unreliable in sending appropriate traffic.

Filtering is used in combination with route redistribution to prevent suboptimal routing and routing loops. The loops might occur on redistribution when routes are redistributed on multiple redistribution points.

Route filtering also prevents remote sites from receiving routes from a local IP address space.

Route Filtering and Internet Connectivity

In large networks, BGP can be used to provide external connectivity, especially when the network is multihomed. When BGP routes are exchanged with multiple ISPs, take care to prevent the network from becoming a transit AS network between the ISPs. Use route filtering to prevent the advertisement of private addresses and addresses that are out of the official address scope.

In an enterprise network, route filtering usually occurs at redistribution points. When redistributing between an IGP and BGP, use redistribution into the BGP domain with filtering to prevent announcement of invalid and private IP addresses. Because routers inside an enterprise network do not need data for every Internet route, route filtering can be applied during redistribution from the BGP domain into the IGP routing protocol. Note, however, that the redistribution between BGP and any IGP is not generally recommended.

Route Summarization

A hierarchy in the network reduces routing traffic and unnecessary route recomputation. To implement a hierarchy, a network can be divided into areas that enable route summarization. This is illustrated in Figure 7-7.

Routing traffic consumes considerable network resources, so a large flat network is not scalable. When a change occurs, it is propagated throughout the network. This scenario requires processing time for route recomputation and bandwidth to propagate routing updates.

With summarization in place, a route recomputation that occurs in one network area does not influence routing in other areas. Instabilities that are caused by topology changes are isolated, and convergence is improved. This reduces the amount of routing traffic, the size of the routing tables, and the memory and processing power that is required for routing.

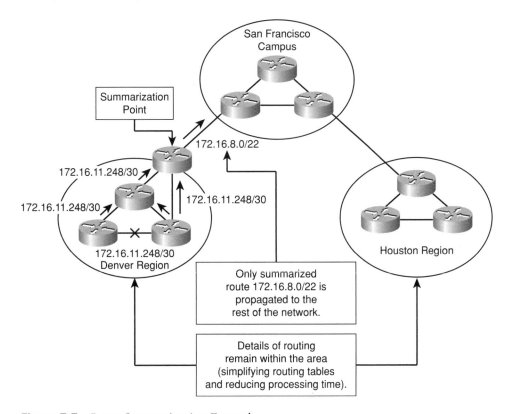

Figure 7-7   *Route Summarization Example*

Summarization can be implemented manually or automatically with routing protocols that provide such options.

Note   The underlying IP addressing plan must be hierarchical to support route summarization.

Recommended Practice: Summarize at the Distribution Layer

It is a recommended practice to configure summarization in a large network from the distribution layer toward the core:

■   Implement summarization at WAN connectivity and remote-access points to the core. For example, summarize remote networks into major networks, and only those major networks are then advertised to the core.

■ Implement summarization at the distribution layer for all networks on all interfaces toward the campus core.

Summarization at the distribution layer optimizes the convergence process. For example, if a link to an access layer device goes down, return traffic to that device will be dropped at the distribution layer until the IGP converges. Summaries also limit the number of peers that an EIGRP router must query or the number of link-state advertisements (LSA) that an OSPF router must process, and thereby limit the speed of the convergence process.

When the core receives two summary routes, the more specific route is installed in the routing table. Therefore, summaries for the primary links must use a longer subnet mask.

Note   Summarization relies on a solid network addressing design.

Recommended Practice: Passive Interfaces for IGP at the Access Layer

Another recommended practice is to limit unnecessary peering across the access layer. By default, the distribution layer switches send routing updates and attempt to peer across the links from the access switches to the remote distribution switches on every VLAN. This is unnecessary and wastes CPU processing time. As a recommended practice, unnecessary routing of peer adjacencies should be limited by configuring the ports toward the access switches as passive, which suppresses the advertising of routing updates. If a remote peer does not receive routing updates from a potential peer on a specific interface, it will not need to process these updates. It will not form a neighbor adjacency with the potential peer.

IPv6 Route Summarization

The larger address space of IPv6 allows the allocation of large address blocks to organizations and makes it necessary to use address aggregation for routing traffic reduction.

IPv6 routing information can be summarized at the boundaries of address spaces in the same manner as IPv4. Each customer site announces to the ISP only the /48 prefix that aggregates all the customer site addresses. The ISP summarizes the address space of all customer sites and announces only a /32 prefix to the global Internet. It allows decreasing of the global routing table entries and allows more scalable and efficient routing.

Within their own networks, customers can manage the address space according to their needs within the 16-bit subnet ID (between prefixes /64 and /48).

Summary

In this chapter, you learned about selecting routing protocols for enterprise networks. The following topics were explored:

- Protocols with hierarchical and link-state attributes support the fastest network convergence.

- EIGRP and OSPF are the recommend IGPs for the enterprise.

- EIGRP is a Cisco-proprietary protocol for routing IPv4, IPv6, IPX, and AppleTalk traffic.

- OSPF is a standardized protocol for routing IPv4 and IPv6 that was developed to replace RIP in larger, more diverse media networks.

- BGP-4 is a representative EGP. It is primarily used to interconnect autonomous systems or to connect enterprises to an ISP.

- Large networks can implement multiple protocols for different modules of the Cisco Network Architectures for the Enterprise.

- Advanced routing features such as redistribution, filtering, and summarization allow multiple routing protocols to coexist and provide greater scalability.

- Redistribution between different routing protocols passes routing knowledge from one protocol to another.

- Route filtering prevents advertisement of certain routes through the routing domain.

- Route summarization and an IP hierarchy reduce routing traffic and unnecessary route recomputation.

- IPv6 route summarization provides aggregation of prefixes that are announced in the global routing table, for efficient and scalable routing.

Review Questions

Answer the following questions, and then see Appendix A for the answers.

1. Which of the different routing protocol types is also referred to as "routing by rumor"?

2. When using RIP version 2, what is the maximum reachable hop count allowed?

3. Which of the available routing protocols uses inter-AS?

4. _____ routing means that the protocol only sends information about advertised networks along major class network boundaries.

5. Which routing protocol is Cisco proprietary and is considered to be a hybrid protocol with features of both distance vector and link-state protocols?

6. When implementing an OSPF network, there must always be a central area called the _____ that is also Area _____ .

7. When implementing an IPv6 network, what are the names and versions of the RIP, OSPF, and EIGRP routing protocols that need to be considered?

8. Which of the possible routing protocols are recommended to be used at the campus core?

9. What is the name of the method for integrating the routes from one routing protocol to another?

10. At which of the hierarchical design layers is it recommended to use route summarization?

Chapter 8

Evaluating Security Solutions for the Network

This chapter discusses network security solutions and contains the following sections:

■ Defining Network Security

■ Understanding Network Security Policy and Processes

Network security is an essential network service that spans the entire network. The modularity of Cisco Network Architectures for the Enterprise provides the ability to focus on a single security problem within a particular network module and integrate a solution into a global network design. A modular approach simplifies the network design and ensures that a security breach in one network module will remain isolated and not affect the entire network.

This chapter introduces the Cisco SAFE architecture strategy for designing network security. The chapter evaluates security from the physical perspective up through individual application security. Logging and monitoring are described as integral parts of any security solution and as preventive mechanisms to detect attacks before serious consequences result.

Defining Network Security

The scope of a network security solution is determined by organizational requirements and potential threats that are evaluated for each network component. To create a secure network, potential threats must be recognized. The following sections discuss the rationale for network security, including threats and risks. They also discuss network components as potential targets and explain how risk assessment is used in a security policy.

Network Security Background

In the distant past, the network was designed to be an open utility, and network security was largely a matter of physical security. As networks become increasingly interconnected and data flows more freely, security services become critical. In the commercial world, connectivity is no longer optional, because the possible risks do not outweigh the benefits. Therefore, security services must provide adequate protection to allow organizations to conduct business in a relatively open environment.

Secure networks are required to defend against attacks and prevent unauthorized access. Legislation, industry regulations, and company policies can also require secure networks to keep data private and make sure that data is not misused. Secure networks should provide the following:

- Prevent external hackers from getting access to the network

- Allow only authorized users into the network

- Prevent those inside the network from executing deliberate or inadvertent attacks

- Provide different levels of access for different types of users

- Protect data from misuse and corruption

To be truly effective, the security design must offer these protections in a way that is transparent to the users, is easy to administer, and does not disrupt business.

Security Legislation

Security legislation and industry standards can define how data has to be managed, how to make sure that private information is protected, and what kind of information can be public. Based on legislative mandates and industry directives, organizations might need to protect customer privacy by encrypting data to help ensure that the network is secure.

Some examples of laws and directives influencing network security include

- **Health Insurance Portability and Accountability Act (HIPAA):** The U.S. HIPAA security regulations apply to protected health information that is electronically maintained or used in an electronic transmission. Thousands of U.S. organizations must comply with the HIPAA Security Rule. The Security Rule is a key part of HIPAA, which is federal legislation that was passed into law in August 1996. The overall purpose of the act is to enable better access to health insurance, reduce fraud and abuse, and lower the overall cost of health care in the United States.

- **European Union Data Protection Directive (EUDPD) 95/46/EC:** This directive states, "In accordance with this Directive, Member States shall protect the fundamental rights and freedoms of natural persons, and in particular their right to privacy with respect to the processing of personal data." It also states, "Member States shall neither restrict nor prohibit the free flow of personal data between Member States for reasons that are connected with the protection afforded under paragraph 1."

- **Sarbanes-Oxley Act of 2002 (SOX):** This U.S. federal law was passed in response to a number of major corporate and accounting scandals. SOX is also known as the Public Company Accounting Reform and Investor Protection Act. SOX establishes new or enhanced auditing and financial standards for all U.S. public company boards, management, and public accounting firms. The act contains 11 sections, ranging from additional corporate board responsibilities to criminal penalties, and it requires the U.S. Securities and Exchange Commission (SEC) to implement rulings on requirements to comply with the new law.

- **Payment Card Industry (PCI) Data Security Standard (DSS):** The PCI DSS was developed to ensure safe handling of sensitive payment information, such as storage and transfer of credit card information. The PCI DSS is the umbrella program for other programs, such as the Visa Cardholder Information Security Program (CISP) and MasterCard Site Data Protection (SDP) program.

Threats and Risks

When designing for security, the types of attacks that can compromise system security and their associated risks need to be recognized. These threats can be classified into three broad categories:

- **Reconnaissance:** Reconnaissance is the active gathering of information about an enemy or target. In the networking security area, it is usually the first step that is accomplished prior to any kind of attack. The idea is to compile as much data as possible regarding the target network and the involved systems.

- **Gaining system access:** After data regarding the target system is established, the next step is getting access to the system by exploiting the system or using "social engineering." Known vulnerabilities in operating systems, services, and physical access can be exploited and privileges can be escalated. Social engineering can be used to obtain confidential information by manipulation of legitimate users. The impact of gaining system access can include these risks:

  - Exposure or compromise of sensitive data or machines

  - Execution of arbitrary commands on the system

- **Denial of service (DoS):** Even if direct access to a system is not possible, another category of threat is DoS. The DoS attack is used to make systems unusable by overloading resources such as CPU or bandwidth to disable the system. When multiple sources are conducting a DoS attack, it is called a distributed DoS (DDoS) attack.

To provide adequate protection of network resources, network procedures and technologies need to address the security risks. They include the following:

- **Confidentiality of data:** Only authorized users should be able to view sensitive information to prevent theft, legal liabilities, and damage to the organization.

- **Integrity of data:** Only authorized users should be able to change sensitive information and guarantee the authenticity of data.

- **System and data availability:** Uninterrupted access to important computing resources should be ensured to prevent business disruption and loss of productivity.

Reconnaissance Attacks

A common technique implemented to locate active targets such as networking devices and end stations is port scanning. A number of different tools can be used to implement port scanning on a target network or host.

The following are some examples of scanning tools:

- **Network Mapper (Nmap):** Nmap is a free, open-source, port-scanning utility for network exploration or security auditing. It was designed to rapidly scan large networks, although it works fine against single hosts.

- **Vistumbler and inSSIDer:** Vistumbler and inSSIDer are tools for Microsoft Windows that facilitate the detection of wireless LANs (WLAN) using the IEEE 802.11b, 802.11a, 802.11n, and 802.11g WLAN standards.

- **SuperScan:** SuperScan is a popular Windows XP or Vista port-scanning tool. It offers high scanning speed, improved host detection, extensive banner grabbing, and Windows host enumeration capability.

- **Kismet:** Kismet is an IEEE 802.11 Layer 2 wireless network detector, sniffer, and intrusion detection system (IDS) that can sniff IEEE 802.11b, 802.11a, 802.11n, and 802.11g traffic. It identifies networks by passively collecting packets and detecting standard named networks, detecting hidden networks, and inferring the presence of nonbeaconing networks through data traffic.

These tools are designed to scan large networks and determine which hosts are up and which services they are offering. They can support many scanning techniques such as

- User Datagram Protocol (UDP)
- TCP connect (open)
- TCP synchronization (TCP SYN) (half open)
- FTP proxy (bounce attack)
- Internet Control Message Protocol (ICMP) (ping sweep)
- FIN
- ACK sweep
- Xmas Tree
- SYN sweep
- IP protocol
- Null scans

After TCP or UDP ports are discovered using one of the scan methods, version detection communicates with those ports to try to determine more about what is actually running.

Figure 8-1 shows a sample Nmap screen (Using Zenmap Windows GUI) that has identified some open ports and the operating system version for a host.

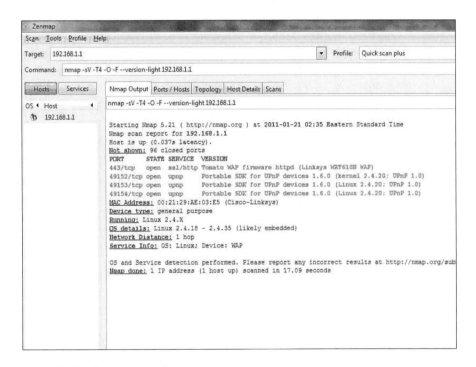

Figure 8-1   *Nmap Example*

Vulnerability Assessment

Vulnerability scanners are used to locate known vulnerabilities in the network. It can be done as passive scanning, where networking traffic is analyzed, or as active testing of systems by sending packets through the network.

The following websites have access to published vulnerability data:

■ **CERT Coordination Center (CERT/CC):** www.cert.org/nav/index_red.html

■ **MITRE:** www.cve.mitre.org

■ **Microsoft:** www.microsoft.com/technet/security/bulletin/summary.mspx

■ **Cisco Security Notices:**
www.cisco.com/en/US/products/products_security_advisories_listing.html

The following tools are used for vulnerability scanning:

- **Nessus:** Nessus is an open-source product that is designed to automate the testing and discovery of known security problems. Although there is a Windows graphical front end available, the core Nessus product requires Linux or UNIX to run.

- **Microsoft Baseline Security Analyzer (MBSA):** Although this tool is not a true vulnerability scanner, companies that rely primarily on Microsoft Windows products can use the freely available MBSA. MBSA scans the system and identifies whether there are any patches missing for Microsoft products, such as the Windows operating systems, Internet Information Services (IIS), SQL Server, Exchange Server, Internet Explorer, Windows Media Player, and Microsoft Office products. MBSA also identifies missing or weak passwords and other common security issues and raises an alarm for them.

- **Security Administrator's Integrated Network Tool (SAINT):** SAINT is a commercial vulnerability assessment tool. In contrast to the Windows-only tools, SAINT runs exclusively on UNIX.

Example Threat: Gaining Unauthorized Access to Systems

There are multiple ways to gain access to systems. A common threat is the knowledge of usernames and passwords by unauthorized persons. Usernames and passwords can be captured or cracked. Default administrative or service accounts can be accessible. If a malicious user gains access to a sufficiently privileged password, he can have access to all the files on the system. He might also be able to exploit other systems, based on user trust relationships across systems.

Another way of gaining access to a system is through social engineering, which is the practice of obtaining confidential information by the manipulation of legitimate users. Examples of social engineering include

- **Physical access to information:** It is possible to get confidential information and passwords by having physical access to the company. Walking inside a facility can allow someone to obtain passwords that are insecurely posted in an office or cubicle.

- **Psychological approach:** Another social engineering approach is using psychological methods to get confidential information. A well-known process is calling and asking for passwords while pretending that the information is required to maintain the account.

It might be possible to decrypt or crack passwords if the system password file is available or if passwords are captured when transmitted over the network.

Example Risk: Integrity Violations and Confidentiality Breaches

Integrity violations occur when the attacker changes sensitive data without proper authorization. For example, the attacker obtains permission to write to sensitive data and changes or deletes it. The owner might not detect the change until there has been a tangible loss. Many companies treat integrity violations as the most serious threat to their business because of the difficulty in detecting changes and the possible cascading consequences of late detection.

Confidentiality breaches occur when an attacker attempts to read sensitive data. These attacks are extremely difficult to detect because the attacker can copy sensitive data without the knowledge of the owner and without leaving a trace.

An example of both types of threats is shown in Figure 8-2.

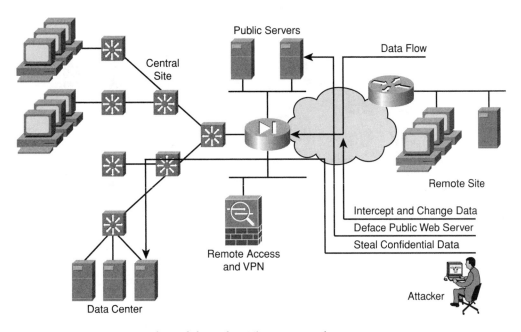

Figure 8-2 *Integrity and Confidentiality Threat Examples*

The risks of both integrity violations and confidentiality breaches are usually managed by enforcing access control in various ways. Here are some examples:

- Limiting access to network resources by using network access control, such as physical separation of networks, restrictive firewalls, and VLANs

- Limiting access to files and objects using operating system–based access controls, such as UNIX host security and Windows domain security

- Limiting user access to data by application-level controls, such as different user profiles for different roles

- Using cryptography to protect data outside the application, such as encryption to provide confidentiality and secure fingerprints or digital signatures to provide data authenticity and integrity

Example Risk: Loss of Availability

DoS attacks attempt to compromise the availability of a network, host, or application. DoS and DDoS attacks are considered a major risk because they can easily interrupt business processes and cause significant loss. DoS attacks are relatively simple to conduct, even by an unskilled attacker. Figure 8-3 shows an example of a DoS attack.

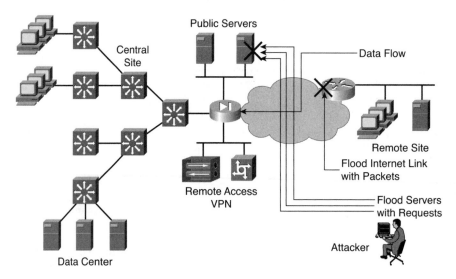

Figure 8-3   *DoS Attack Example*

Most DoS attacks rely on spoofing and flooding techniques. The impact of DoS attacks can be managed in several ways:

■ Use DHCP snooping to verify DHCP transactions and protect against rogue DHCP servers.

■ Use Dynamic Address Resolution Protocol (ARP) Inspection (DAI) to intercept all ARP requests and replies on the untrusted ports. Use the binding information that is built by the DHCP snooping feature to verify that ARP packets have valid IP-to-MAC bindings.

■ Implement Unicast Reverse Path Forwarding (uRPF) checks.

■ Implement access lists to filter traffic.

■ Rate-limit traffic such as incoming ARP and DHCP requests.

DDoS attacks are usually the consequence of one of these failures:

■ The cause might be the inability of a network, host, or application to manage an enormous quantity of data, which renders the system unresponsive or brings it to a halt. The difficulty of defending against such an attack lies in the difficulty of distinguishing legitimate data from attacker data.

■   The cause might be the failure of a host or application to manage an unexpected condition, such as maliciously formatted input data, an unexpected interaction of system components, or simple resource exhaustion.

Everything Is a Potential Target

Given the broad range of threats, everything in the network is a potential target. Hosts are typically the preferred target for worms and viruses. Host files can be corrupted in an attack, and the compromised host can be used to launch attacks against other hosts. However, the network infrastructure, including all network devices and services, offers potential targets for attackers.

Understanding Network Security Policy and Processes

To build a secure network and keep it secure, it is important to understand network security as one part of the system lifecycle.

Network security is a continuous process that is built around a security policy in the system lifecycle. Organizational requirements and risk analysis are used in the development of a security policy. Regardless of the security implications, business needs must be the first priority. If the business cannot function because of security constraints, the organization will have a major problem.

These are the key parameters to consider when designing a secure network:

■   **Business needs:** What does the organization want to do with the network?

■   **Risk analysis:** What is the risk-and-cost balance?

■   **Security policy:** What are the policies, standards, and guidelines used to address business needs and risk?

■   **Industry-recommended practices:** What are the reliable, well-understood, and recommended security practices?

■   **Security operations:** Identify the process for incident response, monitoring, maintenance, and compliance auditing of the system.

Definition of a Security Policy

A security policy consists of a set of objectives, the rules of behavior for users and administrators, and the requirements for the system and management. Collectively, they are designed to ensure the security of computer systems in an organization.

A very good introduction to security policies and the components that should be included in a security policy can be found in RFC 2196, "Site Security Handbook." The RFC is a guide to developing computer security policies and procedures for sites that have systems on the Internet. The purpose of the handbook is to provide practical guidance to administrators who are trying to secure their information and services. The subjects that are covered include policy content and formation, a broad range of technical system and network security topics, and security incident response.

The main purpose of a security policy is to inform users, staff, and managers of company requirements for protecting technology and information assets. The policy specifies the mechanisms through which these requirements are met.

Some questions that might need to be asked in developing a security policy include these:

1. Which data and assets will be covered by the security policy?

2. Under which conditions is communication allowed between networked hosts?

3. How will implementation of the policies be verified?

4. How are policy violations detected?

5. What is the impact of a policy violation?

6. Which actions are required upon a violation of a security policy?

Another purpose of a security policy is to provide a baseline from which to acquire, configure, and audit computer systems and networks for compliance with the policy. Therefore, an attempt to use a set of security tools in the absence of at least an implied security policy is meaningless.

As part of the development of a security policy, a risk assessment and cost-benefit analysis need to be performed. The security system must be designed to accommodate the goals of the business, not hinder them. Risk assessment and cost-benefit analysis can be understood by asking two key questions:

1. What is the cost-benefit analysis of the security system?

2. How will the latest attack techniques affect the network environment?

Risk Assessment and Management

Network security uses risk management to reduce risk to acceptable levels. A risk assessment provides input to a network security policy. Risk assessment and cost-benefit analysis document the level of risk and suggest the methods of managing risk at an acceptable level.

As part of the risk assessment process, the organization should define these issues:

■ Assets to protect

■ Value of the assets

■ Financial loss that would result from a security incident

■ Probability that an attack could be directed against the assets

■ Ability to control or minimize the risk through the security design and policy

The network security policy describes risk management measures as they relate to potential threats. Risk management and security policy development are continuous processes, as the severity and probability of risks change rapidly.

An example policy is the use of cryptography to provide confidentiality through encryption. A company encryption algorithm and the length of the encryption key might require an immediate change if a relatively inexpensive and exceptionally fast code-cracking computer becomes available. The organization will need to choose a stronger algorithm to protect against the new threat.

In the commercial world, it is a common practice to build systems with just enough security to bring potential losses down to the desired level. Alternatively, organizations with higher security requirements, such as legislative bodies, might need to implement stronger measures than might seem economically necessary.

A security designer tries to evaluate the severity of a particular risk, which depends on the damage that a successful attack could cause. However, it is often difficult to associate a value with an asset, as in cases such as these:

■ A medical database of a large hospital system, where there are disastrous consequences if confidentiality is breached

■ A corporate public web page which, if defaced (an integrity violation), can become a public relations nightmare, even though it might not result in a serious breach of confidentiality

Organizations can use a risk index to weigh risks for potential threats.

The risk index is based on these factors, as illustrated in Figure 8-4:

■ Severity of loss in the event of compromise of an asset

■ Probability of risk (likelihood that compromise will occur)

■ Ability to control or manage risk

Figure 8-4 *Risk Index Factors*

One way to develop a risk index is to assign a value to each factor from 1 (lowest) to 3 (highest). For example, the highest severity produces the greatest impact on user groups or particular environments and can even affect an entire site. Moderate severity risks can critically affect user environments or affect an entire site, but mitigating the attack is a reasonably attainable scenario. Low severity risks have a minor impact on user environments and typically can be easily mitigated. A risk index calculation example is shown in Table 8-1.

Table 8-1   *Risk Index Calculation Sheet*

Risk	Probability (P) (Value Between 1 and 3)	Severity (S) (Value Between 1 and 3)	Control (Value Between 1 and 3)	Risk Index (P * S)/C (Value Between 1/3 and 9)
Breach of confidentiality of customer database	1	3	2	1.5
DDoS attack sustained for more than 1 hour against an e-commerce server	2	2	1	4

The risk index is then calculated by dividing the product of the probability and severity factors by the control factor. The formula is as follows:

Risk index = (Probability factor * Severity factor) / (Control factor)

Note   Additional risk levels can be chosen to increase the granularity of the risk levels.

An organization should collaborate with stakeholders and subject matter experts to build the risk matrix. The security policy should outline a plan of activities to control each risk and the actions to take if a security incident occurs.

Example: Security Policy

Figure 8-5 illustrates the organization of a security policy and describes how to divide it into smaller parts that are applicable to the network segments.

A general document describes the overall risk-management policy, and identifies corporation assets and where to apply protection. In addition, the document defines how responsibility for risk management is distributed throughout the enterprise.

Other documents might address more specific areas of risk management. They include

■ **Network access control policy:** Documents how data is categorized (for example, confidential, internal, top secret) and the general principles of access control that are implemented in the network.

- **Acceptable use of network:** Usually written in easy-to-understand language and distributed among end users. This document informs users about their roles and responsibilities in risk management. The acceptable-use policy should be as explicit as possible to avoid ambiguity or misunderstanding.

- **Security management policy:** Defines how to perform secure computer infrastructure management.

- **Incident-handling policy:** Documents the procedures that are used to ensure reliable and acceptable handling of emergencies.

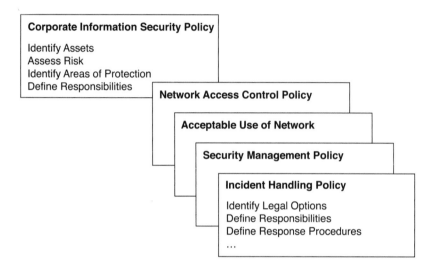

Figure 8-5   *Organization of a Security Policy*

Other areas might also be covered in separate documents, depending on organizational requirements. The security policy should have the acceptance and support of all levels of employees in the organization. Representatives of all key stakeholders and affected management should be involved in creating and revising the security policy.

Network Security Is a Continuous Process

A security policy should be considered as a living document. This means that the document is continuously updated as technology and organizational requirements change.

As part of the security policy, the following four steps build the continuous security process:

Step 1.   **Secure:** A security solution is implemented to stop or prevent unauthorized access or activities and to protect information and assets. Securing the network includes the implementation of filtering, authentication, encryption, vulnerability patching, and additional countermeasures to realize the security policy.

Step 2.   **Monitor:** Monitoring the security solution is required to detect violations of the security policy and involves system auditing and real-time intrusion detection.

Step 3.   **Test:** The effectiveness of the security policy and the implemented security solution is validated by regular system auditing and vulnerability scanning.

Step 4.   **Improve:** The information that is gathered from monitoring and testing the security solution is used to make improvements to the security implementation. This step might involve adjusting the security policy as new security vulnerabilities and risks are identified.

As shown in Figure 8-6, a process consisting of the four steps helps maintain the security policy.

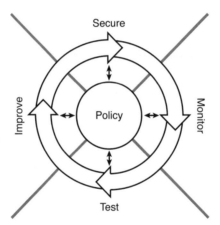

Figure 8-6   *Network Security Is a Continuous Process*

Integrating Security Design and Network Design

Security is more often becoming an embedded part of the network. Security services such as firewalls, intrusion prevention systems (IPS), Secure Socket Layer (SSL), Transport Layer Security (TLS), and IPsec can now reside inside network infrastructure. Security design that is integrated with network design is more manageable than components that are added after the network is implemented. It is now a recommended practice when designing the network to integrate security design.

An integrated security and network design requires coordination not just between the network and security teams but also with all of IT, including the security policy team and desktop operations.

Understanding the Cisco SAFE Approach

The following sections introduce the Cisco SAFE architecture and describe how it can be used to design a secure network. The sections also discuss the Cisco solutions that are available for designing and deploying secure networks.

Cisco SAFE Architecture

As key enablers of business activity, networks must be designed and implemented with security as an integrated design element to ensure the confidentiality, integrity, and availability of data and system resources that support the key business functions. Cisco SAFE provides security design guidelines for building secure and reliable network infrastructures that are resilient to both well-known and new forms of attack.

The main idea behind SAFE is to provide organizations with information regarding the actual design and deployment of secured networks. Based on the principle of deep network security and protection from external and internal attacks, SAFE was created to help network designers analyze their security requirements. This approach focuses not on equipment installation but on the analysis of expected threats and the design of the network security strategy. In addition, SAFE facilitates the creation of a multilayered and modular security system, whereby a breach at one level does not affect the entire system. The SAFE architecture is shown in Figure 8-7.

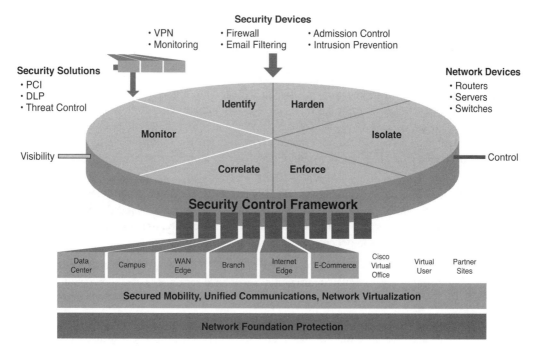

Figure 8-7 *Cisco SAFE Architecture*

Cisco SAFE architecture with maximum accuracy considers both current traffic flow and the future functional requirements of modern corporate networks to achieve the following goals:

■ Policy-based security and threat mitigation

■ Implementation of security mechanisms for all network infrastructure (not just on special devices)

■ Secure management facilities and formation of reports

■ Authentication, authorization, and accounting (AAA) services for access to critical network resources

■ Intrusion prevention for network resources and subnets

■ Support for new applications and tools

The main benefits of Cisco SAFE are as follows:

■ SAFE is a basis for the design of secured high-availability networks.

■ SAFE has an open, modular, expanded, and scaled structure.

■ SAFE simplifies the development, implementation, and management of network security.

The Network as a Platform for Security

Network security begins with a secure network foundation. Because the network touches all parts of the infrastructure, it is the ideal location to implement core and advanced security services. The nucleus of secure network infrastructure solutions includes Cisco ASA adaptive security appliances (Cisco ASA) and routers and switches with security integrated and embedded both in and between them. The following is a more detailed description of which solutions are provided on each of these devices:

■ **Routers:** Incorporate firewall, IPS, IP security (for example, IPsec Virtual Private Network [VPN], Cisco Easy VPN, Dynamic Multipoint VPN [DMVPN]), and SSL VPN services into the routing infrastructure, in addition to features that protect the router if it should become the target of an attack.

■ **Cisco Catalyst switches:** Incorporate firewall, IPS, SSL VPN, IPsec VPN, distributed denial of service (DDoS) mitigation, and virtualization services, allowing unique policies for each security zone.

■ **Cisco ASA adaptive security appliances:** Consolidate all the foundational security technologies (firewall, IPS, IPsec, and SSL VPN) into a single, easily managed platform.

Cisco Security Control Framework

This topic describes the components of the Cisco Security Control Framework (SCF), which is shown in Figure 8-8.

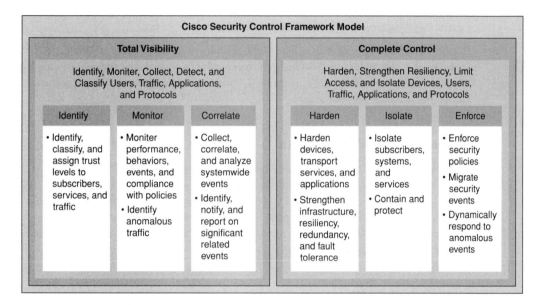

Figure 8-8   *Security Control Framework*

The Cisco Security Control Framework (SCF) is a security framework that is aimed at ensuring network and service availability as well as business continuity. Security threats are an ever-moving target, and the Cisco SCF is designed to address current key threats while tracking new and evolving threats, by using best common practices and comprehensive solutions. Cisco SAFE uses the SCF to create network designs that ensure network and service availability and business continuity. Cisco SCF influences the selection of security products and capabilities and guides their deployment throughout the network where they best enhance visibility and control.

Cisco SCF assumes the existence of security policies that are developed as a result of threat and risk assessments, in alignment with business goals. The security policies and guidelines are expected to define the acceptable and secure use of each service, device, and system in the environment. The security policies should also determine the processes and procedures that are needed to achieve the business goals. The collection of this data defines security operations. It is crucial to business success that security policies, guidelines, and operations do not prevent but rather empower the organization to achieve its goals.

The success of the security policies ultimately depends on the degree to which they enhance visibility and control. Simply put, security can be defined as a function of visibility and control. Without visibility, there is no control, and without control, there is no security. Therefore, the main focus of Cisco SCF is on enhancing visibility and control. In the context of SAFE, SCF influences the selection and deployment of platforms and capabilities to achieve a desirable degree of visibility and control.

Cisco SCF defines six security actions that help enforce security policies and improve visibility and control. Figure 8-8 illustrates how visibility is enhanced through the actions of identifying, monitoring, and correlating. Control is improved through the actions of hardening, isolating, and enforcing.

Trust and Identity Management

Businesses need to effectively and securely manage who and what can access the network, as well as when, where, and how that access can occur. Trust and identity management is critical for organizations and underpins the creation of any secure network or system. It entails providing or denying access to business applications and networked resources, based on the specific privileges and rights of a user. An illustration of trust and identity management solutions is shown in Figure 8-9.

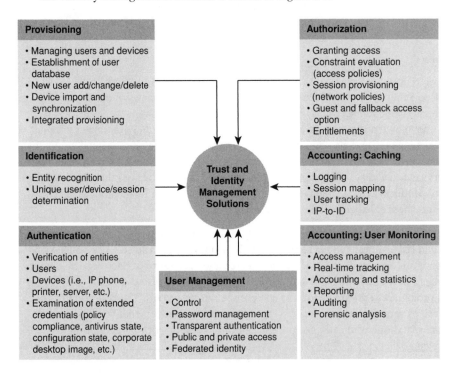

Figure 8-9 *Trust and Identity Management*

Trust and identity management solutions provide secure network access and admission at any point in the network and isolate and control infected or unpatched devices that attempt to access the network.

Trust

Trust is the root of security, because it defines the relationship with which two or more network entities are allowed to communicate. Security policy decisions are based on trust. Trusted entities are allowed to communicate freely. Communication with untrusted entities needs to be carefully managed and controlled because of its higher risk. Security is used to limit risk by enforcing limitations on trust relationships.

Trust relationships can be explicitly defined or informally implied. They can be inherited. In other words, if a user is granted certain privileges on one system, a similar system can extend the same privileges. However, trust and privileges that are granted can be abused.

Domains of trust facilitate network segmentation that is based on similarities of policy and concerns. The required system security can vary in terms of importance to the business and the likelihood of attack. Segments can have different trust models, depending on the security requirements. Consistent security controls should be applied within a segment and define trust relationships between segments.

The gradient of trust determines the trust level between domains. The trust-level difference can range from minor to extreme. The gradient determines the extent of security safeguards and attention to monitoring. This is illustrated in Figure 8-10.

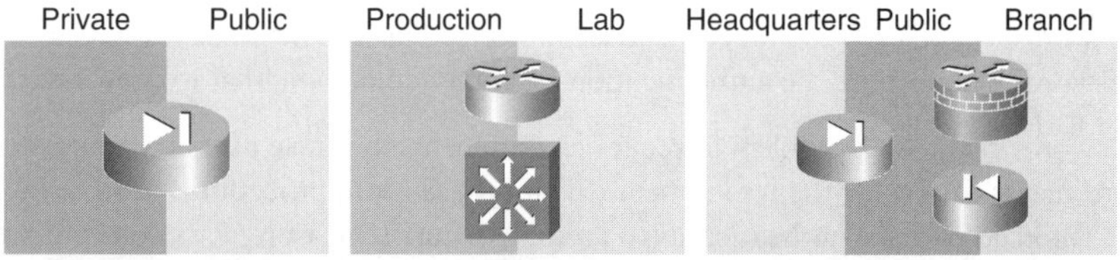

Domains of Trust	Gradient of Trust	Sample Safeguards Needed
Private to Public	Extreme (High Risk)	Advanced firewalling, flow-based inspection, misuse detection (including IPS), constant monitoring
Production to Lab	Minor (Low Risk)	Basic access control, casual monitoring
Headquarters to Branch (over Public)	Steep (Considerable Risk)	Communication security and authentication to alleviate confidentiality and integrity concerns

Figure 8-10 *Domains of Trust Example*

The trust relationship between segments should be controlled at defined points by using some form of network firewall or access control. Mastering domains of trust is a key component in quality network security design.

Identity

Identity can refer to individuals, devices, organizations, or all three. Proper identity usage enables effective risk mitigation and the ability to apply policy and access control in a more granular and accurate manner.

Credentials are pieces of information that are used to verify or authenticate the identity of a network entity. Authentication of identity is traditionally based on one of three proofs:

- **Something that is known to the user:** Involves knowledge of a unique secret, which is usually shared by the authenticating parties. To a user, this secret appears as a classic password known as a personal identification number (PIN) or a private cryptographic key.

- **Something the subject possesses:** Usually involves physical possession of an item that is unique to the subject. Examples include password token cards, smart cards, and hardware keys.

- **A physical characteristic:** Involves verification of a unique physical characteristic of the subject, such as a fingerprint, retina pattern, voice, or face.

The most common identity credentials are passwords, tokens, and certificates.

Passwords can be used to authenticate an authorized user to network resources. Passwords demonstrate the authentication attribute "something that is known to the user."

Passwords can pose a problem in secure environments, because users try to create a password that is easiest for them to remember. Good password procedures need to be created and enforced to make authentication a credible security measure. Password policies and procedures should enforce the use of nondictionary passwords that are changed often.

Passwords should never be shared or posted on a monitor or wall or hidden under a keyboard.

To achieve high assurance in authentication, many trusted systems require "two-factor authentication," where a subject provides at least two types of proof of identity.

An example is an access control system that is based on both a token and a password. With two-factor authentication, the compromise of one factor does not lead to the compromise of the system. A password can become known, but it is useless without the token. Conversely, if the token is stolen, the thief cannot use it without the password.

A token can be a physical device that an authorized user implements to aid in authentication or a software application that generates a one-time authentication password or number.

Access Control

Trust and identity management is also supported by access control. Access control is the ability to enforce a policy that defines which entities can access which network resources. Access control indirectly helps ensure confidentiality and integrity of sensitive data by limiting access to the data. Authorization mechanisms limit the access of an entity to resources, based on subject identity.

Access control mechanisms are usually classified in one of these ways:

- Authentication mechanisms establish subject identity.

- Authorization mechanisms limit access to a network. Such mechanisms can define the granularity of access, such as read-only or write permissions.

- Accounting mechanisms such as an audit trail provide evidence of the actions of the subject and real-time monitoring to provide security services such as intrusion prevention.

Authentication, authorization, and accounting (AAA) are network security services that provide a framework in which access control is set up to the network.

Trust and Identity Management Technologies

Many technologies can be used to support trust and identity management.

The following examples are used for trust and identity management:

- **Cisco Identity-Based Networking Services (IBNS):** An integrated solution combining several Cisco products that offer authentication, access control, and user policies to secure network connectivity and resources.

- **IEEE 802.1X:** An IEEE standard for media-level access control, offering the ability to permit or deny network connectivity, control VLAN access, and apply traffic policy that is based on user or machine identity.

- **Access control lists (ACL):** Lists that are maintained by network devices such as routers, switches, and firewalls to control access through the device. An example is an ACL on a router that specifies which clients, based on their subnet addresses, can connect to a sensitive server in the data center.

- **Cisco Network Admission Control (NAC) appliance:** A set of technologies and solutions that uses the network infrastructure to enforce security policy compliance on all devices seeking to access network computing resources. It limits damage from emerging security threats.

- **Firewall:** A device that is designed to permit or deny network traffic, based on certain characteristics, such as source address, destination address, protocol, port, and application. The firewall enforces the access and authorization policy in the network effectively by specifying which connections are permitted or denied between security perimeters.

Example: Cisco IBNS

The Cisco IBNS solution supports identity authentication and secure network connectivity, dynamic provisioning of VLANs on a per-user basis, guest VLANs, and IEEE 802.1X with port security.

IEEE 802.1X is an open-standards-based protocol for authenticating network clients (or ports) on a user-ID or device basis. IEEE 802.1X runs between end devices and users (called *supplicants*) trying to connect to ports on an Ethernet device, such as a Cisco Catalyst switch or a Cisco wireless access point (called the *authenticator*). Authentication and authorization are achieved with back-end communication to an authentication server such as Cisco Secure Access Control Server (Cisco Secure ACS).

In an IBNS solution, when the Cisco Catalyst switch (authenticator) detects that a user (supplicant) is attempting to connect to the network, the authenticator initiates an Extensible Authentication Protocol over LAN (EAPOL) session requesting the user to provide credentials. The client sends its credentials to the authenticator. The switch (or authenticator) passes the user ID and password to an authentication server using RADIUS.

The authentication server determines whether the user ID and password are valid. It also makes a note of the port and MAC address used. If the user ID and password are correct, the authentication server sends a message to the authenticator to permit the user to connect to the network on a specific VLAN. If the user ID and password are not correct, the server sends a message to the switch to block that port.

If access is allowed, the authenticator opens the communications port, and the user now has access to physical LAN services.

Example: Firewall Filtering Using ACLs

Figure 8-11 illustrates the use of a network firewall to control access, which is a common use of network authorization. An enterprise network is usually divided into separate security domains or zones that include the untrusted Internet, trusted enterprise campus, and perimeters of public and semipublic servers. Because all traffic must pass through the network firewall, the firewall enforces the access and authorization policy in the network effectively by specifying which connections are permitted or denied between security perimeters.

The policy for the Internet interface is shown in the figure. From the Internet, HTTP traffic is permitted to the public web servers, and the public web servers can reply. HTTPS traffic from the Internet is permitted to the e-commerce server. Response HTTPS traffic from the e-commerce server is allowed. Traffic that is initiated from the internal network to the Internet, as well as responses to this traffic, are also permitted. All other traffic is denied.

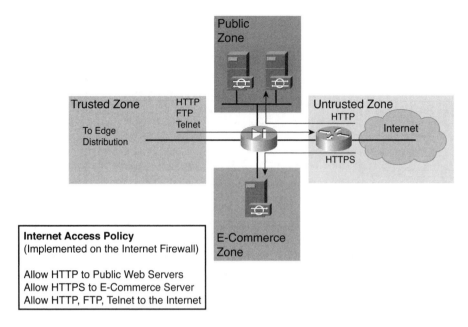

Figure 8-11   *Firewall Filtering Using ACLs*

Example: Cisco NAC Appliance

Customers using the Cisco NAC Appliance permit network access only to compliant and trusted wired or wireless endpoint devices (PCs, servers, and personal digital assistants [PDA], for example) and can restrict the access of noncompliant devices.

Cisco NAC is available in appliance form to meet the technology and operational needs of any organization. The Cisco NAC Appliance is a turnkey solution to control network access based on user authentication and provide wired and wireless endpoint posture compliance with built-in device remediation. The Cisco NAC Appliance identifies whether networked devices such as laptops and PDAs are compliant with the security policies of the network and repairs any vulnerability before permitting access to the network.

Identity and Access Control Deployment Locations

Authentication validation should be deployed as close to the network edge as possible, with strong authentication needed for access from external and untrusted networks. This is illustrated in Figure 8-12.

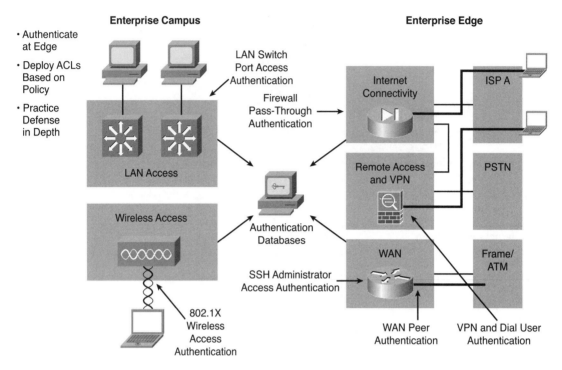

Figure 8-12 *Identity and Access Control Deployment Locations*

Access controls to enforce policy can be deployed at various locations:

- Source-specific rules (with any destination) should be applied as close to the source as possible.

- Destination-specific rules (with any source) should be applied as close to the destination as possible.

- Mixed rules using combinations of specific sources and destinations should be applied as close to the source as possible.

The principle of least privilege should be used, which means that each subject should have only the necessary privileges to perform his defined tasks. Highly distributed rules afford greater granularity and overall performance scalability at the cost of management complexity. However, centralized rules provide easier management at the cost of scalability.

Defense in depth should be practiced. Security mechanisms should back up each other. One example is to use a dedicated firewall that is supplemented with perimeter routers that use ACLs to filter packets, to limit access to resources at a granular level.

Threat Defense

Network security must protect businesses from increasing threats such as access breaches, "Day Zero" worm attacks and viruses, and internal threats. Threats, both known and unknown, continue to become more destructive and frequent than in the past. Internal and external threats, such as worms, DoS attacks, man-in-the-middle attacks, and Trojan horses, have the ability to radically affect business profitability.

The Cisco Threat Defense System (Cisco TDS) provides a strong defense against these known and unknown attacks. Appropriate security technologies, along with advanced networking intelligence, are required to effectively defend against attacks. To be most effective, these technologies must be implemented throughout the network, rather than just in point products or technologies. An attack can start anywhere and instantly spread across all network resources.

The Cisco TDS enhances security in the existing network infrastructure. It adds comprehensive security on the endpoints (both server and desktops) and adds dedicated security technologies to networking devices and appliances. The Cisco TDS proactively defends the business, applications, users, and the network. It protects businesses from operation disruption, lost revenue, and loss of reputation. The Cisco TDS comprises several critical technologies and products, enabling security that is integrated in routers, switches, and appliances. Examples include firewalls, network-based intrusion prevention sensors, detection instrumentation, and traffic isolation techniques.

Incorporating Physical Security

Physical security is critical to successful network security implementation and can significantly influence the strength of the total security design. This topic describes the guidelines for incorporating physical security into an overall security policy.

Physical security restricts physical access to a device or the communications media. A good security policy must anticipate possible physical attacks and assess their relevance in terms of possible loss, probability, and simplicity of attack.

Consider these potential physical threats:

- A network device does not always enforce all of its security settings when an attacker directly accesses the hardware through console access, memory probing, or installation of unreliable software.

- Access to the physical communication medium can allow an attacker to impersonate trusted systems and view, intercept, and change data that is flowing in a network.

- An attacker might use physically destructive attacks against devices and networks such as physical force, attacks over the power network, or electromagnetic surveillance and attacks.

- An attacker might steal a device such as a home office router or laptop computer and use it to access the corporate network.

The traditional method to manage the risk of physical compromise is to deploy physical access controls by using techniques such as locks or alarms. It is important to identify how a physical security breach might interact with network security mechanisms. For example, if an attacker obtains physical access to a switch port in a corporate building and acquires unrestricted access to the corporate network, there could be a significant risk. If the security policy assumes, in error, that only legitimate users can obtain such access, the attacker will be able to connect to the network without authentication and thus bypass network access control.

A security designer must identify the additional consequences that result from device theft in a secure network. For example, if a laptop computer is stolen from a roaming user, does it contain cryptographic keys that enable the attacker to connect to the enterprise network while impersonating a legitimate user? Moreover, does the network administrator have a scalable means to revoke credentials that could be obtained by the attacker through physical theft?

Sometimes, a significant portion of the network infrastructure is outside the physical control of the enterprise, so physical controls are not enforced at the media access level. For example, many enterprises rely on the fact that the physical infrastructure of the Frame Relay network of the service provider is well protected, even though access to its wire conduits is easily available. To protect communications over unsafe networks, cryptography provides confidentiality and integrity protection that are fully under the control of the enterprise.

Infrastructure Protection

To meet business needs, it is critical to utilize security features and services to protect the infrastructure. These services are necessary so that network devices are not accessed or altered in an unauthorized manner and end-to-end network transport and integrated services remain available.

Infrastructure protection consists of measures that are taken to minimize the risks and threats to which the network elements are exposed, to preserve the integrity and availability of the network.

Deploying recommended practices and security policy enforcement that harden network devices helps secure the network foundation by protecting network elements and the integrity of their interactions. To address the increasing complexity of the attacks, Cisco has enhanced Cisco IOS Software security features and services for both network elements and infrastructure. This improves the availability of the network elements and the network.

Secure network infrastructure solutions include Cisco ASA security appliances and Cisco routers and switches with integrated security.

Infrastructure protection practices should be deployed on all network infrastructure devices. There can be different mechanisms available, depending on the device. Typically, there are equivalent functions available. For example, perimeter routers should implement ingress traffic filtering to prohibit DoS attacks, which use forged IP addresses to be propagated from the Internet.

Note   RFC 2827 specifies Internet best current practices for ingress traffic filtering.

All switches should be configured to support bridge protocol data unit (BPDU) guard and root guard, and to set the VLAN Trunking Protocol (VTP) mode to transparent.

More advanced protection mechanisms, such as DAI inspection and DHCP snooping, might be available only on higher-end switches. When supported, infrastructure devices should consider implementing Control Plane Policing (CoPP) to manage the traffic flow of control plane packets on Cisco IOS routers and switches to limit reconnaissance and DoS attacks.

Infrastructure protection should be implemented throughout the network, especially at strategic perimeter points, to control ingress and egress traffic.

Recommended Practices for Infrastructure Protection

Here are some recommended practices for infrastructure protection:

■   Use Secure Shell (SSH) to access devices instead of Telnet.

■   Enable AAA and role-based access control (RADIUS or TACACS+) for access to the command-line interface (CLI) or privileged mode access on all devices.

■   Send syslog messages (event notification messages) from network devices to a syslog server. Collect and archive the logs.

■   When using Simple Network Management Protocol (SNMP), use SNMP version 3 (SNMPv3) for its authentication and privacy features.

■   Disable unused services on network devices:

```
no service tcp-small-servers
no service udp-small-servers
```

■   Use Secure FTP (SFTP) and Secure Copy Protocol (SCP) to move images and configurations around. FTP and TFTP should be avoided when possible.

■   Install virtual terminal (VTY) access lists to limit which addresses can access management and CLI services.

■   Enable protocol authentication where it is available (Enhanced Interior Gateway Routing Protocol [EIGRP], Open Shortest Path First [OSPF], Border Gateway Protocol [BGP], Hot Standby Router Protocol [HSRP], VTP, and so on) in the control plane.

■   Consider using the one-step router lockdown feature in Cisco Router and Security Device Manager (Cisco SDM) to help ensure that all nonessential services in Cisco IOS Software are shut off before the Cisco router is connected to the public Internet or a WAN.

Threat Detection and Mitigation

Threat detection and mitigation technologies are used to provide early notification of unpredicted malicious traffic or behavior. The goals of these technologies include the following:

- To detect, notify, and prevent unauthorized and unpredictable events or traffic

- To help directly preserve the availability of the network, particularly against unknown or unforeseen attacks

Threat detection and mitigation technologies solutions include these:

- **Endpoint protection:** Viruses and worms frequently create network congestion as a by-product of rapid propagation as well as infection of endpoints. In addition, antivirus software allows hosts to detect and remove infections that are based on patterns.

- **Infection containment:** The Cisco ASA 5500 Series Adaptive Security Appliances, Cisco Catalyst 6500 Series Firewall Services Module (Catalyst 6500 Series FWSM), and the firewall feature set in Cisco IOS Software protect the network perimeter and create "islands of security" on the internal network. Strong network admission policies are not a cure-all and do not eliminate the need to continue monitoring devices after they enter a network. Determined attackers can evade just about any admission check, and the network cannot always rely on, or trust, an infected element to turn itself in. Compliant devices can also become infected through various methods (for example, a Universal Serial Bus [USB] key with infected content) when they are members of a network. To further protect the network, the Cisco SAFE architecture is designed to extend the security checks that are performed by the Cisco NAC Appliance at the time of admission for the duration of the network connection. In addition, the Cisco SAFE architecture can rely on other network elements, including other endpoints, to detect when another endpoint is no longer trustworthy.

- **In-line IPS and anomaly detection:** An important area of ongoing security development has been in the area of network intrusion detection systems (NIDS). One of the first Cisco innovations in this area was to integrate NIDS into its router and switching platforms. For NIDS to fully deliver on its capabilities, it must transform into an IPS with in-line filtering capabilities. This provides a mechanism to remove unwanted traffic with fine-grained programmable classification engines. The Cisco IPS 4200 Series sensors, Cisco Catalyst 6500 Series Intrusion Detection System Services Module 2 (IDSM-2), or the Cisco IOS Intrusion Prevention System (IPS) quickly identifies, analyzes, and stops malevolent traffic. The Cisco Traffic Anomaly Detector XT and Guard XT appliances and the Cisco Catalyst 6500/Cisco 7600 Traffic Anomaly Detector Module and Anomaly Guard Module ensure business continuity in the event of DDoS attacks.

- **Application security and content security defense:** Over the past several years, a number of new application layer network products have emerged to help locate new classes of threats that were not adequately addressed by classic firewall and NIDS products. These risks include viruses and worms, junk email and phishing, spyware, web services abuse, IP telephony abuse, and unauthorized peer-to-peer activity. Packet- and content-inspection security services on firewalls and IPS appliances help manage these types of threats and misuse. This convergence brings granular traffic-inspection services to critical network security enforcement points containing malicious traffic before it can be propagated across the network.

Threat Detection and Mitigation Solutions

Many solutions can be used to support threat detection and mitigation, including the following:

- Centralized Policy Management and Monitoring:

    - Cisco Security Monitoring, Analysis, and Response System (Cisco Security MARS)

    - Cisco Security Manager

- Firewall:

    - Cisco ASA Adaptive Security Appliance

    - Cisco ACE Web Application Firewall

    - Cisco IOS Firewall

- Cisco Intrusion Prevention System (Cisco IPS)

- Endpoint Security:

    - Cisco NAC Appliance

- Content Security:

    - Cisco IronPort Web Security Appliance (Cisco WSA)

    - Cisco IronPort E-mail Security Appliance (Cisco ESA)

Threat detection and mitigation solutions can be deployed throughout the network, as shown in Figure 8-13.

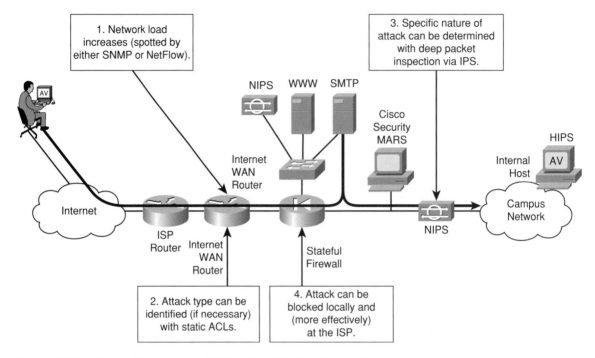

Figure 8-13 *Threat Detection and Mitigation Solutions Example*

For example, the perimeter Internet WAN router is the first line of defense in a worm attack. A network management station can detect an increase in network load through SNMP or NetFlow events from the perimeter router. Specific ACLs can be applied to this router to identify the attack type.

A network intrusion prevention system (NIPS) can use deep-packet examination to determine the specific nature of the attack. Host intrusion prevention systems (HIPS) are typically implemented in software, while NIPS are usually appliances or software features in a network device. Both IPS implementations use in-line, signature-based attack detection. HIPS can also be utilized to provide host policy enforcement and verification.

A stateful firewall can be used to block the attack locally, until the ISP can shut down the attack. A key element to a successful threat detection and mitigation system is to recognize the availability of data from sources such as these:

■ NetFlow

■ Syslog

■ SNMP traps

■ Changes in SNMP values and thresholds

■ Remote Monitoring (RMON)

A good security information manager such as Cisco Security MARS helps aggregate this data and present it in a useful format.

Example: Cisco IronPort ESA

This topic describes how the Cisco IronPort Email Security Appliance (Cisco ESA) can help mitigate network threats that are propagated through emails.

It is well known that email is a medium through which spyware and viruses can be propagated. Junk email and various malicious malware can significantly affect employee productivity. The Cisco ESA is a firewall and threat-monitoring appliance for Simple Mail Transfer Protocol (SMTP) traffic (TCP port 25). In other words, Cisco ESA acts as a Mail Transfer Agent (MTA) or broker within the email delivery process. There are multiple approaches to the deployment of Cisco ESA, depending on the number of interfaces used. The most frequent approach uses a single physical interface to transfer emails to and from both the Internet and the internal mail servers. In this model, Cisco ESA should be logically located in the private demilitarized zone (DMZ) or inside network. However, two physical interfaces can be used if desired—one that is connected to the DMZ and used to send and receive email to and from the Internet, and the other connected to the inside network and used to deliver email to the internal mail server. It is generally recommended that the Cisco ESA be placed as close to the firewall as possible.

The Cisco ESA acts like the SMTP gateway for the enterprise. This means that the Cisco ESA should be located as the first host that receives emails from the Internet and the first hop in the email infrastructure. In addition, the Cisco ESA should be accessible through the Internet through a public email address. Therefore, it is recommended that the Cisco ESA be placed in the Internet edge infrastructure and use static Network Address Translation (NAT) to translate the public IP address to the internal IP address of the Cisco ESA. By using a different MTA as a gateway (as opposed to the Cisco ESA), the Cisco ESA is prevented from determining the sender's IP address. This address is needed to query Cisco SensorBase for the sender's reputation score and to stop junk email.

Example: Cisco IronPort WSA

This topic describes how the Cisco IronPort Web Security Appliance (Cisco WSA) can monitor and mitigate any abnormal web activity between corporate users and the outside world. The Cisco WSA is logically located in the path between corporate web users and the Internet. In effect, the Cisco WSA acts as a web proxy for the corporate users residing inside the network.

This logical placement of the Cisco WSA implies proper configuration of the browser. There are three different ways to use the Cisco WSA with respect to the browser configuration:

- **Explicit mode without the use of proxy autoconfiguration (PAC) files:** This requires manual configuration of the browser to point to the Cisco WSA as its proxy. This choice does not support redundancy, does not work with multiple Cisco WSAs, and requires changes to every browser in the enterprise network. This is the preferred method to test and verify proper operation of the Cisco WSA.

■ **Explicit mode with the use of PAC files:** In this mode, the proxy information is stored in a file that can be downloaded automatically, or the location of the file can be referenced manually. The advantage of this mode is that more than one proxy can be referenced in the files and used by the browser. This allows load balancing and redundancy of Cisco WSAs. DHCP or Domain Name System (DNS) can be used to download the files automatically to the browser. This eliminates the need to manually configure each browser separately.

■ **Transparent mode with Web Cache Communication Protocol (WCCP):** In this mode, the web traffic is transparently directed to the Cisco WSA using WCCP redirection and does not require any adjustments to the browser. It requires the configuration of a WCCP-enabled firewall, router, or Layer 3 switch to direct client traffic to the appliance. Care should be taken when asymmetrical traffic flows exist in the network. This is a good method for load sharing and redundancy.

It is recommended that explicit mode be initially implemented. This mode can be used with the use of PAC files for initial testing, and then transition to WCCP for final implementation.

Secure Connectivity

This topic provides additional details on the secure connectivity element of the Cisco SAFE approach.

As illustrated in Figure 8-14, ensuring the privacy and integrity of all information is vital to businesses today. With increased network connectivity comes increased exposure. As organizations adopt the use of the Internet for intranet, extranet, and teleworker connectivity (such as broadband always-on connections), maintaining security, data integrity, and privacy across these connections is paramount. LAN connections, traditionally considered trusted networks, now also require higher levels of security. In fact, internal threats are ten times more financially damaging than external threats. Preserving the confidentiality and integrity of the data and applications that traverse the wired or wireless LAN is a key element in decisions that businesses make about security.

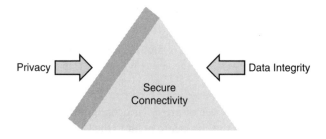

Figure 8-14 *Secure Connectivity*

The Cisco Secure Connectivity System uses encryption and authentication capabilities to provide secure transport across untrusted networks. To protect data, voice, and video applications over wired and wireless media, Cisco offers IPsec, SSL, SSH, and Multiprotocol Label Switching (MPLS)–based VPN technologies. This is in addition to the extensive security capabilities that are incorporated into Cisco wireless and IP telephony solutions to help ensure the privacy of IP communications.

Encryption Fundamentals

Cryptography provides confidentiality through encryption. As shown in Figure 8-15, encryption disguises a message to hide its content.

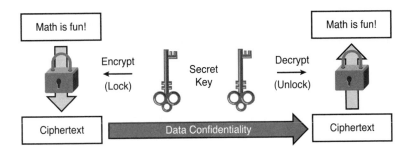

Figure 8-15 *Encryption Example*

With encryption, plain text (the readable message) is converted to cipher text (the unreadable, disguised message) and transferred confidentially from a source to a destination. At the destination, the cipher text is converted back to plain text. The purpose of encryption is to guarantee confidentiality. Only authorized entities can encrypt and decrypt data. With most modern algorithms, successful encryption and decryption require knowledge of the appropriate cryptographic keys. An example of data encryption is the use of encryption algorithms to hide the IP packet payloads that use IPsec security protocols.

For encryption to work, the remote device must have a key to decrypt the encrypted traffic. These are two ways to securely send a key to the remote device:

- Shared secrets
- Public key infrastructure (PKI)

With shared secrets, both sides recognize the same key. The encryption key might be identical to the decryption key or require a simple transform to create the decryption keys. The keys represent a shared secret between two or more parties that can be used to maintain a private information link. The key is carried out of band (OOB) to the remote side. This is the easiest mechanism, but it has some inherent security concerns. Because the keys are potentially subject to discovery, they need to be changed often and kept secure during distribution and while in service. Reliably selecting, distributing, and maintaining shared keys without error or discovery can be difficult.

PKI is another form of encryption. It uses asymmetric keys, where the encryption key is different from the decryption key. Most PKI systems rely on certificates to establish the identity or public key of a party, where a certificate has been issued by a certificate authority (CA) computer whose legitimacy is trusted. Data that is encrypted with the public key can be decrypted with the private key. Data that is encrypted with the private key can be decrypted with the public key.

Note   Data encrypted with the public key cannot be decrypted with the public key with PKI.

The parties who need to encrypt their communications exchange their public keys (contained in the certificate) but do not disclose their private keys. The sending party uses the public key of the receiving party to encrypt the message data and forward the cipher text (encrypted data) to the other party. The receiving party then decrypts the cipher text with the private key. PKI encryption is widely used in e-commerce sites.

VPN Protocols

There are a number of different VPN protocols that can be used. The majority of protocols have specific traits to improve specific situations and designs. Table 8-2 lists the different VPN protocols, the benefits, and when they should be implemented.

Table 8-2   *VPN Protocols*

VPN Protocol	Benefits	Implementation Recommendations
Standard IPsec VPN	Provides encryption between sites and supports quality of service (QoS)	Use when multivendor interoperability is required.
Cisco DMVPN	Simplifies encryption configuration and management for point-to-point GRE tunnels. Provides on-demand spoke-to-spoke tunnels. Supports QoS, multicast, and routing to simplify configuration for hub-and-spoke VPNs while supporting QoS, multicast, and routing. Provides low-scale, on-demand meshing.	Use to simplify configuration for hub-and-spoke VPNs while supporting QoS, multicast, and routing and to provide low-scale, on-demand meshing.

Table 8-2   *VPN Protocols*

VPN Protocol	Benefits	Implementation Recommendations
Cisco Easy VPN	Simplifies IPsec and remote-site device management through dynamic configuration policy-push. Supports quality of service (QoS).	Use when simplifying overall VPN and management is the primary goal (but only if limited networking features are required). Use to provide a simple, unified configuration framework for a mix of Cisco VPN products.
Cisco Generic Routing Encapsulation (GRE)–Based VPN	Enables transport of multicast and the routing of traffic across an IPsec VPN. Supports non-IP protocols. Supports QoS.	Use when routing must be supported across the VPN for the same functions as hub-and-spoke DMVPN but when a more detailed configuration is required.
Group Encrypted Transport (GET) VPN	Simplifies encryption integration on IP and MPLS WANs. Simplifies encryption management through the use of group keying instead of point-to-point key pairs. Enables scalable and manageable any-to-any connectivity between sites. Supports QoS, multicast, and routing.	Use to add encryption to MPLS or IP WANs while preserving any-to-any connectivity and networking features. Use to enable scalable, full-time meshing for IPsec VPNs. Use to enable participation of smaller routers in meshed networks. Use to simplify encryption key management while supporting QoS, multicast, and routing.

Ensuring Privacy

Transmission confidentiality keeps data private while it is being transported over insecure networks. This section describes privacy methods.

When trusted and untrusted networks are connected (for example, when a corporate network connects with the Internet), data can be transmitted among trusted subjects over untrusted networks. Untrusted networks do not support classic access control mechanisms, because a corporation does not have control over the users and network resources. Therefore, data needs to be protected in transmission to ensure that no one in the untrusted network can view or change the transmitted data. Figure 8-16 illustrates an example of transmission privacy.

Figure 8-16 illustrates two sites that are connected over an untrusted network: the Internet. To provide data confidentiality, a VPN technology that supports encryption creates a secured point-to-point association between the sites over the Internet. All packets that leave one site are encrypted, forwarded on to the untrusted network, and decrypted by a device on the remote site. Anyone who is eavesdropping on the untrusted network should not be able to decrypt the packet payloads and read sensitive data.

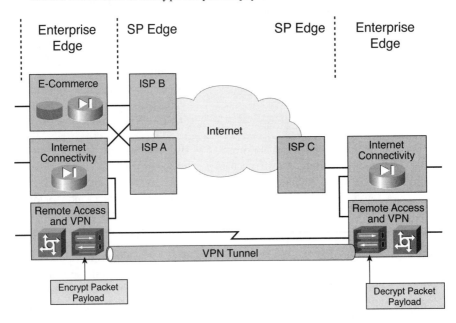

Figure 8-16 *Transmission Privacy Example*

Specific cryptography guidelines to consider when designing and implementing a solution for transmission confidentiality include the following:

- Cryptography can become a performance bottleneck. A careful analysis should be performed to determine where to protect data. In general, if confidential or sensitive data travels over a network where an attacker could easily intercept communications (such as a network outside the physical control of the organization or a network where device compromises are likely), communications need to be protected, as defined in the security policy.

- Although some restrictions still apply, organizations can now export some modern cryptography. Depending on the legal regulations in a country, it is recommended to use the strongest available cryptography to provide sufficient protection. Take care, because some cryptographic algorithms allow extremely long key lengths to be specified, which might not provide worthwhile confidentiality improvements.

- Use only well-known cryptographic algorithms such as Triple Data Encryption Standard (3DES), Advanced Encryption Standard (AES), or RC4, because only well-known algorithms are tested, analyzed, and considered trustworthy.

■   Do not forget that encryption provides only confidentiality, and most organizations view data integrity and authenticity as equally important elements of security. If possible, use both confidentiality- and integrity-guaranteeing cryptographic algorithms.

Example: Providing Confidentiality over the Internet

To decrease communication costs, a health insurance company decides to connect some of its branch offices to its headquarters over the Internet. It needs to protect patient record confidentiality. Because attackers on the Internet are able to intercept communications, the company implements a VPN using the strongest possible encryption algorithms to guarantee data confidentiality. In the event of interception, it is unlikely that the attacker would be able to decrypt messages, which are protected with modern cryptographic algorithms such as 3DES, AES, or RC4.

Example: Protecting Communication over the Public Infrastructure

Enterprises that simultaneously transmit sensitive and nonsensitive data over a public circuit, such as an MPLS or Frame Relay link, can use VPNs. The sensitive traffic to other remote enterprise sites is protected in the VPN when it is routed over the WAN, while traffic outside the enterprise can be sent in the clear.

Example: Network Authentication over a VPN

An organization needs to deploy remote-access services to its network using the Internet. It has implemented remote-access VPN technology and requires proper user authentication before users enter the protected network. The organization has had poor experiences enforcing password updates and wants to deploy a very secure, yet simple, system. One-time password (OTP) generators for remote users might be the ideal solution, because they are secure and simple to use.

Maintaining Data Integrity

This section describes the selection of transmission integrity methods for security design.

Cryptography also provides integrity mechanisms, which can protect data in transmission over untrusted networks. Cryptographic protocols, such as secure fingerprints and digital signatures, can detect any violation of the integrity of sensitive data.

Secure fingerprints attach a cryptographically strong checksum to data, which is generated and verified using a secret key that is known only to authorized subjects. By verifying this checksum when needed, an authorized subject can confirm the integrity of data. For example, a method of secure fingerprints that is known as a Hash-based Message Authentication Code (HMAC) is implemented in the IPsec standards to provide packet integrity and authenticity in IP networks. The HMAC method is very fast and is suitable for real-time traffic integrity and authentication.

Digital signing uses a similar cryptography method and attaches a digital signature to sensitive data. A unique signature-generation key, which is known exclusively to one signer, generates the signature. Other parties use the signature-verification key of the signer to verify the signature. The cryptography behind digital signing guarantees data authenticity and accuracy because the originator signed it. In the financial world, digital signatures also provide nonrepudiation of transactions, where a subject can prove to a third party that a transaction has occurred. Digital signature protocols are based on public-key cryptography and are not used for bulk protection because of their performance limitations.

Example: VPN Tunneling for Data Integrity

Figure 8-17 illustrates a connection between two network sites over the Internet. To provide data integrity, a VPN technology that supports secure fingerprinting creates a secured point-to-point association over the Internet. All packets that leave one site are imprinted with a secure digital fingerprint (similar to a very strong checksum) that uniquely identifies the data at the sender side. The packets are forwarded onto the untrusted network. A device on the remote site verifies the secure fingerprint to ensure that no one has tampered with the packet. Anyone eavesdropping on the untrusted network should not be able to change the packet payloads and change sensitive data without being detected.

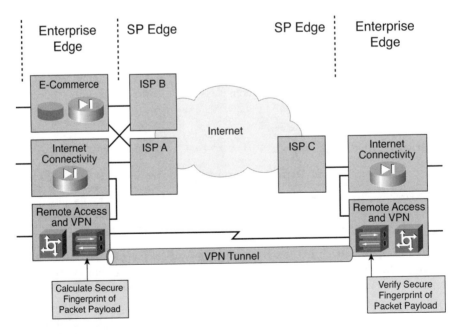

Figure 8-17 *Data Integrity Example*

Apply the same guidelines and warnings as confidentiality mechanisms when using integrity cryptographic mechanisms. Guidelines include the following:

■ Evaluate the need for data integrity carefully, and enforce it only where it is justified by the potential threats.

■ Use the strongest available mechanisms for data integrity, taking the performance effects into account.

■ Use only established and well-known cryptographic algorithms.

Example: Implementation of Digital Signatures

An organization needs to exchange stock market data over the Internet. Confidentiality is not its main concern. The main risk lies in an attacker changing data in transit and presenting false stock market data to the organization. The preferred data exchange application of the organization is email. Therefore, it decides to implement digital signatures of all email messages when exchanging data over the Internet among partners.

Security Management

Security management applications and technologies are used to monitor and control the network. Security management supports the following:

■ It collects, analyzes, and presents network data to the network managers. The tools should allow centrally storing and analyzing the audit results, including logs and traps. In addition to classic logging using the syslog protocol, IPSs can provide automatic correlation and in-depth visibility into complex security events. These features save administrators a considerable amount of time.

■ It offers structured deployment and provisioning of security policies into the security devices.

■ It provides role-based access control (RBAC) and accounts for all activities. Management personnel must be able to implement change control and monitoring and prevent accidental damage.

Security implementation is only as good as the policies used. Organizations must audit changes and create new versions of device configurations and device software according to corporate policies.

The biggest risk to security in properly planned network architecture is policy error. Management personnel must be aware of security policies and defined operational procedures so that they can respond to an incident quickly, reliably, and appropriately.

The Cisco Security Control Framework (SCF) is a common framework that influences the selection of products and capabilities that maximize visibility and control, the two most fundamental aspects driving security for the Cisco SAFE architecture. This framework facilitates the integration of the rich portfolio of Cisco security services that are designed to support the entire solution lifecycle. Key components of this framework include

- **Cisco Security Monitoring, Analysis, and Response System (Cisco Security MARS):** Cisco Security MARS is an appliance-based solution that allows network and security administrators to monitor, identify, isolate, and counter security threats. Cisco Security MARS obtains network intelligence by understanding the topology and device configurations from routers, switches, NetFlow, IPSs, firewalls, and other network devices and by profiling network traffic. The integrated network discovery in the system builds a topology map containing device configuration and current security policies. This enables Cisco Security MARS to model packet flows through the network. Because the appliance does not operate in-line, and it makes minimal use of existing software agents, there is minimal impact on network or system performance.

- **Cisco Security Manager:** This is a powerful but easy-to-use solution for configuring firewall, VPN, and IPS policies on Cisco security appliances, firewalls, routers, and switch modules. Using a GUI, Cisco Security Manager allows security policies to be easily configured per device, per device group, or globally.

- **Cisco NAC Manager:** This is a solution that manages the Cisco NAC Server. It provides a web-based interface for creating security policies and managing online users. It also acts as an authentication proxy for authentication servers on the back end, such as Cisco Secure ACS.

- **Cisco Secure ACS (CS-ACS):** This provides AAA services for routers, switches, firewalls, VPN services, and Cisco NAC clients. In addition, Cisco Secure ACS also interfaces with external back-end Microsoft Active Directory and Lightweight Directory Access Protocol (LDAP) authentication services.

- **System administration host:** This provides configuration, software images, and content changes on devices from a central server.

- **Configuration and software archive host:** This provides a repository for device configuration and system image backup files.

- **Network Time Protocol (NTP) server:** NTP is a server that is used for time synchronization.

- **Cisco Firewall VPN:** This provides granular access control for traffic flows between the management hosts and the managed devices for in-band management. Firewall also provides secure VPN access to the management module for administrators. It is located at the campus, branches, and other places in the network.

As illustrated in Figure 8-18, the SAFE architecture design includes a management network module that is dedicated to carrying control and management plane traffic such as Network Time Protocol (NTP), SSH, SNMP, VPN, TACACS+, syslog, and NetFlow reporting.

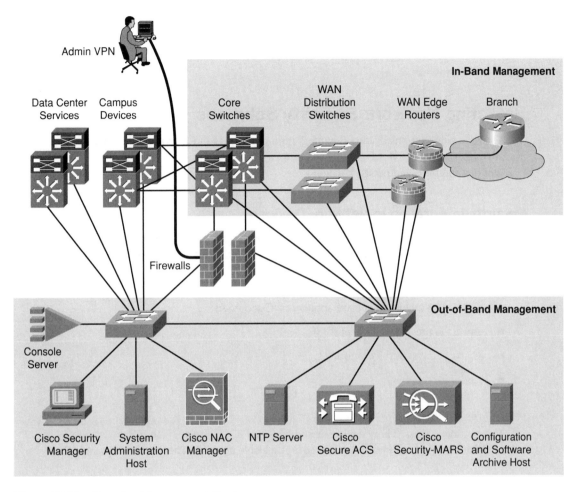

Figure 8-18 *Security Management Design*

The management module provides configuration management for nearly all devices in the network by using two primary technologies: Cisco IOS routers acting as terminal servers and a dedicated management network segment that is implemented either on separate hardware or VLANs. The dedicated management network segment provides the primary method for managing network devices. It uses secure transport protocols such as SSH and HTTPS. Hardened terminal servers provide backup console and CLI access to the network devices using the reverse-Telnet function.

The management network combines OOB management and in-band (IB) management access to manage the various devices. OOB management is used for devices at the head-quarters. OOB management is accomplished by connecting dedicated management ports or spare Ethernet ports on devices directly affixed to the dedicated OOB management network that hosts the management and monitoring applications and services. The OOB management network can be either implemented as a collection of dedicated hardware or based on VLAN isolation. IB management is used for remote devices such as the branch site. Access is provided through the data path using a firewalled connection to the core network module.

Selecting Network Security Solutions

The following sections discuss the integration of security in Cisco network devices. They also describe how to design security solutions for the enterprise network using Cisco security solutions and network devices.

Security Integration in Network Devices

To design and implement a secure network, it is necessary to integrate security in every part of the network environment. Features covered in the following sections include

- Cisco IOS router security

- Cisco ASA adaptive security appliances (Cisco ASA)

- Intrusion prevention system (IPS)

- Cisco Catalyst Services modules

- Endpoint security

Cisco IOS Security

This section discusses how devices based on Cisco IOS Software incorporate various security features to create an integrated and scalable network. These features include the following:

- **Cisco IOS Firewall:** A security-specific option for Cisco IOS Software. The Cisco IOS Firewall provides integrated network security with robust stateful firewall functionality for network perimeters. The Cisco IOS Firewall provides enterprises as well as small- and medium-sized businesses with a very cost-effective option, both in terms of initial capital investment and continuing administrative costs. Cisco IOS Firewalls help businesses guarantee network uptime and security by protecting customer networks against network and application layer attacks, viruses, and worms. At the same time, Cisco IOS Firewalls provide effective control of application traffic flowing through the network. The Cisco IOS Firewall offers sophisticated security and policy-enforcement services for connections within an organization (intranet) and between partner networks (extranets), as well as securing Internet connectivity for teleworker and branch offices.

- **Cisco IOS Intrusion Prevention System (IPS):** An in-line, deep-packet, inspection-based feature that enables Cisco IOS Software to effectively mitigate a wide range of network attacks. As a core facet of the Cisco Self-Defending Network, Cisco IOS IPS enables the network to defend itself with the intelligence to accurately identify, classify, and stop or block malicious or damaging traffic in real time. Cisco IOS IPS operates by loading a set of attack signatures on the router. To assist users in signature selection, Cisco provides prebuilt signature definition files that contain high-fidelity signatures that are based on the memory available on a router. Registered Cisco.com users with a Cisco Service Agreement can download the latest version of the signature definition files and the complete set of Cisco IPS signatures in Cisco IOS IPS signature definition files (SDF). Cisco IOS IPS complements the Cisco IOS Firewall and VPN solutions for superior threat protection at all entry points into the network.

■ **Cisco IOS IPsec:** IPsec functionality provides network data encryption at the IP packet level, offering a robust, standards-based security solution. IPsec provides data authentication and antireplay services in addition to data confidentiality services. It is the only way to implement secure VPNs. Organizations can combine IPsec with other Cisco IOS Software functionality to build scalable, robust, and secure QoS–aware VPNs.

■ **Cisco IOS Software trust and identity services:** Include core technologies that enable network traffic security: AAA; PKI; SSH; SSL; and IEEE 802.1X. Cisco IOS AAA network security services provide the primary framework to set up access control on a router or access server. It is an architectural framework for configuring a set of three independent security functions in a consistent manner. Cisco IOS AAA provides a modular way to perform AAA services. PKI provides strong and robust authentication, authorization, confidentiality, and nonrepudiation for e-business and e-commerce applications. SSH supports Secure Telnet access between applications and router resources. SSL enables a secure path between a web browser and router resources.

Example: Security Hardware Options for ISRs G2

The Cisco Generation 2 Integrated Services Routers (ISR G2) support additional options to enhance security in the network:

■ **Built-in VPN acceleration:** The built-in, hardware-based encryption acceleration offloads the VPN processes to provide increased VPN throughput with minimal impact on the router CPU.

■ **Secure voice:** The digital signal processor (DSP) slots of the ISRs use packet voice DSP modules (PVDM) that provide conferencing, transcoding, and secure voice features. For example, with Secure Real-Time Transport Protocol (SRTP), the entire voice payload is encrypted while the header is still in clear text, to support QoS features.

■ **High-performance advanced integration module (AIM):** The VPN, encryption, and IPS AIMs are a solution for aggregation-type applications, such as Dynamic Multipoint VPN (DMVPN), where large numbers of remote VPN tunnels are required. The VPN and encryption AIMs support Triple Data Encryption Standard (3DES) and Advanced Encryption Standard (AES) and boost router encryption and compression performance.

■ **Universal Serial Bus (USB) port and removable credentials:** The Cisco 1900, 2900, and 3900 Series routers were designed with on-board USB 1.1 ports, enabling important security and storage capabilities. These capabilities help to secure user authentication, store removable credentials for establishing secure VPN connections, securely distribute configuration files, and provide bulk flash memory storage for files and configuration.

■ **Cisco Intrusion Prevention System Network Module Enhanced (IPS NME) for Cisco 1900, 2900, and 3900 Series Integrated Services Routers:** The Cisco IPS NME brings hardware-based intrusion prevention to branch offices and small businesses. With the ever-increasing complexity and sophistication of security threats, every point of the network can be at risk. The Cisco IPS NME can accurately identify, classify, and stop malicious traffic, including worms, spyware, malware, adware, network viruses, and application abuse. Vigilant protection helps ensure business continuity and minimizes the effect of costly intrusions. Running Cisco IPS Sensor Software, the Cisco IPS NME can monitor up to 75 Mbps of traffic and is suitable for multiple T1/E1 and T3 environments. Cisco IPS NME interoperates with various Cisco IOS Software security features.

■ **Cisco NAC Network Module:** Cisco Network Admission Control (NAC) Network Module adds the feature-rich Cisco NAC Appliance Server (Cisco NAS) capabilities, with Cisco 2900 and 3900 Series Integrated Services Routers. The Cisco NAS (formerly Cisco Clean Access Server) is a rapidly deployable NAC product that allows network administrators to authenticate, authorize, evaluate, and remediate wired, wireless, and remote users and their machines before allowing users onto the network. The integration of Cisco NAS capabilities into a network module for Integrated Services Routers allows network administrators to manage a single device in a branch office for data, voice, and security requirements, reducing network complexity, IT staff training, equipment sparing requirements, and maintenance costs.

Security Appliances

The following sections are an overview of the Cisco security appliances.

Cisco ASA Adaptive Security Appliances

The Cisco ASA 5500 Series Adaptive Security Appliances are a high-performance, multi-function security appliance family delivering converged firewall, IPS, network antivirus, and VPN services. As a key component of the Cisco SAFE, these appliances provide proactive threat mitigation that stops attacks before they spread through the network. They also control network activity and application traffic. They deliver flexible VPN connectivity while remaining cost-effective and easy to manage.

The centralized architecture for IPsec and SSL provides ease of management and implementation in deployments that require detailed access controls for numerous deployment scenarios with diverse user communities, including mobile workers, telecommuters, and extranet users.

Cisco Network Admission Control Appliance

Cisco NAC Appliance extends NAC to all network access methods, including access through LANs, remote-access gateways, and wireless access points. It also supports posture assessment for guest users. Cisco NAC can be combined with Cisco NAC Guest Server and Cisco NAC Profiler for additional features.

Intrusion Prevention System

The Cisco IPS solution combines passive intrusion detection, in-line prevention services, and innovative technologies to improve accuracy. The result is confidence in the provided protection of the solution, without the fear of legitimate traffic being dropped.

Cisco IPS 4200 Series sensors offer significant protection to a network by aiding in detection and classification. They block threats, including worms, spyware and adware, network viruses, and application abuse. Using Cisco IPS Sensor Software Version 7.0, the Cisco IPS solution combines in-line intrusion prevention services with innovative technologies that improve accuracy. As a result, more threats can be blocked without the risk of dropping legitimate network traffic. The new software release includes enhanced detection capabilities as well as improved scalability, resiliency, and performance features.

The Cisco IPS appliances offer comprehensive protection of the network through their ability to collaborate with other network security resources, providing a proactive approach to protecting the network. The Cisco IPS appliances support multivector threat identification to protect the network from policy violations, vulnerability exploitation, and anomalous activity. This is provided through detailed inspection of traffic in Layers 2 through 7. The sensors address bandwidth requirements from 65 Mbps to several gigabits per second. The following list discusses the different currently available IPS sensors:

- At 250 Mbps, the Cisco IPS 4240 Sensor can be deployed to provide protection in switched environments on multiple T3 subnets. With the support of multiple 10/100/1000 interfaces, it can also be deployed on partially utilized gigabit links or fully saturated, full-duplex 100-Mbps environments.

- The Cisco 4240-DC Intrusion Prevention Sensor is based on the Cisco IPS 4240 Sensor but supports DC power. The Cisco IPS 4240-DC is Network Equipment Building System (NEBS) compliant and can be deployed in environments that have specific requirements pertaining to NEBS Level 3 compliance.

- The Cisco IPS 4255 Sensor delivers 600 Mbps of performance and can be used to protect partially utilized gigabit subnets and traffic traversing switches that are being used to aggregate traffic from numerous subnets.

- The Cisco IPS 4260 Sensor delivers 1 Gbps of protection performance and can be used to protect both gigabit subnets and aggregated traffic traversing switches from multiple subnets. This purpose-built device supports both copper and fiber network interface card (NIC) environments, providing flexibility of deployment.

■ The Cisco IPS 4270 Sensor provides up to 4 Gbps of intrusion prevention performance. With optional fiber or copper NIC cards for as many as 16 interfaces, multiple segments can be monitored for malicious traffic.

Cisco Catalyst Services Modules

The Cisco Catalyst 6500 Series switching platform provides the option to extend the capabilities with various security-related modules. They include

■ **Cisco Catalyst 6500 Series Firewall Services Module (FWSM):** The Cisco Catalyst 6500 Series FWSM is a high-speed, integrated firewall module for Cisco Catalyst 6500 Series switches and Cisco 7600 Series routers. Up to four Cisco FWSMs can be installed in a single chassis, providing scalability to 20 Gbps per chassis. The Cisco FWSM includes many advanced features, such as multiple security contexts at both the routed levels and in bridging mode. This helps to reduce cost and operational complexity while managing multiple firewalls from the same management platform.

■ **Cisco Catalyst 6500 Series Intrusion Detection System Services Module 2 (IDSM-2):** The Cisco IDSM-2 is part of the Cisco Intrusion Prevention System (Cisco IPS). It works in concert with the other components to efficiently protect the data infrastructure. It supports both in-line (IPS) mode and passive operation (IDS). Up to 500 Mbps of IDS and IPS inspection provide high-speed, packet-examination capabilities and allow more protection of a wider variety of networks and traffic.

■ **Cisco Catalyst 6500 Series SSL Services Module:** The Cisco SSL Services Module is an Integrated Services Module for the Cisco Catalyst 6500 Series switches and Cisco 7600 Series routers. It offloads processor-intensive tasks that are related to securing traffic with SSL. It increases the number of secure connections that are supported by a website and reduces the operational complexity of high-performance web server farms. Up to four Cisco SSL Services Modules can be installed in each chassis.

■ **Cisco IPsec VPN Shared Port Adapter (SPA):** The Cisco IPsec VPN SPA delivers scalable and cost-effective VPN performance for Cisco Catalyst 6500 Series switches and Cisco 7600 Series routers. The Cisco Catalyst 6500 switch or Cisco 7600 router can support up to two Cisco IPsec VPN SPAs. Using the Cisco 7600 Series/Catalyst 6500 Series Services SPA Carrier-400 (Cisco Services SPA Carrier-400), each slot of the Cisco Catalyst 6500 switch or Cisco 7600 router can support up to two Cisco IPsec VPN SPAs. Although the Cisco IPsec VPN SPA does not have physical WAN or LAN interfaces, it takes advantage of the breadth of LAN and WAN interfaces of each of the platforms.

■ **Cisco Catalyst 6500 Series/7600 Series WebVPN Services Module:** This is a high-speed, integrated SSL VPN services module for Cisco Catalyst 6500 Series switches and Cisco 7600 Series routers that addresses the scalability, performance, application support, and security that is required for large-scale, remote-access SSL VPN deployments. Supporting up to 32,000 SSL VPN users and 128,000 connections per chassis, the Cisco WebVPN Services Module can cost-effectively meet the capacity requirements of large enterprises. The unique virtualization capabilities that are integrated into the module simplify the policy creation and enforcement for diverse enterprise user communities and make it an ideal solution for managed service providers. The broad, industry-proven application support and endpoint security that is provided by the Cisco WebVPN Services Module is ideally suited to meet the secure connectivity demands of any organization.

- **Cisco Traffic Anomaly Detector Module:** The Cisco Traffic Anomaly Detector Module uses behavioral analysis and attack recognition technology to proactively detect and identify all types of online assaults. By constantly monitoring traffic that is destined for a protected device, such as a web or e-commerce application server, the Cisco Traffic Anomaly Detector Module compiles detailed profiles that indicate how individual devices behave under "normal" operating conditions. If the Cisco Traffic Anomaly Detector Module detects any per-flow deviations from the profile, it considers the anomalous behavior a potential attack and responds based on user preference. It does this by sending an operator alert to initiate a manual response, by triggering an existing management system, or by launching the Cisco Anomaly Guard Module to immediately begin mitigation services.

- **Cisco Catalyst 6500/Cisco 7600 Router Anomaly Guard Module:** A single Cisco Anomaly Guard Module provides the platform for processing attack traffic at gigabit-per-second line rates. The Cisco Anomaly Guard Module features a unique on-demand deployment model, diverting and scrubbing only traffic that is addressed to targeted devices or zones, without affecting other traffic. Within the module, integrated multiple layers of defense enable the Cisco Anomaly Guard Module to identify and block malicious attack traffic while allowing legitimate transactions to continue flowing to their original destinations.

- **Cisco Catalyst 6500 Series Network Analysis Module (NAM-1 and NAM-2):** The Cisco NAM modules provide visibility into all layers of network traffic by using Remote Monitoring 2 (RMON2) and other advanced MIBs. The Cisco NAMs access the built-in mini-Remote Monitoring (mini-RMON) features of the Cisco Catalyst 6500 Series switches and Cisco 7600 Series routers to provide port-level traffic statistics at the MAC or data link layer. They also deliver the intelligence that is required to analyze traffic flows for applications, hosts, conversations, and network-based services, such as QoS and VoIP.

Endpoint Security Solutions

Endpoint security solutions provide server and desktop protection against new and emerging threats stemming from malicious network activity. Endpoint security solutions should identify and prevent malicious behavior, resulting in the elimination of known and unknown, or "Day Zero," network threats. Endpoint security solutions should provide the aggregation and extension of multiple endpoint security functions by providing intrusion prevention and distributed firewall capabilities, in addition to malicious mobile code protection, system integrity assurance, and audit log consolidation.

Cisco Network Admission Control (NAC) and NAC Appliance integration with trusted QoS provides collaboration with the network to enhance the functionality of Cisco network and security devices and to improve the delivery of mission-critical traffic when the network is under a heavy load. In addition to Cisco products, complete endpoint security solutions are based on a successful integration of products from various third-party vendors, such as Trend, Sophos, Priveon (Bit9).

Securing the Enterprise Network

The following sections review the locations to deploy security devices and solutions in the enterprise network.

Securing the enterprise network involves deploying technologies that support identity and access control, threat defense and infrastructure protection, and security management. These sections provide an overview of where to deploy these technologies.

Example: Deploying Identity and Access Control in the Enterprise Campus

Figure 8-19 illustrates where identity and access control technologies can be deployed in the enterprise campus.

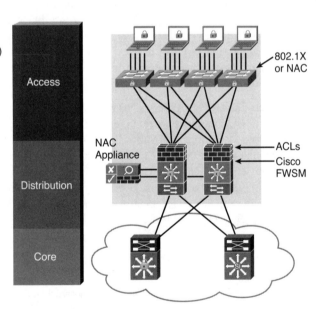

Figure 8-19 *Deploying Identity and Access Control Example*

Example: Deploying Threat Detection and Mitigation in the Enterprise Campus

Figure 8-20 illustrates where threat detection and mitigation technologies can be deployed in the enterprise campus.

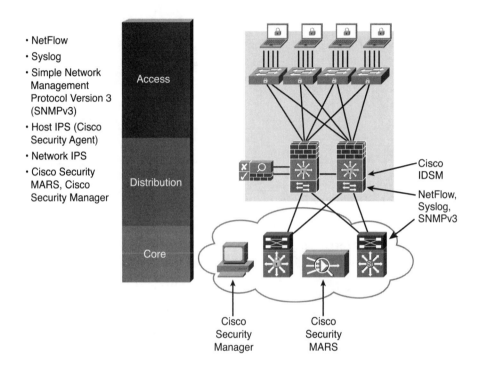

Figure 8-20 *Deploying Threat Detection and Mitigation Example*

Example: Deploying Infrastructure Protection in the Enterprise Campus

Figure 8-21 illustrates infrastructure protection technologies can be deployed in the enterprise campus.

Example: Deploying Security in the Enterprise Campus

An organization has experienced several incidents in which laptop users on the campus network have brought in viruses from home. Some users have attempted to intercept network traffic. Some interns have tried to hack the network infrastructure. As shown in Figure 8-22, to manage the risks, the organization implements identity and access control solutions, threat detection and mitigation solutions, infrastructure protection, and security management.

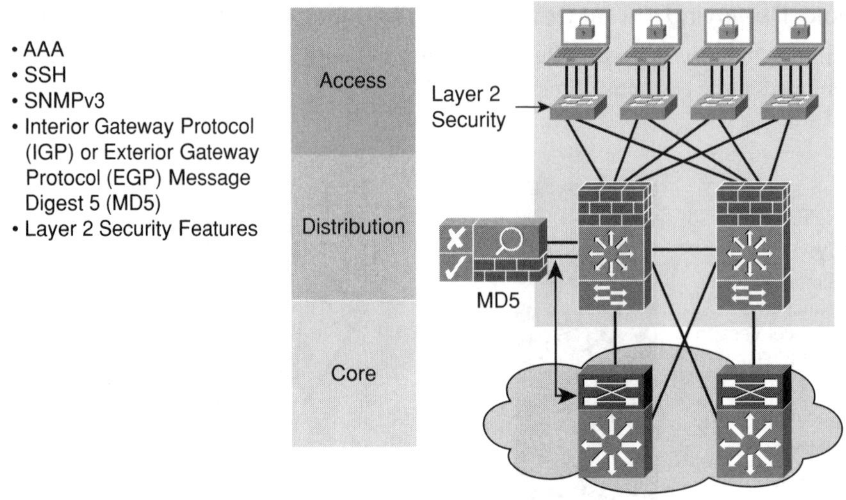

• AAA
• SSH
• SNMPv3
• Interior Gateway Protocol (IGP) or Exterior Gateway Protocol (EGP) Message Digest 5 (MD5)
• Layer 2 Security Features
Access
Distribution
Core
Layer 2 Security
MD5

Figure 8-21 *Deploying Infrastructure Protection Example*

Identity and Access Control:
• IEEE 802.1X, NAC, ACLs, Firewalls
Threat Detection and Mitigation:
• NetFlow, Syslog, SNMP, Cisco Security MARS, Network IPS, Host IPS
Infrastructure Protection:
• AAA, SSH, SNMPv3, IGP or EGP MD5, Layer 2 Security Features
Security Management:
• Cisco Security Manager, Cisco Security MARS
Access
Distribution
Core
802.1X
Layer 2 Security
NAC Appliance
ACLs
Cisco FWSM
Cisco IDSM
NetFlow, Syslog, SNMPv3
MD5
Cisco Security Manager
Cisco Security MARS

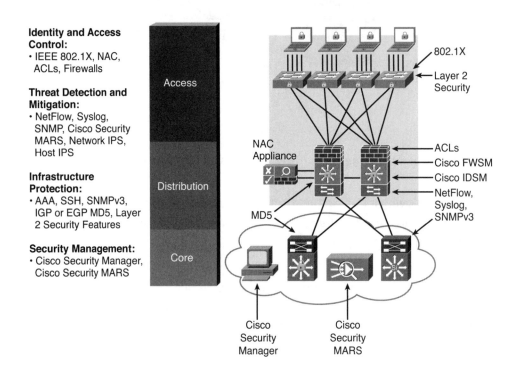

Figure 8-22 *Deploying Security Example*

Example: Deploying Identity and Access Control in the Enterprise Data Center

Figure 8-23 illustrates where identity and access control technologies can be deployed in the enterprise data center.

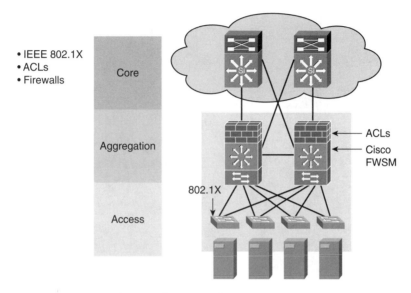

Figure 8-23 *Deploying Identity and Access Control Example*

Example: Deploying Threat Detection and Mitigation in the Enterprise Data Center

Figure 8-24 illustrates where threat detection and mitigation technologies can be deployed in the enterprise data center.

Example: Deploying Infrastructure Protection in the Enterprise Data Center

Figure 8-25 illustrates where infrastructure protection technologies can be deployed in the enterprise data center.

Example: Deploying Security in the Data Center

The data center hosts servers for the main campus network and branch offices. These servers can contain the most sensitive information of the enterprise and are available to many users. Therefore, network performance is usually a critical issue, which can sometimes limit the choice of protection mechanisms. Some specific risks in the data center include

■   Direct compromise of exposed applications and unauthorized access to data

■   Compromise of other hosts from compromised servers in this module

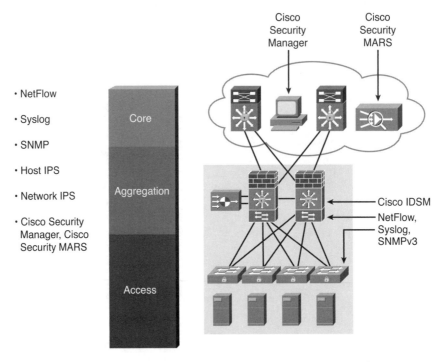

- NetFlow

- Syslog

- SNMP

- Host IPS

- Network IPS

- Cisco Security Manager, Cisco Security MARS

Figure 8-24 *Deploying Threat Detection and Mitigation Example*

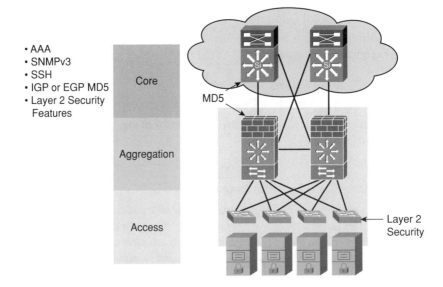

- AAA
- SNMPv3
- SSH
- IGP or EGP MD5
- Layer 2 Security Features

Figure 8-25 *Deploying Infrastructure Protection Example*

To provide security, the organization implements the following:

■   Identity and access control solutions

■   Threat detection and mitigation solutions

■   Infrastructure protection (including Control Plane Policing [CoPP])

■   Security management

An illustration is shown in Figure 8-26.

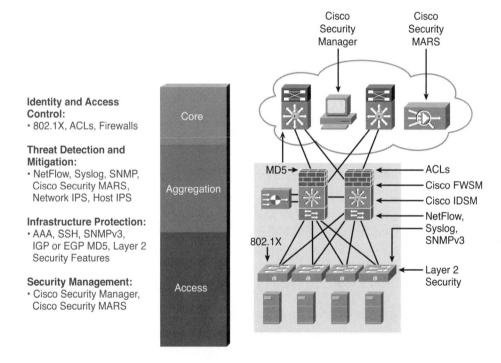

Figure 8-26   *Deploying Data Center Security Example*

Example: Deploying Identity and Access Control in the Enterprise Edge

Figure 8-27 illustrates where identity and access control technologies can be deployed in the enterprise edge. Notice the demilitarized zone (DMZ) in the figure.

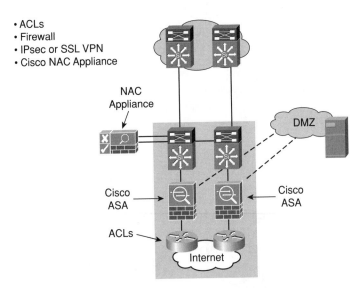

Figure 8-27 *Deploying Edge Identity and Access Control Example*

Example: Deploying Threat Detection and Mitigation in the Enterprise Edge

Figure 8-28 illustrates threat detection and mitigation technologies that can be deployed in the enterprise edge.

Example: Deploying Infrastructure Protection in the Enterprise Edge

Figure 8-29 illustrates infrastructure protection technologies that can be deployed in the enterprise edge.

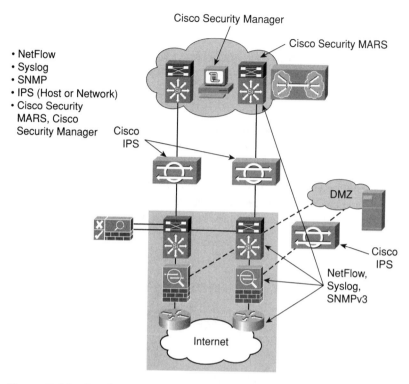

- NetFlow
- Syslog
- SNMP
- IPS (Host or Network)
- Cisco Security
  MARS, Cisco
  Security Manager

Figure 8-28 *Deploying Edge Threat Detection and Mitigation Example*

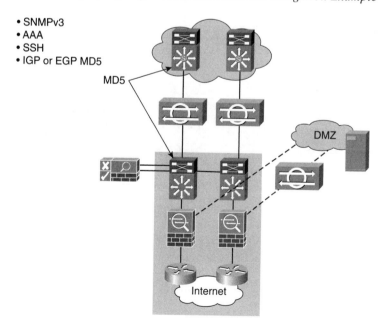

- SNMPv3
- AAA
- SSH
- IGP or EGP MD5

Figure 8-29 *Edge Infrastructure Protection Example*

Example: Deploying Security in the Enterprise Edge

The enterprise edge modules provide WAN connectivity among various parts of the enterprise network. Security is important whenever data is transferred between locations. A summarized illustration of the edge security solutions is shown in Figure 8-30.

Here are some specific risks in the WAN module:

- Data transmission confidentiality and integrity, where an attacker who obtains physical access to the network media or to a service provider WAN switch can intercept WAN connections. An attacker might eavesdrop on any traffic or change data in transit.

- Accidental or deliberate misconfiguration of the WAN network, which can result in the interconnection of different enterprises. Some WAN protocols can establish automatic peering, and unwanted connectivity might become possible.

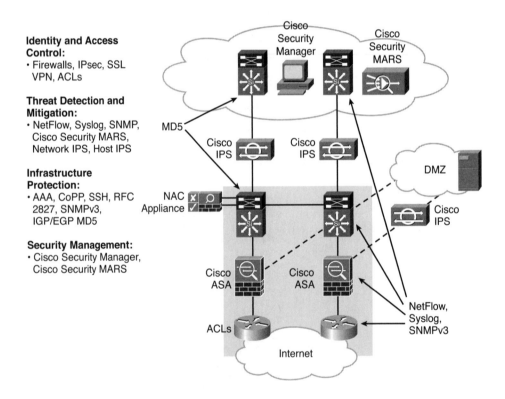

Figure 8-30 *Edge Security Solutions Overview*

Summary

In this chapter, you learned about security design principles with a focus on the following topics:

- Security services must provide adequate protection to conduct business in a relatively open environment:

    - There are many types of security threats and associated risks.

    - Each device on the network, such as a host, router, or switch, is a potential security target.

- Network security is part of the system lifecycle:

    - Network security is a continuous process that is built around a security policy.

    - Security design and network design should be integrated.

- Trust and identity management provide secure network access and admission at any point in the network and isolate and control infected or unpatched devices that attempt to access the network.

- Threat defense provides a strong defense against known and unknown attacks, using security integrated in routers, switches, and appliances.

- Secure connectivity uses encryption and authentication to provide secure transport across untrusted networks.

- Security management is a framework for scalable policy administration and enforcement.

- Cisco has integrated security features into network devices, including ACLs, firewall support, VPNs, IPSs, and event logging.

- The Cisco SAFE architecture and Cisco network devices with integrated security are deployed throughout the enterprise network.

References

For additional information, refer to the following resources:

Cisco, Inc. Cisco SAFE Reference Guide, at
www.cisco.com/en/US/docs/solutions/Enterprise/Security/SAFE_RG/SAFE_rg.html.

Cisco, Inc. Cisco Integrated Services Routers Generation 2 At-a-Glance comparative
overview and security features, at
www.cisco.com/en/US/prod/collateral/routers/ps10538/aag_c45_556315.pdf.

Cisco, Inc. Cisco SAFE Solution Overview, at
www.cisco.com/en/US/docs/solutions/Enterprise/Security/SAFESolOver.html.

Cisco, Inc. Security and VPN: Introduction, at
www.cisco.com/en/US/products/hw/vpndevc/index.html.

Cisco, Inc. Infrastructure Protection on Cisco IOS Software–Based Platforms, at
www.cisco.com/en/US/prod/collateral/iosswrel/ps8802/ps6970/ps1838/prod_white_
paper0900aecd804ac831.pdf.

Cisco Systems, Inc. Cisco Router and Security Device Manager: Introduction, at
www.cisco.com/en/US/products/sw/secursw/ps5318/index.html.

Cisco, Inc. Cisco Adaptive Security Device Manager: Introduction, at
www.cisco.com/en/US/products/ps6121/index.html.

Cisco, Inc. Cisco Intrusion Prevention System: Introduction, at
www.cisco.com/en/US/products/sw/secursw/ps2113/index.html.

Cisco, Inc. CiscoWorks Management Center for Cisco Security Agents: Introduction, at
www.cisco.com/en/US/products/sw/cscowork/ps5212/index.html.

Cisco, Inc. Cisco Secure Access Control Server for Windows: Introduction, at
www.cisco.com/en/US/products/sw/secursw/ps2086/index.html.

Cisco, Inc. Cisco Security Manager: Introduction, at
www.cisco.com/en/US/products/ps6498/index.html.

Cisco, Inc. Cisco Security Monitoring, Analysis, and Response System: Introduction, at
www.cisco.com/en/US/products/ps6241/index.html.

Cisco, Inc. Enterprise Internet Edge Design Guide, at
www.cisco.com/en/US/docs/solutions/Enterprise/Security/IE_DG.html.

Cisco, Inc. Cisco IOS Firewall: Introduction, at
www.cisco.com/en/US/products/sw/secursw/ps1018/index.html.

Cisco, Inc. Cisco IOS IPsec: Introduction, at
www.cisco.com/en/US/products/ps6635/products_ios_protocol_group_home.html.

Cisco, Inc. Cisco IOS Trust and Identity: Introduction, at
www.cisco.com/en/US/netsol/ns463/index.html

Review Questions

Answer the following questions, and then refer to Appendix A for the answers:

1. Which law was enacted in response to a number of major corporate and accounting scandals and establishes new or enhanced auditing and financial standards for all U.S. public company boards, management, and public accounting firms?

2. What security risk involves the alteration of sensitive data?

3. Which tool is used to rapidly scan large networks through the scanning and analysis of network ports?

4. What are the key parameters that should be considered when designing a secure network?

5. What is the name of the security framework that is aimed at ensuring network and service availability and business continuity?

6. What are the three ways that access control mechanisms are usually classified?

7. What are the two ways to securely send a key to a remote device?

8. Which Cisco IOS features enables the device to defend itself with the intelligence to accurately identify, classify and stop or block malicious or damaging traffic in real time?

9. What Cisco Catalyst module uses behavioral analysis and attack recognition technology to proactively detect and identify all types of online assaults?

10. What types of solutions provide server and desktop protection against new and emerging threats stemming from malicious network activity?

Chapter 9

Identifying Voice and Video Networking Considerations

This chapter introduces voice and video design principles and contains the following sections:

- Integrating Voice and Video Architectures

- Identifying the Requirements of Voice and Video Technologies

Many enterprises are integrating their voice and data networks into a single Unified Communications network. Unified Communications networks can run the same applications as telephony networks but in a more cost-effective and scalable manner. To design a network, both voice and data traffic need to be considered.

This chapter reviews traditional voice architectures and features. It explains the reasons for migrating from a traditional architecture to an integrated one. Voice traffic engineering on the Unified Communications network will be examined. The chapter concludes with useful guidelines for preparing the IP infrastructure for voice and video transport.

Integrating Voice and Video Architectures

Packet telephony introduces a new set of terms and standards. Each technology has a specific role to play in the network.

The following sections discuss the main drivers of the new Unified Communications network. They also examine the components that are required to successfully deploy voice and video on an existing data network. They provide an overview of standard voice components that are common to all packet networks. They also cover VoIP components that are found in enterprise packet networks. These aspects will allow a person to be better prepared to design an integrated voice-video-data network.

Differentiating Between Analog and Digital Signaling

The human voice generates sound waves, and the telephone converts the sound waves into analog signals. Analog signaling is not robust because of line noise or inefficient techniques used to reduce line noise. Analog transmissions are boosted by amplifiers because the signal diminishes as it travels farther from the central telephone office. As the signal is boosted, the noise is also boosted, which often causes an unusable connection.

In digital networks, signals are transmitted over great distances and coded, regenerated, and decoded without degradation of quality. Repeaters amplify the signal and clean it to its original condition. Repeaters then determine the original sequence of the signal levels and send the clean signal to the next network destination.

The public switched telephone network (PSTN) is a collection of interconnected voice-oriented public telephone networks, both commercial and government-owned. Presently, the PSTN is almost entirely digital in technology except for the final link from the central (local) telephone office to the user. For clear voice connections over distances, the PSTN converts analog speech to a digital format and sends it over a digital network. At the other end of the connection, the telephone system converts the digital signal back to an analog format, normal sound waves that the ear can pick up.

There are several steps to converting an analog signal into digital format. These are illustrated in Figure 9-1.

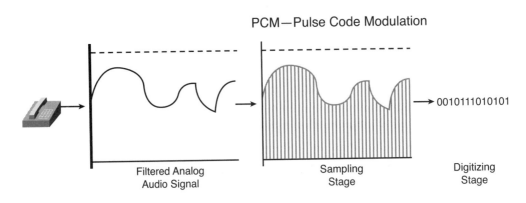

Figure 9-1   *Analog-to-Digital Conversion*

Detailed information is included in the following steps:

Step 1.   **Filtering:** Filters out the speech frequency component of the signal. Most of the energy of spoken language ranges from 300 Hz to (approximately) 3400 Hz. Therefore, early digital telephony researchers established a 3100-Hz bandwidth for standard speech. A coder-decoder (codec) puts the analog waveforms through a voice frequency filter to filter out anything greater than 4000 Hz.

Step 2.   **Sampling:** Samples the filtered input signal at a constant sampling frequency by using a process called pulse amplitude modulation (PAM). This step uses the original analog signal to modulate the amplitude of a pulse train that has a constant amplitude and frequency. The sampling rate is twice the highest frequency of 4000 Hz, which is 8000 times per second, or every 125 microseconds.

Step 3.   **Digitizing:** Digitizes the samples to transmit over a telephony network by using pulse code modulation (PCM). The only difference between PAM and PCM is that PCM takes the process one step further by encoding each analog sample by using binary codewords. PCM has an analog-to-digital converter on the source side and a digital-to-analog converter on the destination side.

The digitizing process is further divided into two subprocesses:

- **Quantization and coding:** A digitizing process that converts each analog sample value into a discrete value that is assigned a unique digital codeword. As the input signal samples enter the quantization phase, they are assigned to a quantization interval. All quantization intervals are equally spaced throughout the dynamic range of the input analog signal. Each quantization interval is assigned a discrete value in the form of a binary codeword. The standard word size utilized is 8 bits, which enables 256 possible quantizing intervals. The 8-bit codewords allow a bit rate of 64 kbps. The rate is calculated by multiplying the sampling rate (twice the input frequency) by the size of the codeword (2 * 4 kHz * 8 bits = 64 kbps).

- **Companding:** A process of first compressing an analog signal at the source and then expanding this signal back to its original size when it reaches its destination. Combining the two terms *compressing* and *expanding* into one word resulted in the term *companding*. During the companding process, input analog signal samples are compressed into logarithmic segments, and then each segment is quantized and coded using uniform quantization. The result is a more accurate value for smaller amplitudes and a uniform signal-to-noise quantization ratio across the input range.

Note The a-law logarithmic companding standard is used in Europe, and μ-law is used in North America and Japan. For communication between a μ-law and an a-law country, the μ-law country must change its signaling to accommodate the a-law country.

Introducing Voice and Video over IP

Although the PSTN has effectively carried voice, there are several business drivers for integrated voice and data networks in the enterprise. This section describes the drivers for migrating from separate voice and data networks to integrated networks.

These events are driving convergence to Unified Communications networks:

- Companies want to reduce WAN costs by migrating to integrated networks that can carry any type of data efficiently.

- Data has overtaken voice as the primary traffic on many voice networks.

- The PSTN architecture that was built for voice is not flexible enough to carry data well. The PSTN cannot create and deploy features quickly enough.

- Data, voice, and video cannot be integrated on the current PSTN structure.

Time-division multiplexing (TDM) networks such as the PSTN cannot allocate bandwidth on demand as packet-switching networks do. A circuit-switched PSTN call uses a dedicated 64 kbps for the entire duration of the call, whether conversation is taking place or not. The low trunk efficiency of circuit-switched networks is a major driver for the migration to unified packet-switched networks, where bandwidth is consumed only when the traffic flows.

Integrating data, voice, and video in a network changes the infrastructure and enables vendors to introduce new features. The Unified Communications network model enables distribution of call routing, control, and applications functions that are based on industry standards. Enterprises can mix and match equipment from multiple vendors and geographically deploy these systems wherever they are needed.

On an IP network, enterprises can locate voice-call servers and application servers virtually anywhere. As voice moves to IP networks that use the public Internet for traffic between enterprises and private intranets for traffic within an enterprise, service providers can host voice-call and application servers.

Unified Communications include Voice over IP (VoIP), rich media, collaboration, and many other functions. They place strict requirements on IP packet loss, packet delay, and delay variation (or jitter). Therefore, most of the quality of service (QoS) mechanisms available on Cisco switches and routers must be enabled throughout the network. For the same reasons, redundant devices and network links that provide quick convergence after network failures or topology changes are also important to ensure a highly available infrastructure. The different network unification pieces are illustrated in Figure 9-2.

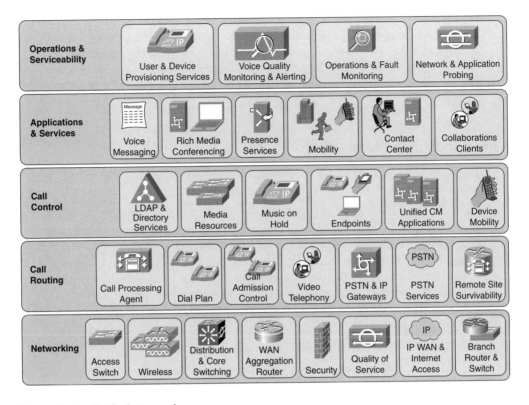

Figure 9-2 *Unified Network*

The following aspects are essential to the topic of Unified Communications networking and are specifically organized here in order of importance and relevance to one another:

■ **Network infrastructure:** Ensures a redundant and resilient foundation with QoS enabled for Unified Communications applications.

■ **Voice security:** Ensures a general security policy for Unified Communications applications and a hardened and secure networking foundation for them to rely upon.

■ **Unified Communications deployment models:** Provides tested models in which to deploy Unified Communications call control and applications, as well as best practices and design guidelines to apply to Unified Communications deployments.

■ **VoIP migration options:** Provides guidelines on how to plan and approach a migration from separate standalone voice, video, and collaboration systems to an integrated Cisco Unified Communications System.

The networking architecture lays the foundation upon which all other layers of the Unified Communications system are deployed. Additional layers, including call routing, call control, applications and services, and operations and serviceability, rely heavily on the readiness of the network to support their services. The networking layer is the single most important aspect of a solid Unified Communications foundation. It provides the quality of service necessary to ensure that applications have uncompromised access to network services. The networking layer also secures the correct deployment of servers and the proper bandwidth for endpoints and services to communicate effectively and securely.

Voice and Video Standards

H.323 is an ITU standard that provides a mechanism for transporting multimedia communications over packet-switched networks. This section describes the features and benefits of the H.323 standard.

By complying with the H.323 standard, multimedia products and applications from multiple vendors can interoperate, which allows users to communicate without concern for compatibility. The H.323 standard is complex and broad in scope. It includes standalone devices (IP telephones, voice gateways), embedded personal computer technology (such as PCs with Microsoft NetMeeting), and point-to-point and multipoint conferences. H.323 addresses call control, multimedia management, and bandwidth management.

H.323 references many other ITU standards, including the following:

- **H.225:** A standard used to describe call signaling and Registration, Admission, and Status (RAS) signaling used for H.323 session establishment and packetization.

- **H.245:** A control standard for multimedia communication that describes the messages and procedures used for opening and closing logical channels for audio, video, and data; capability exchange; control; and indications.

H.323 defines four major components for a network-based communications system:

- Terminals
- Gateways
- Gatekeepers
- Multipoint control units (MCU)

Terminals

Terminals are endpoints that provide real-time, two-way voice (video and data are optional) communications with other endpoints such as H.323 terminals, gateways, or MCUs. An H.323 terminal must be able to transmit and receive standard 64-kbps pulse code modulation (PCM)–encoded voice. An example of an H.323 terminal is a PC with Microsoft Windows NetMeeting software.

Gateways

An H.323 gateway is an optional element. Gateways provide many services such as translation between H.323 endpoints and other non-H.323 devices. This translation allows H.323 endpoints and non-H.323 endpoints to communicate. In addition, the gateway translates among audio, video, and data formats. It converts call setup signals and procedures and converts communication control signals and procedures.

Gateways are not required between two terminal connections because endpoints can directly communicate with each other. Terminals communicate with H.323 gateways by using the H.245 and Q.931 protocols.

Gatekeepers

The gatekeeper is also an optional H.323 element. An H.323 gatekeeper provides call control and services to H.323 endpoints. The scope of endpoints in which a gatekeeper exercises its authority is called a *zone*. H.323 defines a one-to-one relationship between a zone and a gatekeeper. When a gatekeeper is included, it must perform address translation, admission control, bandwidth control, and zone management.

The gatekeeper can also perform call control signaling, call authorization, bandwidth management, and call management. The gatekeeper can make decisions about balancing multiple gateways by integrating their addressing into the Domain Name System (DNS) or through Cisco IOS Software configuration options. For example, if a call is routed through a gatekeeper, that gatekeeper forwards the call to the corresponding gateway based on some routing logic. This function is called Gatekeeper-Routed Call Signaling, where the H.323 gatekeeper functions as a virtual voice switch.

Note Cisco Unified Communications Manager does not support the Gatekeeper-Routed Call Signaling capability.

Gatekeeper Example

Figure 9-3 illustrates various voice design options and emphasizes the importance of a gatekeeper, especially in large voice network designs. Voice network design depends primarily on the number of voice gateways and, consequently, the number of logical connections among them.

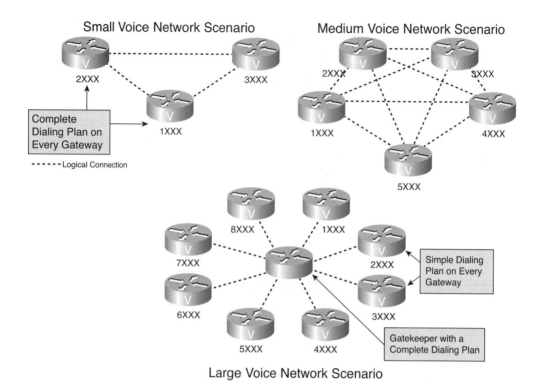

Figure 9-3 *Gatekeeper Example*

The maximum number of logical connections among voice gateways and the complexity of the network are represented by the formula $[N * (N - 1)] / 2$, where N is the number of voice gateways in the system. For example, the maximum number of logical connections among three voice gateways is 3, among five voice gateways is 10, and among eight voice gateways is 28. The complexity grows very fast, and adding one voice gateway to the existing network means reconfiguring all other voice gateways. Therefore, network maintenance can become very difficult.

The Cisco solution to this issue is to use a gatekeeper to store the dial plan for a zone. Gateways then need only to register with the gatekeeper. The gatekeeper provides all call control services to them.

Multipoint Control Units

The MCU is an H.323 endpoint. It incorporates two functional components:

■ **Multipoint controller (MC):** Supports conferences of three or more endpoints. The MC is not modeled as a standalone unit and can be located with an endpoint, terminal or gateway, gatekeeper, or MCU.

■ **Multipoint processor (MP):** Receives multiple streams of multimedia input, switches and mixes the streams, and then retransmits the result to the conference members. Like the MC, an MP resides in an MCU.

When voice is transported across the IP network using traditional telephones, a voice gateway is required on both sides of the IP network. The gateway is a voice-enabled router that performs voice-to-IP and IP-to-voice conversions in a special piece of hardware called a digital signal processor (DSP). After the gateway converts voice into IP packets, it transmits the packets across the IP network. The receiving router converts IP packets back to voice signals and forwards them through the PBX to the destination telephone.

When a network uses H.323-capable devices over IP, a voice gateway is required to provide the conversion capabilities between the IP network and the PSTN.

H.264

H.264 is an ITU standard that defines effective video encoding. The H.264 ITU-T standard, identical to ISO/IEC MPEG4 part 10 and Advanced Video Coding (AVC), defines the most effective algorithm for video compression. The H.264 protocol improves the video resolution quality in the H.323 protocol suite by encoding and transmitting two interlaced fields for each frame (that is, 30 frames per second and 60 fields per second, instead of only 30 fields per second of H.263). This process allows the user to present decoded video that is much more fluid and lifelike. The result of this enhancement is a substantially higher resolution quality that approaches or matches MPEG-2 quality at a 64 percent lower bandwidth cost.

H.264 also handles the encoding of the pixel blocks more efficiently. It practically eliminates the tiling or pixilation seen on current videoconferences when there is a scene change or a lot of motion.

Introducing VoIP

Voice over IP (VoIP) refers to communication services and voice, facsimile, and voice-messaging applications that are transported through the IP network rather than traditional telephony networks. This section describes additional components that are required for VoIP in an enterprise environment. They are illustrated in Figure 9-4.

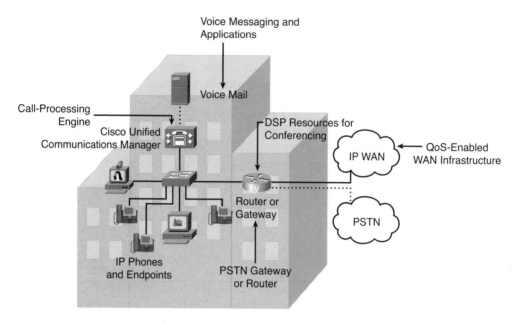

Figure 9-4   *VoIP Components*

VoIP architecture includes these distinct components:

- **Infrastructure:** The infrastructure is based on data link layer and network layer switches and voice-enabled routers that interconnect endpoints with the IP and PSTN network. Endpoints attach to the network using Ethernet switch ports that sense the presence of IP devices, such as Cisco IP Phones and wireless access points that require in-line power. Voice-enabled routers convert voice between circuit-switched (PSTN) and IP networks.

- **Call processing:** Cisco Unified Communications Manager (CUCM) is the software-based, call-processing component of the Cisco enterprise VoIP solution. CUCM provides a scalable, distributable, and highly available enterprise VoIP call-processing solution. CUCM performs in a manner similar to the PBX in a traditional telephone network.

- **Applications:** Applications use the existing VoIP infrastructure and add features to the system. Unified messaging, voicemail, Interactive Voice Response (IVR), Cisco Unified Contact Center, and Auto Attendant are among the applications that are available with VoIP. The open-source application layer allows third-party companies to develop software that interoperates with CUCM.

- **Client devices:** Client devices are IP telephones and software applications that allow communications across the IP network. CUCM centrally manages IP telephones through Ethernet connections in building access switches.

Typical overall design goals of a VoIP network are as follows:

- **To use end-to-end VoIP between sites where IP connectivity is already established:** VoIP can be simply deployed as an overlaid service that runs on the existing infrastructure.

- **To make VoIP widely usable:** Voice quality needs to be on the same level as in traditional telephony systems.

- **To lower long-distance costs:** Enterprises can accomplish this goal by using private IP networks and possibly the public Internet for routing telephone calls.

- **To make VoIP cost-effective:** This goal depends on more efficient use of existing WAN capacity and the cost of upgrading the existing IP network infrastructure to support VoIP. In some cases, enterprises can accomplish this goal by using the public Internet or private IP networks for routing telephone calls.

- **To provide high availability of VoIP:** To meet this goal, make network components redundant and provide backup power to all network infrastructure components, including routers, switches, and IP phones.

- **To offer lower total cost of ownership and greater flexibility than traditional telephony:** Installation costs and operational costs for unified systems are lower than the cost to implement and operate two infrastructures.

- **To enable new applications on top of VoIP through third-party software:** For example, an intelligent phone used for database information access as an alternative to a PC is likely to be less costly to own, operate, and maintain and easier to use.

- **To improve remote worker, agent, and work-at-home staff productivity:** VoIP can extend the productivity-enhancing enterprise telephony features such as voicemail and voice conferencing to the remote teleworker.

- **To facilitate data and telephony network consolidation:** Such consolidation can contribute to operational and equipment savings.

IP Telephony Design Models

There are a number of different ways to deploy VoIP depending on the size and others factors of the specific organization. The options include a single-site deployment, a multisite centralized deployment, or a multisite distributed deployment. Each is covered in the following sections.

Single-Site

Single-site VoIP design consists of a CUCM, IP telephones, switches with in-line power, applications such as voicemail, and a voice-enabled router, all located at the same physical site. A LAN switch powers IP telephones through the Ethernet interface. For users to make off-site calls, gateway trunks are connected to the PSTN. The single-site model is illustrated in Figure 9-5.

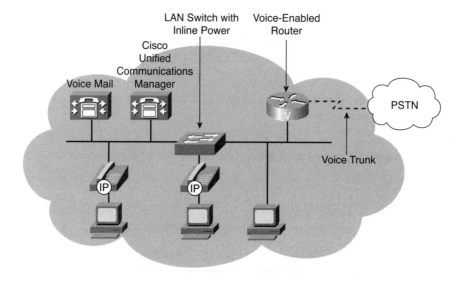

Figure 9-5 *Single-Site VoIP Model*

Single-site deployment allows each site to be completely self-contained. Users place all calls to the outside world and remote locations across the PSTN. If an IP WAN is incorporated into the single-site model, it is for data traffic only. Telephony services are not administered over the WAN. Service cannot be provided if there is an IP WAN failure or if there is insufficient bandwidth. There is no loss of call-processing service or functionality. The only requirements are a PSTN carrier and route diversity within the PSTN network.

As a recommended practice, use this model for a single campus or site with fewer than 30,000 lines.

Centralized Multisite

In the model of a multisite WAN with centralized call processing, remote IP telephones rely on a centralized CUCM that provides services for many sites. It uses the IP WAN to transport voice traffic between the sites. The IP WAN also carries call control signaling between the central site and the remote sites. Applications such as voice mail and Interactive Voice Response (IVR) are also centralized. They reduce the overall cost of ownership and allow centralized administration and maintenance. The multisite WAN with centralized call processing VoIP model is illustrated in Figure 9-6.

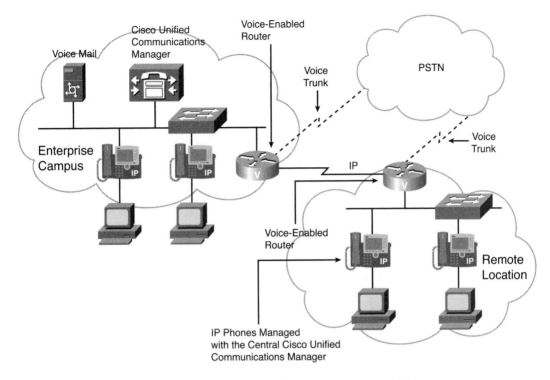

Figure 9-6   *Multisite WAN with Centralized Call Processing VoIP Model*

The remote locations require IP connectivity with the campus network. IP telephones, powered by a local LAN switch, convert voice into IP packets and send them to the local LAN. The local router forwards the packets to the appropriate destination based on its routing table. In the event of a WAN failure, the voice-enabled router at the remote site can provide backup call processing functionality with Cisco Unified Survivable Remote Site Telephony (SRST) services. Cisco Unified SRST allows organizations to extend high-availability VoIP to their small branch offices by providing backup call-processing functionality on voice-enabled routers.

If an enterprise requires high-quality voice communication over the WAN, the service provider must implement QoS mechanisms. Enterprises and service providers usually sign a service-level agreement (SLA) that guarantees bandwidth and latency levels that are suitable for voice transport.

Note   The router in the campus network is voice capable to enable voice communication with the outside world through the PSTN.

As a recommended practice, this model is used for a main site with many smaller remote sites that are connected through a QoS-enabled WAN but that do not require full features and functionality during a WAN outage.

Distributed Multisite

The multisite WAN model with distributed call processing consists of multiple independent sites, each with its own call-processing agent. It is connected to an IP WAN that carries voice traffic between the distributed sites. An IP WAN interconnects all the distributed call-processing sites. The IP WAN in this model does not carry call control signaling between the sites because each site has its own call-processing agent. Typically, the PSTN serves as a backup connection between the sites in case the IP WAN connection fails or does not have sufficient available bandwidth for incremental calls. The multisite WAN with distributed call processing VoIP model is illustrated in Figure 9-7.

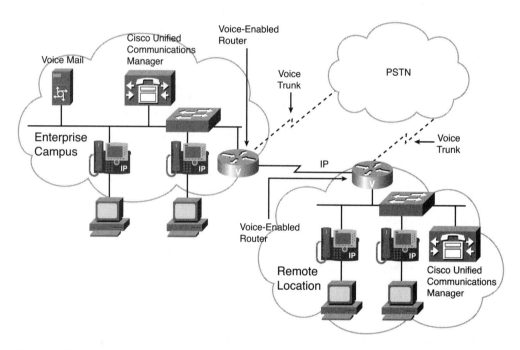

Figure 9-7   *Multisite WAN with Distributed Call Processing VoIP Model*

A site connected only through the PSTN is a standalone site and is not covered by the distributed call-processing model.

As a recommended practice, this model is used for a large central site with more than 30,000 lines or for a deployment with more than six large sites (more than 30,000 lines total) interconnected through a QoS-enabled WAN.

Note   Customers can scale VoIP functionality to a small site or branch office with CUCM Express. CUCM Express is a solution embedded in Cisco IOS Software that provides call processing for up to 450 Cisco Unified IP Phones. The CUCM Express product offers customers a low-cost, reliable, and feature-rich solution for deployment. This option is covered in other Cisco Press books.

Introducing Video Considerations

There is a virtual explosion of media applications on the IP network, with many different combinations of audio, video, and data media. This is illustrated in Figure 9-8. For example, VoIP streams can be standard VoIP, high-definition audio, Internet VoIP, or others. Video streams can range from relatively low-definition webcams to traditional video-over-IP, room-to-room conferencing to high-definition Cisco TelePresence systems. Additionally, there are new IP convergence opportunities occurring that further expand the number of media applications and streams on the IP network.

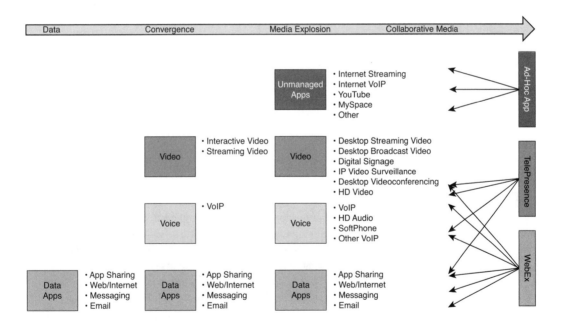

Figure 9-8   *Media Application Convergence Evolution*

Another source of new media streams on the network is "unmanaged" media applications. These are applications that are considered primarily for consumers, but are also used by corporate employees. Many of these unmanaged media applications can fall into a gray area for some companies in terms of usage policies. For example, at first glance, consumer media sharing sites such as YouTube can appear to have clearly consumer-only applicability. However, many of these same services also contain videos that can provide considerable know-how and information that are useful to employees as well.

The explosion of media content, types, and applications, both managed and unmanaged, requires network architects to scrutinize their media application provisioning strategy. Without a clear strategy, the number and volume of media applications on the IP network could very well exceed the ability of the network administrator to provision and manage.

Media Application Models

Various media applications will behave differently and put a variety of different requirements on the network.

The four media applications cover a significant cross section of models of media application behavior. To include additional applications in the inventory, critical questions to consider should include the following:

1. Is the media stored and viewed (streaming) or real-time (interactive)?

2. Where are the media sources and where are the viewers?

3. In which direction do the media flows traverse the network?

4. How much bandwidth does the media application require? And how much burst?

5. What are the service-level tolerances (in terms of latency, jitter, and loss)?

6. What are the likely media application usage patterns?

7. Are there requirements to connect to other companies (or customers)?

8. In what direction is the media application likely to evolve in the future?

Delivery of Media Application

Because of the high amount of compression and motion-compensated prediction utilized by H.264, even a very small amount of packet loss can result in visible degradation of the video quality. Traditional network designs supporting data applications can have a targeted packet loss of less than 1–2 percent. For VoIP, network designs were tightened to have only 0.5–1 percent of packet loss. For media-ready networks, especially those supporting high-definition media applications, network designs need to be tightened again by an order of magnitude, targeting a 0–0.05 percent packet loss. This is illustrated in Table 9-1.

Table 9-1   *Media Application Delivery Requirements Table*

Traffic Type	Sensitivity to Multisecond Interruption	Packet Loss Target
Data	Tolerant	1–2%
Voice	Less tolerant	< 1%
Video	Intolerant	< 0.05%

However, an absolute target for packet loss is not the only consideration in high-availability network design. Loss, during normal network operation, should effectively be 0 percent on a properly designed network. In such a case, it is generally only during network events such as link failures and/or route-flaps that packet loss would occur. Therefore, it is usually more meaningful to express availability targets not only in absolute terms, such as <0.05 percent, but also in terms of convergence targets, which are sometimes also referred to as the Mean-Time-to-Repair (MTTR) targets.

Architectural Framework for Media Services

A medianet is built upon an architecture that supports the different models of media services and applications. It optimizes their delivery, such as those shown in the architectural framework. This framework is illustrated in Figure 9-9.

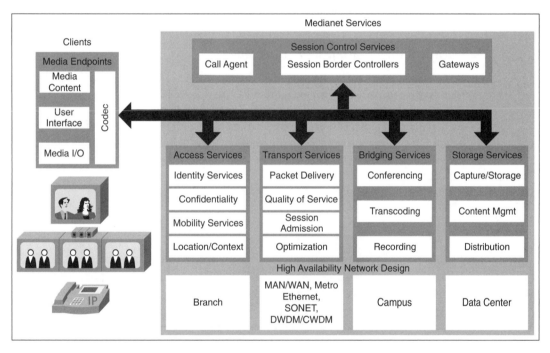

Figure 9-9 *Architectural Framework for Media Services*

A medianet framework starts with an end-to-end network infrastructure designed and built to achieve high availability, including the data center, campus, WAN, and branch office networks. The network provides a set of services to video applications, including

■   **Access services:** Provide access control and identity of video clients, as well as mobility and location services

- **Transport services:** Provide packet delivery, ensuring the service levels with QoS and delivery optimization

- **Bridging services:** Transcoding, conferencing, and recording services

- **Storage services:** Content capture, storage, retrieval, distribution, and management services

- **Session control services:** Signaling and control to set up and tear down sessions, as well as gateways

When these media services are made available within the network infrastructure, endpoints can be multipurpose and rely upon these common media services to join and leave sessions for multiple media applications. Common functions such as transcoding and conferencing different media codecs within the same session can be deployed and leveraged by multiple applications, instead of being duplicated for each new media application.

Call Control and Transport Protocols

Voice communication over IP also relies on control signals. The various call control and transport protocols are shown in Figure 9-10. Control signals and data require reliable TCP/IP transport because users must receive the signals in the order in which they were sent, without any loss. However, voice loses its value with time. If a voice packet is delayed, it can lose its relevance to the recipient. Thus, voice conversations (noncontrol packets) use the more efficient, unreliable User Datagram Protocol (UDP)/IP transport.

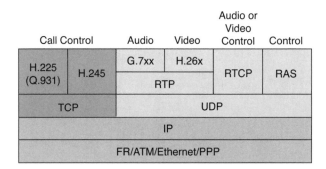

Figure 9-10 *Call Control and Transport Protocols*

Call Control Functions with H.323

Call control functions with H.323 include signaling for call setup, capability exchange, signaling of commands and indications, and messages to open and describe the content of logical channels. Overall system control is provided by separate signaling functions such as

- **H.225 call-signaling channel:** Uses Q.931 to establish a connection between two terminals.

- **H.245 control channel:** A reliable channel that carries control messages that govern voice operation, including capabilities exchange, opening and closing of logical channels, preference requests, flow control messages, and general commands and indications. Capabilities exchange is one of the fundamental capabilities in the ITU recommendation.

- **RAS signaling:** The Registration, Admission, and Status (RAS) protocol performs registration, admission, bandwidth changes, status, and disengagement procedures between endpoints and gatekeepers. The RAS protocol runs on UDP/IP. RAS is used only if an H.323 gatekeeper is present.

- **Real-Time Transport Protocol Control Protocol (RTCP):** Provides a mechanism for hosts that are involved in a Real-Time Transport Protocol (RTP) session to exchange information about monitoring and controlling the session. RTCP monitors quality for such elements as packet counts, packet loss, and interarrival jitter.

Voice Conversation with RTP

RTP, which runs on top of UDP/IP, carries voice conversation between two IP endpoints. Because of the time-sensitive nature of voice transport, UDP/IP is the logical choice to carry voice.

With voice conversation, more data is required on a packet-by-packet basis than UDP offers. Therefore, RTP carries packet sequence and time-stamping information. It uses sequence information to determine whether the packets are arriving in order, and it uses the time-stamping data to determine the interarrival packet time (jitter). These two pieces of information are essential for high-quality VoIP conversations.

Using RTP is important for real-time traffic; however, a few drawbacks exist. The IP, UDP, and RTP packet header sizes are 20, 8, and 12 bytes, respectively. These packet header sizes add up to a 40-byte header, which can be twice as large as the compressed voice payload. This large header adds considerable overhead to the voice traffic and reduces voice bandwidth efficiency.

Note Large IP/UDP/RTP headers can be compressed by using RTP header compression (compressed Real-Time Transport Protocol [cRTP]) to 2 bytes without UDP checksums or to 4 bytes with UDP checksums.

Call Control Functions with SSCP

Skinny Client Control Protocol (SCCP) is a Cisco-proprietary terminal control protocol used for messaging between IP phones and CUCM. An illustration of SCCP in use is shown in Figure 9-11.

By default, CUCM uses SCCP to signal Cisco IP Phones. Examples of SCCP clients include the Cisco Unified IP Phone 7900 Series phones, such as the Cisco Unified IP Phone 7960 Series, Cisco Unified IP Phone 7970 Series, Cisco Unified IP Phone 7985, and the 802.11b Cisco Unified Wireless IP Phone 7920 phones. SCCP is a lightweight protocol that uses TCP/IP for efficient communication. CUCM acts as a signaling proxy for the SCCP clients for call events initiated over other common protocols such as H.323, Session Initiation Protocol (SIP), and Media Gateway Control Protocol (MGCP).

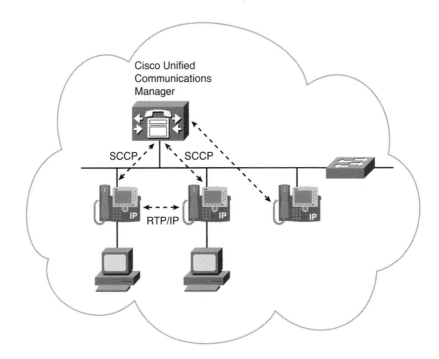

Figure 9-11   *SCCP Control*

During registration, a Cisco IP Phone receives its line and all other configurations from CUCM. After it registers, the Cisco IP Phone is notified of new incoming calls and can make outgoing calls. The SCCP protocol is used for VoIP call signaling and enhanced features such as the Message Waiting Indicator (MWI).

Media connections between devices involved in a call utilize RTP for the streaming sessions.

Call Control Functions with SIP

SIP is the Internet Engineering Task Force (IETF) standard for multimedia conferencing over IP. SIP is an ASCII-based application layer control protocol (defined in RFCs 3261, 3262, 3263, 3264, and 3265) that can be used to establish, maintain, and terminate calls between two or more endpoints. SIP was developed as a simple lightweight replacement for H.323. An illustration of SIP in use is shown in Figure 9-12.

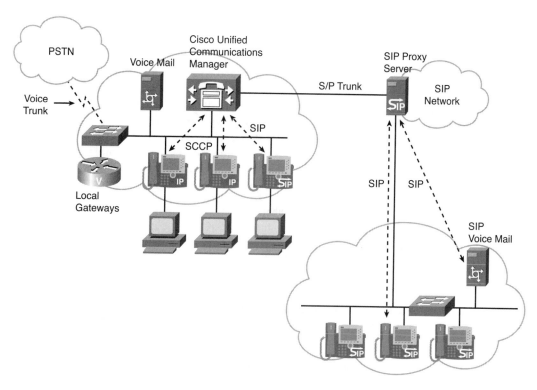

Figure 9-12 *SIP Control*

The Cisco SIP Proxy Server is a software application that provides call-routing services in a VoIP network. Enterprises can use the Cisco SIP Proxy Server for internal VoIP in a SIP network where SIP user agents communicate with the SIP proxy server. The SIP proxy server can also provide integrated communications with a CUCM and enterprise voice gateways. SCCP and SIP phones can register with the CUCM in a VoIP network.

Like other VoIP protocols, SIP is designed to address the functions of signaling and session management within a packet telephony network. Signaling allows call information to be carried across network boundaries. Session management provides the ability to control the attributes of an end-to-end call. SIP utilizes requests and responses to establish communication among the various components in the network and to ultimately establish a conference between two or more endpoints.

SIP integrates with other Internet services, such as email, web, voicemail, instant messaging, multiparty conferencing, and multimedia collaboration. When used with an IP infrastructure, SIP helps to enable rich communications with numerous multivendor devices and media. It can set up individual voice or conference calls, videoconferences and point-to-point video-enabled calls, web collaboration and chat sessions, and instant-messaging sessions among any number of SIP-enabled endpoints.

Users in a SIP network are identified by unique SIP addresses. They register with a registrar server using their assigned SIP addresses. The registrar server provides this information to the location server upon request.

The basic elements of a SIP system are user agents and proxy servers. The SIP user agent is software that is implemented in end-user devices and server components to manage the SIP connection. User agents include endpoints such as IP phones, SIP media gateways, conferencing servers, and messaging systems. SIP proxy servers route SIP requests from user agents to their appropriate destinations. Proxies are typically colocated with a SIP registrar, which maintains a list of contacts for specific users or accounts within a specific IP domain. SIP uses RTP to transfer packetized voice, video, and data in real time between user agents. SIP-compliant devices such as IP phones can register directly with CUCM.

A SIP network uses the following components:

- **User Agent (UA):** SIP is a peer-to-peer protocol. The peers in a session are called UAs. A UA is a combination of a UA client (UAC) and a UA server (UAS) that initiates and receives calls. A UAC initiates a SIP request. A UAS, a server application, contacts the user when it receives a SIP request. The UAS then responds on behalf of the user. CUCM can act as both a server and a client (a back-to-back UA).

- **SIP proxy server:** The proxy server works as an intermediate device that receives SIP requests from a client and then forwards the requests on behalf of the client. Proxy servers can provide functions such as authentication, authorization, network access control, routing, reliable request retransmission, and security.

- **Redirect server:** The redirect server provides the client with information about the next hop or hops that a message should take, and the client then contacts the next-hop server or UAS directly.

- **Registrar server:** The registrar server processes requests from UACs for registration of their current location. Redirect or proxy servers often contain registrar servers.

Call Control Functions with MGCP

MGCP is a client/server protocol defined in an informational (nonstandard) IETF document, RFC 3661, that allows call agents such as CUCM to centrally control media gateways. An illustration of MGCP in use is shown in Figure 9-13.

The two components of MGCP are endpoints and call agents. Endpoints are any of the voice ports on a gateway, while call agents are the control devices that administer the gateways. An MGCP gateway manages translation between audio signals and the packet network. With MGCP, the call agent recognizes and controls the state of each individual port on the gateway. MGCP allows complete control of the dial plan from CUCM, including per-port control of connections to the PSTN, legacy PBX and voicemail systems, plain old telephone service (POTS) phones, and so on. This control is implemented with the use of a series of plain-text commands sent over UDP port 2427 between the CUCM and the gateway.

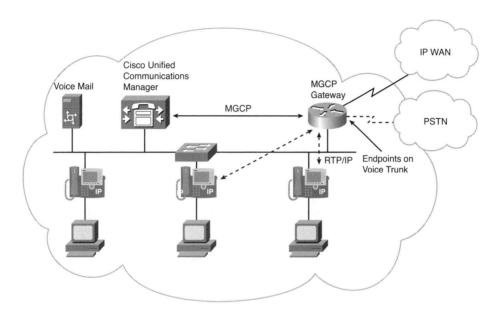

Figure 9-13   *MGCP Control*

The two basic MGCP constructs are endpoints and connections. An endpoint is a source for call data (RTP/IP) that is flowing through the gateway. A common type of endpoint is found at the physical interface between the PSTN and the gateway. This type of endpoint might be an analog voice port or a channel on a digital trunk. There are other types of endpoints, including logical endpoints.

MGCP uses RTP/UDP for establishing audio connections over IP networks. For any MGCP call, a call agent must create a connection either between an endpoint and the packet network or two endpoints. When a connection is made to an endpoint, the gateway assigns a connection identifier for each connection.

Identifying the Requirements of Voice and Video Technologies

Various factors that affect voice traffic must be analyzed to create a proper integrated network design. The following sections focus on the types of delay, bandwidth restrictions, and quality of service (QoS) issues that affect voice communications. They discuss the importance of encoding, which affects bandwidth consumption and voice and video quality. These sections also introduce mechanisms that impact voice and video quality.

To design a network to transport voice and video, delay, packet loss, jitter, and the impact that QoS can have on maintaining voice quality need to be analyzed.

Minimizing Delay, Jitter, and Loss

Voice quality in an IP network is directly affected by delay, jitter, and packet loss. Solutions are available to address all three issues.

When designing networks that transport Voice over IP networks, the delay components in the network must be considered. Correctly accounting for all potential delays ensures that overall network performance will be acceptable.

The two major types of delay are fixed delay and variable delay.

One-Way Network Delay Recommendations

The generally accepted limit for good-quality voice connection delay is 150 ms one way. As delays increase, the communication between two people is compromised. For example, they speak at the same time or both wait for the other to speak. This "delayed" condition is called talker overlap. The ITU G.114 recommendation for network delay is illustrated in Table 9-2.

Table 9-2   *ITU G.114 Recommendations for Network Delay Considerations*

One-Way Delay (ms)	Description
0–150	Acceptable for most user applications.
151–400	Acceptable provided that organizations are aware of the transmission time impact on the transmission quality of user applications.
401+	Unacceptable for general network planning purposes; however, it is recognized that in some exceptional cases, this limit will be exceeded.

The ITU describes network delay for voice applications in recommendation G.114. This recommendation, shown in Table 9-2, defines three bands of one-way delay.

Voice packets will be delayed if the network is congested because of poor network design, traffic congestion, or insufficient bandwidth.

Fixed network delay includes three components: propagation delay, serialization delay, and processing delay.

Propagation Delay

Propagation delay is the delay of signals between the sending and receiving endpoints. It can typically be ignored, which is limited by the speed of light, for most designs, because it is relatively small compared to other types of delay.

Note   Propagation delay has a noticeable impact only to the overall delay on satellite links.

Serialization Delay

Serialization delay results from the delay of placing the bits on the circuit. The higher the circuit speed, the less time it takes to place the bits on the circuit. Stated simply, the higher the speed, the lower the serialization delay.

Serialization delay is a constant function of link speed and packet size. Calculate serialization delay by dividing the packet length by the bit rate. This formula shows how large a serialization delay can occur as a result of slow links or large packets. Serialization delay is always predictable; for example, using a 64-kbps link and an 80-byte frame, the delay is exactly 10 ms.

Note   Serialization delay is a factor only on slow-speed links up to 1 Mbps.

Processing Delay

Processing can also greatly affect the delay that traffic is subject to when being transported across a networking device. Processing delays include the following:

- **Coding, compression, decompression, and decoding delays:** These functions are performed in either hardware or software, based on the algorithm that is used. By using specialized hardware, such as digital signal processors (DSP), quality can be dramatically improved and the delay that is associated with various voice compression schemes can be reduced.

- **Packetization delay:** Packetization delay results from the process of holding the digital voice samples to place into the payload until enough samples are collected to fill the packet or cell payload. To reduce excessive packetization delay that is associated with some compression schemes, the voice gateway can send partial packets.

Variable network delay is more unpredictable and difficult to calculate than fixed network delay. Three factors that contribute to variable network delay include

- Queuing delay
- Dejitter buffers
- Variable packet sizes

Queuing Delay

Congested output queues on network interfaces are the most common sources of variable delay. Queuing delay occurs when a voice packet waits for others to be serviced first on the outgoing interface. This waiting time is statistically based on the arrival of traffic. The more inputs, the more likely that packets will contend for the trunk. Queuing delay is also based on the size of the packet that is currently being serviced.

For example, a 1500-byte data packet is queued before the voice packet. The voice packet must wait until the entire data packet is transmitted, which produces a delay in the voice path. If the link is slow (for example, 64 kbps or 128 kbps), the delay can be more than 200 ms, which is unacceptable for voice.

Variable delay is also influenced by the size of the packet that is currently being serviced. Larger packets take longer time to transmit than smaller packets. Therefore, a queue that combines large and small packets experiences varying lengths of delay.

Link Fragmentation and Interleaving (LFI) is a solution for queuing delay situations. With LFI, the voice gateway fragments large packets into smaller frames and interleaves them with small voice packets. A voice packet does not experience a delay waiting for the entire data packet to be sent. LFI reduces delay and ensures a more predictable voice delay.

LFI fragments packets into frames of equal size to solve the delay problem that is caused by variable packet size. Configure LFI on a link to provide a fixed 10-ms delay. Set the fragment size so that voice packets do not become fragmented.

Dejitter Buffers

Because congestion can occur at any point within a network, packets can fill interface queues instantaneously. This situation leads to a difference in delay times between packets in a single voice stream. This variable delay, called jitter, is illustrated in Figure 9-14.

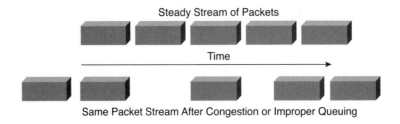

Figure 9-14 *Jitter Example*

Dejitter buffers work at the receiving end to smooth delay variability and allow time for decoding and decompression. On the first talk spurt, the dejitter buffer provides smooth voice playback. Setting the dejitter buffer too low causes overflows and loss of data, while setting it too high causes excessive delay.

In effect, a dejitter buffer reduces or eliminates delay variation by converting it to fixed delay. However, a dejitter buffer always adds delay to the total budget, depending on the variance of the delay.

Dejitter buffers work most efficiently when packets arrive in a fairly uniform delay. QoS congestion-avoidance mechanisms can be used to manage delay and avoid network congestion. Dejitter buffers can be disabled and the constant delay can be reduced if there is no delay variance.

> **Note**   Delay is always added to the total delay budget when dejitter buffers are used. Keep the dejitter buffer as small as possible to keep total delay to a minimum.

Jitter is defined as a variation in the delay of received packets. The originating voice gateway sends the packets in a continuous stream, spaced evenly apart. Because of network congestion, improper queuing, or configuration errors, the delay between each packet can vary instead of remaining constant.

When a voice gateway receives an audio stream for VoIP, it must compensate for the jitter that it encounters with the playout delay buffer. The playout delay buffer must buffer the packets and then play them out in a steady stream to the DSPs, which then convert the voice back to an analog audio stream. The playout delay buffer is also referred to as the dejitter buffer.

Packet Loss

Packet loss causes voice and video clipping and skips. Loss can occur because of the following:

- Congested links

- Improper network QoS configuration

- Poor packet buffer management on the routers and switches

- Routing problems

- Additional issues in both the WAN and the LAN

If queues get saturated, VoIP packets can be dropped, resulting in effects such as clicks or lost words.

The industry-standard codec algorithms that are used in the Cisco DSP can correct for up to 30 ms of lost voice. Cisco VoIP technology, by default, uses 20-ms samples of voice payload per VoIP packet. For the codec correction algorithms to be effective, only a single packet can be lost during any given time. For packet losses as small as one packet, the DSP interpolates the conversation with what it thinks the audio should be, and the packet loss is not audible.

Because of the high amount of compression and motion-compensated prediction utilized by video codecs, even a small amount of packet loss can result in visible degradation of the video quality. Packet loss tolerances for good video quality are highly subjective and can depend on a variety of factors such as

- Video resolution

- Frame rate

- Configured data rate

- Codec implementation

- The specific PC upon which the videoconferencing application is running

However, values between 0.1 and 1 percent often yield acceptable video quality.

Preventing Echo

In a voice telephone call, an echo occurs when callers hear their own words repeated. An echo is the audible leak of the voice of the caller into the receive (return) path.

Echo is a function of delay and magnitude. The echo problem worsens as the delay and the loudness of the echo grow. When timed properly, echo is reassuring to the speaker. If the echo exceeds approximately 25 ms, it can be distracting and cause breaks in the conversation.

These elements in a voice network can affect echo:

- **Hybrid transformers:** Hybrid transformers in an analog phone are often prime culprits for signal leakage between analog transmit and receive paths. Echo is normally caused by a mismatch in impedance from the four-wire network switch conversion to the two-wire local loop. This type of echo is typically the result of an impedance mismatch in a PBX.

- **Telephones:** The analog telephone presents a load to the PBX. This load should match the output impedance of the source device (Foreign Exchange Station [FXS] port). Some inexpensive telephones are not matched to the output impedance of the FXS port and are sources of echo. Headsets are particularly notorious for poor echo performance.

When digital telephones are used, the point of digital-to-analog conversion occurs inside the telephone. Extending the digital transmission segments closer to the actual telephone decreases the potential for echo.

> **Note**   Digital segments of the voice network do not cause echo. Technically, voice gateways cannot be the source of echo.

To improve the quality of telephone conversation, an echo canceller might need to be placed in the network. An echo canceller in a voice gateway reduces the level of echo that has leaked from the receive path into the transmit path. The more latency in receiving the speech, the worse the echo seems to the user. Echo cancellers are built into low-bit-rate codecs and are operated on each DSP. Echo cancellers are limited, by design, by the total amount of time that they wait for the reflected speech to be received. This is known as an echo trail. The echo cancellation time (echo trail) is normally between 16 and 32 ms.

Echo Canceller Example

Assume that user A is talking to user B. When the speech of user A hits an impedance mismatch or other echo-causing environment, it bounces back to user A. User A can hear the delay several milliseconds after speaking.

To remove the echo from the line, the router of user A must keep an inverse image of the speech of user A for a certain amount of time. This image is called inverse speech. The echo canceller in the router listens for sound coming from user B and subtracts the inverse speech of user A to remove any echo.

Echo Cancellation Guidelines

The ITU-T defines an "irritation zone" of echo loudness and delay. A short echo of approximately 15 ms does not need to be suppressed, but higher echo delays require strong echo suppression. Therefore, echo cancellation is required in all networks that produce one-way time delays greater than 16 ms.

The appropriate echo-cancellation time also needs to be configured. If the echo-cancellation time is set too low, callers still hear echo during the telephone call. If the configured echo cancellation timer is set too high, it takes longer for the echo canceller to converge and eliminate the echo. Attenuating the signal below the noise floor can also eliminate echo.

Voice Coding and Compression

Voice communication over IP relies on voice that is coded and encapsulated into IP packets. This section provides an overview of the various coder-decoders (codecs) that are used in packet telephony networks.

As the quality of transmitted voice can be subjective, Mean Opinion Score (MOS) is used as a common benchmark that defines the quality of the voice. MOS ranks the quality of a codec on a scale from 1 to 5, with 1 being the lowest quality and 5 being the highest.

Table 9-3 displays information on the commonly used codecs and their requirements and scores.

Table 9-3 *Voice Codecs*

Codec	ITU Standard	Data Rate	MOS
PCM	G.711	64 kbps	4.1
ADPCM	G.726/G.727	16/24/32/40 kbps	3.85 or less
LD-CELP	G.728	16 kbps	3.61
CS-ACELP	G.729	8 kbps	3.92
ACELP/MPMLQ	G.723.1	6.3/5.3 kbps	3.9/3.65

*Note: Data rates shown are for digitized speech only and do not include overhead RTP, UDP, IP, and Layer 2 headers.

A codec is a device or software that encodes and decodes a signal into digital data stream.

> **Note**   In addition to the coded digital stream, headers are needed for RTP, UDP, IP, and Layer 2 packets and framing.

Each codec provides a certain quality of speech. Advances in technology have greatly improved the quality of compressed voice, which has resulted in a spectrum of coding and compression algorithms. They are illustrated in Table 9-4.

Table 9-4   *Coding and Compression Algorithms*

Algorithm	Advantage	Savings
Pulse Code Modulation (PCM)	The toll-quality voice that is expected from the public switched telephone network (PSTN). PCM runs at 64 kbps, provides no compression, and therefore provides no opportunity for bandwidth savings. Most Cisco implementations use G.711 on the LAN link because of its good compression and high-quality results, approaching toll quality.	—
Adaptive Differential Pulse Code Modulation (ADPCM)	Provides three levels of compression. Some fidelity is lost as compression increases.	Depending on the traffic mix, cost savings are generally 25 percent for 32-kbps ADPCM, 30 percent for 24-kbps ADPCM, and 35 percent for 16-kbps ADPCM.
Low-Delay Code-Excited Linear Prediction (LD-CELP) compression	An algorithm that models the human voice.	Depending on the traffic mix, cost savings can be up to 35 percent for 16-kbps LD-CELP.
Conjugate-Structure Algebraic Code-Excited Linear Prediction (CS-ACELP)	Provides eight times the bandwidth savings over PCM. CS-ACELP is a more recently developed algorithm that is modeled after the human voice and delivers quality comparable to LD-CELP and 32-kbps ADPCM.	Cost savings are approximately 40 percent for 8-kbps CS-ACELP. Most Cisco implementations use G.729 on WAN links because of its good compression and high-quality results, approaching G.711.
Code-Excited Linear Prediction (CELP) compression	Provides huge bandwidth savings over PCM.	Cost savings can be up to 50 percent for 5.3-kbps CELP.

The ITU defines a series of standards for voice coding and compression. They are listed in Table 9-5.

Table 9-5 *ITU Series of Standards for Codecs*

Codec	Requirements	Description
G.711	Uses the 64-kbps PCM voice-coding technique	G.711-encoded voice is already in the correct format for digital voice delivery in the public telephone network or through PBXs.
G.726	Uses ADPCM coding at 40, 32, 24, and 16 kbps	ADPCM voice can also be interchanged between packet voice networks and public telephone or PBX networks, provided that the latter have ADPCM capability.
G.728	Uses LD-CELP voice compression, which requires only 16 kbps of bandwidth	CELP voice coding must be transcoded to a PCM-based coding before delivery to the PSTN for delivery to or through the telephone networks.
G.729	Uses CS-ACELP compression, which enables voice to be coded into 8-kbps streams	There are various forms of this standard, and all provide speech quality similar to that of 32-kbps ADPCM. For example, in G.729a, the basic algorithm was optimized to reduce the computation requirements. In G.729b, voice activity detection and comfort noise generation was added. G.729ab provides an optimized version of G.729b, requiring less computation.
G.723.1	Uses a dual-rate coder for compressing speech at very low bit rates	This standard has two bit rates that are associated with it: 5.3 kbps using Algebraic Code-Excited Linear Prediction (ACELP) and 6.3 kbps using Multipulse Maximum Likelihood Quantization (MPMLQ).

A newer, more objective measurement is available that is quickly overtaking MOSs as the industry quality measurement of choice for coding algorithms. Perceptual Speech Quality Measurement (PSQM), which is specified in ITU standard P.861, provides a rating on a scale of 0 to 6.5, where 0 is best and 6.5 is worst. PSQM works by comparing the transmitted speech to the original input to produce a score.

PSQM is implemented in test equipment and monitoring systems that provide a PSQM score for a test voice call over a particular packet network. Some PSQM test equipment converts the 0-to-6.5 scale to a 0-to-5 scale to correlate to MOS.

Codec Complexity, DSPs, and Voice Calls

Codec technology for compressing and decompressing data can be implemented in DSPs. Some codec compression techniques require more processing power than others. Codec complexity is divided into low, medium, and high complexity. The difference between a low-, medium-, or high-complexity codec is the amount of processor power required to process the codec algorithm and the number of voice channels that a single DSP can support.

The number of calls supported depends on the DSP and the complexity used. For example, the Cisco High-Density Packet Voice/Fax DSP Module (AS54-PVDM2-64) helps Cisco voice gateways provide high-density voice connectivity supporting 24 to 64 channels (calls), depending on the codec compression complexity. Table 9-6 illustrates the complexity of the different available codecs and shows how many channels of voice would possible if using the AS54-PVDM2-64 module.

Table 9-6   *Codec Complexity (AS54-PVDM2-64)*

Low Complexity (Maximum 64 Calls)	Medium Complexity (Maximum 32 Calls)	High Complexity (Maximum 24 Calls)
G.711 a-law	G.729a	G.723.1: 5.3K and 6.3K
G.711 mu-law	G.729ab	G.723.1A: 5.3K and 6.3K
Fax pass-through	G.726: 16K, 24K, and 32K	G.728
Modem pass-through	T.38 fax relay	Modern relay
Clear-channel codec	Cisco Fax Relay	AMR-NB: 4.75K, 5.15K, 5.9K, 6.7K, 7.4K, 7.95K, 10.2K, 12.2K, and silence insertion descriptor

Note   To help calculate the number of DSPs required, refer to the DSP Calculator found at www.cisco.com/cgi-bin/Support/DSP/dsp-calc.pl.

Bandwidth Considerations

A primary WAN issue when network designers are designing VoIP networks is bandwidth availability. The amount of bandwidth per call increases or decreases greatly, depending on which codec is used and the number of voice samples that are required per packet. However, the best coding mechanism does not necessarily result in the best voice quality. For example, the better the compression, the worse the voice quality. The organization must decide which is more important: better voice quality or more efficient bandwidth consumption.

To reduce the amount of traffic per voice call, and to use available bandwidth more efficiently, an effective voice coding and compression mechanism can be used. Use the compressed Real-Time Transport Protocol (cRTP) and suppress silence using Voice Activity Detection (VAD).

Reducing Voice Traffic with cRTP

All voice packets that are encapsulated into IP consist of two components: voice samples and IP/UDP/RTP headers. Although the DSP compresses voice samples, which vary in size based on the codec that is used, the headers are a constant 40 bytes. Compared to the 20 bytes of voice samples in a default G.729 call, the headers constitute a considerable amount of overhead. cRTP compresses the headers to 2 or 4 bytes, which offers significant bandwidth savings. cRTP is sometimes referred to as "RTP header compression." RFC 2508, at http://tools.ietf.org/html/rfc2508, discusses cRTP; an illustration of cRTP is shown in Figure 9-15.

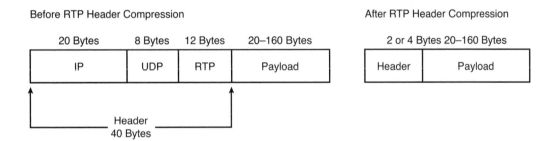

Figure 9-15 *cRTP Example*

Enabling compression on a low-bandwidth serial link can greatly reduce the network overhead and conserve WAN bandwidth if there is a significant volume of RTP traffic. In general, it is recommended to enable cRTP on slow links up to 768 kbps. However, cRTP is not recommended for higher-speed links because of its high CPU requirements.

Note Because cRTP compresses VoIP calls on a link-by-link basis, configure cRTP on all links on the path.

Reducing Voice Traffic with VAD

On average, about 35 percent of all calls produce silence. In traditional voice networks, all voice calls use a fixed bandwidth of 64-kbps links, regardless of the amount of the conversation that is speech or silence. With VoIP networks, all conversation and silence is packetized. VAD suppresses packets of silence. Instead of sending VoIP packets of silence, VoIP gateways interleave data traffic with VoIP conversations to use network bandwidth more effectively.

Voice Bandwidth Calculation

The voice bandwidth needed per call can be estimated with the following calculations:

- Voice packet size = (Layer 2 header) + (IP/UDP/RTP header) + (Voice payload)

- Voice packets per second (pps) = Codec bit rate / Voice payload size

- Bandwidth = (Voice packet size) * (pps)

Make these assumptions in bandwidth calculations:

- IP/UDP/RTP headers are 40 bytes.

- RTP header compression can reduce the IP/UDP/RTP headers to 2 or 4 bytes.

- A WAN Layer 2 header adds 6 bytes.

Voice Bandwidth Calculation Example

The bandwidth calculation for a G.729 call (8-kbps codec bit rate) with cRTP and a default 20 bytes of voice payload is as follows:

- Voice packet size (bytes) = (Layer 2 header of 6 bytes) + (Compressed IP/UDP/RTP header of 2 bytes) + (Voice payload of 20 bytes) = 28 bytes

- Voice packet size (bits) = (28 bytes) * (8 bits per byte) = 224 bits

- Voice packets per second (pps) = (8-kbps codec bit rate) / (160 bits) = 50 pps

- Bandwidth per call = Voice packet size (224 bits) * (50 pps) = 11.2 kbps

- Result: The G.729 call with cRTP requires 11.2 kbps of bandwidth.

A more precise estimate of voice codec bandwidth can be developed using the Cisco Voice Codec Bandwidth Calculator, available at http://tools.cisco.com/Support/VBC/do/CodecCalc1.do.

Figure 9-16 shows a portion of the results of the Cisco Voice Codec Bandwidth Calculator for the G.729 codec. This calculation includes 5 percent additional overhead to accommodate bandwidth for signaling and is using RTP compression.

It might seem logical, from a bandwidth consumption standpoint, to convert all calls to low-bit-rate codecs, which saves bandwidth and decreases infrastructure costs. However, both expected voice quality and bandwidth consumption must be considered when choosing the optimum codec. The disadvantages of strong voice compression should also be evaluated. One of the main disadvantages is signal distortion after multiple encodings. For example, when a G.729 voice signal is encoded three times, the MOS drops from 3.92 (very good) to 2.68 (unacceptable). Another drawback can be codec-induced delay introduced from low-bit-rate codecs.

Codec Information		
Codec Bit Rate	8 kbps	= (Codec Sample Size * 8) / (Codec Sample Interval)
Codec Sample Size	10 bytes	size of each individual codec sample
Codec Sample Interval	10 msec	the time it takes for a single sample
Bandwith Per Call (VoIP)		
Voice Packets Per Second	50	(Codec Bit Rate / Voice Payload Size)
Bandwidth Per Call (RTP Only)	11.6 kbps	(Total Packet Size(bits) + Flag(bits))* (Packets Per Second)
5% Additional Overhead	0.58 kbps	5% additional overhead per call to accomodate bandwidth for signaling (for example: RTCP/H225/H245 messages on H.323 networks).
Bandwith Per Call + 5.0% Additional Overhead	12.18 kbps	Overhead + Bandwidth Per call
Total Bandwith Required (VoIP)		
Bandwidth Used for All Calls (RTP Only)	11.6 kbps	(Bandwidth per Call) * (Number of Calls)
Total Bandwidth (including Overhead)	12.18 kbps	Same as above + 5.0% Overhead
Packet Size Calculation		
Total Packet Size	28 bytes	Excluding Frame Flag
Voice Payload Size	20 bytes	Size of the Codec Samples per packet
Layer2 Overhead	6 bytes	Layer2 Overhead including CRC
Compressed Header	2 bytes	IP/UDP/RTP Compressed header
Frame Flag (7E)	1 byte	Most modern framers can handle a single flag between frames (ie... no beginning flag)

Figure 9-16   *Voice Codec Bandwidth Calculator Example*

Note   G.729 is the recommended voice codec for most WAN networks that do not support multiple encodings because of its relatively low bandwidth requirements and high MOS.

Table 9-7 illustrates the codecs, their payload size, and the required bandwidth with and without RTP header compression. The last column indicates the number of uncompressed and compressed calls that could be made on a 512-kbps link with the given codec.

Table 9-7   *Advantages and Limitations of Deploying an IPS in Inline Mode*

Compression	Payload Size (kb)	Bandwidth (kbps)	Bandwidth w/cRTP (kbps)	Number of Calls on a 512-kbps Link Without cRTP/with cRTP
G.711 (64 kbps)	160	83	68	6/7
G.726 (32 kbps)	60	57	36	8/14
G.726 (24 kbps)	40	52	29	9/17
G.728 (16 kbps)	40	35	19	14/26
G.729 (8 kbps)	20	27	12	19/46
G.723 (6.3 kbps)	24	18	8	28/64
G.723 (5.3 kbps)	20	17	7	30/73

Typical Video Resolution and Bandwidth

The sending station determines the video's resolution and, consequently, the load on the network. This is irrespective of the size of the monitor used to display the video. Observing the video is not a reliable method to estimate load. Common high-definition formats are 720i, 1080i, 1080p, and so on. The numerical value of the format represents the number of rows in the frame. The aspect ratio of high-definition is 16:9, which results in 1920 columns. Video load on the network is likely to increase over time because of the demand for high-quality images. In addition to high resolution, there is also a proliferation of lower-quality video that is often tunneled in HTTP or, in some cases, HTTPS and Secure Socket Layer (SSL). Typical resolutions include CIF (352x288) and 4CIF (704x576). An illustration of the typical video formats is shown in Table 9-8.

Table 9-8 *Typical Video Formats*

Format	Resolution	Typical Bandwidth
QCIF (1/4 CIF)	176 x 144	260 kbps
CIF	352 x 288	512 kbps
4CIF	704 x 576	1 Mbps
720 HD	720 x 1280	1–8 Mbps
1080 HD	1080 x 1920	5–8 Mbps H.264 >12 Mbps MPG2

The impact of resolution on the network load is generally a squared term. An image that is twice as big will require four times the bandwidth. In addition, the color sampling, quantization, and the frame rate also impact the amount of network traffic. Standard rates are 30 frames per second (actually 29.97), but this is an arbitrary value chosen based on the frequency of AC power. In Europe, analog video is traditionally 25 FPS. Cineplex movies are shot at 24 FPS. As the frame rate is decreased, the network load is also decreased and the motion becomes less lifelike. Video above 24 FPS does not noticeably improve motion. Finally, the sophistication of the encoder has a large impact on video load. H.264 encoders have great flexibility in evaluating the ideal way to encode video. This can result in complexities when trying to determine the optimal method. H.264 coding of real-time CIF video will drive all but the most powerful laptops well into the 90 percent CPU range without dedicated media processors.

Bandwidth Requirements of H.264 Video Streams

The bandwidth requirements for video as a 1-second smoothed average are fairly well known. The H.264 protocol uses higher video compression than other protocols and at the same time improves the video resolution quality. It encodes 30 frames per second (can be variable), but there are some variances for bandwidth requirements because of resolution and video source in use.

Table 9-9 illustrates the typical bandwidth requirements for different video sources and resolutions. The last column indicates bandwidth for video stream and does not take into account audio or auxiliary channels.

Table 9-9   *Bandwidth Requirements of H.264 Video Streams*

Video Source	Resolution	Typical Load
Cisco TelePresence System 3000	1080p	12.3 Mbps
Cisco TelePresence System 3000	720p	6.75 Mbps
Cisco TelePresence System 1000	1080p	4.1 Mbps
Cisco TelePresence System 1000	720p	2.25 Mbps
Cisco 4500 Series Video Surveillance IP Camera	1080p	4–6 Mbps
Cisco DMS - Digital Sign SD (HTTP)	720 x 480	1.5–2.5 Mbps
Cisco DMS - Digital Sign HD (HTTP)	1080p	8–12 Mbps
Cisco Unified Video Advantage	CIF	768 kbps
YouTube HD	720p	2 Mbps

Using QoS for Voice and Video

This section describes QoS mechanisms to provide effective service for voice and video traffic. RFC 5865 outlines 12 classes of media applications that have unique service-level requirements. The following six are directly related to voice and video:

- **VoIP Telephony:** This service class is intended for VoIP telephony (bearer-only) traffic (VoIP signaling traffic is assigned to the "Call-Signaling" class). Traffic assigned to this class should be marked EF. This class is provisioned with an Expedited Forwarding (EF) Per-Hop Behavior (PHB). The EF PHB, defined in RFC 3246, is a strict-priority queuing service and, as such, admission to this class should be controlled (admission control is discussed in the following section). Example traffic includes G.711 and G.729a.

- **Broadcast Video:** This service class is intended for broadcast TV, live events, video surveillance flows, and similar "inelastic" streaming video flows ("inelastic" refers to flows that are highly drop sensitive and have no retransmission and/or flow control capabilities). Traffic in this class should be marked Class Selector 5 (CS5) and can be provisioned with an EF PHB; as such, admission to this class should be controlled. Example traffic includes live Cisco Digital Media System (DMS) streams to desktops or to Cisco Digital Media Players (DMP), live Cisco Enterprise TV (ETV) streams, and Cisco IP Video Surveillance.

- **Real-Time Interactive:** This service class is intended for (inelastic) room-based, high-definition interactive video applications and is intended primarily for voice and video components of these applications. Whenever technically possible and administratively feasible, data subcomponents of this class can be separated out and assigned to the "Transactional Data" traffic class. Traffic in this class should be marked CS4 and can be provisioned with an EF PHB; as such, admission to this class should be controlled. An example application is Cisco TelePresence.

- **Multimedia Conferencing:** This service class is intended for desktop software multimedia collaboration applications and is intended primarily for voice and video components of these applications. Whenever technically possible and administratively feasible, data subcomponents of this class can be separated out and assigned to the "Transactional Data" traffic class. Traffic in this class should be marked Assured Forwarding (AF) Class 4 (AF41) and should be provisioned with a guaranteed bandwidth queue with DSCP-based Weighted-Random Early Detect (DSCP-WRED) enabled. Admission to this class should be controlled; additionally, traffic in this class can be subject to policing and remarking.

- **Multimedia Streaming:** This service class is intended for Video-on-Demand (VoD) streaming video flows, which, in general, are more elastic than broadcast/live streaming flows. Traffic in this class should be marked AF Class 3 (AF31) and should be provisioned with a guaranteed bandwidth queue with DSCP-based WRED enabled. Admission control is recommended on this traffic class (though not strictly required), and this class can be subject to policing and remarking. Example applications include Cisco Digital Media System Video-on-Demand (VoD) streams.

- **Call-Signaling:** This service class is intended for signaling traffic that supports IP voice and video telephony. Traffic in this class should be marked CS3 and provisioned with a (moderate, but dedicated) guaranteed bandwidth queue. WRED should not be enabled on this class, as call-signaling traffic should not be dropped (if this class is experiencing drops, the bandwidth allocated to it should be reprovisioned). Example traffic includes SCCP, SIP, H.323, and so on.

Table 9-10 shows an example of how these different classes can be used.

Table 9-10   *DSCP Example*

Application Class	Per-Hop Behavior	Admission Control	Queuing and Dropping	Media Application Examples
VoIP Telephony	EF	Requested	Priority Queue (PQ)	Cisco IP Phones (G.711, G.729)
Broadcast Video	CS5	Requested	(Optional) PQ	Cisco IP Video Surveillance/Cisco Enterprise TV
Real-Time Interactive	CS4	Requested	(Optional) PQ	Cisco TelePresence
Multimedia Conferencing	AF4	Recommended	BW Queue + DSCP WRED	Cisco Unified Personal Communicator
Multimedia Streaming	AF3	—	BW Queue + DSCP WRED	Cisco Digital Media System (VoDs)
Network Control	CS6	—	BW Queue	EIGRP, OSPF, BQP, HSRP, IKE
Signaling	CS3	—	BW Queue	SCCP, SIP, H.323
Ops/Admin Mgmt (QAM)	CS2	—	BW Queue	SNMP, SSH, Syslog
Transactional Data	AF2	—	BW Queue + DSCP WRED	Cisco WebEx/MeetingPlace/ERP Apps
Bulk Data	AF1	—	BW Queue + DSCP WRED	Email, FTP, Backup Apps, Content Distribution
Best Effort	DF	—	Default Queue + RED	Default Class
Scavenger	CS1	—	Min BW Queue	YouTube, iTunes, Bit Torrent, Xbox Live

To provide high-quality voice and to take advantage of the full voice feature set, access layer switches should provide support for these features:

- 802.1Q trunking and 802.1p are needed for the proper treatment of Layer 2 CoS packet marking on Layer 2 ports with IP phones connected.

- Multiple egress queues are needed to provide priority queuing of RTP voice packet streams.

- The ability to classify or reclassify traffic and establish a network trust boundary is required.

- Layer 3 awareness and the ability to implement QoS access control lists (ACL) might be required if certain IP telephony endpoints are being used, such as a PC running a software-based IP phone application that cannot benefit from an extended trust boundary.

When deploying voice, it is recommended that two VLANs are enabled at the access layer switch: a data VLAN for data traffic and a voice VLAN under Cisco IOS Software (called an auxiliary VLAN under the Catalyst operating system) for voice traffic.

Separate voice and data VLANs are recommended for the following reasons:

- Private addressing of phones on the voice VLAN ensures address conservation and ensures that phones are not accessible directly through public networks. PCs and servers can be addressed with publicly routed subnet addresses. However, voice endpoints should be addressed using RFC 1918 private subnet addresses.

- QoS trust boundaries can be selectively extended to voice devices without extending the trust boundaries to PCs and other data devices.

- VLAN access control, 802.1Q, and 802.1p tagging can provide protection for voice devices from malicious internal and external network attacks such as worms, denial of service (DoS) attacks, and attempts by data devices to gain access to priority queues through packet tagging.

- Separate VLANs for voice and data devices at the access layer provide ease of management and simplified QoS configuration.

Note   In-line power capability is highly recommended for the access layer switches to support IP phones.

Figure 9-17 illustrates the different available QoS networking mechanisms.

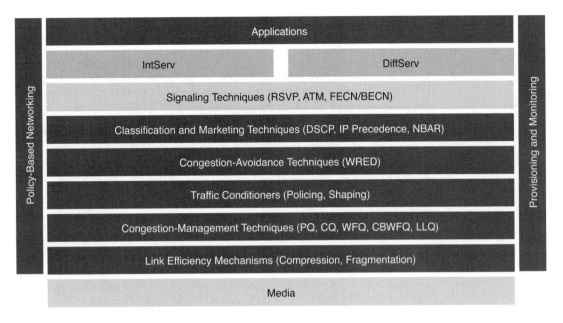

Figure 9-17 *QoS Networking Mechanisms*

These are the categories of QoS mechanisms:

■ **Classification and marking:** Classification is the process of identifying the class or group to which a packet belongs. Network devices use various match criteria to place traffic into a certain number of classes. Classification is accomplished with class maps, ACLs, or route maps and sets the IP precedence bits to the matched packets. Matches can be based on the following criteria:

   ■ Protocol, such as a stateful protocol or a Layer 4 protocol

   ■ Input port

   ■ IP precedence or Differentiated Services Code Point (DSCP)

   ■ Ethernet 802.1p CoS

■ **Congestion avoidance:** Congestion-avoidance techniques monitor network traffic loads in an effort to anticipate and avoid congestion at common network and internetwork bottlenecks before they become a problem. Congestion-avoidance techniques provide preferential treatment for premium (priority) class traffic under congestion situations while concurrently maximizing network throughput and capacity utilization and minimizing packet loss and delay. Weighted Random Early Detection (WRED) and Distributed Weighted Random Early detection (DWRED) are the Cisco IOS QoS congestion-avoidance features.

- **Traffic conditioners:** Policers and shapers usually identify traffic descriptor violations in an identical manner. They usually differ in the way that they respond to violations, as these examples show:

  - A policer typically drops traffic. For example, the Committed Access Rate (CAR) rate-limiting policer will either drop the packet or rewrite its IP precedence and reset the CoS bits in the packet header.

  - A shaper typically delays excess traffic by using a buffer or queuing mechanism to hold packets and shape the flow when the data rate of the source is higher than expected. For example, generic traffic shaping uses a weighted fair queue to delay packets to shape the flow. Frame Relay Traffic Shaping (FRTS) uses either a priority queue, a custom queue, or a First In, First Out (FIFO) queue, depending on how it is configured.

- **Congestion management:** To manage congestion, network devices use a queuing algorithm to segregate traffic and determine a method to prioritize it on an output link. Configure QoS to provide sufficient bandwidth and priority forwarding for delay-sensitive traffic. Examples of congestion management techniques are FIFO, Weighted Fair Queuing (WFQ), Priority Queuing (PQ), Custom Queuing (CQ), Class-Based Weighted Fair Queuing (CBWFQ), and Low Latency Queuing (LLQ).

- **Link efficiency:** Link efficiency mechanisms reduce delay on slower-speed WAN links by breaking up large datagrams and interleaving low-delay traffic packets with the smaller packets that result from the fragmented datagram.

Mechanisms for classification, congestion management, and congestion avoidance need to be considered to meet network service requirements over constrained network resources.

LLQ sends delay-sensitive data, such as voice, to be dequeued and sent first (before packets in other queues are dequeued) and gives delay-sensitive data preferential treatment over other traffic. Because of this, LLQ is the recommended queuing mechanism for supporting voice on IP networks. Voice traffic should be classified in the priority queue. Video traffic should be classified depending on video type (for example, real-time video should be classified in the priority queue).

Figure 9-18 illustrates how LLQ combines CBWFQ and PQ. Strict PQ sends delay-sensitive data first.

The advantage of LLQ is that its policing mechanism guarantees bandwidth for voice and real-time video and gives them a priority. LLQ reduces jitter in voice and video conversations. The rest of the traffic is classified by using CBWFQ.

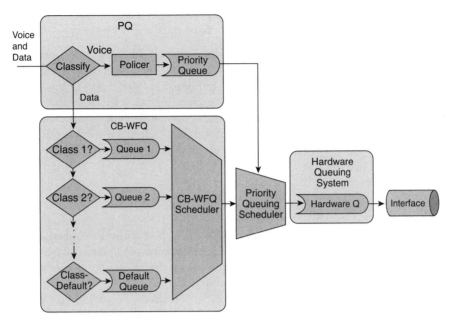

Figure 9-18 *LLQ Example*

QoS Considerations for Voice and Video in the WAN

In addition to providing adequate bandwidth for all required applications, traffic classification, and voice priority queuing and scheduling, the WAN infrastructure typically requires additional mechanisms such as traffic shaping, link efficiency techniques, and call admission control (CAC).

Traffic shaping is used to ensure that WAN links are not sent more traffic than they can manage, which could cause dropped packets.

Link efficiency can be applied to WAN paths. For example, Link Fragmentation and Interleaving (LFI) can be used to prevent small voice packets from being queued behind large data packets, which can lead to delays on low-speed links.

CAC is an essential component of any IP telephony system that involves multiple sites connected through an IP WAN. After the provisioned voice and video bandwidth has been fully utilized in the WAN, the IP video-telephony system must reject subsequent calls to avoid oversubscription of the priority queue on the IP WAN link. This would cause quality degradation for all calls. This function is provided by CAC. It is essential to guarantee good voice and video quality in a multisite deployment involving an IP WAN.

To preserve a satisfactory end-user experience, the CAC function should always be performed during the call setup phase. If network resources are unavailable, a message can be presented to the end user or the call can be rerouted across a different network (such as the PSTN).

CAC mechanisms extend QoS capabilities to protect voice traffic from being negatively affected by other voice traffic. It also keeps excess voice traffic off the network.

If the WAN access link between two PBXs has the bandwidth to carry only two VoIP calls, admitting a third call will impair the voice quality of all three calls. The queuing mechanisms that provide policing cause this problem, not CAC. If a voice gateway receives packets that exceed the configured or allowable rate, it tail-drops these packets from the queue. The queuing mechanism cannot distinguish which IP packet belongs to which voice call. The voice gateway drops packets that exceed the given arrival rate within a certain period of time. Thus, all three calls experience packet loss, which end users perceive as clipped speech.

Call Rerouting Alternatives

When implementing CAC, the outgoing gateway detects that insufficient network resources are available to process a call. The gateway rejects additional calls, and the originating gateway must find another way to manage the call. In the absence of any specific configuration, the outgoing voice gateway sends a reorder tone to the calling party. The PSTN switch or PBX can then announce, "All circuits are busy. Please try your call again later."

The outgoing voice gateway can be configured to accomplish the following tasks:

- Reroute the call through an alternate packet network path, if such a path exists

- Reroute the call through the PSTN path

- Return the call to the originating time-division multiplexing (TDM) switch with the reject cause code

Call Admission Control Examples

The first example illustrated in Figure 9-19 shows a VoIP network without CAC. Suppose that the WAN access link between two PBXs has the bandwidth to carry only two VoIP calls. Admitting the third call impairs the voice quality of all three calls.

The second example illustrated in Figure 9-19 shows a VoIP network with CAC. If the outgoing gateway detects that insufficient network resources are available to allow a call to proceed, the gateway automatically reroutes the call to the PSTN, which maintains the voice quality of the two existing calls.

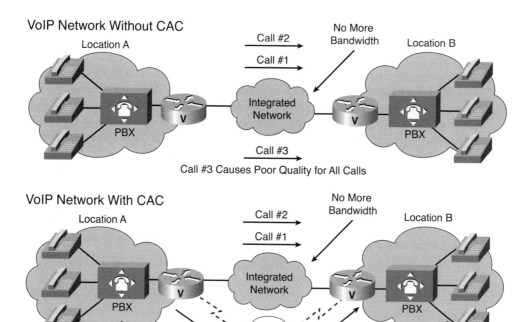

Figure 9-19   *Call Admission Control Examples*

Implementing CAC with RSVP

CAC can also be implemented with the Resource Reservation Protocol (RSVP). RSVP is an industry-standard signaling protocol that enables an application to reserve bandwidth dynamically across an IP network. RSVP, which runs over IP, was first introduced by the Internet Engineering Task Force (IETF) in RFC 2205 and updated by RFCs 2750, 3936, and 4495. Using RSVP, applications can request a certain amount of bandwidth for a data flow across a network (for example, a voice call) and can receive an indication of the outcome of the reservation based on actual resource availability. RSVP performs resource reservation for a given data flow across a network. It is accomplished by defining signaling messages that are exchanged between the source and destination devices for the data flow, and that are processed by intermediate routers along the path. The RSVP signaling messages are IP packets that are routed through the network according to the existing routing protocols.

Not all routers on the path are required to support RSVP, because the protocol is designed to operate transparently across RSVP-unaware nodes. On each RSVP-enabled router, the RSVP process intercepts the signaling messages and interacts with the QoS manager for the router interfaces involved in the data flow to "reserve" bandwidth resources. When the available resources are insufficient for the data flow anywhere along the path, the router signals the failure back to the application that originated the reservation request.

For example, a branch office router can have a primary link with an LLQ provisioned for ten calls and a backup link that can accommodate two calls. RSVP can be configured on both router interfaces so that the RSVP bandwidth matches the LLQ bandwidth. The call-processing agent at the branch can be configured to require RSVP reservations for all calls to or from other branches. Now calls are admitted or rejected based on the outcome of the RSVP reservations, which automatically follow the path determined by the routing protocol. Under normal conditions (when the primary link is active), up to ten calls will be admitted; during failure of the primary link, only up to two calls will be admitted.

Policies can typically be set within the call-processing agent to determine what to do in the event of a CAC failure. For example, the call could be rejected, rerouted across the PSTN, or sent across the IP WAN as a best-effort call with a different DSCP marking.

Cisco Unified Communications Manager version 5.0 and later versions support the Cisco RSVP Agent, which enables more efficient use of networks. Cisco RSVP Agent provides an additional method to achieve CAC other than location-based CAC. RSVP can manage more complex topologies than location-based CAC, which supports only hub-and-spoke network topologies.

Voice Traffic Engineering Overview

Traffic engineering is a science of selecting the appropriate number of lines and the proper types of service to accommodate users.

Effective capacity-planning design minimizes degraded voice service in integrated networks by considering all network resources, from trunks and DSPs to WANs and the campus infrastructure. Several concepts and terms are used in traffic engineering to better assist voice traffic engineers to determine how to provision trunks:

- **Grade of service (GoS):** The probability that a voice gateway will block calls while attempting to allocate circuits during the busiest hour is the GoS. It is written as a decimal fraction, called the Pxx blocking factor, or blockage, where xx is the percentage of calls that are blocked for a traffic system. For example, traffic facilities that require a P01 grade of service define a 1 percent probability of callers being blocked.

- **Erlang:** One erlang equals one full hour, or 3600 seconds, of telephone conversation. If a trunk carries 12.35 erlangs during an hour, an average of a little more than 12 lines (connections) are busy. In the traffic calculation, one erlang implies a single resource in continuous use. The traffic measured in erlangs is used to determine whether a system has too many or too few resources provisioned.

- **Centum Call Seconds (CCS):** A centum (one hundred) call second represents 1/36 of an erlang. To calculate the CCS, multiply the number of calls per hour by their average duration in seconds and divide the result by 100. A system port that can manage a continuous one-hour call has a traffic rating of 36 CCS. Station traffic varies greatly among users, but the typical range is about 6 to 12 CCS per port. If exact statistical data cannot be obtained, assume that the average typical trunk traffic is 30 CCS per port.

■ **Busy hour:** The 60-minute period in a given 24-hour period during which the maximum total traffic load occurs. This is sometimes called the peak hour.

■ **Busy-Hour Traffic (BHT):** The BHT value represents the number of hours of traffic that is transported across a trunk group in its busiest hour. This value is expressed in erlangs.

■ **Blocking probability:** The blocking probability value describes the calls that are not completed because insufficient lines are available. A value of 0.01 means that the voice gateway will block 1 percent of calls.

■ **Call Detail Record (CDR):** A CDR is a record containing information about recent system usage, such as the identities of sources (points of origin), the identities of destinations (endpoints), the duration of each call, the amount billed for each call, the total usage time in the billing period, the total free time remaining in the billing period, and the running total charged during the billing period. The format of the CDR varies among telecom providers and call-logging software. Some software allows the CDR format to be configured by the user.

To determine the appropriate number of trunks that are required to transport the traffic given the desired grade of service, consult erlang traffic engineering tables.

Erlang tables show the amount of traffic potential for specified numbers of circuits, including the probability of receiving a busy signal. The calculation results are usually stated in CCS. Erlang tables combine offered traffic, number of circuits, and grade of service in the following traffic models:

■ **Erlang B:** This is the most common traffic model. It is used to calculate the number of lines that are required if the traffic figure is known (in erlangs) during the busiest hour. The model assumes that all blocked calls are immediately cleared.

■ **Extended Erlang B:** This model is similar to Erlang B, but it considers the additional traffic load that is caused when blocked callers immediately try to call again. The retry percentage can be specified.

■ **Erlang C:** This model assumes that all blocked calls stay in the system until the voice gateway can manage them. The Erlang C model can be applied to a call center design where calls enter a queue if an agent is not available.

Figure 9-20 shows the nonlinear relationship among the amount of traffic in erlangs, the number of circuits (simultaneous connections), and the QoS.

	Number of Erlangs Increases with the Increased Blocking Probability			Number of Erlangs Increases with the Number of Simultaneous Connections		
GOS= Blocking Probability	.003	.005	.01	.02	.03	.05
Number of Circuits						
1	.003	.006	.011	.021	.031	.053
2	.081	.106	.153	.224	.282	.382
3	.289	.349	.456	.603	.716	.900
4	.602	.702	.870	1.093	1.259	1.525
5	.996	1.132	1.361	1.658	1.876	2.219
6	1.447	1.822	1.900	2.278	2.543	2.961
7	1.947	2.158	2.501	2.936	3.250	3.738
8	2.484	2.730	3.128	3.627	3.987	4.543
9	3.053	3.333	3.783	4.345	4.748	5.371
10	3.648	3.961	4.462	5.084	5.530	6.216

Busy Hour Traffic (BHT) in Erlangs

Figure 9-20   *Erlang B Table Example*

The Erlang B table can help with the following examples:

■ For ten circuits with a GoS of P01 (1 percent block probability), 4.462 erlangs of traffic is offered. The 4.462 erlangs equals approximately 160 CCS (4.462 * 36). Assuming that there are 20 users in the company, every user talks for about 13.4 minutes per hour. (4.462 * 36 * 100 / 60) / 20 = 13.4 minutes.

■ 2.961 erlangs are managed by six circuits at a GoS of P05. The 2.961 erlangs equals approximately 107 CCS (2.961 * 36). Assuming that there are ten users in the company, every user talks for about 17.8 minutes every hour. (2.961 * 36 * 100 / 60) / 10 = 17.8 minutes.

Note   For information on erlangs and how to use online erlang calculators, refer to www.erlang.com.

Summary

In this chapter, you learned about voice and video design principles. The following topics have been covered:

■ Business demands are driving the need for unified voice, video, and data networks not on the PSTN.

■ The H.323 standard is a foundation for audio, video, and data communications across IP-based networks, including the Internet.

- The H.264 standard defines the most effective algorithm for video compressing.

- IP telephony refers to communication services and voice, facsimile, and voice-messaging applications that are transported through the IP network rather than the PSTN.

- Voice communication over IP relies on control protocols such as H.323, SCCP, SIP, and MGCP.

- Voice and video quality in an IP network is directly affected by delay, jitter, and packet loss.

- An echo is the audible leak of the voice of the caller into the receive (return) path.

- Because of the high amount of compression utilized by video codecs, packet loss extremely affects video.

- Unified Communications over IP relies on voice and video that are coded and encapsulated into IP packets.

- When network designers are designing voice and video on IP networks, a primary WAN issue is bandwidth availability.

- QoS mechanisms are important for networks that carry voice and video.

- Traffic engineering is a science of selecting the appropriate number of lines and the proper types of service to accommodate users.

- New voice and video over IP solutions must integrate into existing environments and provide similar functionality.

- Business needs are driving the need for unified networks supporting Unified Communications.

- There are many issues that affect voice and video traffic, such as delay, jitter, packet loss, congestion, and slow-speed links. Compression techniques, LFI, and QoS mechanisms can alleviate many of these issues.

References

For additional information, refer to these resources:

Cisco Systems, Inc. Cisco Unified Communication Manager: Introduction, at www.cisco.com/en/US/products/sw/voicesw/ps556/index.html.

Cisco Systems, Inc. Cisco Unified Communications 8x SRND, at www.cisco.com/en/US/docs/voice_ip_comm/cucm/srnd/8x/uc8x.html.

Cisco Systems, Inc. Understanding Codecs: Complexity, Hardware Support, MOS, and Negotiation, at www.cisco.com/en/US/tech/tk1077/technologies_tech_note 09186a00800b6710.shtml.

Davidson, J. and J. Peters. *Voice over IP Fundamentals*. Indianapolis, Indiana: Cisco Press; 2000.

Cisco Systems, Inc. Voice Network Signaling and Control, at www.cisco.com/en/US/tech/tk652/tk653/technologies_tech_note09186a00800a6210.shtml.

Cisco Systems, Inc. Understanding Delay in Packet Voice Networks, at www.cisco.com/warp/public/788/VoIP/delay-details.html.

Cisco Systems, Inc. Voice over IP—Per-Call Bandwidth Consumption, at www.cisco.com/en/US/tech/tk652/tk698/technologies_tech_note09186a0080094ae2.shtml.

Cisco Systems, Inc. Cisco IOS Voice, Video, and Fax Configuration Guide, Release 12.2, at www.cisco.com/en/US/docs/ios/12_2/voice/configuration/guide/fvvfax_c.html.

Cisco Systems, Inc. Traffic Analysis for Voice over IP, at www.cisco.com/univercd/cc/td/doc/cisintwk/intsolns/VoIPsol/ta_isd.htm.

Cisco Systems, Inc. High-Density Packet Voice/Fax Digital Signal Processor Module, at www.cisco.com/en/US/products/hw/univgate/ps501/products_data_sheet0900aecd80458049.html.

Cisco Systems, Inc. Cisco Voice Codec Bandwidth Calculator, at http://tools.cisco.com/Support/VBC/do/CodecCalc1.do.

Cisco Systems, Inc. QoS Design Recommendations for Medianet, at www.cisco.com/en/US/docs/solutions/Enterprise/Video/qosmrn.html.

Cisco Systems, Inc. Enterprise Medianet Quality of Service Design 4.0—Overview, at www.cisco.com/en/US/docs/solutions/Enterprise/WAN_and_MAN/QoS_SRND_40/QoSIntro_40.html.

Review Questions

Answer the following questions, and then refer to Appendix A for the answers.

1. What steps are involved in converting analog signals to digital format?

2. What H.323 element provides audio, video, and data format translation between endpoints?

3. What ITU standard defines the most effective current algorithm for video compression?

4. What is the packet loss target for video traffic types?

5. What protocol is used to carry voice conversations between IP endpoints?

6. What are the names of the different components used by SIP?

7. What is the range of acceptable one-way delay for voice in most user applications?

8. What is the name used to describe the situation when the traffic from a voice stream is received with variable delay?

9. What DSCP per-hop behavior is typically given to VoIP telephony traffic?

10. What voice engineering concept equals one full hour of a telephone conversation?

Chapter 10

Identifying Design Considerations for Basic Wireless Networking

This chapter describes wireless network design principles and includes the following sections:

- Cisco Unified Wireless Network Review

- Wireless Network Controller Technology

- Designing Wireless Networks Using Controllers

This chapter introduces the Cisco Unified Wireless Network architecture and discusses wireless design principles to provide the necessary guidelines for successful wireless network design. The chapter starts with an introduction of the Cisco Unified Wireless Network and then discusses wireless network controller technologies. It concludes with useful guidelines for designing wireless networks with controllers for enterprise environments.

Cisco Unified Wireless Network Review

The following sections review the Cisco Unified Wireless Network. They also cover the fundamental architectural concepts and deployment considerations necessary to design a basic Cisco Unified Wireless Network solution.

Cisco Unified Wireless Network Architecture

A wireless LAN (WLAN) provides network connectivity over radio waves. Wireless stations such as PCs and Personal Digital Assistants (PDA) connect to a wireless access point using half-duplex transmissions. The access point connects to the wired network. Organizations are deploying WLANs to increase employee productivity, enhance collaboration, and improve responsiveness to customers.

Traditionally, each access point in a WLAN operates as a separate autonomous node configured with Service Set Identifier (SSID), RF channel, and RF power settings. There are some disadvantages to this approach. Scaling to large, contiguous, coordinated WLANs and adding higher-level applications are challenging with autonomous access points. For example, if an autonomous access point recognizes a nearby access point operating on the same channel, the autonomous access point cannot determine whether the adjacent access point is part of the same network or a neighboring one. Some form of centralized coordination is needed to allow multiple access points to operate across rooms and floors.

Cisco Unified Wireless Network Elements

The Cisco Unified Wireless Network architecture allows the WLAN to operate as an Intelligent Information Network and support advanced mobility services. It is composed of five interconnected elements that work together to deliver a unified, end-to-end, enterprise-class wireless solution.

Beginning with a base of client devices, each element adds capabilities as network needs evolve and grow. They interconnect with the elements above and below to create a comprehensive, secure WLAN solution. These are the five interconnected elements of the Cisco Unified Wireless Network architecture:

- **Client devices:** With more than 90 percent of shipping client devices certified as Cisco compatible, almost any client device that is selected will support Cisco equipment's powerful advanced features. Secure client devices provide out-of-the-box wireless security through Cisco Compatible Certified components.

- **Access points:** Dynamically configured access points provide ubiquitous network access in all environments. Enhanced productivity is supported through plug and play with Lightweight Access Point Protocol (LWAPP) and Control and Provisioning of Wireless Access Points Protocol (CAPWAP). Cisco access points are a proven platform with a large installed base and market share leadership. All Cisco lightweight access points support mobility services, such as fast secure roaming for voice and location services for real-time network visibility.

- **Network unification:** Integration of the wired and wireless network is critical for unified network control, scalability, security, and reliability. Seamless functionality is provided through wireless integration into all major switching and routing platforms, including Cisco Wireless LAN Controllers, Cisco Wireless LAN Controller Modules for Integrated Services Routers, and Cisco Catalyst 6500/7600 Series Wireless Services Module (WiSM).

- **World-class network management:** The same level of security, scalability, reliability, ease of deployment, and management for WLANs as for wired LANs is provided through network management systems such as Cisco Wireless Control System (WCS), which visualizes and helps secure the air space. Context-aware mobility services are provided with the Cisco Mobility Service Engine.

- **Mobility services:** Unified Mobility services deliver enhanced mobility services, including advanced security threat detection and mitigation, voice services, context-aware mobility services, and guest access.

Benefits of the Cisco Unified Wireless Network architecture include

- Ease of deployment and upgrades

- Reliable connectivity through dynamic RF management

- Optimized per-user performance through user load balancing

- Guest networking

- Layer 2 and 3 roaming

- Embedded wireless intrusion detection system (IDS)

- Location services

- Voice over IP

- Lowered total cost of ownership (TCO)

- Wired and wireless unification

An enterprise network can start with the base components of client devices, lightweight access points, and wireless LAN controllers (WLC). As an organization's wireless networking requirements grow, the organization can then add further elements, such as Cisco WCS and the Cisco Mobility Service Engine.

Cisco WCS is an optional network management component that works in conjunction with Cisco Aironet lightweight access points and Cisco Wireless LAN Controllers. With Cisco WCS, network administrators have a single solution for RF prediction, policy provisioning, network optimization, troubleshooting, user tracking, security monitoring, and WLAN systems management. Cisco WCS includes tools for WLAN planning and design, RF management, basic location tracking, Intrusion Prevention System (IPS), and WLAN systems configuration, monitoring, and management.

The Cisco Mobility Service Engine integrates with Cisco WCS for enhanced location tracking of many wireless devices to within a few meters. This appliance also records historical location information that can be used for location trending, rapid problem resolution, and RF capacity management.

CAPWAP and LWAPP Fundamentals

LWAPP is an Internet Engineering Task Force (IETF) draft protocol that defines the control messaging for setup and path authentication and runtime operations between access points and controllers. LWAPP also defines the tunneling mechanism for data traffic.

LWAPP defines how the access point will communicate with the controller, including these messages:

■ **LWAPP data messages:** Encapsulated and forwarded data frames from and to wireless clients. These messages use UDP port 12222.

■ **LWAPP control messages:** Management messages exchanged between the WLAN controller and the access point. These messages use UDP port 12223.

The LWAPP tunnel uses Layer 3 transport.

In controller software release 5.2 or later, Cisco lightweight access points use the IETF standard Control and Provisioning of Wireless Access Points protocol (CAPWAP) to communicate between the controller and other lightweight access points on the network. Controller software releases prior to 5.2 use the Lightweight Access Point Protocol (LWAPP) for these communications.

CAPWAP, which is based on LWAPP, is a standard, interoperable protocol that enables a controller to manage a collection of wireless access points.

CAPWAP is very close to LWAPP in its behavior. One of the major differences is that CAPWAP utilizes Datagram Transport Layer Security (DTLS) to protect traffic between access points and controllers, instead of Advanced Encryption Standard (AES) as with LWAPP. DTLS is a derivation of the Secure Socket Layer (SSL) protocol built with UDP support. DTLS ensures that a secured session is established and maintained between the access points and the controller. CAPWAP information sent between controllers and APs is encrypted with DTLS.

Another important difference is that CAPWAP features a dynamic maximum transmission unit (MTU) discovery mechanism. With this system, CAPWAP access points and controllers can discover the MTU on the links between controllers and APs and adjust their encapsulated packet size accordingly. Follow these guidelines when using CAPWAP:

■ If the firewall is currently configured to allow traffic only from access points that use LWAPP, the rules of the firewall must be changed to allow traffic from access points that use CAPWAP.

■ Make sure that the CAPWAP UDP ports 5246 and 5247 are enabled and are not blocked by an intermediate device. These ports are used by the access points to communicate with the controller. LWAPP used UDP ports 12222 and 12223.

■ If access control lists (ACL) are in the control path between the controller and its access points, the CAPWAP protocol ports need to be opened to prevent access points from being stranded.

The access points use a random UDP source port to reach these destination ports on the controller. In controller software release 5.2, LWAPP was removed and replaced by CAPWAP, but with a new out-of-the-box access point, it could try to use LWAPP to contact the controller before it downloads the CAPWAP image from the controller. After the access point downloads the CAPWAP image from the controller, it uses only CAPWAP to communicate with the controller. A WLC can manage and operate a large number of lightweight access points. In addition, the WLC can coordinate and collate information across a large wireless network and even across a WAN. The WLC supplies both the configuration information and firmware updates to the access points, if needed.

CAPWAP control and data packets are carried over the IP network encapsulated in UDP packets. This is called "Layer 3 CAPWAP transport mode." Unlike LWAPP, CAPWAP only supports this mode and does not support a Layer 2 option. The CAPWAP tunnel uses the IP address of the access point and the IP address of the AP manager interface on the WLC as endpoints.

By default, Cisco lightweight access points get an IP address through DHCP. On the access point side, both CAPWAP control and data messages use an ephemeral port that is derived from a hash of the access point MAC address as the UDP port. On the WLC side, CAPWAP data messages always use UDP port 5247. On the WLC side, CAPWAP control messages always use UDP port 5246. This configuration allows access points to communicate with a WLC across subnets as long as these UDP ports are not filtered by a firewall.

Split Media Access Control

The Cisco Unified Wireless Network architecture centralizes WLAN configuration and control on a device called a wireless LAN controller (WLC). In this architecture, access points are "lightweight," meaning that they cannot act independently of a WLC. When a WLAN client sends a packet, it is received by an access point, decrypted if necessary, encapsulated with a CAPWAP header, and forwarded to the WLC. At the controller, the CAPWAP header is stripped off and the frame is switched from the controller onto an appropriate VLAN in the campus infrastructure. When a client on the wired network sends a packet to a WLAN client, the packet first goes into the WLC. Here it is encapsulated with a CAPWAP header and then forwarded to the appropriate access point. The access point strips off the CAPWAP header, encrypts the frame if necessary, and then bridges the frame onto the RF medium.

Much of the traditional WLAN functionality has moved from access points to a centralized WLC under the Cisco Unified Wireless Network architecture. CAPWAP splits the MAC functions of an access point between the WLC and the lightweight access point. The split-MAC functionality allows the access points to be deployed in a "zero-touch" fashion, where individual configuration of access points is not required.

Figure 10-1 illustrates split-MAC architecture.

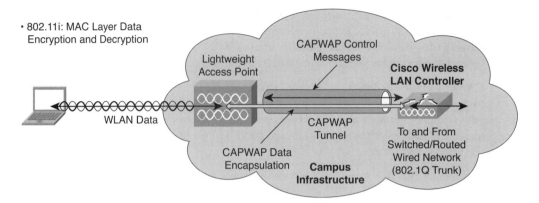

Figure 10-1 *Split-MAC Architecture*

With split MAC, CAPWAP splits the different MAC functionalities as shown:

■ **Controller:**

   ■ 802.11 MAC management: Association requests and actions

   ■ 802.11e resource reservation

   ■ 802.11i authentication and key management

■ **Access point:**

   ■ 802.11: Beacons, probe response

   ■ 802.11 control: Packet acknowledgment and transmission

   ■ 802.11e: Frame queuing and packet prioritization

   ■ 802.11i: MAC layer data encryption and decryption

Local Media Access Control

CAPWAP also supports local MAC, which can be appropriate for branch wireless deployments. Local MAC supports implementing full 802.11 functionality at the access point. Unlike split MAC, the access point provides the MAC management support for association requests and actions.

Local MAC allows decoupling the data plane from the control path by terminating all client traffic at the wired port of the access point. This permits direct wireless access to resources local to the access point. It also provides link resiliency by allowing the CAPWAP control path (the link between access point and controller) to be down while wireless service persists. This functionality is particularly useful in small remote and branch offices across WAN links, where only a handful of access points are needed and the cost of a local controller is not justified.

Local MAC architecture is shown in Figure 10-2.

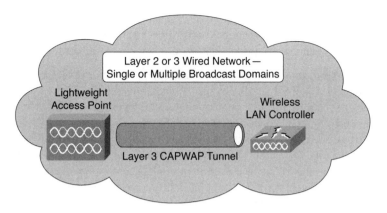

Figure 10-2 *Local MAC Architecture*

With local MAC, CAPWAP splits the different MAC functionalities as shown here:

- **Controller:**
    - 802.11 proxy association requests and actions
    - 802.11e resource reservation
    - 802.11i authentication and key management
- **Access point:**
    - 802.11: Beacons, probe response
    - 802.11 control: Packet acknowledgment and transmission
    - 802.11e: Frame queuing and packet prioritization
    - 802.11i: MAC layer data encryption and decryption
    - 802.11 MAC management: Association requests and actions

Access Point Modes

Only the default LWAPP/CAPWAP access point mode has been discussed to this point. LWAPP/CAPWAP access points support several modes.

Access points can be configured to operate in various modes, depending on their intended usage:

- **Local mode:** This is the default mode of operation. When an access point is placed into local mode, the access point spends 60 ms on channels that it does not operate on every 180 seconds. During this time, the access point performs noise floor measurements, measures interference, and scans for IDS events.

- **H-REAP mode:** Hybrid Remote Edge Access Point (H-REAP) mode enables an access point to reside across a WAN link and still be able to communicate with the

WLC and provide the functionality of a regular lightweight access point. Currently, hybrid REAP is supported on the Cisco Aironet 1130, 1140, 1240 AG, and 1250 AG Series lightweight access points. This mode allows local MAC functionality.

- **Rogue detector mode:** Access points that operate in rogue detector mode monitor rogue access points. They do not transmit or contain rogue access points. The rogue detector should be able to recognize all the VLANs in the network, because rogue access points can be connected to any of the VLANs in the network (it is connected to a trunk port). The switch sends all the rogue access point or client MAC address lists to the rogue detector. The rogue detector then forwards the lists to the WLC to compare with the MACs of clients that the WLC access points have heard over the air. If MACs match, the WLC comprehends that the rogue access point to which those clients are connected is on the wired network.

- **Monitor mode:** Monitor mode is a feature designed to allow specified CAPWAP-enabled access points to exclude themselves from managing data traffic between clients and the infrastructure. With their radio set to a "receive only" mode, they act as dedicated sensors for Context-Aware Mobility Services, rogue access point detection, and intrusion detection. When access points are in monitor mode, they cannot serve clients and continuously cycle through all configured channels listening to each channel for approximately 60 ms. In monitor mode, the access point can send packets to a rogue access point to deauthenticate end users.

- **Sniffer mode:** A CAPWAP-enabled access point that operates in sniffer mode functions as a protocol sniffer and captures and forwards all the packets on a particular channel to a remote machine that runs AiroPeek. These packets contain information about time stamp, signal strength, packet size, and so on. The sniffer mode feature should be enabled only if running AiroPeek, a third-party network analyzer software that supports decoding of wireless data packets.

- **Bridge mode:** The bridge mode feature on the Cisco Aironet 1130 and 1240 Series (typically indoor usage) and the Cisco Aironet 1500 Series (typically outdoor usage) provides cost-effective, high-bandwidth wireless bridging connectivity. Applications supported are point-to-point bridging, point-to-multipoint bridging, point-to-point wireless access with integrated wireless backhaul, and point-to-multipoint wireless access with integrated wireless backhaul.

Additional information on selecting an access point based on the intended use is covered in the section "Designing Wireless Networks Using Controllers."

Wireless Infrastructure

This section overviews how the base Cisco Unified Wireless Network components are connected to the enterprise network; Figure 10-3 illustrates the different deployment options.

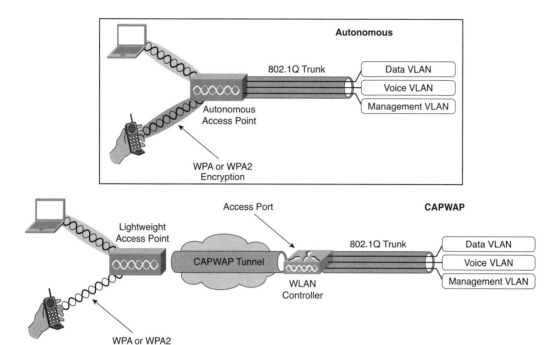

Figure 10-3   *Wireless Deployment Options*

Autonomous access points act as 802.1Q translational bridges. The access points are responsible for taking the wireless client RF traffic into the appropriate local VLAN in the wired network.

In the Cisco Unified Wireless Network architecture, which is a CAPWAP deployment, the Cisco Wireless LAN Controllers are the network devices responsible for placing the wireless client traffic into the appropriate VLAN.

The lightweight access point takes wireless client RF traffic and sends it inside a CAPWAP tunnel on the wired network to the Cisco Wireless LAN Controller. From the perspective of the access point, the controller is a CAPWAP tunnel endpoint with an IP address. At the end of the CAPWAP tunnel, the Cisco Wireless LAN Controller is an 802.1Q bridge that collects RF traffic and puts it on the appropriate VLAN in the wired network.

Although the Cisco Wireless LAN Controller always connects to 802.1Q trunks on a switch or a router, Cisco lightweight access points do not recognize VLAN tagging (except in H-REAP mode). They should be connected only to untagged access ports on a neighbor switch.

Note   If a statically addressed access point is moved to a different IP subnet, it is not capable of forwarding traffic because it is not able to form a CAPWAP tunnel with a WLC.

Stations connect to lightweight access points using RF signals. As a recommended practice for the enterprise, this connection should be authenticated and encrypted. The Cisco Unified Wireless Network provides full support for Wi-Fi Protected Access (WPA) and Wi-Fi Protected Access 2 (WPA2) with its building blocks of 802.1X Extensible Authentication Protocol (EAP) mutual authentication and Temporal Key Integrity Protocol (TKIP) or Advanced Encryption Standard (AES) encryption.

Wireless Authentication

In the Cisco Unified Wireless Network architecture, the supplicant or end device communicates with the Cisco Wireless LAN Controller as the EAP authenticator. After the wireless client associates with the access point, the access point blocks the client from gaining access to anything (except the authentication server) on the network until the client has logged in and authenticated. The process of wireless authentication is illustrated in Figure 10-4.

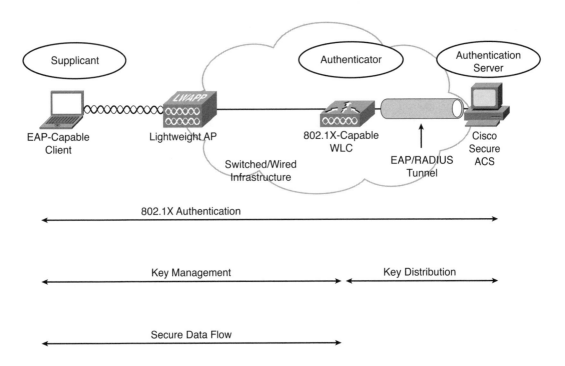

Figure 10-4   *Wireless Authentication*

The client supplies network login credentials such as a user ID and password to the authenticator. The Cisco Wireless LAN Controller communicates to an authentication server such as Cisco Secure Access Control Server (ACS) using EAP. A set of exchanges then occurs between the supplicant, the authenticator, and the server. If the authentication succeeds, the authenticator allows network access to the supplicant through the port. The Cisco Wireless LAN Controller informs the lightweight access point which dynamic interface and policies to use for the client.

After mutual authentication has been successfully completed, the client and RADIUS server each derive the same encryption key, which is used to encrypt all data exchanged. Using a secure channel on the wired LAN, the RADIUS server sends the key to the Cisco Wireless LAN Controller, which stores it for the client. The result is per-user, per-session encryption keys, with the length of a session determined by a policy defined on the RADIUS server. When a session expires or the client roams from one access point to another, reauthentication occurs and generates a new session key. The reauthentication is transparent to the user.

Several 802.1X authentication types exist, each providing a different approach to authentication while relying on the same framework and EAP for communication between a client and the authentication server.

Cisco Unified Wireless Network products support multiple EAP types, including

- **EAP-Transport Layer Security (EAP-TLS):** EAP-TLS is an IETF open standard and is well supported among wireless vendors but rarely deployed. It uses Public Key Infrastructure (PKI) to secure communications to the RADIUS authentication server using TLS and digital certificates.

- **Protected Extensible Authentication Protocol (PEAP):** PEAP was a joint proposal by Cisco Systems, Microsoft, and RSA Security as an open standard. PEAP-Microsoft Challenge Handshake Authentication Protocol version 2 (MSCHAPv2) is the most common version and is widely available in products and widely deployed. It is similar in design to EAP-Tunneled TLS (TTLS), requiring only a server-side PKI certificate to create a secure TLS tunnel to protect user authentication. PEAP-Generic Token Card (GTC) allows more generic authentication to a number of databases, such as Novell Directory Services (NDS).

- **EAP-TTLS:** EAP-TTLS was codeveloped by Funk Software and Certicom. It is widely supported across platforms and offers very good security, using PKI certificates only on the authentication server.

- **Cisco Lightweight Extensible Authentication Protocol (LEAP):** LEAP is an early proprietary EAP method supported in the Cisco Compatible Extensions program. It is vulnerable to dictionary attack.

- **EAP-Flexible Authentication via Secure Tunneling (EAP-FAST):** EAP-FAST is a proposal by Cisco Systems to fix the weaknesses of LEAP. EAP-FAST uses Protected Access Credentials (PAC), and the use of server certificates is optional in EAP-FAST. EAP-FAST has three phases. Phase 0 is an optional phase where the PAC can be provisioned manually or dynamically. In Phase 1, the client and the authentication, authorization, and accounting (AAA) server use the PAC to establish a TLS tunnel. In Phase 2, the client sends user information across the tunnel.

Each EAP type has advantages and disadvantages. Trade-offs exist between the security provided, EAP type manageability, the operating systems supported, the client devices supported, the client software and authentication messaging overhead, certificate requirements, user ease of use, and WLAN infrastructure device support.

Organizations should evaluate their networks and security environments to select the best EAP authentication type for their 802.1X deployment. Areas to evaluate when selecting an EAP type include

■ Type of security mechanism used for security credentials

■ User authentication database

■ Client operating systems in use

■ Available client supplicants

■ Type of user login needed

■ Use of RADIUS or AAA servers

Overview of WLAN Controllers

The Cisco Unified Wireless Network architecture is based on the Cisco Wireless LAN Controllers. Cisco Wireless LAN Controller documentation identifies its components with these terms:

■ **Ports:** A Cisco Wireless LAN Controller port is a physical entity that connects the Cisco Wireless LAN Controller to the neighbor switch in the wired campus infrastructure. Each port is by default an 802.1Q VLAN trunk port. The controller connects WLANs from the access points over a trunk port to the enterprise network. There can be multiple physical ports on a Cisco Wireless LAN Controller. Some Cisco Wireless LAN Controllers support link aggregation (LAG). LAG, based on the IEEE 802.3ad port aggregation standard, allows aggregation of all the ports on a Cisco Wireless LAN Controller into a single port-channel interface. The system can dynamically manage traffic load balancing and port redundancy with LAG. When the controller ports are set to LAG, the switch to which the controller connects should be set to EtherChannel unconditionally (mode on). Some Cisco Wireless LAN Controllers also have a 10/100 copper service port. The service port is reserved for out-of-band management of the Cisco Wireless LAN Controller and system recovery and maintenance. Use of the service port is optional.

■ **Interfaces:** A Cisco Wireless LAN Controller interface is a logical entity on the Cisco Wireless LAN Controller that maps to a VLAN on the wired network. There are several kinds of interfaces. An interface has multiple parameters associated with it, including IP address, default gateway (for the IP subnet), primary physical port, secondary physical port, VLAN tag, and DHCP server. When LAG is not used, each interface is mapped to at least one primary physical port and an optional secondary port. Multiple interfaces can be mapped to a single Cisco Wireless LAN Controller port. When LAG is used, the system dynamically maps the interfaces to the aggregated port channel.

■ **WLANs:** A WLAN is a logical entity that associates a Service Set Identifier (SSID) to an interface on the Cisco Wireless LAN Controller. A WLAN is configured with security, quality of service (QoS), radio policies, and other wireless network parameters. There can be up to 16 access point WLANs configured per Cisco Wireless LAN Controller.

There are several types of Cisco Wireless LAN Controller interfaces:

■ **Management interface:** (Static, configured at setup, mandatory). The management interface is the default interface for in-band management of the Cisco Wireless LAN Controller and for connectivity to enterprise services such as AAA servers. If the service port is in use, the management interface must be on a different subnet from the service port. The management interface is also used for discovery between access points and the Cisco Wireless LAN Controller. The management interface is the only in-band interface IP address on the Cisco Wireless LAN Controller that can be pinged consistently from the access points.

■ **AP manager interface:** (Static, configured at setup, mandatory except for 5508 WLC). A Cisco Wireless LAN Controller has one or more AP manager interfaces. They are used for all Layer 3 communications between the Cisco Wireless LAN Controller and the lightweight access points after the access point discovers the controller. The AP manager IP address is used as the tunnel source for CAPWAP packets from the Cisco Wireless LAN Controller to the access point and as the destination for CAPWAP packets from the access point to the Cisco Wireless LAN Controller. The AP manager interface must have a unique IP address. Usually it is configured on the same subnet as the management interface, but this is not necessarily a requirement.

■ **Dynamic interface:** Dynamic interfaces are created by the network administrator and are designed to be analogous to VLANs for WLAN client devices. The Cisco Wireless LAN Controller supports up to 512 dynamic interface instances. Each dynamic interface must be assigned to a unique IP subnet and VLAN. Each dynamic interface acts as a DHCP relay for wireless clients associated with WLANs mapped to the interface.

■ **Virtual interface:** (Static, configured at setup, mandatory). The virtual interface is used to support mobility management, DHCP relay, and embedded Layer 3 security, such as guest web authentication and Virtual Private Network (VPN) termination. The virtual interface must be configured with an unassigned and unused gateway IP address. A typical virtual interface is 1.1.1.1. The virtual interface address cannot be pinged and should not exist in any routing table in the network. If multiple Cisco Wireless LAN Controllers are configured in a mobility group, the virtual interface IP address must be the same on all Cisco Wireless LAN Controller devices to allow seamless roaming.

■ **Service port interface:** (Static, configured at setup, optional). The service port interface is statically mapped by the system only to the physical service port. The service port interface must have an IP address on a different subnet from the management interface, AP manager interface, and any dynamic interfaces. The service port interface can obtain an IP address through DHCP or it can be assigned a static IP address, but a default gateway cannot be assigned to the service port interface. Static routes can be defined in the Cisco Wireless LAN Controller for remote network access to the service port. The service port interface is typically reserved for out-of-band management in the event of a network failure. It is also the only port that is active when the controller is in boot mode. The physical service port is a copper 10/100 Ethernet port and is not capable of carrying 802.1Q tags, so it must be connected to an access port on the neighbor switch.

Figure 10-5 illustrates the relationships among WLANs, interfaces, and ports on a Cisco Wireless LAN Controller. Interfaces must be assigned to a port for connectivity to the enterprise network. Multiple WLANs can be assigned to an interface. Multiple interfaces can be assigned to the same port. An interface can be assigned to only one port. The service port interface is associated only with the physical service port. The virtual interface is not associated with any port. The AP manager interface and the management interface can be in the same subnet.

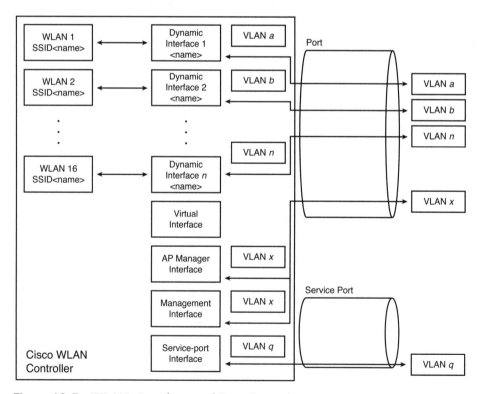

Figure 10-5 *WLANs, Interfaces, and Ports Example*

Cisco has many wireless controller products. For example, the Cisco 2100 Series Wireless LAN Controllers manage up to 25 lightweight access points. The Cisco Wireless LAN Controller Module also manages up to 25 Cisco Aironet lightweight access points and is supported on Cisco 2800 and 3800 Series Integrated Services Routers.

The Cisco Catalyst 3750G Integrated Wireless LAN Controller integrates WLC functions into the Cisco Catalyst 3750G switches. The two models supported are

- The Cisco Catalyst 3750G 24WS (WS-C3750G-24WS-S25), with 24 10/100/1000 Power over Ethernet (PoE) ports, two Small Form-factor Pluggable (SFP) module slots, and an integrated Cisco Wireless LAN Controller supporting up to 25 Cisco lightweight access points.

- The Cisco Catalyst 3750G 24WS (WS-C3750G-24WS-S50), with 24 10/100/1000 PoE ports, two SFP module slots, and an integrated Cisco Wireless LAN Controller supporting up to 50 Cisco lightweight access points.

The Cisco 4400 Series Wireless LAN Controllers are designed for medium to large enterprise facilities. The Cisco 4400 Series controllers are available in two models:

- The Cisco 4402 Wireless LAN Controller with two Gigabit Ethernet ports comes in configurations that support 12, 25, and 50 lightweight access points.

- The Cisco 4404 Wireless LAN Controller with four Gigabit Ethernet ports supports 100 lightweight access points.

The Cisco Catalyst 6500 Series Wireless Services Module (WiSM) supports up to 300 lightweight access points per module.

The Cisco 5500 Series Wireless LAN Controllers are designed for medium to large enterprise facilities. Cisco 5508 Wireless Controllers deliver reliable performance, enhanced flexibility, and zero service loss for mission-critical wireless. 802.11n offers up to nine times the performance of 802.11a/g networks. The Cisco 5508 Wireless LAN Controller supports 12, 25, 50, 100, 250, or 500 access points for business-critical wireless services at locations of all sizes.

Access Point Support and Scaling

Depending on the Cisco Wireless LAN Controller platform, different numbers of access points are supported. Figure 10-6 illustrates some of the current access point offerings. Cisco provides different access points and bridges for various physical environments. Every environment is different, which precludes a one-size-fits-all product line. In addition to controller-based and standalone access points (depending on the ISR model), Cisco has integrated access points into the Integrated Service Routers (ISR) with either built-in standalone access point or wireless controller network modules for external controller-based access points.

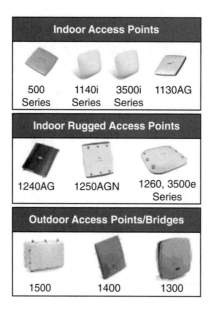

Figure 10-6   *Current Access Point Offerings*

All Cisco Aironet controller-based access points connect to any Cisco Wireless LAN Controllers. Customers can mix and match access points within their network, and still take advantage of all the rich Cisco Unified Wireless Network capabilities in an integrated manner using controller-based products. Alternatively, standalone access points are manageable through CiscoWorks Wireless LAN Solution Engine (WLSE) or CiscoWorks WLSE Express, offering core security and roaming.

Cisco has access point products for the carpeted enterprise, rugged environments, and challenging environments such as the outdoors. Examples are as follows:

■   Cisco Aironet 500 Series, 1130AG, 1140 AGN, and 3500i Series Access Points are for the carpeted enterprise that has little environmental variability and operates within a controlled environment.

■   Cisco Aironet 1240AG, 1250AGN, 1260AGN, and 3500e Series Access Points are for challenging environments that need a rugged enclosure such as manufacturing, loading docks, and warehouses.

■   Cisco Aironet 1500 Series Lightweight Outdoor Mesh Access Points are for cost-effective, scalable deployment of secure outdoor wireless LANs for network connections within a campus area, outdoor infrastructure for mobile users, or public access for outdoor areas. The 1500 Series supports autoconfiguring and self-healing wireless mesh deployments.

■ Cisco Aironet 1300 Series Outdoor Access Point/Bridge or Cisco Aironet 1400 Series Wireless Bridges offer high-speed, high-performance outdoor bridging for line-of-sight applications. They both have a rugged enclosure optimized for harsh outdoor environments with extended operating temperature ranges.

Access Point Scalability Considerations

Cisco 4400 Series Wireless LAN Controller platforms normally supports a maximum of 48 access points per port.

This limitation applies to the 4400 Series appliance controllers (4402-50, 4404-100), the Cisco Catalyst 3750G Integrated Wireless LAN Controller, and the Cisco Catalyst 6500 Series WiSM. There are two ways to scale beyond 48 access points per physical port on a Cisco Wireless LAN Controller:

■ **Use multiple AP manager interfaces:** This option is supported only on 4400 Series appliance controllers.

■ **Use Link Aggregation (LAG):** This option is supported on the 4400 Series appliance controllers and is the default and only option on the Cisco Catalyst 3750G Integrated Wireless LAN Controller and the Cisco Catalyst 6500 Series WiSM.

The 4400 Series appliance controllers can use LAG or multiple AP manager interfaces. With LAG enabled, the logical port on a Cisco 4402 controller supports up to 50 access points, and the logical port on a Cisco 4404 controller supports up to 100 access points.

Multiple AP Manager Interface Example

As shown in Figure 10-7, with multiple AP manager interfaces, two or more AP manager interfaces are created on a 4400 Series appliance controller. Each AP manager interface is mapped to a different physical port. All AP manager IP addresses are included in the CAPWAP discovery response message from a Cisco Wireless LAN Controller to an access point, along with information on the number of access points that are currently using each AP manager IP address. The access point selects an AP manager IP address to use for the CAPWAP tunnel request, preferring the least-loaded AP manager interface. Therefore, the access point load is dynamically distributed across the multiple AP manager interfaces.

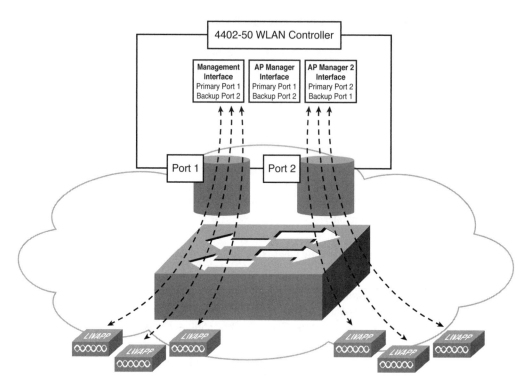

Figure 10-7   *Multiple AP Manager Interfaces Example*

Multiple AP manager interfaces can exist on the same VLAN and IP subnet, or they can be configured on different VLANs and IP subnets. It is recommended that all AP manager interfaces be configured on the same VLAN and IP subnet.

One advantage to multiple AP manager interfaces is that the Cisco Wireless LAN Controller platform can be connected to more than one neighbor device.

Using multiple AP manager interfaces affects port and Cisco Wireless LAN Controller redundancy engineering. For example, the Cisco 4402-50 Controller supports a maximum of 50 access points and has two ports. To support the maximum number of access points, two AP manager interfaces need to be created. A problem occurs if supporting port redundancy is requested.

The static AP manager interface is assigned port 1 as the primary port and port 2 as the secondary. The second AP manager interface is assigned port 2 as the primary and port 1 as the secondary. If either port fails, a situation arises where the Cisco Wireless LAN Controller is trying to support 50 access points on a port that supports only 48 access points. Two access points will be unable to communicate with the Cisco Wireless LAN Controller and will be forced to look for an alternate controller. This limitation must be taken into consideration when engineering redundancy.

Link Aggregation (LAG) with a Single AP Manager Interface Example

As shown in Figure 10-8, when LAG is enabled, the system dynamically manages port redundancy and load-balances access points across an EtherChannel interface transparently. The limit of 48 access points per port does not apply when LAG is enabled. LAG simplifies controller configuration because primary and secondary ports for each interface no longer need to be configured. If any of the controller ports fail, traffic is automatically migrated to one of the other ports. As long as at least one controller port is functioning, the system continues to operate, access points remain connected to the network, and wireless clients continue to send and receive data.

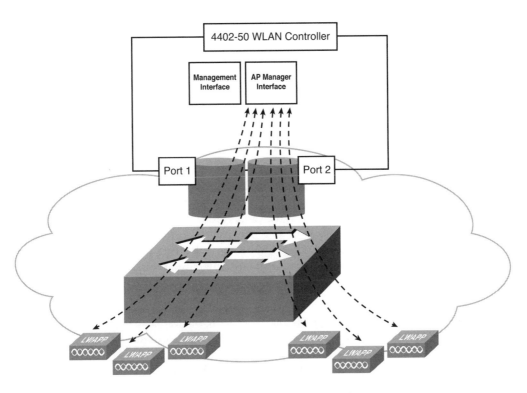

Figure 10-8 *LAG with a Single AP Manager Interface Example*

One limitation with LAG is that the Cisco Wireless LAN Controller platform supports only one LAG group per controller. Therefore, when LAG is enabled, all the physical ports, excluding the service port, are included in the bundle. This means that a Cisco Wireless LAN Controller in LAG mode cannot be connected to more than one neighbor device.

Note   When possible, it is recommended that LAG be used to support access point scaling rather than using multiple AP manager interfaces.

Wireless Network Controller Technology

The following sections describe wireless networks using controllers. They explain how access points and controllers integrate into an enterprise network.

Lightweight Access Point Connectivity to a WLC

Lightweight access points are "zero-touch" deployed and are not configured directly. After a lightweight access point is physically installed and connected to an access port on an infrastructure switch, the access point goes through a WLC discovery and join phase using an exchange of CAPWAP messages.

These are the steps in the WLC discovery process:

Step 1.   A CAPWAP-enabled access point starts the discovery process to find a controller using CAPWAP.

Step 2.   After 60 seconds of trying to join a controller with CAPWAP, the access point starts the discovery process in LWAPP.

Step 3.   If the access point cannot find a controller using LWAPP within 60 seconds, it returns to Step 1.

CAPWAP controllers and LWAPP controllers can be deployed on the same network. The CAPWAP-enabled software allows access points to join either a controller that runs CAPWAP or LWAPP. The only exception is the Cisco Aironet 1140 Series Access Point, which supports only CAPWAP and therefore joins only controllers that run CAPWAP. For example, an 1130 Series Access Point can join a controller that runs either CAPWAP or LWAPP, whereas the 1140 Series Access Point can join only a controller that runs CAPWAP. Notice that newer access points will only utilize CAPWAP discovery. Older access points only use LWAPP.

The access points use a random UDP source port to reach destination UDP ports on the controller. In controller software release 5.2, LWAPP was removed and replaced by CAPWAP, but a new out-of-the-box access point could try to use LWAPP to contact the controller before it downloads the CAPWAP image from the controller. After the access point downloads the CAPWAP image from the controller, it uses only CAPWAP to communicate with the controller.

WLC Selection

The CAPWAP discovery and selection process is important, because it provides a mechanism for network administers to manage which access point is joined to which WLC. It is also important for design, because the CAPWAP join mechanisms must be chosen for deployment.

WLCs embed important information in the CAPWAP discovery response. That data includes the following:

- Controller sysName

- Controller type

- Controller access point capacity and its current access point load

- Master controller status

- AP manager IP addresses

The access point then selects a WLC that will send a CAPWAP join request from the candidate WLC list, based on the embedded information, as shown in the following steps:

Step 1. If the access point has previously been configured with a primary, secondary, or tertiary controller, the access point examines the controller sysName field (from the CAPWAP discovery responses), attempting to find the WLC configured as primary. If the access point finds a matching sysName, it sequentially tries to join the primary, secondary, and tertiary controllers.

Step 2. If primary, secondary, or tertiary controllers have not been configured for an access point, if these controllers cannot be found in the candidate list, or if the CAPWAP join requests to those controllers have failed, the access point then looks at the Master Controller status field in the CAPWAP discovery responses from the candidate WLCs. If a WLC is configured as a master controller, the access point selects that WLC and sends it a CAPWAP join request.

Step 3. If the access point is unsuccessful at joining a WLC based on the criteria in Steps 1 and 2, it attempts to join the WLC with the greatest capacity for access point associations. The access point first tries to discover as many controllers as it possibly can, to maximize its chances to find a primary, secondary, tertiary, or master controller. The access point then tries to open an encrypted communication (CAPWAP/DTLS tunnel) with one or several controllers (for example, the primary and the secondary). Each WLC validates the access point and then sends a CAPWAP response to the access point. The access point validates the WLC to complete the tunnel establishment process. The validation on both the access point and the WLC is a mutual authentication mechanism. An encryption key derivation process is subsequently initiated. The encryption key is used to secure future CAPWAP messages. The access point then sends a CAPWAP join request within one of the established tunnels to the controller it wants to join. The chosen WLC replies with a join response and a status message (success or failure). If the status is success, the access point joins the WLC and receives its configuration from the WLC. If the result is failure, the access point tries to join another WLC.

Lightweight Access Point Operations

The access point downloads firmware from the WLC if its running code version does not match the WLC. The access point always matches its code revision to the WLC.

The WLC then provisions the access point with the appropriate Service Set Identifier (SSID), security, quality of service (QoS), and other parameters that have been configured at the WLC. At this point, the access point is ready to serve WLAN clients.

The WLC periodically queries its joined access points for statistics using CAPWAP control messages. These statistics are used for dynamic Radio Resource Management (RRM), alarming, reporting, and other tasks.

The access point periodically sends a CAPWAP heartbeat control message to the WLC. The WLC responds with a CAPWAP acknowledgment to the heartbeat. The heartbeat interval is 30 seconds by default (configurable). When two consecutive heartbeat acknowledgments from the controller are missed, the access point resends the heartbeat up to five more times at one-second intervals. If no acknowledgment is received after five retries, the access point declares the controller unreachable, releases and renews its IP address, and looks for a new controller.

Note   The heartbeat mechanism is important, because it is used to support controller redundancy designs. These designs are discussed later in this chapter.

Mobility in the Cisco Unified Wireless Network

One significant benefit derived from wireless networks is mobility, the ability of end devices to move to new locations and remain networked without reassociation and DHCP delays.

Roaming occurs when a wireless client moves association from one access point and reassociates with another. In a low-quality roaming experience, mobility involves a new association with an access point, a new IP address, and possibly reestablishing security credentials. These steps take noticeable time, and clients can lose network connectivity or drop voice calls.

For a high-quality roaming experience, a WLAN client must be able to maintain its association seamlessly from one access point to another securely and with as little latency as possible. The roaming event is triggered on signal quality, not proximity. When the signal quality for a client drops as a result of movement, the client device roams to another access point.

Mobility introduces challenges in a network implementation. Roaming must be supported when the wireless client roams from one access point to another, whether both access points are joined to the same WLC (intracontroller) or to different WLCs (intercontroller). Depending on the application, the Cisco Unified Wireless Network might need to support Layer 2 or Layer 3 roaming. A high-quality roaming experience should also be seamless to the client and preserve the security context and associations.

Intracontroller Roaming

When a wireless client associates to an access point and authenticates through a WLC, the WLC places an entry for that client in its client database. This entry includes the MAC and IP addresses of the client, security context and associations, QoS context, and WLAN and associated access point. The WLC uses this information to forward frames and manage traffic to and from the wireless client.

When the wireless client moves its association from one access point to another on the same WLC, the WLC simply updates the client database with the new associated access point. If necessary, new security context and associations are established as well. With intracontroller roaming, an IP address refresh is not needed. An illustration of intracontroller roaming is shown in Figure 10-9.

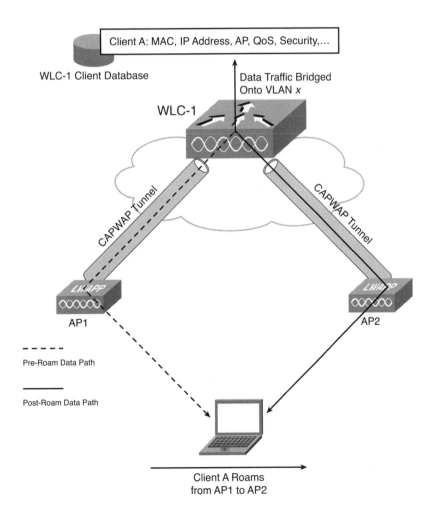

Figure 10-9   *Intracontroller Roaming*

WLAN clients are always reauthenticated by the system in some way on a roam. This process is always necessary to protect against client spoofing. When wireless clients support Pairwise Master Key (PMK) caching, as defined in the 802.11i and Wi-Fi Protected Access version 2 (WPA2) specifications, Cisco Wireless LAN Controllers support full, secure roaming and rekeying without reauthenticating the client with the authentication, authorization, and accounting (AAA) server in the back end. This is true for both Layer 2 and Layer 3 intracontroller and intercontroller roaming. The proactive caching (before the client roaming event) of the PMK that is derived during a client 802.1x or Extensible Authentication Protocol (EAP) authentication at the access point is called Proactive Key Caching (PKC). Although no special client-side software is required to support roaming, PKC requires client-side supplicant support.

Intercontroller Roaming—Layer 2

Intercontroller roaming occurs when a client roams from an access point joined to one WLC to an access point joined to a different WLC. This event can be Layer 2 or a Layer 3 roaming.

Figure 10-10 illustrates an intercontroller Layer 2 roam. A Layer 2 roam occurs when the client traffic is bridged to the same IP subnet provisioned through the LAN interfaces on both WLCs. When the client reassociates to an access point connected to a new WLC, the new WLC exchanges mobility messages with the original WLC and the client database entry is moved to the new WLC. New security context and associations are established if necessary, and the client database entry is updated for the new access point. With Layer 2 intercontroller roaming, an IP address refresh is not needed. This process is transparent to the end user.

Note   Both forms of intercontroller roaming require the controllers to be in the same mobility group. A description of mobility groups is provided later in this section.

Intercontroller Roaming—Layer 3

Layer 3 roaming occurs when the client associates to an access point on a different WLC and the traffic is bridged to a different subnet.

Figure 10-11 illustrates an intercontroller Layer 3 roam.

When the client associates to an access point joined to a new controller, the new controller exchanges mobility messages with the original controller and the client database entry is copied to the new controller. New security context and associations are established if necessary, and the client database entry is updated for the new access point. This process remains invisible to the user. This process occurs whether both controllers are in the same subnet or in different subnets.

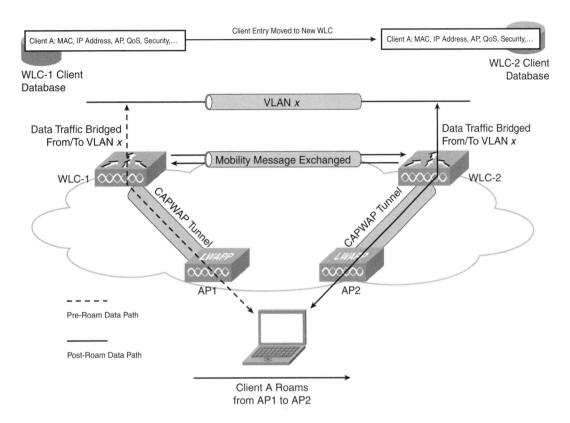

Figure 10-10 *Intercontroller Roaming - Layer 2*

Symmetric roaming is the default mechanism in controller code v5.2 and later. In this mode, traffic received on the foreign controller through AP 2 is first sent back to controller 1, the anchor controller, before being forwarded to the network. Traffic coming from the network for the roaming client is received on the anchor controller before being forwarded through a CAPWAP tunnel to the wireless client. With symmetric roaming, from the wired network perspective, the wireless client never left its initial controller.

Note Although a 2100 Series controller cannot be designated as an anchor for a WLAN when using autoanchor mobility, it can serve as an anchor in symmetric mobility tunneling to process and forward the upstream client data traffic tunneled from the foreign controller.

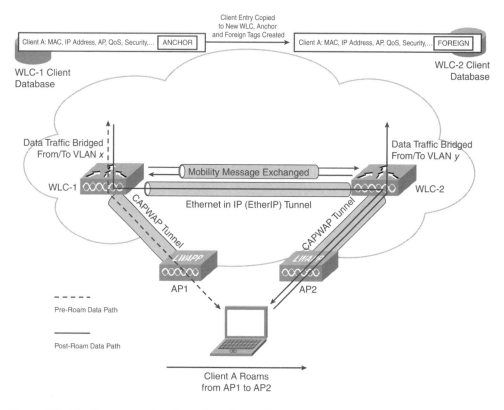

Figure 10-11   *Intercontroller Roaming - Layer 3*

Mobility Groups

A set of WLC devices can be configured as a mobility group. A mobility group allows the deployment of multiple WLC devices in a network and has the devices dynamically share important data among them. The shared information includes context and state of the client device and WLC loading information. With this information, the network can support intercontroller WLAN device roaming, access point load balancing, and controller redundancy. A mobility group also supports forwarding of data traffic through EtherIP tunnels when intercontroller layer 3 roaming occurs.

Each WLC in a mobility group is configured with a list of the other members of the mobility group. Each WLC device builds a neighbor relationship with every other member of the group. When client data is forwarded between members of a mobility group to support Layer 3 roaming, the packets are carried over an EtherIP tunnel.

A mobility group can include up to 24 WLCs. The number of access points supported in a mobility group is bounded by the number of controllers and controller types in the group. For example, a mobility group made up of 24 Cisco 4404-100 Wireless LAN Controller devices will support up to 2400 access points, because each 4404-100 Controller supports up to 100 access points (24 * 100 = 2400 access points). A mobility group made up of 12 4402-25 and 12 4402-50 Wireless LAN Controller devices will support up to 900 access points, because the 4402-25 device supports up to 25 access points and the 4402-50 device supports up to 50 access points (12 * 25 + 12 * 50 = 300 + 600 = 900 access points) and so on. A Cisco Catalyst 6500 Series Wireless Services Module (WiSM) controller module counts as two controllers in a mobility group, so a maximum of 12 Cisco Catalyst 6500 Series WiSM modules can be supported in a single mobility group.

Each controller is configured with a mobility domain name. Two controllers belong to the same mobility group if they are configured with the same mobility domain name. Roaming can occur between these controllers if they are familiar with each other's management interface IP address and MAC address. Two controllers belong to the same mobility list (but not the same mobility group) if they are configured with different mobility domain names and know each other's management interface IP address and built-in MAC address. Controller software release 5.1 and later support up to 72 controllers in a controller's mobility list and seamless roaming across multiple mobility groups. During seamless roaming, the client maintains its IP address across all mobility groups. However, Cisco Centralized Key Management (CCKM) and public key cryptography (PKC) are supported only for intramobility-group roaming. When a client crosses a mobility group boundary during a roam, the client is fully authenticated, but the IP address is maintained, and EtherIP tunneling is initiated for Layer 3 roaming. Typically, WLCs should be placed in the same mobility group when an intercontroller roam is possible. If there is no possibility of a roaming event, it might make sense to not put WLCs in the same mobility group. For example, suppose that two separate WLCs in two buildings have been deployed, with each WLC managing the access points in its building. If the buildings are separated by a large parking area with no RF coverage, a WLAN client is not going to roam from an access point in one building to an access point in the other building. These WLCs do not need to be members of the same mobility group.

As a recommended practice, redundant WLCs should be in the same mobility group. When an access point joins a WLC, it learns the IP addresses of the other WLCs in the mobility group from its joined WLC. These addresses are remembered and used the next time the access point does an LWAPP/CAPWAP discovery.

Mobility Group Requirement Example

IP connectivity between the WLCs should be verified by pinging the WLCs. Care should be taken to verify that each WLC in the mobility group has the same virtual interface IP address. The case-sensitive Mobility Group Name parameter must be the same on all WLCs in the mobility group. For each WLC, the MAC address and IP address parameters for the other WLC devices in the mobility group need to be entered manually. The WLCs need unrestricted access to UDP port 16666 for unencrypted messages and UDP port 16667 for encrypted messages between WLCs through any firewalls or access control lists (ACL).

Note   The UDP ports used for WLC-to-access (CAPWAP) point communications are 5246 (control) and 5247 (data).

Recommended Practices for Supporting Roaming

When designing roaming support in the network, try to minimize intercontroller roaming. When intercontroller roaming is required, follow these guidelines:

- Design the network to support a round-trip time (RTT) of less than 10 ms between controllers.

- Strive to use Layer 2 intercontroller roaming, maintaining traffic on the same subnet for more efficiency.

Because wireless LAN clients are always reauthenticated by the system in some way on a roam, use client-side supplicants that support key caching to speed and secure the roaming process. For example, if a PMK for a given WLAN client is already present at an access point when presented by the associating client, full 802.1x or EAP authentication is not required. Instead, the WLAN client can simply use the WPA four-way handshake process to securely derive a new session encryption key for communication with that access point. The distribution of these cached PMKs to access points is greatly simplified in the unified wireless deployment. The PMK is simply cached in the controller and is available to all access points that connect to that controller. It is also available between all controllers that belong to the mobility group of that controller in advance of a client roaming event.

Cisco Centralized Key Management is an earlier Cisco standard supported by Cisco Compatible Extensions clients to provide fast secure roaming. The principal mechanism for accelerating roaming is the same as PKC—by using a cached PMK—but the implementation is slightly different, and the two mechanisms are not compatible.

PKC or Cisco Centralized Key Management enables WLAN clients to quickly roam between access points. The WLC caches session credentials (security keys) derived for a client session and uses them for reauthentication and rekeying when a client roams within the mobility group. Caching this information rather than forcing the client to do a full authentication reduces the authentication time and the total time required for roaming. This can enhance application transparency because the impact of roaming is reduced and less likely to impact either the application or the user.

Note   Either PKC or Cisco Centralized Key Management should be implemented to assist in seamless Layer 3 roaming.

Client roaming capabilities vary by vendor, driver, and supplicant. The client must match both security (PMK or Cisco Centralized Key Management) and the SSID.

The Cisco Compatible Extensions program for WLAN client devices allows program participants to implement support for all features in a Cisco specification of the latest WLAN standards and Cisco innovations. These products are submitted to an independent lab for rigorous testing. The Cisco Compatible Extensions program ensures the widespread availability of client devices that are interoperable with a Cisco WLAN infrastructure and take advantage of Cisco innovations for enhanced security, mobility, QoS, and network management. The current Cisco Compatible Extensions feature set is Cisco Compatible Extensions version 4.

Controller Redundancy Design

Cisco Wireless LAN Controllers can support either dynamic or deterministic redundancy. With dynamic redundancy, the access point attempts to join the WLC with the greatest availability for access point associations. With deterministic redundancy, the access point attempts to join the WLC that supports deterministic redundancy.

The next attempt is to join a WLC configured as a master controller. This technique is typically used only on the initial access point deployment to a find an initial controller, at which time the access point with its deterministic controllers can be configured.

Finally, the access point join decision algorithm attempts to dynamically choose a WLC based on the greatest availability for access point associations.

Deterministic Controller Redundancy

With deterministic controller redundancy, the network administrator statically configures a primary, secondary, and optionally, a tertiary controller. This configuration can be accomplished statically at each access point level or dynamically at the controller global level. The configuration of primary, secondary, and tertiary WLCs can be performed somewhat laboriously on each access point or with more ease using templates with the Cisco Wireless Control System (WCS).

When an access point determines that its primary controller is unreachable because of missed heartbeat acknowledgments, it attempts to join the secondary controller. If the access point fails to join the secondary controller, it attempts to join the tertiary controller. If the primary, secondary, and tertiary controllers are not available, the access point resorts to the dynamic LWAPP/CAPWAP algorithms to connect to the least-loaded available controller.

Note   Failover to a defined secondary or tertiary controller is more rapid than dynamic failover to the least-loaded controller.

This design supports easier operational management, because the network administrator can deterministically predict the results of an access point reassociation. The network is designed for WLC infrastructure redundancy, and extra capacity on the secondary or tertiary controllers can be provisioned in the event of a catastrophic failure.

The Cisco Wireless LAN Controllers have a configurable parameter for access point fallback. When the AP Fallback option is enabled, access points return to their primary controllers after a failover event when the primary controller comes back online. This feature is enabled by default, and some administrators choose to leave the AP Fallback default value in place.

However, when an access point falls back to its primary controller, there is a brief window of time, usually about 30 seconds, during which service to wireless clients is interrupted because the access points are rejoining the primary WLC. Also, if connectivity to the primary WLC has become unstable for some reason, the access point might end up "flapping" back and forth between the primary and backup WLCs. Many wireless LAN administrators prefer to disable the AP Fallback option and move the access points back to the primary in a controlled manner during a scheduled service window.

Deterministic Controller Redundancy Example

Figure 10-12 illustrates three access points configured with primary, secondary, and tertiary WLCs. If WLC-B fails, its attached access point connects to WLC-C. While WLC-B is down, if WLC-A fails, its access point connects to WLC-C.

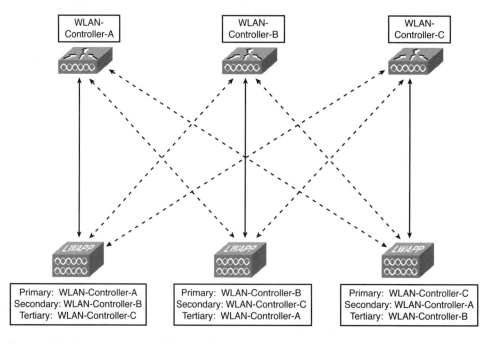

Figure 10-12 *Deterministic Controller Redundancy Example*

Dynamic Controller Redundancy

The LWAPP and CAPWAP protocols allow dynamic redundancy and load balancing. In the controller CAPWAP discovery response, the WLC embeds data on its current access point load (defined as the number of access points joined to it at the time), its access point capacity, and the number of wireless clients connected to the controller. As long as the WLC has the AP Fallback parameter enabled, an access point can decide to change to a less-loaded WLC. Under dynamic load balancing, the access point attempts to join the least-loaded controller, defined as the controller with the greatest available access point capacity.

This dynamic load balancing can be a basis for a dynamic controller redundancy scheme. When an access point misses a heartbeat acknowledgment, and after up to five resent heartbeat messages, the access point releases and renews its IP address and initiates a new WLC hunting and discovery process to find a new controller. This process is how the system supports dynamic WLC redundancy.

This useful algorithm can help dynamically balance the access point load across the mobility group. However, it is important to consider that it could also have some unintended consequences. With dynamic load balancing, the access points can join controllers in any order or sequence. These designs can be perfectly acceptable if there are not many roaming clients. However, if many clients are roaming, there will be many intercontroller roaming events that can have a potential impact on aggregate network performance.

The traffic patterns from wireless clients will be unpredictable. They can make it difficult to implement stateful security mechanisms in the infrastructure and take advantage of some other security features in Cisco switches.

If the access points are enabled sequentially with dynamic redundancy, the network can develop a salt-and-pepper access point design, where adjacent access points are joined to different controllers. This also will lead to many intercontroller roaming events that can have a potential impact on aggregate network performance.

Because of some of these characteristics of dynamic load balancing and redundancy, as a recommended practice, most customers choose to override the dynamic behavior of CAPWAP by assigning access points to specific controllers to balance the load, assigning access points a primary, secondary, and possibly, tertiary controller. This process causes WLC redundancy behavior to be deterministic. Furthermore, when an access point has a primary, secondary, and optionally, tertiary WLC configured, access point failover occurs more quickly.

Dynamic Controller Redundancy Example

Figure 10-13 illustrates the salt-and-pepper access point design concept. Every odd-numbered access point is joined to WLC1, and every even-numbered access point is joined to WLC2. In theory, this design provides dynamic traffic load balancing across WLCs and coverage redundancy in the event of a WLC failure.

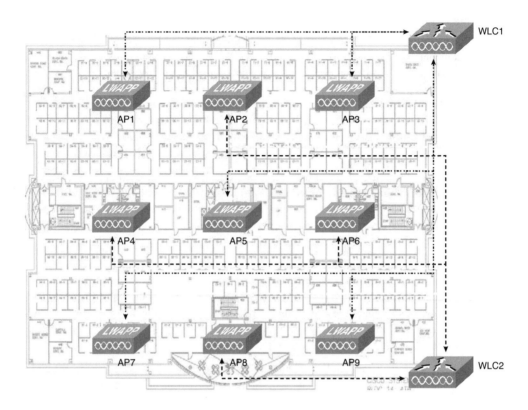

Figure 10-13 *Dynamic Controller Redundancy Example*

In actual practice, salt-and-pepper designs can result in a large number of intercontroller roaming events and so are not widely recommended or deployed. Equivalent performance and resiliency can be obtained without a salt-and-pepper design.

> **Note**   Link aggregation (LAG) can support both access port scaling and controller redundancy. For access point scaling to support more than 48 access points per physical WLC port, it is recommended that LAG be used rather than multiple AP manager interfaces. For controller redundancy, it is recommended that deterministic controller redundancy with predefined primary, secondary, and tertiary controllers be used rather than dynamic controller redundancy supported by LAG.

N + 1 Redundancy Design

In the N + 1 redundancy configuration, one controller backs up N controller. This is illustrated in Figure 10-14. In this configuration, the redundant controller is placed in a network operations center (NOC) or data center and acts a backup for multiple WLCs. Each access point is configured with a WLC as primary, and all access points point to the single redundant controller as secondary.

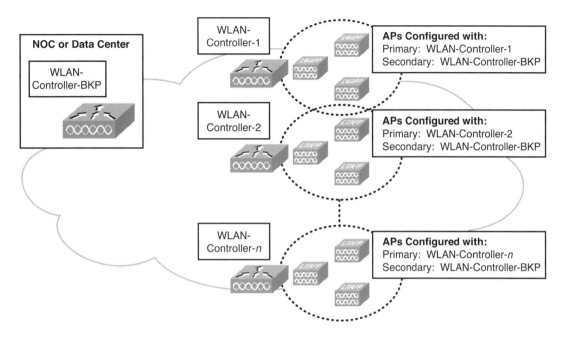

Figure 10-14 *N+1 Redundancy Example*

One issue with this design is that the redundant controller could become oversubscribed with access points in the unlikely event of multiple primary WLC failures. When a WLC has reached the maximum number of joined access points, it does not accept any more LWAPP or CAPWAP join requests. When the backup WLC becomes oversubscribed, some access points might be without a WLC. When designing an N + 1 redundant solution, the risks of multiple WLC failures and the consequences of an oversubscribed backup WLC should be assessed.

N + N Redundancy Design

In the N + N redundancy configuration, N controllers back up N controllers. For example, in Figure 10-15, there are two controllers. Some of the access points are configured with controller A as primary and controller B as secondary. The other access points are configured to use controller B as primary and controller A as secondary.

In this design, try to load-balance the access point capacity across both controllers. But also try to logically group access points on controllers to minimize intercontroller roaming events. For example, if supporting a four-floor building with two redundant controllers, the access points on floors 1 and 2 can be configured to use one controller as primary and the access points on floors 3 and 4 to use the other controller as primary.

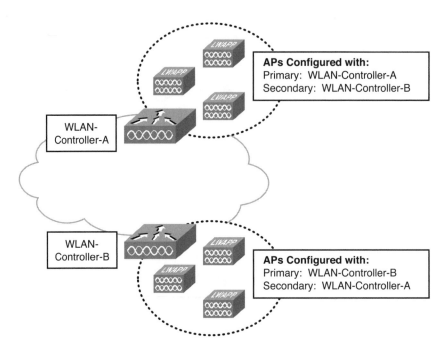

Figure 10-15   *N+N Redundancy Example*

> **Note**   There should be enough excess capacity on each controller to manage a failover situation.

N + N + 1 Redundancy Design

In the N + N + 1 redundancy configuration, N controllers back up N controllers as secondary, and one controller backs up all N controllers as tertiary.

For example, in Figure 10-16, some of the access points are configured with controller A as primary and controller B as secondary. Some of the access points are configured with controller B as primary and controller A as secondary. All the access points are configured to use the same backup controller as tertiary. Typically, the primary and secondary controllers are placed at the network distribution level, and the single tertiary controller is placed in an NOC or data center. Multiple distribution blocks can be configured with the same tertiary controller.

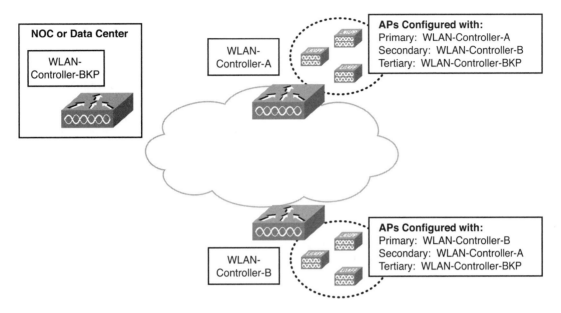

Figure 10-16 *N+N+1 Redundancy Example*

When selecting a redundancy option, the risks of WLC failure and the service-level agreement (SLA) required to be maintained by the WLAN should be considered. The design solution should provide a more robust redundancy scheme for a higher SLA.

Radio Resource Management (RRM) and RF Groups

Access point capacity is impacted by the application. For example, a recommended practice is for an access point to support roughly seven to eight Voice over WLAN (VoWLAN) calls, depending on the codec, or about 20 data devices, because all clients must share the available bandwidth. The most common response to strained network capacity is to add more access points. However, wireless is a fixed resource, because there are only three channels that can be used without causing interference between access points as part of the 802.11b/g standards. To minimize cochannel interference, channels 1, 6, and 11 are usually the only ones utilized in medium- and high-density enterprise deployments. Adding more 802.11b/g access points using only three channels with too much RF power can actually increase RF performance problems as opposed to correcting them. This situation can be somewhat improved by managing 802.11b/g RF power or using 802.11a, which provides significantly more channels than 802.11b/g because it propagates over a shorter distance. Some enterprise designs reserve 802.11a for VoWLAN support.

The user experience in a wireless network is dependent on radio propagation and other building characteristics affecting connection speeds and error rates. The RF environment is transient. An office looks dramatically different at 10 a.m., when hundreds of people are walking around contending for network resources, than at 3 a.m., when doors are closed, no people are present, and neighboring offices are not generating RF interference. Wireless and RF propagation issues directly affect the QoS delivered to users.

Cisco RRM allows the Cisco Unified Wireless Network architecture to continuously analyze the existing RF environments. Also, it automatically adjusts the access point power and channel configurations to help mitigate cochannel interference, signal coverage problems, and so on. RRM also reduces the need to perform exhaustive site surveys, increases system capacity, and provides automated self-healing functionality to compensate for RF dead zones and access point failures.

Real-time RF management is a foundation of the Cisco lightweight wireless solution. The Cisco Wireless LAN Controllers use dynamic RRM algorithms to create an environment that is completely self-configuring, self-optimizing, and self-healing. This makes Cisco WLANs ideal for the delivery of secure and reliable business applications.

RRM information is exchanged between access points and the controller they are associated to, and between controllers that are a part of the same RF group. An RF group is a subset of a mobility group. Mobility groups and mobility group members are configured first; then each controller is assigned an RF group name. The controllers that belong to the same RF group within one mobility group exchange information about the RF environment. Up to 20 controllers can belong to the same RF group.

When designing the wireless network, only those controllers that have access points in range of one another and need to coordinate their effort to improve the RF coverage should be put in the same RF group. For example, two controllers with access points in different buildings do not have a reason to belong to the same RF group. Two controllers with access points on the same open-space floor should probably belong to the same RF group and exchange information about the RF environment they share.

The RRM algorithm works to offer an optimal coverage. Optimal is understood as a uniform coverage with smooth transition from one access point cell to the next. For this purpose, one function of the RRM algorithm is to reduce the AP power level if it is too high. An ideal target is that each access point detects its neighbor's signal at a level of –70 dBm. Each access point needs to detect at least three neighbors for this algorithm to be triggered. If the neighboring access point signal is too high, interferences can occur and the controller will try to lower some of the access points' power level. The controller can also change the access point channel (operating frequency) to avoid RF interferences.

If several clients are detected below a configurable signal level, the controller can detect whether these clients are leaving the coverage area and increase the access point power level to dynamically adapt and maintain coverage for these clients.

RF Grouping

An RF group is another critical deployment concept. As illustrated in Figure 10-17, it is a cluster of WLC devices that coordinate their dynamic RRM calculations on a per-802.11 physical layer (PHY) type. An RF group exists for each 802.11 PHY type. Clustering

WLCs into RF groups allows the dynamic RRM algorithms to scale beyond a single WLC and span building floors, buildings, and even campuses. RF groups are formed with the following process:

1. Lightweight access points periodically send out neighbor messages over the air. The message includes an encrypted shared secret that is configured on the WLC and pushed to each access point.

2. Access points sharing the same secret are able to validate messages from each other. When access points on different WLCs hear validated neighbor messages at a signal strength of –80 dBm or stronger, the controllers dynamically form an RF group.

3. The members or controllers of an RF group elect an RF group leader to maintain a "master" power and channel scheme for the RF group. The RF group leader analyzes real-time radio data collected by the system and calculates the master power and channel plan.

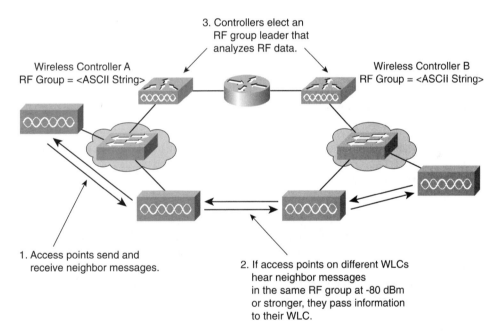

Figure 10-17 *RF Grouping*

The RF group leader and members exchange RRM messages at a specified updated interval, which is 600 seconds by default. Between update intervals, the RF group leader sends keepalive messages to each of the RF group members and collects real-time RF data. These messages use UDP port 12214 for 802.11b/g and UDP port 12115 for 802.11a. Verify that these ports are not restricted by firewalls or filters between RF group members.

On controller software code 7.0 and later, new access points are available (Cisco 3500 Series) that can detect non-802.11 interferences. The controllers can detect those interferences and trigger the RRM algorithm based on their detection. This process is called Event-Driven Radio Resource Management (ED-RRM) and is part of the general CleanAir family of features.

One limitation of this design is that only the new Cisco 3500 Series Access Points, deployed in a uniform fashion, can participate in non-802.11 interference detection, location, and mitigation. The consequence is that there are two possibilities when designing wireless networks:

■ If the network already contains access points, some Cisco 3500 Series Access Points can be added, to be able to detect interferences and get alarms and reports. The network will not be able to react to those interferences. The administrator will have to manually apply remedies by changing the AP channels in the affected areas.

■ Design greenfield coverage with only Cisco 3500 Series Access Points and controller code 7.0 or later. In that configuration, the ED_RRM will be fully operational, and the network will automatically react to non-802.11 interferences to dynamically change the affected AP's channels and report the issue and its mitigation.

Access Point Self-Healing

With access point self-healing, the WLC uses RRM to raise the power levels and adjust the channel selection of neighbor access points to compensate for lost coverage of a failed access point.

An in-depth discussion of the mechanics of RF self-healing is beyond the scope of this book. However, an access point is determined to be lost when the neighbor access points no longer see RF neighbor messages at –70 dBm from the access point. Lost neighbor access points are reported to the WLC. RRM is used to automatically increase power on surrounding access points to fill the gap created by the loss in coverage.

It is important to note that the system must be designed and installed with greater access point density to support self-healing capabilities. Specifically, access points must be placed so that the system has at least one power level available to step up if RF self-healing is triggered. It is also important to note that access point self-healing works only for access points configured to be in the same RF group.

Designing Wireless Networks Using Controllers

The following sections review designing wireless networks with controllers.

RF Site Survey

An RF site survey is the first step in the design and deployment of a wireless network and the most important step to ensure desired operation. A site survey is a process where a surveyor studies the facility to determine the RF characteristics in the environment. The surveyor plans and reviews RF coverage areas, checks for RF interference, and determines the appropriate placement of wireless infrastructure devices.

In a wireless network, many issues can arise that prevent the RF signal from reaching all parts of the facility. Examples of RF issues include multipath distortion, hidden node problems, and near and far issues. To address these issues, the regions where the issues occur need to be located. A site survey assists in defining the contours of RF coverage in a particular facility. It helps discover regions where multipath distortion can occur and areas where RF interference is high. It helps find solutions to eliminate such issues. The Cisco Wireless Control System (WCS) can detect RF interference and optimize around it. However, it cannot analyze the RF interference to provide the information necessary to identify and locate the source. A spectrum analysis tool such as Cognio Spectrum Expert can provide analysis to classify the interference, determine the impact of the interference on the Wi-Fi network, and enable the administrator to physically locate the source of interference and take action.

A site survey that determines the RF coverage area in a facility also helps in choosing the number of wireless infrastructure devices as well as the deployment locations that an organization needs to meet its business requirements.

The customer wireless requirements should be defined as part of the site survey. Access points should be placed to support the locations and numbers of wireless LAN (WLAN) clients.

RF Site Survey Process

The typical steps in an RF site survey are as follows:

Step 1. Define customer requirements in terms of devices to support, sites where wireless devices will be located, and service levels expected. Peak requirements such as support for conference rooms should also be defined.

Step 2. Obtain a facility diagram to identify the potential RF obstacles. Based on the customer requirements, identify planned wireless coverage areas.

Step 3. Visually inspect the facility to look for potential barriers to the propagation of RF signals, such as metal racks, elevator shafts, and stairwells.

Step 4. Identify user areas that can be intensively used, such as conference rooms, and areas that are not used as heavily, such as stairwells.

Step 5. Determine preliminary access point locations. These locations include the power and wired network access, cell coverage and overlap, channel selection, and mounting locations and antenna.

Step 6. Perform the actual surveying to verify the access point location. Make sure to use the same access point model for the survey that is in use or that will be used in production. While the survey is being performed, relocate access points as needed and retest.

Step 7.   Document the findings. Record the locations and log signal readings as well as data rates at outer boundaries.

Defining the Customer Requirements

As part of the site survey, the customer requirements need to be identified. As part of defining the customer requirements, these questions should be asked:

1. What type and number of devices need to be supported wirelessly?

    a. Is there current WLAN or RF equipment in place? Existing WLAN equipment will need to be integrated, and the impacts of existing RF devices should be mitigated.

    b. Will the WLAN be used only for data, or will wireless phones also be supported? If wireless phones are being used, the wireless network needs to be built with better receive signal strength for quality of service (QoS).

    c. Are there peak periods to support? Use of wireless services in a conference room will peak during meetings.

2. Will users be stationary or on the move while using the WLAN? If users are mobile, high-quality hand-off during client roaming is a requirement.

3. Where should wireless coverage be supported? How many buildings, floors, and areas should be supported? Are outdoor bridged links needed?

4. What level of support should be provided? What level of redundancy and self-healing is needed in the wireless infrastructure?

These questions are important to define the scope of the wireless infrastructure design.

Identifying Coverage Areas and User Density

The next step in the RF site survey is identifying planned coverage areas on the facility diagram. An illustration of this is shown in Figure 10-18.

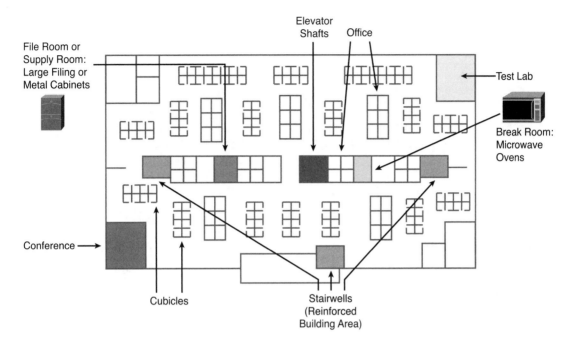

Figure 10-18   *Identifying Coverage Areas*

Part of the site survey report should include a floor plan, showing coverage areas, as well as marking areas that the customer has defined as no-coverage areas. This information provides the customer, the installer, and a troubleshooter with some indication of what coverage each access point should be providing. The expected density of wireless devices should be identified, which might be one or two per office and 20 or more per conference room. As a general principle, an access point can support seven to eight wireless phones or about 20 data-only devices.

The facility should be visually inspected to look for potential issues, such as elevator shafts, stairwells, and microwave equipment.

Determine Preliminary Access Point Locations

The next step in the RF site survey is identifying preliminary access point locations based on the planned coverage area and user density. An example is shown in Figure 10-19.

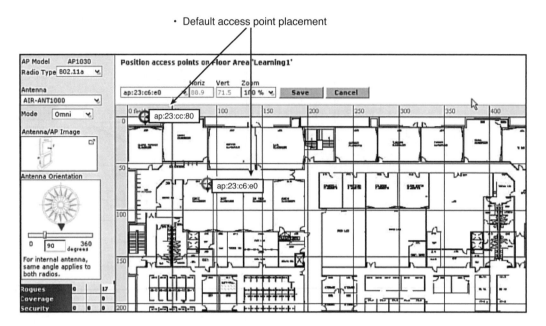

Figure 10-19   *Determining Preliminary Access Point Locations*

This process can be supported with several tools. For example, the Cisco Wireless Control System (WCS) can import real floor plans. RF characteristics can be assigned to building components to increase design accuracy. Cisco WCS has a planning mode feature that uses this map to estimate how many access points are needed for a given floor in a building. The planning mode feature takes into account the following when predicting range and coverage:

- Protocol 802.11b/g, 802.11a, or 802.11n

- Coverage or capacity

- Throughput

- Square feet

> **Note**   After implementation, the Cisco Unified Wireless Network has the ability to adjust power and channels so that access points create the least amount of interference with each other.

Cisco WCS can be used as a starting point to estimate the number and preliminary locations of access points at the start of a site survey. This approach is most successful in simple carpeted office environments that are less RF challenging than other environments, such as warehouses.

Cisco WCS also provides an integrated RF prediction tool that can be used to visualize the detailed WLAN design, including lightweight access point placement, configuration, and performance and coverage estimates. Graphical heat maps help IT staff visualize anticipated WLAN behavior for easier planning and faster rollout. This is shown in Figure 10-20.

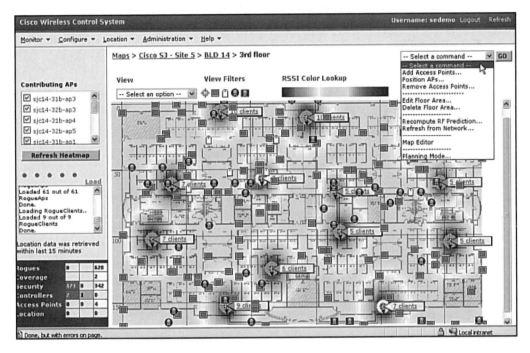

Figure 10-20   *Visualizing RF Coverage*

Note   The accuracy of this heat map greatly depends on the effort made to adjust RF loss characteristics of the building components such as walls, solid doors, and stairways.

Perform the Actual Survey

The next step in the RF site survey process is to conduct the actual survey to determine coverage based on the planned access point locations. To establish the coverage characteristics of an enterprise office site, several measurements are required:

■   Measure the radius of the coverage range for a given data rate.

■   Move the client from the corner to the edge of coverage and check the data rate.

■   Determine the coverage range behind stairwells, offices, supply rooms, cubicles, and so on.

- With as many access points as available, build the planned wireless coverage.

- Establish nonoverlapping channels as often as possible to reduce contention.

- Repeat this process until all the required coverage areas are set up.

A tool such as AirMagnet Survey Pro can be utilized. It performs a manual site survey per access point or access points and receiving results on these measures:

- Signal strength

- Noise level

- Signal-to-noise ratio

- Channel interference

- Data rate

- Retry rate

- Loss rate

The mapping tools in Survey Pro can provide effective surveys if enough data points are taken.

An available free tool is the Cisco Aironet Site Survey Utility. This tool is designed for the Cisco 802.11a/b/g/n client cards. The following information is provided by the tool:

- Access point IP and MAC address

- Channel

- Signal strength

- Noise level

- Signal-to-noise ratio

- Link speed

Peak coverage holes are areas where clients cannot receive a signal from the wireless network. When deploying wireless networks, there is a trade-off between the cost of the initial network deployment and the percentage of coverage hole areas. A reasonable coverage criterion for launch is between 2 and 10 percent coverage holes. This means that between 2 and 10 test locations out of 100 random test locations might receive marginal service. After launch, Cisco Radio Resource Management will identify these coverage hole areas and report them to the network manager. This allows the network manager to fill holes based on user demand.

Documenting the Findings

After the manual survey is completed, the final step in the process is to document the findings. A proper site survey provides detailed information that includes the following:

- Customer requirements

- Coverage

- Interference sources

- Equipment placement

- Power considerations

- Wiring requirements

The site survey documentation serves as a guide for the wireless network design and for the installation and verification of the wireless communications infrastructure.

The site survey report should also contain a list of the parts that will be needed. This list should include the following:

- The total number of access points for the installation and a recommendation for a spare to be kept on hand in case of emergency

- The total number and type of antennas and mounting solutions that are required

- The network components that have been proposed

The site survey should include diagrams representing the facility, access point locations, and proposed cable runs. Whenever possible, include photographs of the planned access point location or proposed antenna installation to make it very clear how and where the equipment should be installed.

With the introduction of voice to a predominantly wireless data network, the methodology of site surveys needs to be altered. For example, wireless data is less susceptible to disruption than wireless voice when it comes to cell overlap, RF noise, and packet delay. Surveying for wireless voice coverage requires more effort and time than for data-only coverage at the same site. A voice survey requires planning coverage plus planning capacity.

Note Further discussion of site surveys to support voice over WLAN (VoWLAN) is beyond the scope of this book. Additional information is available in Design Principles for Voice over WLAN, at www.cisco.com/en/US/solutions/collateral/ns340/ns394/ns348/net_implementation_white_paper0900aecd804f1a46.html.

Design Considerations for Campus Wireless Networks

The basis of the Cisco Unified Wireless Network is client devices connected to Cisco lightweight access points connected to Cisco Wireless LAN Controllers.

To develop a design, several questions need to be answered:

1. How many access points are needed?

   Sufficient access points need to be available to provide RF coverage and the features required to support the needs of the wireless clients. Different access points have different features, including internal or external antenna, single or dual radios, and devices supported. In the optimal case, more access points than required by the client density requirements (overdeployment) would be deployed to ensure seamless coverage and higher capacity. The Cisco WLAN can compensate for RF overlap. A couple of extra access points can be used to cover unforeseen coverage holes or as spares.

2. Where should the access points be placed?

   The access points should be placed where WLAN clients will be located. Access points should be placed in central locations that can cover several walled offices or cubicle areas. Access points are typically not as effective when deployed in a wiring closet as when placed close to users. An access point deployed in a meeting room can support peak wireless requirements during a meeting better than an access point in an adjacent hallway that might also be used for day-to-day office requirements.

3. How will the access points receive power?

   Power over Ethernet (PoE) is a typical deployment choice to minimize power cabling requirements for access points, especially those mounted on the ceiling. Traditional power sources can be used as well.

4. How many WLCs will be needed?

   The number of access points that a controller can support varies depending on the selected controller. Enough controllers should be provisioned to support the access points and provide high availability through redundancy based on the reliability requirements of the location. Higher redundancy is needed for mission-critical applications and Voice over WLAN (VoWLAN).

5. Where should the WLCs be placed?

   WLCs should be placed in secure areas such as a wiring closet or data center. Placing WLCs in multiple wiring closets helps with reliability in the event of a power loss to one wiring closet.

CAPWAP Access Point Feature Summary

Table 10-1 illustrates a summary of CAPWAP access point features.

Table 10-1   *CAPWAP Indoor Access Point Features*

	AP 1130	AP 1140	AP 3500i	AP 1240	AP 12050	1260	3500e
Integrated CleanAir	No	No	Yes	No	No	No	Yes
Data Uplink (Mbps)	10/100	10/100/1000	10/100/000	10/100	10/100/1000	10/100/1000	10/100/1000
Power Requirement	802.3af	802.3af	802.3af	802.3af	E-PoE 802.3af	802.3af	802.3af
Installation	Carpeted	Carpeted	Carpeted	Rugged	Rugged	Rugged	Rugged
Temp. Range	0 to +40°C	0 to +40°C	0 to +40°C	–20 to +55°C	–20 to +55°C	–20 to +55°C	–20 to +55°C
Antennas	Internal	Internal	Internal	External	External	External	External
Wi-Fi Standards	a/b/g	a/b/g/n	a/b/g/n	a/b/g	a/b/g/n	a/b/g/n	a/b/g/n
DRAM, MB	32	128	128	32	64	128	128
Flash, MB	16	32	32	16	32	32	32

Controller Placement Design

Controllers in the enterprise campus can be administered in the distribution layer or centralized in the core layer. As much as possible, controllers should be placed to minimize intercontroller roaming and latency of traffic flow over the wireless media.

LWAPP/CAPWAP tunneling separates the physical controller placement from the subnets, so the WLCs can be positioned where they are connected, secured, and powered and where traffic flows work well. Controllers should be deployed using deterministic redundancy to avoid unnecessary intercontroller roaming that can result from salt-and-pepper designs.

Distributed controller deployment can work well with existing networks or focused wireless coverage areas.

The general recommendation is to use a centralized design for controller placement to minimize operational complexity and support. Centralize controllers to potential roaming sites. For example, if one site has two buildings between a possible roaming area, centralize all the controllers for that site in the same physical location. If the same location has a third building, but if no roaming is expected between this third building and the first two, the controllers for the third building do not need to be at the same location as the controllers for the first two buildings.

The controller centralization occurs at a site level. If using regional deployments, the controllers at the collapsed core can also be centralized. If the existing design uses a distributed model, growth can be obtained with a hybrid deployment, keeping the existing distributed controllers and centralizing the new, additional controllers.

Centralized WLC Placement Example

Figure 10-21 illustrates a centralized WLC design with the placement of access points in the access layer and WLCs in a service block in the core layer.

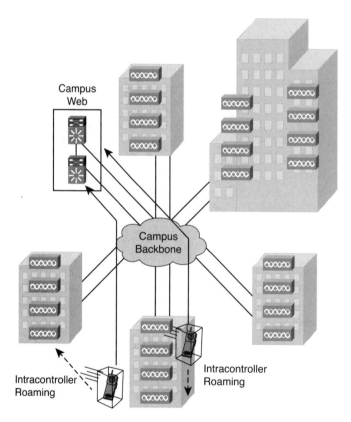

Figure 10-21 *Centralized WLC Design Example*

The centralized WLC design supports simplified management with fewer endpoints and fewer locations to manage issues such as high availability, routing, and power requirements. Centralized WLC design also supports the most efficient mobility.

Distributed WLC Design Example

Figure 10-22 illustrates a distributed WLC design with the placement of access points in the access layer and WLCs in the distribution layer.

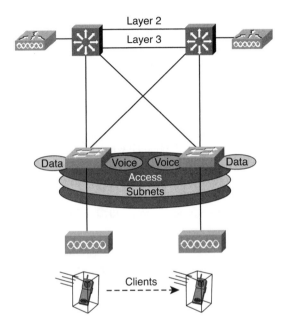

Figure 10-22 *Distributed WLC Design Example*

The distributed WLC design can easily support coverage areas isolated by construction where mobility between buildings is not implemented.

Campus Cisco Wireless LAN Controller Options

Depending on the size of the campus and whether integration with Layer 3 infrastructure devices is desired, one of two categories of WLCs is typically deployed.

Appliance controllers from the Cisco 4400 Series can be used to support from 6 to 100 access points. These controllers can support from 40 to 2000 wireless devices, depending on the mix of data and voice clients. Layer 3 routing is supported on another platform. The Cisco 4400 Series connects to the enterprise network using an 802.1Q trunk.

Appliance controllers from the Cisco 5500 Series can be used to support up to 500 access points and 7000 clients. It is a highly scalable and flexible platform that enables system-wide services for mission-critical wireless in medium- to large-sized enterprises and campus environments. Designed for 802.11n performance and maximum scalability, the 5500 Series offers enhanced uptime with RF visibility and protection, the ability to simultaneously manage up to 500 access points, superior performance for reliable stream-ing video and toll-quality voice, and improved fault recovery for a consistent mobility experience in the most demanding environments.

Controllers integrated in Layer 3 devices, such as the Cisco Catalyst 3750G Integrated Wireless LAN Controller or the Cisco Catalyst 6500 Series WiSM, support from 25 to 300 access points. In this case, Layer 3 routing can be supported on the same platform. The integrated controllers support Layer 2 connections internally and can use Layer 2 or Layer 3 connections to the wired enterprise network.

Design Considerations for Branch Wireless Networks

There are several key design considerations for branch networks. The number of access points that are required to support the branch wireless clients must be defined. The ports must be available on the local switch to support the connection between the access points and the wired network. Power must also be provided to the access points, either through Power over Ethernet (PoE) or traditional power cabling. Controller cost is likely a consideration as well. It might not be economically feasible for small sites to implement local controllers.

Sufficient bandwidth to support wireless traffic to corporate resources must be available. If the decision to use a centralized controller to support branch office access points is made, the latency between the access point and the WLC should not exceed 300 ms round-trip time (RTT). If using centralized controllers, only H-REAP access points should be used.

Connecting lightweight access points to a WLC over a WAN is not recommended unless the AP is set to H-REAP mode.

Hybrid REAP

Hybrid Remote Edge Access Point (H-REAP) is another option for branch office and remote office deployments. H-REAP enables customers to configure and control a few access points in a branch or remote office from the corporate office through a WAN link without deploying a controller in each office. The H-REAP access points can switch client data traffic and perform client authentication locally when their connection to the controller is lost. When they are connected to the controller, they can also send traffic back to the controller.

H-REAP operates in two modes:

- **Standalone mode:** When the controller is not reachable by H-REAP, the device goes into the standalone state and performs client authentication by itself. In standalone mode, H-REAP supports WPA-PSK and WPA2-PSK for client authentication.

- **Connected mode:** When H-REAP can reach the controller, so that it is in a connected state, H-REAP gets help from the controller to complete client authentication. In con-nected mode, H-REAP supports WPA-PSK, WPA2-PSK, Virtual Private Networks

(VPN), Layer 2 Tunneling Protocol (L2TP), Extensible Authentication Protocol (EAP), and web authentication for client authentication.

H-REAP is delay-sensitive. Round-trip latency must not exceed 300 ms between the access point and the controller. CAPWAP control packets must be prioritized over all other traffic.

Note   Controller code changed the RTT value for the H-REAP from 100 ms to 300 ms.

H-REAP is supported on all the CAPWAP controllers but only on the Cisco Aironet 1130 AG, 1140, 1240 AG, and 1250 Series Access Points.

H-REAP Deployment Example

Figure 10-23 illustrates a typical H-REAP deployment. H-REAP access points should be connected using trunk points to support switched VLANs.

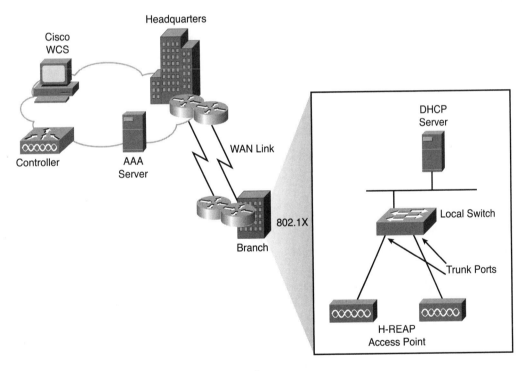

Figure 10-23   *H-REAP Deployment Example*

Note   To better organize and manage the hybrid-REAP access points, hybrid-REAP groups can be created and specific access points can be assigned to them. Per controller, up to 20 hybrid-REAP groups with up to 25 access points per group can be configured.

Branch Office Cisco Wireless LAN Controller Options

Depending on the size of the branch and whether integration with Layer 3 infrastructure devices is desired, one of two categories of WLCs is typically deployed.

Appliance controllers, such as the Cisco 2100 Series, the Cisco 4400 Series, and the Cisco 5500 Series, are often used to support up to 25 access points for the Cisco 2100 Series, up to 100 access points for the Cisco 4400 Series, and up to 500 access points for the Cisco 5500 Series. These controllers typically support up to 7000 wireless devices, depending on the mix of data and voice clients.

Controllers integrated in Layer 3 devices, such as the Cisco Wireless Controller Module for Integrated Services Routers (ISR) or the Cisco Catalyst 3750G Integrated Wireless LAN Controller, also support up to 25 access points.

For remote teleworkers, more than one controller per location might need to be deployed. A secure (VPN-based) connection to the corporate office might need to be provided, and at the same time offer wireless coverage with the corporate SSID at the remote location. All the remote access points can be controlled from one single interface.

The Cisco OfficeExtend is a secure, simple, and cost-effective solution that extends the corporate wireless network to remote sites. It provides mobile connectivity to workers at temporary workspaces or locations outside of the traditional corporate office, including teleworkers, full- and part-time home office workers, and mobile contractors. The OfficeExtend access point plugs into a router that provides an Internet connection. It establishes a secure tunnel to the corporate network so that remote employees can access data, voice, video, and applications for a mobility experience consistent with that at the corporate office. An illustration of OfficeExtend is shown in Figure 10-24.

The OfficeExtend consists of remote site and corporate office components. The components at the remote site are

- A router with an Internet connection

- Cisco Aironet 1140 Series or Cisco Aironet 1130AG Series Access Point

- Cisco Unified Wireless IP Phone (optional)

The corporate office components are

- Cisco 5500 Series Wireless LAN Controller

- Cisco Wireless Control System

- Cisco Secure Access Control Server

The same services that are available on the wireless network at the corporate office can be securely accessed on the OfficeExtend solution at a remote location. Data, voice, and video as well as applications such as Cisco Unified MeetingPlace conferencing, Cisco WebEx technology, and dual-mode phones are all supported by the OfficeExtend solution. For the initial setup at a home office, the remote worker plugs the access point into the router. The OfficeExtend access point is provisioned in advance by a network administrator using the Cisco Wireless Control System (WCS). It will automatically set up a secure tunnel to the corporate headquarters with the Cisco 5500 Series Wireless Controller. A preregistered corporate IP phone will also automatically connect with the Cisco Unified Communications Manager to access the corporate phone number, voicemail, and user settings.

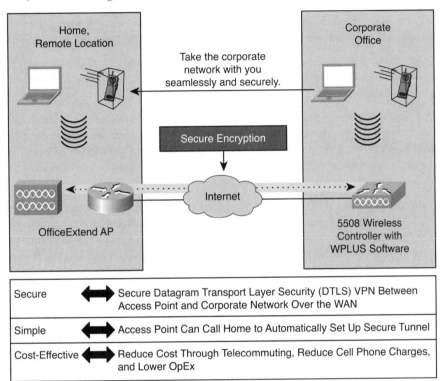

Figure 10-24 *OfficeExtend Example*

The OfficeExtend solution establishes a secure Datagram Transport Layer Security (DTLS) connection between the access point and the controller. The solution also offers the following:

■ Remote WLAN connectivity using the same profile as at the corporate office.

■ Voice service using a Cisco Unified Wireless IP Phone and any voice-over-Wi-Fi phone. The voice services also support Call Aware functionality (the ability to track call statistics).

■ A personal Service Set Identifier (SSID), in addition to the corporate SSID, allow noncorporate devices to access the Internet.

■ Support for M-Drive technology to help ensure wireless quality of service (QoS) and reliable connections.

Design Considerations for Guest Services in Wireless Networks

Providing guest services over a wired network to traditional autonomous access points can pose significant challenges. To maintain internal corporate network security, guest traffic must be restricted to the appropriate subnet and VLAN. These guest VLANs must extend throughout the infrastructure to reach every location where guest access is required in addition to regular employee VLANs. Reconfiguration of the access switches that serve conference rooms, offices, and cubicles where the network is needed can involve many network staff hours to selectively adjust VLANs for guest access.

The Cisco Unified Wireless Network supports simplified configuration and deployment of guest access for customers, vendors, and partners through deployment of lightweight access points.

In a basic scenario, the guest access solution segregates internal user traffic from guest user traffic with VLANs using WLCs to centralize configuration and management of the access points. With this architecture, VLAN and subnet configuration must occur only at the access switch that the controller is connected to. This results in a dramatic reduction in time for reconfiguration of the network.

If the guest network SSID is the only broadcast, unauthorized users might make fewer attempts to access the internal, private WLANs. To increase security, the Cisco Unified Wireless Network ensures that all clients gain access within a certain number of attempts as set by the administrator. If a client fails to gain access within that limit, it is automatically excluded (blocked from access) until the administrator-set timer expires.

However, traffic isolation is provided by VLANs only up to the switch where the controller is connected. For many enterprises, guest traffic isolation through a VLAN might not provide a sufficient level of security.

In this case, the Cisco Unified Wireless Network can provide path isolation using a Layer 2 tunnel to direct all guest traffic to a controller dedicated to guest services in a demilitarized zone (DMZ). The DMZ is a secured network zone between the private (inside) network and a public (outside) network. Guest users can be tunneled to a guest wireless LAN controller (WLC), which then applies the appropriate policies before Internet access is granted. Corporate wireless use policies are managed by the WLCs internal to the enterprise.

Path isolation allows the guest traffic to be separated and differentiated from the corporate internal traffic. It also allows the guest traffic be securely transported across the internal network infrastructure.

Design Considerations for Outdoor Wireless Networks

Traditional outdoor deployment options include point-to-point bridging between buildings and point-to-multipoint bridging between buildings. These are both illustrated in Figure 10-25.

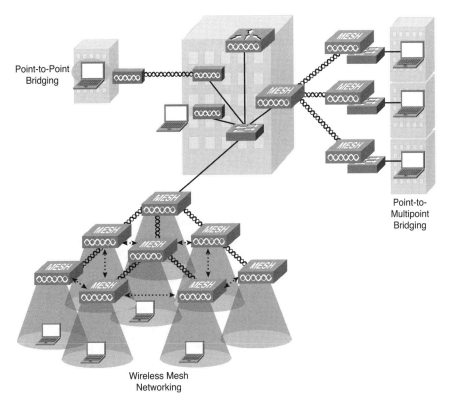

Figure 10-25 *Outdoor Wireless Deployment Options*

Outdoor mesh is a new model, where the access points are connected in a mesh with many redundant connections between nodes. Mesh access points discover each other automatically and select the best path in the mesh for maximizing system capacity and minimizing latency. Access points continuously communicate with other nodes in the mesh, evaluating the potential of each link to improve performance. If a link is degraded, the access point determines whether a better path exists and routes traffic through a more optimal node. A mesh network eliminates the need to wire every access point in the network, making it easier and more cost-effective to extend the reach of the network. The Cisco Wireless Mesh Networking Solution also makes it easy to connect an existing indoor wired or wireless network with the outdoor mesh network. It allows users to roam from one area to another without reconnecting. Perhaps more importantly, administrators can set up one access policy that works across all environments, increasing security and making the system-wide network infrastructure more manageable.

Wireless Mesh Components

The outdoor mesh solution extends the existing Cisco Unified Wireless Network architecture. The CAPWAP-enabled Cisco Mesh Networking Solution enables two or more indoor or outdoor Cisco CAPWAP-enabled mesh access points to communicate with each other over one or more wireless hops to join multiple LANs or to extend IEEE 802.11b/g wireless coverage. Cisco CAPWAP-enabled mesh access points are configured, monitored, and operated from and through any Cisco Wireless LAN Controller deployed in the Cisco Mesh Networking Solution.

The wireless mesh solution is based on the Cisco Unified Wireless Network. That solution consists of several components:

- **Cisco Wireless Control System (WCS):** This easy-to-use and intuitive software for wireless mesh management enables network-wide policy configuration and device management. Cisco WCS provides the overall view of the wireless mesh. Cisco WCS supports Simple Network Management Protocol (SNMP) and syslog.

- **Cisco Wireless LAN Controllers:** The Cisco Wireless LAN Controllers manage multiple access points, mitigate radio interference between access points, manage security, and provide Layer 3 mobility.

- **Root Access Points (RAP):** The RAP is connected to the wired network and serves as a root or gateway to the wired network. RAPs are typically located on rooftops or towers. The RAP uses a wireless interface to communicate with neighboring mesh access points.

- **Mesh Access Points (MAP):** MAPs are the remote access points that provide access for wireless client devices. MAPs are typically located on top of a pole, such as a lamppost, and connect through a wireless interface to a RAP for a gateway to the wired network.

MAP-to-RAP Connectivity Example

The outdoor component of the Cisco Wireless Mesh Networking Solution is based on the Cisco Aironet 1500 Series, an outdoor Wi-Fi (802.11/a/b/g) MAP using the Cisco patent-pending Adaptive Wireless Path Protocol (AWPP).

The Cisco Aironet 1500 Series uses a dedicated two-radio design where the radios have dedicated roles. One radio provides local access for client devices, and the second radio provides the wireless backhaul for network connectivity. The overall throughput of the network is controlled by topology and path considerations in the mesh network.

During bootup, an access point tries to become a RAP if it is connected to the wired network. If a RAP loses its wired network connection, it attempts to become a MAP and searches for an appropriate RAP. By default, the backhaul interface on the RAP uses the 802.11a 5-GHz radio frequency and is set to a speed of 24 Mbps. RAPs utilize the backhaul wireless interface to communicate with neighboring MAPs. A RAP is the parent node to any bridging or mesh network and connects a bridge or mesh network to the wired network. By default, only one RAP can exist for any bridged or mesh network. There is a mesh algorithm that enables the access points to find the least-cost path back to the controller or RAP. This standard product feature minimizes latency and maximizes usable bandwidth. The algorithm takes into account total hop count and throughput at each hop to determine the best path to a RAP. An example of MAP-to-RAP connectivity is shown in Figure 10-26.

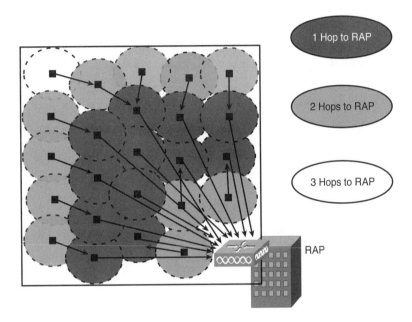

Figure 10-26   *MAP-to-RAP Connectivity Example*

MAPs have no wired connectivity to a WLC. MAPs can be completely wireless. They can support clients that are communicating to other MAPs or RAPs, or they can be wired and serve as bridges to a remote wired network. MAPs are typically installed in places where a wired connection cannot be provided but power can be provided. The MAP provides IEEE 802.11b/g client access through the 2.4-GHz radio frequency and connects wirelessly to the root access point through an 802.11a backhaul radio. MAPs can connect to a RAP using one or multiple hops, providing a broader coverage area than a typical wireless bridge device.

Mesh Design Recommendations

The MAP connection to the RAP can support eight hops on a Cisco Aironet 1500 Series Access Point, although four or fewer hops are recommended for best performance because each hop can produce 1 to 3 ms of latency.

RAPs can connect up to 32 MAPs, but it is recommended that only 20 to 25 MAPs are connected to a RAP. For best performance, connect only 20 MAPs to a RAP.

Summary

In this chapter, the wireless design principles were reviewed. The following topics were explored:

- Defining the requirements for wireless support: The number of end-user devices that should be supported for each location in the network needs to be determined.

- Conducting an RF site survey to define the RF characteristics in the environment: Identify potential areas of interference or coverage holes.

- Defining access point deployment locations based on the site survey and customer requirements.

- Determining wireless LAN (WLAN) controller (WLC) design using recommended practices:

  - Implementing deterministic redundancy using primary, secondary, and potentially, tertiary WLCs

  - Placing the WLCs in the distribution layer

  - Determining whether remote sites will use local or centralized controllers

- Determining the number of mobility groups that will be needed: Mobility groups are needed for seamless roaming.

- Planning how to support internal VLANs and guest access if needed (based on the customer requirements).

- Seeing how the Cisco Unified Wireless Network architecture centralizes WLAN configuration and control on WLCs that control CAPWAP access points.

- Understanding how the Cisco Unified Wireless Network provides transparent roaming supporting both intracontroller and intercontroller roaming. Deterministic controller redundancy with integrated RRM provides the highest-quality roaming experience.

- Reviewing how an RF survey in a wireless network design determines the characteristics of the wireless network and access point placement to provide optimal RF coverage for wireless clients.

References

For additional information, see the following resources:

Cisco Systems, Inc. Wireless LAN Controller (WLC) FAQ, at www.cisco.com/en/US/products/ps6366/products_qanda_item09186a008064a991.shtml.

Cisco Systems, Inc. Enterprise Mobility 3.0 Design Guide, at www.cisco.com/univercd/cc/td/doc/solution/emblty30.pdf.

Cisco Systems, Inc. Cisco Wireless LAN Controller Configuration Guide, Release 4.1, at www.cisco.com/en/US/docs/wireless/controller/4.1/configuration/guide/ccfig41.html.

Cisco Systems, Inc. Radio Resource Management Under Unified Wireless Networks, at www.cisco.com/en/US/tech/tk722/tk809/technologies_tech_note09186a008072c759.shtml.

Cisco Systems, Inc. Cisco Wireless Control System: Introduction, at www.cisco.com/en/US/products/ps6305/index.html.

Cisco Systems, Inc. Achieving Business Goals and Enhancing Customer Relationships with a Secure Guest Access Wi-Fi Network, at www.cisco.com/en/US/products/ps6366/products_white_paper0900aecd8047180a.shtml.

Cisco Systems, Inc. All Cisco Wireless Products, at www.cisco.com/en/US/products/hw/wireless/index.html#~all-prod.

Review Questions

Answer the following questions, and then see Appendix A for the answers.

1. What are the five interconnected elements of the Cisco Unified Wireless Network Architecture?

2. When using CAPWAP, which ports must be enabled and not blocked by intermediate devices?

3. What are the different types of Cisco Wireless LAN Controller interfaces?

4. What are the three different types of roaming?

5. How many wireless LAN controllers can be included in a mobility group?

6. When using RF groups, what is the default interval that RRM messages are exchanged between the group leader and the members?

7. What Cisco system can detect RF interference and optimize around it?

8. What does the planning mode of the Cisco Wireless Control System (WCS) take into account when predicting range and coverage?

9. What mode should be used by lightweight access points that reside on branch networks with their respective WLCs located at a central location?

10. What are the different components that are used to create a wireless mesh based on the Cisco Unified Wireless Network?

Answers to Review Questions

Chapter 1

1. Layers 5 through 7

2. Layer 3

3. Fast Ethernet

4. Leased Line

5. UDP

6. 128 bits

7. RIPv1 and v2, EIGRP, OSPF, Integrated IS-IS, and BGP

8. 10.0.0.0 through 10.255.255.255, 172.16.0.0 through 172.31.255.255, and 192.168.0.0 through 192.168.255.255

9. Unique Local Unicast address type

10. Root bridge

Chapter 2

1. Return on investment, regulation, competitiveness

2. Functionality, scalability, availability, performance, manageability, and efficiency

3. Prepare phase: 5

   Plan phase: 2

   Design phase: 4

Implement phase: 1

Operate phase: 6

Optimize phase: 3

4. Identify customer requirements, characterize the existing network and sites, design the network topology and solutions

5. Identifying network applications and network services, defining organizational goals, organizational constraints, technical goals, assess technical constraints

6. Budget, availability of personnel, policies, schedule availability

7. Site location/name, site address, site shipping address, site contact information, site ownership and maintenance information, Is the site staffed?, site hours, site and room access procedures, special security/safety procedures, union/labor requirements or procedures, equipment location information

8. A

9. D

10. B

Chapter 3

1. The role of each layer in the hierarchical network model is as follows:

   The access layer provides local and remote workgroup or user access to the network.

   The distribution layer provides policy-based connectivity.

   The core (or backbone) layer provides high-speed transport.

2. A, B, and F

3. With the introduction of the virtual switch concept, the distribution switch pair can now be configured to run as a single logical switch. By converting the redundant physical distribution switches into a single logical switch, a significant change is made to the topology of the network. Using an access switch configured with two uplinks to two distribution switches requires a control protocol to determine which of the uplinks to use. Now the access switch has a single Multichassis EtherChannel (MEC) upstream link (using two or more physical links—one to each physical switch) that is connected to a single virtual distribution switch.

4. Enterprise Campus

   Enterprise Edge

   Service Provider

   Remote

5. E-Commerce

Internet Connectivity

WAN and MAN Site-to-Site VPN

Remote Access and VPN

6. E-commerce module: Web servers, firewalls, NIPS appliances

Internet Connectivity module: SMTP mail servers, web servers, firewalls or firewall routers, public FTP servers, DNS servers

Remote Access and VPN module: ASA security appliances, NIPS appliances, firewalls or firewall routers

7. Device redundancy, including card and port redundancy

Redundant physical connections to workstations and servers

Route redundancy

Link redundancy

8. Cisco WAE appliances are products that provide global LAN-like access to enterprise applications and data.

9. Statistics, History, Alarm, Host, hostTopN, Matrix, Filters, Packet capture, and Events (not including Token Ring)

10. Syslog defines the following severity levels:

Emergency (level 0, which is the highest level)

Alert (level 1)

Critical (level 2)

Error (level 3)

Warning (level 4)

Notice (level 5)

Informational (level 6)

Debugging (level 7)

Chapter 4

1. The conventional 80/20 rule underlies traditional network design models. The 80/20 rule says that 80 percent of the traffic is local to the LAN segment and 20 percent leaves the segment.

Client–data center applications apply the 20/80 rule, where only 20 percent of the traffic remains on the local LAN segment and 80 percent leaves the segment to reach centralized servers, the Internet, and so on.

2. Campus core and data center modules

3. One solution is to simply provide sufficient bandwidth on the link. However, an alternative is to implement a QoS mechanism to classify, mark, and police the traffic on the building distribution switch.

4. A multilayer switch should be used as the building distribution layer in the basement to route between the VLANs, route to the WANs, and take advantage of the intelligent network services, such as QoS and traffic filtering, which must be supported at the distribution layer.

5. The recommended best practices related to managing VLANs and STP in the building access layer includes the following:

   Limit VLANs to a single wiring closet whenever possible.

   Use RPVST+ (even if STP is not required at the access layer, it is best to run it to ensure that user-side loops can't be formed).

6. The building distribution layer aggregates the building access layer, segments workgroups, and isolates segments from failures and broadcast storms. This layer implements many policies based on access lists and QoS settings.

7. As a recommended practice, a dedicated campus core layer should be deployed to connect three or more buildings in the enterprise campus, or four or more pairs of building distribution switches in a very large campus. The campus core helps make scaling the network easier. With a campus core, new building distribution switches would need connectivity only to the core, rather than full-mesh connectivity to all the distribution switches.

8. The edge distribution module isolates and controls access to devices that are located in the enterprise edge and enterprise WAN modules. The enterprise edge servers are closer to the external users and, therefore, introduce a higher risk to the internal campus.

9. The data center aggregation (distribution) layer aggregates the uplinks from the access layer to the data center core layer and is the critical point for control and application services.

10. **10 Gigabit Ethernet density:** Without a data center core, there might not be enough 10 Gigabit Ethernet ports to support both the campus distribution and the data center aggregation modules.

    Administrative domains and policies: Separate cores help to isolate campus distribution layers from data center aggregation layers for troubleshooting, administration, and implementation of polices (such as quality of service [QoS], ACLs, troubleshooting, and maintenance).

    Anticipation of future development: If a separate data center core layer is expected to be implemented in the future, it might be worthwhile to install a core layer at the beginning of the design.

Chapter 5

1. A WAN is a communications network that covers a relatively broad geographic area.

2. Time-division multiplexing (TDM)

3. Digital Subscriber Line Access Multiplexer (DSLAM)

4. OC-12

5. Network-Based Application Recognition (NBAR)

6. Star topology (also called hub-and-spoke)

7. Dynamic Multipoint VPN (DMVPN)

8. MPLS Layer 3 VPNs

9. Virtual Private LAN Services (VPLS)

10. Cisco Wide Area Application Services (WAAS)

Chapter 6

1. 32

2. Internet connectivity, e-commerce, remote access, and Virtual Private Network modules.

3. $2^N - 2$, where N is the number of bits set to 0 (the mask)

4. Manual, automatic, and dynamic

5. Using a DNS server or a HOSTS file

6. 2003:0000:4321:0000:0000:0000:0002:0001

7. Unicast, anycast, and multicast

8. Link-local addresses

9. Dual-stack

10. Hybrid model example 2

Chapter 7

1. Distance vector

2. 15

3. BGP

4. Classful

5. EIGRP

6. Backbone, 0

7. RIPng, OSPFv3, and EIGRP for IPv6

8. EIGRP or OSPF

9. Redistribution

10. Distribution

Chapter 8

1. Sarbanes-Oxley Act of 2002

2. Breach of integrity

3. Nmap

4. Business needs, risk analysis, security policy, industry-recommended practices, and security operations

5. Cisco Security Control Framework (SCF)

6. Authentication, authorization, and accounting

7. Shared secrets, public key infrastructure

8. Cisco IOS Intrusion Prevention System (IPS)

9. Cisco Traffic Anomaly Detector Module

10. Endpoint security solutions

Chapter 9

1. Filtering, sampling, digitizing

2. Gateway

3. H.264

4. <0.05%

5. RTP

6. User Agent (UA), SIP proxy server, redirect server, registrar server

7. 0–150 ms

8. Jitter

9. EF

10. Erlang

Chapter 10

1. Client devices, access points, network unification, world-class network management, Mobility services

2. UDP ports 5246 and 5247

3. Management interface, AP manager interface, dynamic interface, virtual interface, and service port interface

4. Intracontroller, Intercontroller–Layer 2, and Intercontroller–Layer 3

5. 24

6. 600 seconds

7. Cisco Wireless Control System (WCS)

8. Protocol, coverage, throughput, and square feet

9. Hybrid REAP (H-REAP)

10. Cisco Wireless Control System (WCS), Cisco Wireless LAN Controllers (WLC), Roof Access Points (RAP), and Mesh Access Points (MAP)

Acronyms and Abbreviations

This appendix lists abbreviations, acronyms, and initialisms used in this book and in the internetworking industry. Many of these acronyms and other terms are also described in the Cisco Internetworking Terms and Acronyms resource, available at www.cisco.com/univercd/cc/td/doc/cisintwk/ita.

Acronym	Expanded Term
mu-sec	Microsecond
1RU	One rack unit
3DES	Triple Data Encryption Standard
3G	Third-generation
6PE	IPv6 on the MPLS PE routers
6to4	IPv6-to-IPv4 tunnel
AAA	Authentication, authorization, and accounting
ABR	Area border router
AC	Alternating current
ACD	Automatic call distribution
ACELP	Algebraic Code–Excited Linear Prediction
ACL	Access control list
ACNS	Application and Content Networking System
ACS	Access control server
AD	Advertised distance
ADPCM	Adaptive Differential Pulse Code Modulation
ADSL	Asymmetric DSL
AES	Advanced Encryption Standard

Acronym	Expanded Term
AIM	Advanced integration module
ALG	Application-level gateway
AMR-NB	Adaptive Multi-Rate Narrow Band
ANS	Application Networking Services
ANSI	American National Standards Institute
AON	Application-Oriented Networking
AP	Access point
API	Application programming interface
APS	Automatic protection switching
ARCnet	Attached Resource Computer Network
ARP	Address Resolution Protocol
AS	Autonomous system
ASA	Adaptive Security Appliance
ASBR	Autonomous system boundary router
ASDM	Adaptive Security Device Manager
ASIC	Application-Specific Integrated Circuit
ATM	Asynchronous Transfer Mode
AWPP	Adaptive Wireless Path Protocol
B	Bearer
BASc	Bachelor's degree in applied science
BCMSN	Building Cisco Multilayer Switched Networks
BECN	Backward explicit congestion notification
BER	Bit error rate
BGP	Border Gateway Protocol
BGP-4	BGP Version 4
BGP4+	Multiprotocol extensions to BGP version 4
BHT	Busy-hour traffic
BIA	Burned-in address
BOM	Bill of materials
BOOTP	Bootstrap Protocol
BPDU	Bridge protocol data unit
BRI	Basic Rate Interface
BSCI	Building Scalable Cisco Internetworks
BSS	Basic Service Set
BSSID	Basic Service Set Identifier

Acronym	Expanded Term
CA	Collision Avoidance Certificate authority
CAC	Call admission control
CAM	Content-addressable memory
CAR	Committed access rate
CAS	Channel-associated signaling
CatOS	Catalyst Operating System
CATV	Cable TV
CBC-DES	Cipher-block chaining data encryption standard
CBWFQ	Class-based weighted fair queuing
CCDA	Cisco Certified Design Associate
CCDP	Cisco Certified Design Professional
CCIE	Cisco Certified Internet Expert
CCITT	Consultative Committee for International Telegraph and Telephone
CCK	Complementary Code Keying
CCKM	Cisco Centralized Key Management
CCNA	Cisco Certified Network Associate
CCNP	Cisco Certified Network Professional
CCS	Common channel signaling Centum Call Second
CCSI	Cisco Certified Systems Instructor
CCX	Cisco-Compatible Extensions
CD	Collision detection
CDMA	Code Division Multiple Access
CDP	Cisco Discovery Protocol
CEF	Cisco Express Forwarding
CELP	Code Excited Linear Prediction Compression
CGMP	Cisco Group Management Protocol
CIDR	Classless interdomain routing
CIR	Committed information rate
CISP	Cardholder Information Security Program
CKIP	Cisco Key Integrity Protocol
CLI	Command-line interface
CLNP	Connectionless Network Protocol
CLNS	Connectionless Network Service
CMIC	Cisco Message Integrity Check
CMTS	Cable Modem Termination System

Acronym	Expanded Term
CNS	Cisco Network Service
CO	Central office
CoPP	Control Plane Policing
CoS	Class of service
CPE	Customer Premises Equipment
CQ	Custom queuing
CRTC	Canadian Radio-television and Telecommunications Commission
cRTP	RTP header compression, or compressed RTP
CS-ACELP	Conjugate Structure Algebraic Code Excited Linear Prediction Compression
CSC-SSM	Content Security and Control Security Services Module
CSMA	Carrier sense multiple access
CSMA/CD	Carrier sense multiple access collision detect
CST	Common Spanning Tree
CTI	Computer telephony integration
CTS	Clear to send
D	Delta
DAI	Dynamic ARP Inspection
dB	Decibel
dBi	dB isotropic
dBm	dB milliwatt
dBw	dB watt
DDoS	Distributed denial of service
DDR	Dial-on-demand routing
DEC	Digital Equipment Corporation
DES	Digital Encryption Standard
DESGN	Designing for Cisco Internetwork Solutions
DHCP	Dynamic Host Configuration Protocol
DHCPv6	DHCP for IPv6
DID	Direct Inward Dialing
DiffServ	Differentiated Services
DMVPN	Dynamic Multipoint VPN
DMZ	Demilitarized zone
DNS	Domain Name Service, or Domain Name System
DOCSIS	Data Over Cable Service Interface Specification

Acronym	Expanded Term
DoS	Denial of service
DPNSS	Digital Private Network Signaling System
DRED	Distributed random early detection
DS0	Digital signal level 0
DSCP	Differentiated Services Code Point
DSL	Digital subscriber line
DSLAM	DSL access multiplexer
DSP	Digital signal processor
DSS	Data Security Standard
DSTM	Dual-Stack Transition Mechanism
DSU	Data service unit
DTMF	Dual-tone multifrequency
DTP	Dynamic Trunking Protocol
DUAL	Diffusing Update Algorithm
DWDM	Dense wavelength division multiplexing
E	Ear
E&M	recEive and transMit; sometimes also known as Ear and Mouth
E911	Enhanced 911
EAP	Extensible Authentication Protocol
EAP-FAST	EAP Flexible Authentication via Secure Tunneling
EAPoL	Extensible Authentication Protocol over LAN
EAP-TLS	EAP Transport Layer Security
EAP-TTLS	EAP Tunneled Transport Layer Security
EBGP	External BGP
ECN	Explicit congestion notification
EGP	Exterior gateway protocol
EIGRP	Enhanced Interior Gateway Routing Protocol
EIRP	Effective Isotropic Radiated Power
ERP	Enterprise resource planning
ES	End system
ESA	Extended service area
ESP	Encapsulating Security Payload
EtherIP	Ethernet in IP
ETSI	European Telecommunications Standards Institute
EUI-64	Extended universal identifier 64-bit

Acronym	Expanded Term
FCC	Federal Communications Commission
FCIP	Fiber Channel over IP
FD	Feasible distance
FDM	Frequency division multiplexing
FEC	Forwarding Equivalence Class
FECN	Forward Explicit Congestion Notification
FIB	Forwarding Information Base
FICON	Fiber Connection
FLSM	Fixed-length subnet masking
FQDN	Fully qualified domain name
FRR	Fast reroute
FRTS	Frame Relay Traffic Shaping
FS	Feasible successor
FWSM	Firewall Services Module
FX	Foreign exchange
FXO	Foreign Exchange Office
FXS	Foreign Exchange Station
Gbps	Gigabits per second
GE	Gigabit Ethernet
GLBA	U.S. Gramm-Leach-Bliley Act of 1999
GLBP	Gateway Load-Balancing Protocol
GoS	Grade of service
GPRS	General Packet Radio Service
GPS	Global Positioning System
GRE	Generic Routing Encapsulation
GSM	Global System for Mobile
GSS	Global Site Selector
GTC	Generic Token Card
GTS	Generic Traffic Shaping
HDLC	High-Level Data Link Control
HDSL	High-data-rate DSL
HDSL-2	Second generation of HDSL
HIDS	Host-based intrusion detection system
HIPAA	Health Insurance Portability and Accountability Act
HIPS	Host-based intrusion prevention system

Acronym	Expanded Term
HMAC	Hash-based Message Authentication Code
HMAC-MD5	Hash-based Message Authentication Code Message Digest 5
HMAC-SHA	Hash-based Message Authentication Code Secure Hash Algorithm
H-REAP	Hybrid Remote Edge AP
HSRP	Hot Standby Router Protocol
HSSI	High-speed serial interface
HTTPS	HTTP secured by SSL
HVAC	Heating, ventilation, and air conditioning
HWIC	High-speed WAN interface card
Hz	Hertz
IANA	Internet Assigned Numbers Authority
IAPP	Inter-Access Point Protocol
IBGP	Internal BGP
IBNS	Identity-Based Networking Services
ICMP	Internet Control Message Protocol
ID	Identifier
IDF	Intermediate distribution frame
IDM	Cisco Intrusion Prevention System Device Manager
IDS	Intrusion detection system
IDSL	ISDN DSL
IEEE	Institute of Electrical and Electronics Engineers
IETF	Internet Engineering Task Force
IGMP	Internet Group Management Protocol
IGP	Interior gateway protocol
IGRP	Interior Gateway Routing Protocol
IIS	Internet Information Server
IKE	Internet Key Exchange
IPC	IP Communications
IPCC	IP Contact Center
IPFIX	IP Flow Information Export
IPS	Intrusion prevention system
IPsec	Internet Protocol Security
IP/TV	Internet Protocol Television
IPv4	IP version 4
IPv6	IP version 6

Acronym	Expanded Term
IPX	Internetwork Packet Exchange
IS	Intermediate system
ISDN	Integrated Services Digital Network
IS-IS	Intermediate System–to–Intermediate System
IS-ISv6	IS-IS version 6
ISL	Inter-switch link
ISM	Industrial, Scientific, and Medical
ISP	Internet service provider
ISR	Integrated Services Router
ISSU	In-Service Software Upgrade
IVR	Interactive Voice Response
kbps	Kilobits per second
kHz	Kilohertz
km	Kilometer
L1	Level 1
L1/L2	Level 1/Level 2
L2	Layer 2
	Level 2
L2F	Layer 2 Forwarding
L2TP	Layer 2 Tunneling Protocol
LAC	L2TP Access Concentrator
LACP	Link Aggregation Control Protocol
LAG	Link aggregation
LAPB	Link Access Procedure Balanced
LBS	Location-based services
LD-CELP	Low-Delay Code Excited Linear Prediction Compression
LDP	Label Distribution Protocol
LEAP	Cisco Lightweight Extensible Authentication Protocol
LFI	Link Fragmentation and Interleaving
LLC	Logical Link Control
LLQ	Low-latency queuing
LNS	L2TP Network Server
LRE	Long-Reach Ethernet
LSA	Link-state advertisement
LSDB	Link-state database

Acronym	Expanded Term
LSP	Label Switched Path
	Link-state packet
LSR	Label Switched Router
LSU	Link-state update
LWAPP	Lightweight AP Protocol
LZS	Lempel-Ziv Stack
M	Mouth
MAN	Metropolitan-area network
MAP	Mesh AP
MARS	Cisco Security Monitoring, Analysis, and Response System
MASc	Master's degree in applied science
Mbps	Megabits per second
MBSA	Microsoft Baseline Security Analyzer
MC	Multipoint controller
MCU	Multipoint control unit
MD5	Message Digest 5
MDS	Multilayer Directors and Fabric Switches
MGCP	Media Gateway Control Protocol
MHz	Megahertz
MIC	Message Integrity Check
MIR	Minimum information rate
MISTP	Multiple-Instance STP
MLP	Multilink Point-to-Point Protocol
MLS	Multilayer switching
MLSP	Multilayer Switching Protocol
MLS-RP	MLS Route Processor
MLS-SE	MLS Switching Engine
MM	Multimode
MoH	Music on Hold
MOS	Mean opinion score
MP	Multilink Protocol
	Multipoint processor
MP3	MPEG-1 Audio Layer 3
MPCC	Microsoft Point-to-Point Compression
MPEG	Moving Picture Experts Group

Acronym	Expanded Term
MPLS	Multiprotocol Label Switching
MPMLQ	Multipulse Maximum Likelihood Quantization
MPPP	Multilink Point-to-Point Protocol
MRTG	Multi-Router Traffic Grapher
ms	Milliseconds
MSB	Most significant bit
MSCHAPv2	Microsoft Challenge Handshake Authentication Protocol version 2
MTBF	Mean time between failures
MTTR	Mean time to repair
MTU	Maximum transmission unit
mW	Milliwatt
MW	Megawatt
MWI	Message Waiting Indicator
NAC	Network Admission Control
NAD	Network Access Device
NAM	Network Analysis Module
NANP	North American Numbering Plan
NAP	Network Access Provider
NAS	Network Attached Storage Network Access Server
NAT	Network Address Translation
NAT-PT	NAT Protocol Translation
NBAR	Network-Based Application Recognition
NBMA	Nonbroadcast multiaccess
NDS	Novell Directory Services
NEBS	Network Equipment Building System
NFC	NetFlow Collection Engine
NIC	Network interface card
NIDS	Network intrusion detection system
NIPS	Network-based intrusion prevention system
NMS	Network management system
NOC	Network operations center
NPA	Numbering Plan Area
NSF	Nonstop Forwarding
NSP	Network service provider

Acronym	Expanded Term
NSSA	Not-so-stubby area
NTP	Network Time Protocol
OC	Optical carrier
ODR	On-Demand Routing
OFDM	Orthogonal frequency division multiplexing
ONS	Optical Networking Solutions
OS	Operating system
OSI	Open Systems Interconnection
OSPF	Open Shortest Path First
OSPFv2	OSPF version 2
OSPFv3	OSPF version 3
OTAP	Over-the-Air Provisioning
OTP	One-time password
OUI	Organizational Unique Identifier
PAC	Protected Access Credential
PAgP	Port Aggregation Protocol
PAM	Pulse amplitude modulation
PAN	Personal-area network
PAT	Port Address Translation
PCI	Payment Card Industry
PCM	Pulse code modulation
PDA	Personal digital assistant
PDM	Protocol-Dependent Module
PDU	Protocol data unit
PE	Provider Edge
PEAP	Protected Extensible Authentication Protocol
PHY	Physical layer
PIM	Protocol-Independent Multicast
PIN	Personal identification number
PIPEDA	Canadian Personal Information Protection and Electronic Documents Act
PKC	Proactive Key Caching
PKI	Public key infrastructure
PMK	Pair-wise Master Key
PoE	Power over Ethernet
POP	Point of Presence

Acronym	Expanded Term
POP3	Post Office Protocol version 3
POS	Packet over SONET/SDH
POTS	Plain old telephone service
PPDIOO	Prepare, Plan, Design, Implement, Operate, Optimize
PPPoA	PPP over ATM
PPPoE	PPP over Ethernet
pps	Packets per second
PPTP	Point-to-Point Tunneling Protocol
PQ	Priority queuing
PRC	Partial Route Calculation
PSK	Preshared key
PSQM	Perceptual Speech Quality Measurement
PSTN	Public switched telephone network
PTK	Pairwise Transient Key
PVC	Permanent virtual circuit
PVDM	Packet voice DSP module
PVST	Per-VLAN spanning tree
QoS	Quality of service
QPPB	QoS Policy Propagation on BGP
QSIG	Q Signaling
RAP	Rooftop AP
RARP	Reverse Address Resolution Protocol
RAS	Registration, Admission, and Status
RC4	Rivest Cipher 4
RDMA	Remote Data Memory Access
RDP	Router Discovery Protocol
REAP	Remote edge AP
RED	Random early detection
RF	Radio frequency
RFI	Request for Information
RFP	Request for Proposal
RIP	Routing Information Protocol
RIPng	RIP new generation
RIPv1	Routing Information Protocol version 1
RIPv2	Routing Information Protocol version 2

Acronym	Expanded Term
RME	Resource Manager Essentials
RMON	Remote Monitoring
RMON2	Remote Monitoring 2
ROI	Return on investment
RP	Rendezvous point
RPF	Reverse Path Forwarding
RPVST+	Rapid Per-VLAN Spanning Tree Plus, or RSTP with Per-VLAN Spanning Tree Plus
RRM	Radio resource management
RSP	Route Switch Processor
RSSI	Received signal strength indicator
RSTP	Rapid Spanning Tree Protocol
RSVP	Resource Reservation Protocol
RTCP	Real-time Transport Control Protocol
RTP	Real-time Transport Protocol
RTS	Request to send
RTT	Round-trip time
SAA	Service assurance agent
SAINT	Security Administrator's Integrated Network Tool
SAN	Storage-area network
SCCP	Skinny Client Control Protocol
SCP	Secure Copy
SDF	Signature definition file
SDH	Synchronous Digital Hierarchy
SDM	Security Device Manager
SDP	Site Data Protection
SDSL	Symmetric DSL
SEC	U.S. Securities and Exchange Commission
SFP	Small Form Factor Pluggable
SFS	Server Fabric Switching
SFTP	SSH FTP
SIP	Session Initiation Protocol
SLA	Service-level agreement
SM	Single-mode
SMDS	Switched Multimegabit Data Services

Acronym	Expanded Term
SMI	Structure of Management Information
SMTP	Simple Mail Transfer Protocol
SNA	Systems Network Architecture
SNAP	Subnetwork Access Protocol
SNMP	Simple Network Management Protocol
SNMPv1	SNMP version 1
SNMPv2	SNMP version 2
SNMPv3	SNMP version 3
SNR	Signal-to-noise ratio
SOA	Service-oriented architecture
SOHO	Small office, home office
SONA	Service-Oriented Network Architecture
SOX	U.S. Sarbanes-Oxley Act of 2002
SP	Service provider
SPA	Shared Port Adapter
SPF	Shortest path first
SRST	Survivable Remote Site Telephony
SRTP	Secure Real-Time Transport Protocol
SS7	Signaling System 7
SSH	Secure Shell
SSID	Service Set Identifier
SSL	Secure Socket Layer
SSO	Stateful Switchover
STAC	Stacker
STP	Spanning Tree Protocol
SVC	Switched virtual circuit
TCO	Total cost of ownership
TDM	Time-division multiplexing
TDMA	Time-division multiple access
TKIP	Temporal Key Integrity Protocol
TLV	Type, length, value
ToS	Type of service
TTL	Time to live
UA	User agent
UAC	UA client

Acronym	Expanded Term
UAS	UA server
uBR	Universal Broadband Router
UDLD	Unidirectional Link Detection
UDP	User Datagram Protocol
U/L	Universal/Local
UMTS	Universal Mobile Telephone Service
UNII	Unlicensed National Information Infrastructure
URI	Uniform Resource Identifier
uRPF	Unicast Reverse Path Forwarding
USB	Universal Serial Bus
UTP	Unshielded twisted-pair
UWN	Unified Wireless Network
V	Volt
v9	Version 9
VACM	View-based Access Control Model
VAD	Voice activity detection
VC	Virtual circuit
VDSL	Very-high-data-rate DSL
VIP	Versatile Interface Processor
VLSM	Variable-length subnet mask
VMPS	VLAN Membership Policy Server
VMS	VPN/Security Management Solution
VoATM	Voice over ATM
VoD	Video on Demand
VoFR	Voice over Frame Relay
VoIP	Voice over IP
VoWLAN	Voice over WLAN
VPDN	Virtual private dialup network
VPN	Virtual Private Network
VRRP	Virtual Router Redundancy Protocol
VTP	VLAN Trunking Protocol
W	Watt
WAAS	Wide-Area Application Services
WAE	Wide-Area Application Engine
WAFS	Wide-Area File Services

Acronym	Expanded Term
WAP	Wireless access point
WCS	Wireless Control System
WEP	Wired Equivalent Privacy
WFA	Wi-Fi Alliance
WFQ	Weighted fair queuing
WIC	WAN interface card
WiSM	Wireless Services Module
WLAN	Wireless LAN
WLANA	WLAN Association
WLC	WLAN controller
WLCM	Cisco WLC module
WLSE	Wireless LAN Solutions Engine
WoW	Workstation on wheels
WPA	Wi-Fi Protected Access
WRED	Weighted Random Early Detection

Index

D

G

H

I

M

P

X

Z

FREE Online Edition

Your purchase of **Designing for Cisco Internetwork Solutions (DESGN) Foundation Learning Guide** includes access to a free online edition for 45 days through the Safari Books Online subscription service. Nearly every Cisco Press book is available online through Safari Books Online, along with more than 5,000 other technical books and videos from publishers such as Addison-Wesley Professional, Exam Cram, IBM Press, O'Reilly, Prentice Hall, Que, and Sams.

SAFARI BOOKS ONLINE allows you to search for a specific answer, cut and paste code, download chapters, and stay current with emerging technologies.

Activate your FREE Online Edition at www.informit.com/safarifree

> **STEP 1:** Enter the coupon code: DRTZNVH

> **STEP 2:** New Safari users, complete the brief registration form.
> Safari subscribers, just log in.

If you have difficulty registering on Safari or accessing the online edition, please e-mail customer-service@safaribooksonline.com

Addison Wesley   Adobe Press   ALPHA   Cisco Press   FT Press   IBM Press   lynda.com   Microsoft Press   New Riders

O'REILLY   Peachpit Press   PRENTICE HALL   QUE   Redbooks   SAMS   SAS Publishing   Sun microsystems   WILEY